A HISTORY OF THE THIRTY YEARS' PEACE

The Development of Industrial Society Series

Harriet Martineau

Title **A HISTORY OF THE THIRTY YEARS' PEACE**
1816-1846

Volume 2

IRISH UNIVERSITY PRESS
Shannon   Ireland

First edition London 1849-50
Second edition London 1858
Third edition London 1877-78

This IUP reprint is a photolithographic facsimile of
the third edition and is unabridged, retaining the original
printer's imprint.

All forms of micropublishing
© *Irish University Microforms Shannon Ireland*

ISBN 0 7165 1753 1 Four volumes
ISBN 0 7165 1754 X Volume 1
ISBN 0 7165 1755 8 Volume 2
ISBN 0 7165 1756 6 Volume 3
ISBN 0 7165 1757 4 Volume 4

T M MacGlinchey Publisher
Irish University Press Shannon Ireland

PRINTED IN THE REPUBLIC OF IRELAND BY
ROBERT HOGG PRINTER TO IRISH UNIVERSITY PRESS

BOHN'S STANDARD LIBRARY.

A HISTORY OF THE

THIRTY YEARS' PEACE.

VOL. II.

A HISTORY

OF THE

THIRTY YEARS' PEACE.

A.D. 1816–1846.

By HARRIET MARTINEAU.

IN FOUR VOLUMES.

Vol. II. (From 1824–1833).

LONDON: GEORGE BELL AND SONS, YORK STREET,
COVENT GARDEN.
1877.

LONDON:
PRINTED BY WILLIAM CLOWES AND SONS,
STAMFORD STREET AND CHARING CROSS.

CONTENTS.

BOOK II. (*Continued*).

CHAPTER VIII.

CHAPTER IX.

CHAPTER X.

CHAPTER XI.

CHAPTER XII.

BOOK III.

FROM THE NEW PARLIAMENT IN 1827 TO THE END OF THE REIGN OF GEORGE IV.

CHAPTER I.

CHAPTER II.

CHAPTER III.

CHAPTER IV.

CHAPTER V.

CHAPTER VI.

CHAPTER VII.

CHAPTER VIII.

CHAPTER IX.

CHAPTER X.

CHAPTER XI.

BOOK IV.

FROM THE ACCESSION OF WILLIAM IV. TO THE BURNING OF THE HOUSES OF PARLIAMENT.

CHAPTER I.

CHAPTER II.

CHAPTER III.

CHAPTER IV.

CHAPTER V.

HISTORY OF THE PEACE.

BOOK II.—(*Continued.*)

CHAPTER VIII.

Speculation—Joint-Stock Companies—Collapse—Panic—Crash—Issue of Small Notes and Coin—King's Speech—Arrangement with Bank of England—Suppression of Small Notes—Scotch Banks—Branch and Joint-Stock Banks—Advances on Goods—Position of Ministers—Suffering of the Period.

WE now enter upon a chapter of modern English history which the moralist regards, and will for a century to come regard, with wonder and shame. It shows how childish the mind of a nation can be; as crises of another kind show how brave and noble it can be, according to the appeal made to its lower or its higher faculties. The same people who had been calm and courageous when their national existence appeared to be in peril, magnanimous and disinterested when the partition of European territory was going on abroad after the peace, staunch and loyal in the cause of a persecuted queen, and well principled in liberty when a new course of foreign policy was entered upon, were now to prove themselves very children under the temptation of sudden prosperity, amidst extraordinary facilities for gambling. It was not altogether rapacity which instigated the follies of 1824 and 1825. Too many were eager for gain, making haste to be rich; and of these the sharpers of society made an easy prey; but with many more, the charm was in the excitement—in the pleasure of sympathy in large enterprises—in the rousing of the faculties of imagination and conception, when their field

of commerce extended over the Pampas and the Andes,
and beyond the furthest seas, and among the ice-rocks of
the poles. When the grey-haired merchant grew eloquent
by his fireside about the clefts of the Cordillera, where the
precious metals glitter to the miner's torch, it was not his
expected gains alone that fired his eye and quickened his
utterance, but that gratification of his conceptive faculty
to which his ordinary life had ministered but too little.
When the professional man perilled his savings to cut
through the Isthmus of Panama, he gloried in helping on
a mighty work; and described, like a poet, the pouring of
the one vast ocean into the other, and the procession of the
merchant-ships of the world riding through on the new-
made current. And so with the aged ladies and retired
servants, who gave from their pittance of property and
income whatever they could squeeze out, to hold shares in
steam-ovens, steam-laundries, or milk-and-egg companies.
They had their visions of domestic comfort and luxury,
and looked joyfully for the time when the good things of
the table and the wardrobe should abound with little
expense of toil. Now was the time for those who make
their market of the unwary to come forth and be busy.
Needy speculators and scheming attorneys, and gamblers
of every class, used their opportunity, first for exciting the
gambling spirit everywhere within their reach, and then
for introducing themselves into a society where at other
times they could have obtained no admittance. They
knew that their opportunity was short; and they used it
diligently. Seasons of speculation and reaction may be
observed in the history of every nation, and may be
expected to recur till nations have grown much wiser
than they are; but such a spectacle of intoxication and
collapse as is offered by the years 1824–1826 will hardly,
we may hope, be equalled again in England.

Among the records of the time we have the following
picture of the state of society in its material aspect, amidst
which the fever of speculation arose :

'The increased wealth of the middle classes is so
obvious, that we can neither walk the fields, visit the
shops, nor examine the workshops and storehouses, without
being deeply impressed with the changes which a few

years have produced. We see the fields better cultivated, the barns and stackyards more fully stored, the horses, cows, and sheep, more abundant and in better condition, and all the implements of husbandry improved in their order, their construction, and their value. In the cities, towns, and villages, we find shops more numerous and better in their appearance, and the several goods more separated from each other; a division that is the infallible token of increased sales. We see the accumulation of wares of every kind adapted to the purses, the wants, and even the whims of every description of customers. This vast increase of goods, thus universally dispersed, is an indication and exhibition of flourishing circumstances. It may be traced into all the manufactories, and observed in the masses of raw materials in each, in commodities of every kind in their several stages of preparation, and in all the subdivisions of those stages, by which not only the increase of wealth is manifested, but the modes by which it is acquired are practically illustrated. If we could ascend a little higher, and examine the accounts of the bankers in the metropolis, and in the provincial towns, small as well as large, we should find that the balances of money resting with them, ready to embrace favourable changes in the price of any commodity, or to be placed at interest as beneficial securities present themselves, are increased to an enormous amount. This, indeed, may be fairly inferred from the low rate of interest in the floating public securities, from the prices of the funds, from the avidity with which every project for the employment of capital is grasped at, and from the general complaint, almost the only complaint heard, that there is now no way of making interest of money. The projects for constructing tunnels, railroads, canals, or bridges, and the eagerness with which they are embraced, are all proofs of that accumulation from savings which the intermediate ranks of society have, by patience and perseverance, been enabled to form. The natural effect of this advancement in possessions has been an advance in the enjoyments which those possessions can administer; and we need not be surprised at the general diffusion of those gratifications which were formerly called luxuries, but which, from their familiarity, we now

describe by the softened, and exclusively English term,
comforts. This is manifested in our houses, in their finish-
ing, in their decorations, and especially in the numerous
conveniences with which they are stored. The merchants
of London forty or fifty years since lived in the dark lanes
in which their counting-houses are still to be found, ate
with their clerks a hasty meal at two o'clock, and returned
to the desk to write their letters, by which they were often
occupied till midnight. The shopkeepers lived behind
their shops, their best floor was let to lodgers, and few
only of the wealthier of them could afford a retreat from
the bustle and the cares of the city to the surrounding
villages of Islington, Hackney, or Camberwell. The
watering-places which have sprung up on the whole coast
of Kent and Sussex were then unknown to those classes of
traders, who now, by occasionally resorting to them, and
spending there a part of what they can spare from their
annual savings, contribute largely to maintain the inhabitants in comfort and respectability. If we visit the country,
we experience the same pleasing emotions as are communicated on the contemplation of the increased enjoyments of
the city. We do not see indeed among the farmers such
great strides, but we see universal advancement. The
profits on their capitals are necessarily lower, and their
growth consequently less rapid; but in the last forty or
fifty years they, too, have made considerable progress.
Whilst they have exchanged the work of the hands for
that of the head, they have exchanged also the round frock
of the ploughman for garments more suitable to their improved condition. Their houses are more commodious and
better furnished; carpets, china plates, and glasses are to
be seen, instead of stone floors, trenchers, and drinking-
horns. Their wives and daughters, upon whom the refinement of society mainly depends, are generally better
educated, and are able to attract their husbands and
brothers from the fairs and the markets at an earlier hour
and with less frequent breaches of the rules of sobriety
than were practised in the last generation. The country
inn is no longer superior in neatness or comfort to the
farmer's own house. Among the manufacturers, we see
some with princely yet well-merited fortunes. But there

is a numerous class inferior to them, who have amassed, and are amassing, considerable wealth, and dispensing employment to thousands of their poorer neighbours. We have had occasion before to notice the increased population of Manchester, Leeds, Birmingham, and several other places which have been the scenes of their operations. Forty years ago, we were well acquainted with those places, with the fortunes which were then enjoyed, and the habits then prevailing. On recent visits, after a long absence, we felt a degree of astonishment which we cannot describe, at the changes which have taken place. We do not speak of the numerous individuals, whose fathers or grandfathers had, almost within recollection, hardly emerged from the condition of day-labourers, and whom we now found the owners of magnificent establishments; for single instances prove little in a case like this; but we allude to the immense addition to the buildings, the improvement in their construction, and the general advance which the owners had made in all the liberal tastes and enjoyments of life.'

Such was the buoyant tone of the time. Such was the record, much of which was to merge into silent dismay, tho gazette, and the obituary.

Early in the spring of 1824, gold and silver were exported to South America; yet nobody appeared to observe that there was too much money abroad. In June and July, there was a decided fall in the exchanges with the continent; yet no one seemed to take the alarm. The Bank of England went on increasing its issues through the whole of 1824, and for three months of the next year; and it was not till the end of that time, in the spring of 1825, that even sagacious men of business began audibly to prophesy the evil to come. At that time, some few declared their belief that a terrible revulsion might be looked for soon. But it was then too late. Between June, 1824, and October, 1825, from ten to twelve millions of coin and bullion were exported; and during the greater part of that time, the Bank of England was still putting out its notes; and the provincial banks issued as many as they could, till the country was deluged with paper-money. Many a man set up for a banker who would, at another time, have as soon thought of setting up for a king. Lord Liverpool

complained, after the crisis, of the system which allows
any petty tradesman, any cobbler, or cheesemonger, to
usurp the royal prerogative, and to issue money without
check or control. There was a perfect mania of competition in making paper issues. Many of the country
bankers, who afterwards failed, discounted the paper that
was brought to them by the wildest and wickedest speculators, and paid a large commission to persons who undertook to promote the circulation of their notes. This inordinate supply of money followed upon a deficiency of
currency in 1821 and 1822; in which latter year an act
was passed permitting the circulation of small notes
beyond the date originally fixed. This extension of time
tempted the bankers to increase their issues, instead of
providing for the withdrawal of some of their paper. In
1825, there was from thirty to forty per cent. more paper
out than in 1822. Just at that time, the Bank of England, followed by other banks, lowered the rate of interest.
Thus there was money in abundance, which its owners did
not know what to do with. The rate of interest was low.
Prices had been so low for two years that they were sure
to rise, suddenly and vastly, while so much money was
abroad; and the opportunity for speculating was one which
few men of enterprise, engaged in trade, were able to
resist.

It would have been well if the rage for speculation had
been confined to men engaged in trade. The madness
spread everywhere. Retired professional men, living on
their acquired fortunes, ladies deriving all their income
from the funds, families who had lent their money on
mortgages, looked at the low interest on money on the one
hand, and the enormous profits made by speculation on the
other, and grew dissatisfied. Hundreds who had before
been content with their moderate incomes, and had blessed
God that their lot had lain between poverty and riches,
now watched with jealousy the opportunities of their
neighbours; were offended if shares in some joint-stock
company were not offered to them, or sighed if obliged to
admit that they were not rich enough to pledge themselves
to a series of calls. Some who went on in their ordinary
course, untouched by the madness of the time, were re-

proached for injustice to their families, in declining to help themselves from the stores of wealth which were poured out all around. These were justified in the end; but they suffered, more or less, with the rest; for this is a case in which the suffering can never be confined to those who err. The scheming attorneys, the needy speculators, the excitable professional men and ladies, and the ignorant small capitalists whom they led astray, were the sinners; but many an honourable and sagacious merchant, who saw whither things were tending, and did his utmost to preserve himself and his neighbours, was half ruined, or wholly ruined, by the consequences of other people's folly. He, like others, suffered by the stoppage of the banks, the sudden contraction of the currency, and the prodigious depreciation of every kind of stock.

While the rate of interest was lowest, the possessors of capital were easily tempted to invest their money in some scheme which should yield them an abundant return. While the rate of interest was lowest, men were tempted to borrow larger sums than they would otherwise have ventured on, wherewith to carry on their speculations. And, again, this was the time, when bankers were willing to discount bills at very long dates, for speculators to buy up goods, hold them back for the high prices expected to ensue, and thus enhance the prices yet further by creating an artificial scarcity   At the very time when even reasonable people were discontented with the low interest they obtained for their money, while threatened with high prices to come, they saw their neighbours making fortunes almost in a day, by skilful buying and selling among the projects afloat. A young lady, whose brother had encouraged her to take a share of £100 in some joint-stock project, might pay her first instalment of £5 with some trembling, and wonder when the next call would come. But if her brother brought her £140 in a few days, with the news that he had sold out for her while the premium was thus high, would she sit down content with having for once gained £35 by her £5? Would she not be as eager to invest again as the managers could be that she should? Thus it was with many thousands of ladies, and gentlemen as inexperienced as they. Some selfish wretches knew well enough what must happen, and only wanted to get rich before the crash—to use the madness while it might serve their turn. The greater number were seduced into the gambling game; but all, guilty, thoughtless, and innocent together, suffered more or less under the inevitable retribution.

As for what the speculation was like, it can hardly be recorded, even at this day, on the open page of history, without a blush. Besides the joint-stock companies who undertook baking, washing, baths, life-insurance, brewing, coal-portage, wool-growing, and the like, there was such a rage for steam-navigation, canals, and railroads, that in the session of 1825, 438 petitions for private bills were presented, and 286 private acts were passed. Part of the retribution of the national folly lay in the decline of the character of the House of Commons, too many of whose members acted, in regard to these bills, with a recklessness which subjected them to a suspicion that they, like others, had forgotten themselves, and had sacrificed their legislative conscience to the interests of themselves and their friends. The acknowledgment of the independence of some of the South American states at this time turned the stream of speculation in that direction. Companies were formed to obtain gold and silver from mountain tops and clefts, where there were no workmen or tools to do the work, no fuel for the fires, and no roads or carriages to bring away the produce. There were to be pearls from the coast of Columbia; and such precious articles were to come from the other hemisphere, that sober persons began to fear too great a change in the affairs and the mind of the English people. There would be so much gold and silver, that, after the chancellor of the exchequer had paid off the national debt, the value of money in England and all Europe would be essentially changed. Gems and pearls were to abound to such a degree that the jewels of ancient families were soon to be shamed. The higher orders began to look about them, when these things were said; and, finding that the middle and lower classes were to become very rich in a short time, they too rushed into the scramble for the wealth of South America. It is on record that a single share of the Real del Monte mine, on which

£70 had been paid, yielded £2000 per cent., having risen speedily to a premium of £1400 per share.

People who declined the grosser kind of gambling—by Stock Exchange speculations—attached themselves to the idea of growing rich by trading with the new markets opened on the other side of the Atlantic. At Rio Janeiro more Manchester goods arrived in a few weeks than had been before required for twenty years; and merchandise—much of it perishable—was left exposed on the beach, among thieves and under variable weather, till the overcrowded warehouses could afford room for its stowage. It is positively declared, that warming-pans from Birmingham were among the articles exposed under the burning sun of that sky; and that skates from Sheffield were offered for sale to a people who had never heard of ice. China and cut-glass were, in some places, pressed upon the natives, as preferable to the cocoa-nut shells and cow-horns, which had hitherto been their dishes and drinking-vessels. A work of the time, written by a lively observer of things on the spot, gives an idea which may be exaggerated, but which must have some truth in it, of how these South American projects were set on foot, and carried out:

'We had all sorts of English speculations in South America, some of which were really amusing. Besides many brother companies which I met with at Buenos Ayres, I found a sister association of milkmaids. It had suddenly occurred to some of the younger sons of John Bull, that, as there were a number of beautiful cows in the United Provinces of Rio de la Plata, a quantity of good pasture, and as the people of Buenos Ayres had no butter to their bread, a churning company would answer admirably; and before the idea was many months old, a cargo of Scotch milkmaids were lying becalmed under the line on their passage to make butter at Buenos Ayres.' When arrived, 'the difficulties they had to contend with were very great. Instead of leaning their heads against patient domestic animals, they were introduced to a set of lawless, wild creatures, who looked so fierce that no young woman who ever sat upon a three-legged stool could dare to approach, much less to milk them. But the guachos attacked the cows, tied their legs with strips of hide, and as soon as they became quiet, the shops of Buenos Ayres were literally full of butter. But now for the sad moral of the story. After the difficulties had been all conquered, it was discovered, first, that the butter would not keep; and, secondly, that, somehow or other, the guachos and natives of Buenos Ayres liked oil better!' This gentleman was himself a victim of the spirit of the time. He went out as manager of one of the mining associations; left two cargoes of English and German miners at Buenos Ayres, and rode on to explore, galloping a thousand miles here, and twelve hundred miles there, in search of a fit spot to which to transport his miners. He found, as others did, that between fraud and folly, there was no hope, and there had never been any solid ground for speculation to build on. Some of the Germans wished to remain in the country; the whole of the rest, English and Germans, returned without having gone into the interior at all; and the company was dissolved, with a loss of at least £50,000. These are mere single specimens of a folly and rashness which were the epidemic of the time. The reaction was not long in coming.

On the 6th of July 1825, the lord chancellor read the king's speech, dismissing the parliament for the session. The speech avowed that the 'general and increasing prosperity on which his majesty had the happiness of congratulating' his parliament at the opening of the session, continued 'to pervade every part of the kingdom.' Yet there were a good many people in the kingdom who were in a very different state of spirits about this prosperity from that which they had been in at the opening of the session. In the early spring, the funds had begun to decline; and soon the prices of almost all commodities were lowered. Cotton, wine, silk, and other foreign products came into the market in such vast quantities, that it must be long before they could be sold off; and their prices fell incessantly, both from the superabundance, and from the eagerness of the holders to sell. No returns came in from the great speculations in foreign countries; no gold and silver from the Andes; no profits from the butter of the Pampas; no tolls from the canal which was to unite the Atlantic and Pacific; no pearls from the coast of Columbia. Again, a multitude of traders had exhausted their credit in obtain-

ing capital which they had locked up in enterprises extending far into the future; and their immediate want of
money was pressing. Without it, they could not await the
release of the capital they had locked up. They importuned
the bankers for further advances; but the bankers were as
much hampered as anybody; they had been tempted, some
months before, by the abundance of money, and the low
rate of interest, to discount bills of extremely long dates,
and to lend accommodation on securities of which they
could make no use, in the present state of the market.
Just at this most critical time, the Bank of England began
to draw in. Her issues had been profuse when money was
too plentiful, and gold was rapidly leaving the country.
Now, when money was wanted in abundance to rescue
commercial credit on all hands, she began to be stiff about
discounting, and to contract her issues. Panic first, and
then despair, were the consequence. Every man seemed
ready to seize his debtor by the throat, and say : 'Pay me
that thou owest.' The hilarity and openness of heart and
hand which had made England such a sunny place a year
ago, were gone; and instead, there was now the suspicion
with which every man regarded his debtor and his creditor;
the daily dread of the post; the eager glance at the gazette;
the walking out to await the mail; the laying down of
pony-carriage and new footman; the giving up the visit
to the sea, and the subscription to the book-club and
concert; and even, too often, the humbling inquiry of
servants, whether they could wait a while for their wages.
The manufacturer looked round on his overloaded shelves,
and for every thousand pounds' worth of goods now reckoned
five hundred. The widow lady and her daughters, who
had paid ready money all their lives, now found themselves
without income for half a year together, and could not enjoy
a meal, because the butcher's and baker's bill was running
on. The dying man, who could not wait for better days,
altered his will with a sigh, lessening his children's portions
by one-half or two-thirds. Young lovers, who were to
have had a jocund wedding this autumn, looked in one
another's faces, and saw that it must not be thought of at
present. But worse was to come.

Here and there, the failure of a commercial house was

announced. First, the failures were of houses which nobody supposed to be very stable; but presently one firm
after another stopped payment: one known to possess
enormous landed estates; another to be the proprietor of
rich mines; a third to have great wealth, fixed or afloat,
in foreign lands. In these cases, the same story was
always told; that it was merely a temporary embarrassment, and that the firms possessed property far exceeding
in value their entire liabilities. But so many of these
embarrassments occurred, each spreading disorder over its
own range of influence, that it presently became doubtful
what any kind of property was really worth, for any
practical purpose. Then, of course, came the turn of the
banks—the securities they held for their vast and rash
advances having become, for the time, little better than
waste-paper. In a country-town, one market-day, the
aspect of the market-place was very unlike its wont.
The country-people were leaving their stalls, and collecting in groups, while some made haste to pack up their
produce, and put to their horses, and hie home as if they
expected to be robbed if they stayed. Here, a man passed
with a gloomy face, and a bank-note clutched in his hand;
there a woman wrung her hands, and wept; and an actual
wail of many voices was heard amidst the hubbub of the
place. The bank of the district had stopped payment.
The hopeful went about telling all they met that it was
only for a time, and that everybody would be paid at last;
the desponding said that now it had begun there was no
saying where it would stop, and that everybody would
be ruined; and neither the hopeful nor the desponding
could suggest anything to be done. Buying and selling
came almost to a stand; for the country people looked
at every kind of bank-note as if it would burn their
fingers, and thought they would rather go home than sell
anything at all. Before going home, however, all who
had money in any bank ran to get it out. The run
upon the banks spread from district to district, and very
soon to London. Lombard Street was full of men of
business standing about waiting to hear the disasters of
the day; or of persons even of great wealth who were
hastening to their bankers to draw out their deposits. It

was a time which tried the faith and courage and generosity of the rich.   Some did not trouble their bankers by
any kind of application; and some few drove up in their
carriages and carried away heavy bags of gold with or
without apparent shame.   On the 5th of December the
news spread with the speed of the wind that the banking-
house of Sir Peter Pole and Company had stopped.   This
must occasion many failures in the provinces, as this firm
had accounts with forty-four country-banks.   The funds
went down immediately; and faster still next day when
the bank of Williams and Company stopped.   From this
time the crash went on without intermission, till in five or
six weeks from sixty to seventy banks had stopped payment.
    The question now was how to get money to go on with
from day to day; a question which involved that of the
very life of the working-classes through the winter.
There seemed to be nothing before millions of them but
absolute starvation, unless commerce could be set agoing
again more or less.   If they could not earn they must
starve; for even those of them who had some property
could not sell.   The pawnbrokers' houses were crammed
from the rafters to the door-step, till they would not hold
one article more; and if they had, the pawnbrokers had no
money any more than other people.   It was a touching
thing to those who had acquaintance among the poor to
see, that winter, the bride-housewife who had lately looked
forward to a marriage of substantial comfort, polishing up
her new furniture or looking for something to mend in
her own or her husband's new clothes, while the faces of
both were wan with hunger.   It was touching to see how
long the pride of the decent dressmaker, and the skilled
weaver and his wife, leaning faint against their idle loom,
stood out against the charity soup and loaf—declaring,
even till it became no longer true, that they could point
out some neighbours who would be glad of tickets, but
that, for themselves, they could not say they had ever
wanted bread.   These things were seen and heard from
street to street of every town, throughout that winter, even
after government and generous-hearted capitalists had
done all that could be done to stop the derangement of the
national affairs.

On the failure of Pole and Co.'s bank, meetings of the cabinet took place, and went on with unusual frequency, till the disorder began to subside. Ten days after the stoppage of Pole's bank, an issue was made of one and two pound bank-notes for country circulation; and the Mint was set to work to coin sovereigns as fast as its machinery would go. For above a week the coinage amounted to 150,000 sovereigns per day. At the same time the most influential and secure men of business in London and in the great towns held meetings, where they adopted resolutions pointing to the support of commercial credit. This show of confidence, and the somewhat increased supply of money, raised the spirits and allayed the panic of society; and by the end of the year—the year which had opened so brilliantly!—the nation began to think it might, one way or another, struggle through; resolving, with the desperate earnestness natural at such crises, if it once got out of this scrape, never to fall into such a one again; a resolution which, in this case, as in that of an individual sinner, lasted only till the next season of strong temptation.

The first days of the new year were, however, dark enough. Though the banks no longer broke by the half-dozen a day, the crash was not over. Here and there, one which had struggled on, and hoped to get through, was obliged to give up at last; and on every such occasion, there was a spread of distress through the district. Still there was no employment for the poor, except such as was created for them; and some of the Lancashire operatives rose, to destroy the machinery which they supposed to be the cause of the glut in the markets. The shipowners charged the same fact upon the relaxation of the navigation-laws, and clamoured accordingly. On the whole, however, the patience and fortitude shown by the most suffering parties were as remarkable as the rashness and selfishness of the speculators who had plunged them into their misery.

It was the business of parliament to see what it could, and what it could not, do in such cases as the present; how much of the mischief was occasioned by bad, or could be prevented by good laws; and how much was independent of legislative action altogether. This inquiry was recommended in the king's speech, delivered by commission on the 2nd of February; and both Houses began to debate the matter at once.

Some few members of each House were eager to bring forward their favourite topics, in connection with the prevalent distress, which was, indeed, large enough to hang every political idea upon; but the greater number were anxious to hear what the ministers had to say, in explanation of the past, and proposal for the future. Lord Liverpool stated the fact, that the issue of paper by country-banks was more than double in 1825 what it had been in 1823. During the years 1821, 1822, and 1823, the value of notes stamped for country-bankers had been, on an average, a little above four millions. In 1824 it had reached six millions; and in 1825 it exceeded eight millions. The Bank of England was at the same time augmenting its issues, though less remarkably. It was now to be proposed by government, to prohibit the circulation of £1 and £2 notes, after a certain period; and next, to negotiate with the Bank of England for an alteration of the terms of its privileges. The charter of the Bank was not to expire till 1833; but it was proposed to induce the directors to establish branch banks in the commercial centres of the provinces, and to permit an extension of the powers of the private banks, whose firms had hitherto not been permitted to consist of more than six partners. The same explanations were made in the other House by the chancellor of the exchequer. A difficulty occurred at once in regard to the suppression of small notes. If a day was fixed by law, after which no more small notes should be stamped, there was evidence in the hands of government to show that such an amount would be stamped in the interim as would render the law altogether nugatory. The government, therefore, stopped the stamping process immediately, though many bankers had paid for their licences to issue notes up to the next 10th of October. Of course, the ministers were called to account for this high-handed proceeding—this 'unconstitutional exercise of power'— this 'violation of a statutory guarantee.' They admitted the justice of these descriptive terms; acknowledged that an act of indemnity might be required, and pleaded, in their defence, the urgent necessity of the case.   After a little complaint and remonstrance, the government heard no more of the matter—the state of the commercial world being such as to make the most vigilant politicians less scrupulous than usual about 'statutory guarantees' being strictly observed.   It was a question of an act like that of blowing up a private house, without leave asked, to stop a conflagration.   Anything was better than running the risk of a deluge of small-note paper in the year to come, like that of the year that was gone.   Lord Liverpool and the chancellor of the exchequer explained that in 1825 the amount of small country note paper had not been less than six millions.   Since the crash, it had been reduced to four millions; the vacancy having been supplied by coin; and now there was no reason to expect that there would be any difficulty in replacing the other four millions by coin; a measure most desirable for the benefit of the poorer classes, who, as the principal holders of small notes, were always the first to suffer, while the least able to bear the suffering, from such a crisis as had just taken place.   In some essential points of the discussion, almost all the members of both Houses agreed: that the present question was in fact of a metallic currency at all, as it was invariably found that, under an unrestricted small note currency, gold and silver were driven out of circulation by an equal amount of paper —Lancashire, where no small notes existed, being the only part of the country which had hitherto had a metallic circulation at all; and the coin, which had been issued with great expense and trouble, being sent back to London by return of the mail which had carried it down; that the present was the time for the restriction to be made—the work being, as Mr. Brougham observed, already half-done by the panic and crash; and that the present was the moment, for another reason—the severe test which had been just applied to the stability of the country banks which had stood the shock, and which could therefore easily stand the gradual withdrawal of the outstanding notes.   The opposition, led by Mr. Baring, numbered only 39 votes against 222; and when the opinion of the majority was thus decisively declared, the minority abstained from further objection.

Some needless difficulty arose, from the imprudent conduct of certain of the country-bankers, who withdrew their small notes from circulation too hastily, allowing no time for the new metallic currency to supply their place.   In some districts this created great difficulty about carrying on the smaller transactions of commerce.   To meet it, an enactment was proposed, and passed by a large majority, by which the Bank of England was enabled to continue stamping small notes during the interval till the 10th of October.   This liberty did not affect the term fixed for the circulation of small notes; and the enlarged power of preparation of notes for that term was sure not to be abused; for the Bank of England found its small-note circulation a pure inconvenience.   The purpose of the enactment was merely to enable the bank to furnish a small currency in particular districts, where it might be urgently wanted during the period of change, when the country-bankers were drawing in their £1 and £2 notes.

One of the strangest arguments brought against the new measures was by Lord Carnarvon in the Upper House.   He gravely urged, that with a return to a metallic currency, highwaymen would again come out upon the roads.   At a time within his recollection, before the common use of small notes, 'a friend of his had been robbed on the highway; another had been wounded by a shot fired at him by a footpad; and a third had narrowly escaped with his life, by seizing the muzzle of the pistol which the robber had thrust into his carriage, and wresting it out of his hand.'   This objection was easily met by proofs of the extent of thefts, even on the high-road, of bank-notes; and of the great amount of the easy crime of forgery.   Lord Carnarvon probably derived his plea from the celebrated *Letters of Malachi Malagrowther*, as Sir Walter Scott chose to style himself.   In these letters, which pleaded against the abolition of the small-note currency of Scotland, the author drew pictures of the probable robberies of bankers' chests in the Highland glens.

The prohibition of the small-note currency was not made to extend to Scotland.   The banking system of Scotland had all along been essentially different from that

of England. Its firms had been under no limitation with
regard to the number of partners; and banking was
carried on by large companies of capitalists, under a
system which admitted the commercial world to a much
fuller knowledge of the affairs of the banks than is
thought of in England, or would there be compatible with
the practices of commerce. Small banking firms in
Scotland must, therefore, consist of men known to be
wealthy and trustworthy; and their responsibility in
issuing small notes is understood to be complete. During
the crash of 1825 and 1826, not a single Scotch bank
failed; and there was evidently no need to interfere with
a system which worked so well in its own locality—however inapplicable it might be elsewhere.

After much negotiation between the government and
the Bank of England, the further changes introduced
into the English banking system were these. The bank
established branches in many of the large trading towns;
a measure which has proved highly useful. Banking firms
might henceforth include any number of partners except
within sixty-five miles of London. These changes, with
the suppression of small notes, would, it was hoped, obviate
much of the danger of insecure banking, from which the
country had suffered so grievously.

As for the relief that should be given on the instant to
the commercial world, the ministers were unwilling to
authorise an issue of exchequer bills; because they thought
the remedy a fallacious one under the circumstances; but
they offered to bear the bank harmless through a purchase
of exchequer bills to the amount of two millions. The
bank did not stir; nor did it meet favourably the government proposition that it should make advances on deposits
of goods. But affairs pressed; times were not mending;
the merchants of London and the large provincial towns
were growing desperate; the government was called,
even in parliament, hard and cruel. Something must be
done to revive confidence, and bring out the hoarded gold,
which was above everything wanted. It was no longer
possible to refuse what the general opinion required; and
before February was out, the bank had agreed to make
advances on deposits of merchants' goods. A great

pawning transaction was entered upon; the advances of the bank being limited to three millions. Commissioners were appointed to conduct the business in the principal trading districts. It was presently found that many of these commissioners would have little or nothing to do. As soon as it was found that the money could be had, it appeared that little of it would be wanted. The restoration of credit was the thing required. On the strength of this new resource, men of high commercial character began to trust one another. The example spread; and in a short time the alarm subsided, and fair and prudent trading began to revive.

Good as were the consequences of this arrangement, the government had the judgment and sympathy of the best men in the country with them in their unwillingness to have recourse to it. The prime-minister declared in his place his serious objection to inducing merchants to look anywhere for aid in commercial difficulties, but to themselves and the banks of the country; and that 'nothing justified the interference of the government in mercantile embarrassments, unless the distress was occasioned by some great public calamity inflicted by the hand of God, or some political event of a very extraordinary nature.' Their position was a very hard one; one so hard that it must be hoped that no government may ever again be made to suffer in like manner by the folly and cupidity of the society they have to govern. First, the ministers had to witness large preparations for the failure of their own wisest policy; preparations with which they had no right or power to interfere. Before the admission of foreign silks, there was such a rage for building silk-mills, each costing from £10,000 to £15,000, that many of them stood still unroofed at the close of the panic and crash. In 1825, the population of Macclesfield amounted to about 20,000; and in the newspapers of February of that year may be seen advertisements to 'overseers, guardians of the poor, and families desirous of settling in Macclesfield. Wanted immediately, from four to five thousand persons, from seven to twenty years of age, to be employed in the throwing and manufacturing of silk.' Again: 'Wanted to be built immediately, one thousand houses.' This was

only a single example of those speculations which, to use
Mr. Canning's words, 'at the time fixed the public gaze,
and so immediately excited their appetency, as to cover
the nation, in the eyes of foreign states, if not with disgrace, at least with ridicule. The most wild and incoherent
schemes were started; projects which sprang with the
dawn, and expired before the setting of the sun, in whose
beams they glittered for a few hours, and then fell; a puff
of vapour sent them soaring towards the skies; the
puncture of a pin brought them to the earth.' In the
midst of the intoxication the government uttered warnings,
strenuously and incessantly, but in vain; and because
these warnings were in vain, those who uttered them
were blamed for not having put forth the strong hand to
restrain the madness of the nation. 'I really do not know,
sir,' declared Mr. Canning, 'what legislative interference
could possibly effect in such a case. I do not know how a
measure could be framed, to deal with those speculations
of unreasoning avarice, which would not, at the same
time, have borne so hard on honest industry and rational
enterprise, that it would have been likely to do more harm
than good. The inordinate appetite for gain, if left to
itself, could not fail to work its own cure, through its own
certain disappointment.' And then, when the meteor
schemes had all exploded, and left nothing behind but
darkness and stifling odours, the sufferers who refused
timely warnings would have it that the ministers might
make the sun rise, and bring wholesome breezes if they
would; and taxed them with obstinacy and hard-hearted-
ness. If they would issue exchequer bills, or do this and
that which none but a despotic government would think
of doing, all might be well in a moment. 'It is most
unfair,' said Mr. Canning, 'to infer from any hesitation on
the part of government to adopt any particular remedy,
under such circumstances, that there exists, therefore, on
their part, an insensibility to the extent or nature of the
existing evil. For myself and for my colleagues, I totally
disdain to answer such insinuations. I impute to no man
who now hears me, that he is insensible; but, sir, for
others to impute it to those upon whom, every day and
every night, care and anxiety are brought by the con

sideration of those distresses, in addition to the common
sympathy in which they share as men, is to impute to
them, not only a want of feeling, but a want of sense,
which would unfit them, not merely for the situations
which they fill in the government of the country, but to
appear here, in the midst of those whom I have the honour
of now addressing.'

Such was the share which the government had to endure
of the pain of the crisis; the foreboding—the heavy heart
in a time of delirious joy; the haunting care which cast
its cold shadow by day, and sat on the pillow at night; the
inability to ward off the mischief, and the discredit of it
when it came; the strain put upon their principles; and
the reproach cast upon their steadfastness—such was their
share of the suffering of the time.   But if they suffered
more than the careless, they suffered less than the guilty.
There were many hundreds, many thousands in the country
who might well envy them their very cares.   Perhaps even
they, with all their means of knowledge, amidst all the
press of evil tidings which rushed in from day to day,
could not be so well aware as those in an humbler station
of the worst miseries of the time.   They had the gazette
under their eyes, and the clamour of the commercial world
in their ears; they had before them the diminishing returns
of the taxes, and the increasing returns of pauperism; but
they were saved the anguish of witnessing the individual
traits which most wring the heart in a season of national
calamity.   It is not he who sees from afar the cloud of
dust from an earthquake, and who faintly hears the murmur
of confused sounds, and who knows that so many churches,
and so many dwellings, and even so many people, have
perished, that can feel the deepest horror of the scene.   It
is rather he who, in some narrow street, meets the spectacle
of the writhing of a crushed sufferer here, a childless
mother there, a surviving lover, a forlorn infant wailing
among ruins and flames, who has the best understanding of
what has befallen.   And so it was with this social convulsion in England.   There are some now of the most comfortable middle-class order, who cannot think of that year
without bitter pain.   They saw many parents grow white-
haired in a week's time; lovers parted on the eve of

marriage; light-hearted girls sent forth from the shelter of
home, to learn to endure the destiny of the governess or
the sempstress; governesses, too old for a new station,
going actually into the workhouse; rural gentry quitting
their lands; and whole families relinquishing every prospect in life, and standing as bare under the storm as Lear
and his strange comrades on the heath. They saw something even worse than all this. They saw the ties of
family honour and harmony snapped by the strain of
cupidity first, and discontent afterwards, and the members
falling off from one another as enemies. They saw the
hope of the innocent, the faith of the pious, the charity of
the generous, the integrity of the trusted, giving way.
They saw the most guilty rewarded, and the most virtuous
involved as deeply as any in the retribution. But it would
be an endless task to adduce the sorrows of that time; nor
can their issue ever be recognised. After a weary and
dreary season of suspense, affairs began to mend; but so
heavily, that even the king's speech, which is understood
to make the best of everything at all times, declared, in
the next November, that the depression had abated more
slowly than his majesty had thought himself warranted in
anticipating. Still, the depression did pass away. Our
ships were once more abroad upon the sea; and the clack
of the loom and the roar of the forge were again heard in
our towns. But the heart-wounds of such a time can no
more be healed than the whitened hair can resume its
colour. The impoverished might grow rich, and many a
laden mind might throw off its cares; but the estranged
could not be reunited; the dishonoured could not be rein-
stated; the grave could not give back the broken-hearted,
nor prosperity reassure some who had suffered too fearfully. To a few who were strong enough, this adversity
may, like other discipline, have ministered increased
strength; 'to him that hath much shall more be given;'
but the strong are everywhere the few; and in this case
their lot is only the single ray in the dark place—the
strong tower which outstood the earthquake.

Men are wont to talk glibly of commercial crises when
they are past, in a tone quite different from that in which
they speak of a pestilence or a famine. In this case, it can

hardly be so—the calamity was so fearful, the folly so humbling, and the guilt now so clear.   There is a certain Scripture text about the temptations and destruction of those 'that would be rich,' which must have haunted many a man's mind, and rung in his ears like a judicial sentence, after the season of passionate cupidity was past. To the more disengaged mind of the guiltless observer, the whole crisis must have been a significant text, from which he could preach eloquently the great truth, how little governments can do for the welfare of nations, in the absence or abeyance of individual virtue and intelligence; how necessary it is that men should rule their own spirits, before they can enjoy that social welfare which a wise government may help to secure, but can never confer.

CHAPTER IX.

Riots—Release of Bonded Corn—Opening the Ports—Emigration—
Colonial Office—Emigration Committee.

THE history of 1825 and 1826 has shown us the state of English capitalists; the rapacity and ignorance of some, and the consequent sufferings of all.   How was it with the labourers, among whom it is natural to look for a worse cupidity, a deeper ignorance, and a fiercer suffering?

From the time when the false prosperity of the country began to decline, there was much rioting.   The first impulse of sufferers too ignorant to know the causes of their suffering, is to rebel against the order of things under which their misery takes place.   The first serious rioting was at Sunderland, in August 1825, just after the tide of prosperity was seen to have turned.   The association of seamen, who were not on good terms with the shipowners, saw a collier quietly leaving the port, manned by strangers, and went out to attack the vessel.   The principal shipowners, who had been sworn in as special constables, put off after them, but could make little resistance against overwhelming numbers; the rioters being at least four hundred.

The shipowners, and all the obnoxious crew, except the master and the mate, were thrown into the sea, whence they were picked up in no condition for further fight. A party of dragoons was brought up; the Riot Act was read; but on the opposite side of the river from that where the proceedings of the rioters had collected a mob of men, women, and children. Some stones were thrown from the midst of this mob, who had not heard the reading of the Riot Act. The soldiers fired, and five persons were killed; one of whom was a carpenter, at work on his stage, and another a labourer, returning from the field. The funeral of the victims was solemn, with banners and flags, and a band of singers; and for mourners, twelve hundred seamen, with each a crape round the left arm, walking hand in hand, two and two. The circumstances had, however, been too fatal for the courage of the men; and they yielded the points for which they had struck.

A more successful stand against authority and law was made in the Isle of Man the next November, when the island was kept in a state of uproar for a week, by the resistance of the poor to the collection of the tithe of potatoes by the proctors of the bishop. The people overturned the laden carts, stood guard over the potatoes, pursued the bishop's proctors, rescued such of their own body as were apprehended, defied the constables, evaded the magistrates and military, and obtained from the bishop, at the end of a week, the following written declaration, which was delivered by his lordship himself into the hands of a deputation from the malcontents: 'Whereas it has been reported by evil-minded persons, that a tithe of potatoes will be taken from the poor tenants of this island, and from persons little able to pay the same—they are hereby assured that such tithe will not be demanded from them, either this year or at any future time.' These poor people needed only the assurance that their potatoes should not be taken from their children to be given to the church; and the bishop saw that it would be little for the advantage of religion to give the food of the poor to the church. So there was grace on the one side, and cheering on the other; and the affair was over for the time.

By the spring of the next year, 1826, there was such

fearful suffering among the poor of the manufacturing districts, that no one could wonder much at the spirit of violence which broke out in Lancashire. The people rose up against the power-looms, which they believed to be the cause of their distress; and in one day, every power-loom in Blackburn, and within six miles of it, was destroyed. It is worthy of note, that the rioters took the utmost care not to injure any spinning-machinery. Time was when the hand-spinners were as much exasperated against spinning-jennies as the hand-loom weavers now were against power-looms. They had discovered the value of the spinning-machinery by this time, but could not be persuaded that they should ever derive any benefit from weaving-machinery. It was a mournful spectacle in Lancashire, that week in April; the mob going from town to town, from factory to factory; snatching their food from bakers' shops and public-houses; throwing stones at the soldiers, and being shot down, rather than give up their object, believing sincerely that their very lives depended on the destruction of these looms; leaping from two-story windows to escape the soldiery, after having cut up every web, and hewn down every beam and stick within; striking at their pursuers with table-knives made into pikes; with scythes and sledge-hammers; swimming canals, hiding in woods, parading the streets of towns, to the number of 10,000 at a time, frightening the night with cries of hunger and yells of rage—all this was terrible; but it came at the end of many months of such sore distress as rouses the fiercest passions of men. On the first day, three persons were killed by the soldiers; on another day, nine: here, it might be seen that wounded men were carried away across the fields; there, the street was found, when emptied, to be 'much stained with blood.' Here, a poor creature was loading his rusty gun with marbles, while the manufacturers were bringing up cannon to plant round their factories; there, haggard men were setting buildings on fire, and snatching buckets from the hands of those who would have supplied water to the engines. Between Monday morning and Saturday night, a thousand power-looms were destroyed. The immediate money-value of this machinery was £30,000; but it had a greater value as the only means of bread of a large number of people who were now left idle and destitute.

In the first week in May, the Manchester operatives rose again; and then the Bradford wool-combers and weavers met to consider 'the present unparalleled distress and famishing condition of the operatives,' and could think of no way of mending it but by breaking windows. There were inquests first, and trials afterwards; but no relief. In Lanarkshire, the noblemen, magistracy, and gentry of the county, assembled to consult upon the wretched and helpless state of the Glasgow operatives, knew no better than to throw the blame on the invention of machinery. In Dublin, the starving silk-weavers formed in procession, to exhibit their hunger in the streets. Their idea of a remedy was, that the public subscription raised for them should be applied in the purchase of the manufacturers' stocks; and thus, when the shelves were cleared, they thought a new demand must at once ensue. At Trow-bridge, the people were dismayed at a rise in the price of potatoes in May, and would have it that the gardeners and greengrocers were hoarding the potatoes. On market-day, they attacked the gardeners' stalls so vigorously, that by eleven o'clock not a vegetable was left in the place. The frightened butchers removed—the soldiers came—window-breaking went on all night—a prisoner was released by unroofing the prison, and two more were sent off to Salis-bury for trial at the assizes. At Carlisle, the starving weavers mobbed one of the candidates for the city, clamour-ing for a repeal of the corn-laws and radical reform; and a riot ensued, in which a woman standing at her own door, with a key in her hand, and a little girl in the street, were shot through the head. The inquests in these cases were not ceremonies tending to tranquillise the exasperated. In the iron districts there were strikes and readings of the Riot Act, and a scouring of the country by soldiery. In Bethnal Green, the thieves of the metropolis congregated, and robbed everybody in the name of the distressed weavers. In Norwich, the unemployed weavers, who would not take work at the wages which the manufacturers could afford, kept watch at the city-gates for goods brought in from the country. They destroyed one cart-load in the street, and

threw the cart into the river; broke the manufacturers'
windows; cooped in a public-house three men from the
country who had silk canes about them; and kept the
magistracy busy and alarmed for some weeks. About
12,000 weavers in Norwich were then unemployed, and
the whole city in a state of depression, the more harassing
from its contrast with the activity and high hope of the
preceding year.

While these scenes of disorder and wretchedness were
witnessed from end to end of the kingdom, the ministers
adhered to the principle on which they had refused to issue
exchequer bills, and declined to purchase popularity by
the offer of any apparent assistance, while convinced that
they could afford none that was real and effectual. They
were confident that the mischief must work its own cure,
and could not be cured in any other way. Yet, something
might be done to relieve the despair of the hungering,
who saw large stores of wheat laid up in bond in Liverpool, Hull, and other ports, while the prospects of the
harvest were very doubtful, and parliament was about to
be dissolved; leaving the people without advocacy to the
care of the government for an interval of months before
the new parliament could assemble. The ministers and
parliament had agreed, early in the session, that it would
be improper to bring forward the whole question of the
corn-laws while the country was in a state of high
excitement and on the eve of a general election. But it
was thought by ministers that the 300,000 quarters of
corn in bond in the ports might be let out without
tampering with the great question, and without doing any
appreciable injury to the agricultural interest; while the
manufacturers declared that even the small imports of
foreign corn which would follow upon such a measure
would afford just the stimulus to their business that was
wanted. They were ready to resume business if they
could obtain any returns from abroad of the only commodity which their foreign customers could at present
send with advantage. It was decided, after eager and
protracted discussions, that the people should have the
prospect of a supply of food, under arrangements which
met the objections of both the parties who were constantly

opposed to each other on all branches of the question of the corn-laws. The manufacturers were to be gratified by the letting out of bond of the 300,000 quarters already in the ports; and the agricultural interest obtained the point, that no prices and amounts of duty should be fixed in relation to the further supply of 500,000 quarters which the ministers were authorised to import, if necessary, within the space of two months. The responsibility in regard to the prices and duties was thrown wholly upon the ministers by the agriculturists, lest any fixing of these by parliament should be made a precedent in any future action for the repeal of the corn-laws. This period of two months was short; and the amount of 500,000 quarters was less than half of the largest previous importation; so that the arrangement was not so formidable but that the landed interest were brought to agree to it, under the extreme pressure of the times, while the manufacturers were thankful for even this slight relaxation of the laws to which they were willing to ascribe almost the whole of their distresses. The opposition to both bills was strong in the House of Lords; but the premier made an earnest appeal to them in view of a possible scarcity of food during the recess, following upon all the recent disasters which had afflicted the country; and at last both bills passed their Lordships' House on the 26th of May.

The object of the ministers, real and avowed, in urging these bills, was to obtain a constitutional permission to do that which they might otherwise be compelled to do without authority, and on the chance of procuring indemnity when the new parliament should meet. They foresaw that they should be compelled to open the ports, during the recess, whether they obtained leave beforehand or not; and of course they were extremely anxious for such authorisation. But, after all, it did not answer their purpose. The hot summer of 1826 is well remembered. It was not very unfavourable to wheat, of which there was about an average crop. But the barley crop was far below the average; and at one time it appeared as if there would be no oats or pulse at all. Oats are generally highest in June, when the preceding year's crop is coming to an end. This year, oats were 22s. 11d. in the middle of June; and the price went on rising, instead of falling, through July and August, till, on the 1st of September, it had risen to 30s. There was so little grass, that the cattle were fed on dry fodder on the richest meadowlands in England, which were brown and burnt as if a fire had passed over them. The deer in noblemen's parks died of drought; ponds and reservoirs were shrunk to muddy pools; hard-working people sat up all night to watch the springs—some to carry home drink to their children— others to have a commodity of cold water to sell in the morning. In some high-lying towns, the richest people made presents to one another of little pitchers of fresh water; and the consumption of beer increased much among those who were disgusted with the warm and stagnant water yielded by the brooks when the wells were all dry. All the accounts from the north of Europe told of a rise in the price of oats and pulse, like that at home; and this increased the alarm. By the 1st of September, the importation price was passed; but before the ports could be opened, the average must be struck of the price above the importation price; and the first average would not be struck till the 15th of November. The ministers decided not to wait for the quarterly average, but to issue an order in council at once for the admission of oats, rye, beans, and peas. What was in bond was brought into the market immediately; and the fresh imports were subjected to additional duties to be confirmed by parliament when it should meet. Thus, after all, ministers were reduced to forestall the action of parliament and to seek an act of indemnity for themselves. Such a necessity was not without its good results. It tended, like every perplexity and irregularity of the kind, to disgust sensible people with that system of restriction on food which was to be put an end to by a member of the administration of that time.

The miserable are always restless. Hunger roams from land to land, as pain tosses on the bed it cannot leave. The famished and cold cannot sit still on the bare ground while there is life within them, and a capacity of hope which points to food and warmth which may be had elsewhere. The poor Irish, with their wistful looks and

their tatters, are poured out upon the coasts of England
and Scotland every year; and when they are too many for
the existing work and food, or when the work and food fall
short from other causes, the grave and decent poor of
England and Scotland wander away too, shipping themselves off westwards, or to our furthest settlements in the
east. The subject of emigration must, sooner or later,
become one of interest and importance to every civilised
state; and soonest to an insular kingdom. It may be
theoretically a question whether, if the English nation had
been altogether wise—had assumed the conduct of its own
civilisation, instead of being the subject, and in some sense
the victim, of its own civilisation—the time would have
yet arrived for sending abroad any of its people. It may
be a question whether, if we were all wise and all of one
mind about social affairs, there is not enough for every one
to do and to enjoy on his native soil. This is a theoretical
question now, which may become a practical one any day;
and the sooner the better. But it has, for a course of
years now, been a prominent question how best to arrange
matters for the needy among our people, who will and
must roam, because they have no food for their little ones,
and no home for their own hearts. The restlessness which
forces upon us the question of emigration is of course
greatest in seasons of adversity; and in the adversity of
the year 1826, it was fierce enough to originate what may
prove to be an important period in our national history.

In 1825, it was announced to the country that the
business of the colonial office had so increased of late
years, that it had become necessary to have an additional
under-secretary of state. Mr. R. Wilmot Horton was the
existing under-secretary; and Mr. R. W. Hay was now
appointed in addition. It may be well that a future time
should see what amount of business was apportioned to
our colonial secretaries in 1825, when emigration, in the
modern import of the word, first began seriously to engage
the attention of society. It is still our way to approve of
our colonial minister as we approve of ministers for home
offices, on account of his general character and qualifications, without much regard to his capacity for a function
requiring a special and elaborate training. It is still our

way to permit our colonial minister to go out and come in at short intervals, as if the stability of the administration were not of the highest importance, when his administration extends over various and distant countries. It is still too probable that a colonial minister's first business is to shut himself up in his study, and find out on the globe where the territories lie which he has to set about governing. But we are beginning to learn how absurd it is to expect the machinery of the colonial office to do the necessary work; to understand the growing magnitude of the business of colonisation, and to be prepared for a reconstitution and prodigious enlargement of the office which is to superintend it. When this impending change is made, men will look back with astonishment on this list furnished in 1825, of the colonies whose affairs at headquarters had to be managed by Mr. Wilmot Horton and Mr. Hay.

Mr. R. Wilmot Horton: Jamaica, Barbadoes, St. Christopher, Nevis and Tortola, Antigua and Montserrat, Dominica, Grenada, St. Lucia, St. Vincent, Tobago, Trinidad, Demerara and Essequibo, Berbice, Honduras, Bahamas, Bermuda, Lower Canada, Upper Canada, Nova Scotia and Cape Breton, New Brunswick, Prince Edward's Island, Newfoundland. Commission of Inquiry and Criminal Justice, West Indies; and Apprenticed Africans.

Mr. Hay: Gibraltar, Malta, Ionian Isles, Marocco, Algiers, Tunis, Tripoli, Missions to the Interior of Africa, Sierra Leone, Gold Coast, Cape of Good Hope, Heligoland, New South Wales, Van Diemen's Land, Ceylon, Mauritius, East Indies. Commission of Inquiry, Cape, Mauritius and Ceylon; Sierra Leone.

The work of assisting emigration was henceforth to be looked forward to by the colonial office as a part of its business. Since 1822, government had given occasional aid to emigration to Canada; and now it heard on every side of expectations from individuals and societies that it would assist in conveying the needy to new fields of labour. The landowners of a Scotch county applied to ministers for encouragement to their poor to emigrate; and the working-men formed themselves into societies, in many parts of the country, whose object was to obtain funds for emigration from rich neighbours and from the government. Government was compelled to deliberate on this important subject. It would not do to go on giving sums of money here and there, without inquiring what was done with it. It was not right to continue supplying grants without knowing how the former schemes had issued. It was not possible to keep at home the poor creatures, rendered desperate by want, who were resolved to try their fortunes abroad; and it was cruel to let them go wholly unprepared and destitute. It became known by this time how piteous was the lot of the emigrant when he found himself among the snows of Canada, with the remnant of his family about him—the few whom hardship and fever and the miseries of the voyage had spared—and no possessions whatever but the axe on his shoulder and the tatters they wore. It became known how the Irish who flock to the United States are naturally regarded as a nuisance in their ports; and how they die in the swamps, digging canals which the Americans will not work at, and crouching in shanties which no American would enter —unless it were the missionary and the priest. Society had not yet awakened to the perception of what emigration ought to be; had not yet admitted the conception of a small, complete society, removed with all needful appliances to a new scene where it would be bound together as at home by its mutual wants and aids; by its capital and its labour; its church, its schools, its gradations of ranks and employments, and sufficient powers of self-government. Such a conception as this had not yet entered the mind of the government or of the nation; but all were aware that the desperate and random emigration of the time was bad, and must give place to something better.

On the 14th of March, 1826, Mr. R. Wilmot Horton moved 'that a select committee be appointed to inquire into the expediency of encouraging emigration from the United Kingdom.' He detailed the circumstances of the experiments of the years 1823 and 1825, when, first, 268 persons emigrated from Ireland to Canada at the expense of £22 each; and next, 2024 persons followed at an expense of £20 each. It had never been the intention of government to go on making grants for the removal of paupers in this mode; but it was thought that the issue of these first attempts was sufficiently favourable to indicate further inquiry and consideration.   As the scheme was advocated on the ground of its being a successful method of removing paupers, it was opposed as an expensive and fruitless remedy for pauperism, as the numbers removed could never perceptibly reduce the superabundance of labour at home.   The wider considerations of the benefits of calling new regions into fertility, and of creating new markets, and thus feeding and employing many who remained behind; the considerations of the proper ages of those who were to go; of their mutual apportionment and co-operation as capitalists and labourers; of the means of making emigration presently self-supporting and expansive —these points were not yet discussed, because they were not yet thought of.   The great subject which was soon to become a science was as yet treated superficially, partially, and empirically.   But a beginning was made.   The committee asked for was appointed; and it presented its report and evidence before the dissolution of parliament, with a recommendation that the subject should be pursued without loss of time.

It was a disastrous year, this year 1826; but if we have seen what miseries marked its progress, we have witnessed, too, the birth of a great redeeming blessing.   It is possible that from the woes and the terror and the clamour of that fearful season may have sprung the fertilisation and peopling of vast new regions abroad, and the redemption of future generations at home.

CHAPTER X.

Catholic Question reviewed—State of Opinion in 1824—Catholic Asso-
ciation—Catholic   Deputation—Mr. O'Connell—Progress of the
Question—Sir F. Burdett's Relief Bill—Duke of York's Declaration
—Bill lost—Catholics and Dissenters—Aspect of the Question.

THE year 1825 was marked by nothing more conspicuously
than by a great change in the aspect and conduct of the
Catholic question.   In a preceding page of this History,
a promise was given of a brief narrative of this great question ; and here, at the beginning of its final stage, we seem
to be at the right point for a rapid review of its history.

The difficulty of most or all perilous political questions
lies in the relation they bear to the long distant past; a
past which did not involve social principles that have since
become of primary importance, and by whose rule the
matter must be finally disposed of.   For long before the
present date, there had been an incessant and unmanageable
confusion, in the general mind of the anti-Catholic party,
between the religious and political mischiefs of admitting
the Catholics to an equality of civil rights with the Protestants; and this confusion itself was modern, compared with
the sufferings of the Catholics.   This was because the
sufferings of the Catholics began in an age when there was
no distinction between civil and religious rights.   When
the distinction rose into recognition, the Romanists were
actively persecuted, sometimes on the religious, and sometimes on the political ground; and when the persecution
became negative, and therefore confined to the political
ground, their enemies had still not arrived at any clearness
of thought, or any common agreement, as to the basis of
their opposition to the Catholic claims.   This is illustrated
by the whole course of the history of those claims.

The Reformation is, of course, the point from which the
separate story of the Catholic body must date.   When
Henry VIII., by his emissaries, demolished the holy shrine
of St. Kieran, and turned out its relics into the street, and

burned the costly crosier of St. Patrick, he did not persecute the Irish Catholics as Irish, but as Catholics; but his acts had the immediate effect of uniting in a general hostility to England the chiefs and tribes who were before incessantly at feud with each other. Nobody then thought of the distinction which grew up in a subsequent age. There was so little call for a religious reformation in Ireland, that we have it on good authority that there were not sixty Protestants in the island when Elizabeth became queen. During her 'vigorous rule' in Ireland, she and her ministers made no nice distinctions between her functions of head of the Church and head of the State, in the penal laws decreed against the Irish Catholics, and the legalised force by which she put down the Irish malcontents. In spite of the talk of the reformed religion in both countries, and the laws against the exercise of the Catholic religion, the conflicting parties were evidently full of political matters, and not of religious. The English government employed Catholic officials in the most important and confidential services in Ireland; even, if they belonged to the Pale, in repelling the Spanish invasions which took place on account of her anti-Catholic laws and policy. The Catholics of the Pale fought against those out of the Pale; and in the reign of James I., as a fierce Catholic, O'Sullivan, tells us, ' the eyes even of the English Irish '—the Catholics of the Pale—' were opened, and they cursed their former folly for helping the heretic.' Elizabeth's wars were waged against the chiefs of savages; chiefs whose tribes knew nothing of tillage, of homes, of property, or comforts; who, in the remoter parts of the island, went almost unclothed, and lay down round fires to sleep on the ground. These chiefs had lands to be robbed of. ' There will be lands for those who want,' said Queen Elizabeth, by way of stirring up her officials, when there were tidings that O'Neal was about to rise; and it would, no doubt, have been exactly the same—the whole course of her conquest of the rebels, whatever had been their religion, of all that existed, from pole to pole. Meantime, her Protestant Church of sixty members did not expand to her wish, though she gave bounties to it, and proscribed its enemies. When it did expand, it was not from con-

versions in Ireland, but by the accession of the colonists
of her successor, and the settlement of the soldiers of
Cromwell.

The confusion which arose after the incursion of these
new dwellers gave rise to the Act of Settlement, by which
7,800,000 acres of land were transferred from Irish
Catholic to English Protestant proprietors. At the first
possible moment—that is, during the brief season when
James II. held up his head in Ireland—the native parliament, in which only six Protestants sat, repealed the Act
of Settlement, against the will of the king. The battle of
the Boyne presently overthrew whatever had been done;
and it is not to be wondered at that the popery laws which
succeeded were excessively severe. Though they said a
great deal about religious error, they were imposed in
dread of a political foe, whose physical force was truly
formidable. ' The Protestant ascendency of Ireland,' says
the *Edinburgh Review* of Sir J. Throckmorton's work on the
Catholic question, ' cared very little about purgatory and
the seven sacraments. They acted upon principles simply
political; and their severity was not derived from polemi-
cal rancour, but from the two great springs of bitterness,
which turn the milk of human nature into gall—revenge
and fear. They knew what the vanquished had done in
the hour of success; they looked at their numbers with
dread, and sought to strengthen the barriers of law against
the rude arm of physical power. The system of the popery
laws, indeed, in Ireland, must be looked at as a whole.
In their present state (1806) they are folly, caprice, feeble
and petulant tyranny. As they stood originally, they were
vigorous and consistent; the firm, well-riveted fetters of
conquest, locking into one another, and stretching down
the captive giant to the floor.'

More forfeitures ensued as soon as King William had
driven out his enemy. The estates transferred on this
occasion are declared to have covered 1,060,793 acres.
The one circumstance which softened their political adversity to the Irish was that, by the Treaty of Limerick,
framed when the struggle was over, the free exercise of
their religion was secured to them for the future, on the
strength of the king's guarantee for himself, his heirs, and

successors, as far as in him lay. By the words of the treaty
it was expressly declared, that 'the Roman Catholics
should enjoy such privileges in the exercise of their
religion as are consistent with the laws of Ireland, or as
they did enjoy in the reign of Charles II.; and their
majesties, as soon as they can summon a parliament in this
kingdom, will endeavour to procure the said Roman
Catholics such further security in that particular as may
preserve them from any disturbance on account of their
religion.' These articles, afterwards published in letters-
patent under the great seal, were signed by the English
general on the 3rd of October, 1691 ; and for three weeks
the Irish Romanists were hopeful and happy. But it was
only for three weeks; and then followed a season of
oppression so cruel as to provoke the question how it
could have been borne, in an age of the world so advanced.
Of the English government of that time, Burke says: ' The
severe and jealous policy of a conqueror in the crude
settlement of his new acquisition, was strangely made a
permanent rule for its future government.' And of the
oppressed party, Swift declared that it was 'just as in-
considerable in point of power as the women and children.'
In this weakness lay their strength. It was nourishing
the germ of that future Catholic question which was soon
to begin disturbing cabinets, and with more and more
power, till, a century after, it should be looked upon with
constant dread as the explosive force which was to shatter
one administration after another for five-and-thirty years
together, and threaten at last to revolutionise the empire.
Little did the government of Queen Anne foresee the
consequences of setting its heel on the neck of the Catholic
interest; but, though it could not foreknow how it would
perplex and destroy a succession of administrations, and
craze the feeble brain of a sovereign, and invite invasion
again and again, it might have remembered how dangerous
it is to sink individuals, and, yet more, whole classes, so
low, that they can fall no lower, and will therefore make
desperate efforts to raise themselves. They might have
taken to heart Swift's words : ' General calamities, without
hopes of redress, are allowed to be the great uniters of
mankind; since nature hath instructed even a brood of

goslings to stick together, while the kite is hovering over their heads. It is certain that a firm union in any country where every man wishes the same thing with relation to the public, may, in several points of the greatest importance, in some measure supply the defect of power; and even of those rights which are the natural and undoubted inheritance of mankind.'

On the 3rd of October 1691, as we have said, the Treaty of Limerick, including provisions favourable to the Catholics, was signed. On the 22nd of the same month, the English parliament decreed that Irish members of both Houses should take the oaths of supremacy; an enactment which excluded Catholics from both the Irish Houses of parliament. King William forgot his pledge to recommend the liberties of the Catholics to the attention of parliament. Three years after that pledge was given, and when nothing had been done to redeem it, a set of enactments was passed which left the Romanists in such a condition that the wonder is that they did not spring at the throats of their oppressors, and peril everything for a savage revenge. All Catholics were disarmed, and the priests banished : that much might have been borne; but the whole body were deprived of all means of educating their children, and were prohibited from being the guardians, not only of other people's children, but of their own. As this was endured, other privations followed in 1704. Every son who would turn Protestant might now succeed to the family estate, which was stringently secured to him. A boy of ten years old, or younger, might thus dispossess his family, if he declared himself a Protestant. A Catholic could no longer purchase land, or enjoy a long lease, or make more than a certain income by his land, or marry a Protestant, or take his place in a line of entail, or hold any office, civil or military, or vote at elections, or, except under certain conditions, dwell in Limerick or Galway. Five years after, more penalties were added; and again in the next reign. Any son of a Catholic might bring his father into chancery, force him to declare on oath the value of his property, and to settle such an allowance upon the family informer as the court should decree, not only for the father's life, but the son s. This

was a zeal for religion indeed, which could slight morality,
and set up a new commandment in the place of the old
one, which enjoins honour to father and mother. Catholics
keeping schools were to be prosecuted as convicts; and
papists were bound to furnish Protestant watchmen for
the towns, and horses for the militia. Any priest celebrat-
ing marriage between a papist and a Protestant was to be
hanged. No Catholics were to enter the profession of the
law; and any lawyer marrying a Catholic was to be held
a papist. If it makes the heart sick now to read these
things, done little more than a century ago, and done in
the name of the religion professed by both parties, what
must it have been to have endured them? What must
have been the interior of Catholic households in those
days? If the blessing of education had been left them,
we might understand their patience; and we can but hope
that circumstances were to them an education sufficient for
their needs; for the children did not rise against their
parents, nor the oppressed against their oppressors. There
was no rebellion during the series of years which added
weight to the oppression with every new parliament.
These Catholic households had, in the absence of learning,
their faith, which they found sufficient to bind them
together in love, to strengthen them against temptation,
and under poverty; to nerve them to courage, and fortify
them for endurance. Thus it was at the time, while the
spirit of confessorship was fresh and strong among them.
But it is the first-fruits of adversity only, or chiefly, that
are blessed. In course of time, the enforced ignorance
began to tell upon the mind, and the unrelieved oppression
upon the temper, of the Catholic body; and we see the
results now in those moral defects of the Irish which per-
petuate their social miseries after the oppression has been
removed. It should be remembered, on the other hand,
that the spirit of the Reformation, which attributed all
the evils in the world to papistry, had not died out; that
the memory of the worst days of the Inquisition was fresh,
and the horror of the Gunpowder Plot, and the dread of
the Stuarts. It was a mistake to suppose that the evils
which took place under the prevalence of the Catholic faith
were all attributable to that faith; and it was another

mistake to suppose that any faith can be extirpated by persecution; but those were not days of philosophical statesmanship; and it would be unreasonable to look for the springing up of political philosophy by the light of Guy Fawkes's lantern, on the footsteps of successive Pretenders.

The first dawn of promise of better days appears to have followed upon the quietness of the Irish in the two Stuart rebellions. While Scotland and the north of England were up in arms, the Catholics of Ireland gave no trouble; and the Brunswick sovereigns were gratified and grateful. It was during their reigns that the Catholics had been deprived of the franchise; but that act had been an advert-ing again to a political from a religious ground. The English faction had for some time been becoming Irish in its habits and predilections. As Mr. Burke said: 'The English, as they began to be domiciliated, began also to recollect that they had a country; what was at first strictly an English interest, by faint and almost insensible degrees, but at length openly and avowedly, became an inde-pendent Irish interest.' The government feared a union between the two classes of Irish residents, which might become formidable to English rule; and they rendered the Catholic class politically powerless, by depriving them of the only remnant of social influence they still held—the franchise. But, when the Irish remained quiet during the two rebellions, they procured for themselves a degree of good-will from the English government which opened the way for their final emancipation. Their quietness was called 'loyalty;' a term which it would be no credit to them to accord; for they owed no faith to a sovereignty which had kept none with them, but had humbled them from the rank of subjects to that of slaves. By whatever name it may be called, their demeanour obtained for them some countenance from George II. and his minister, Wal-pole; and in 1757 they first reappeared as a distinct moving body in the state—presenting an address at Dublin Castle, during the viceroyalty of the Duke of Bedford.

The 'restraining system' continued, however, without material relaxation, for twenty years longer. By that time, a young champion of liberty had risen up, ready to make use of, and to ripen, a better state of ideas and feelings than had existed in the days of his fathers. By lapse of time, men's minds had become enlarged, and their hearts freed from some old fears and hatreds; and Grattan was one to make the most of improved facilities, and to win over the best minds to the right side. After obtaining the removal of some restrictions on Irish commerce, he carried in the Irish parliament, in 1780, the memorable resolution: 'That the king's most excellent majesty, and the Lords and Commons of Ireland, are the only competent power to make laws to bind Ireland.' Many disqualifying statutes were repealed in the few subsequent years; and the admission of Catholics to a freer possession and disposal of land was the cause of that development of agriculture to which Ireland owes the greater part of the improvement in her material resources from that day to this.

Some students of history look upon this year 1780 as the date of an Irish revolution as important to the Irish as that of 1688 had been to Great Britain. Like most revolutions, it was achieved by the use of irregular instruments. It is not our business here to give over again the history of the Irish volunteers; but merely to point to them and their agency, as a precedent which must be kept in view when we come to the contemplation of future volunteer associations in Ireland. The volunteers of the last century achieved a great work with little or no damage or discredit; they were repeatedly thanked by parliament; they were honoured and praised by the best part of society, in both England and Ireland; and there can be no reasonable wonder, after this, at the formation of future volunteer societies, when further liberties had to be contended for, and must, in the nature of things, be won. From the date of the victories of 1780, it was certain that the questions of Irish and Catholic disqualifications could never again be put aside. Complete equality with Englishmen and Protestants, or complete separation, was thenceforth assured to the Catholics of Ireland. The English government had relinquished, under whatever compulsion, the function of oppressor. There could be no rest now till it assumed that of liberator. And till the liberation was accomplished, there *was* no rest. During the interval of delay, the mind of the sovereign was perturbed—once to the point of insanity; every cabinet was first distracted and then broken up; and parliament was agitated by the perpetual renewal of the Catholic demand for justice, and the spectacle of the gradual strengthening of the claim which could never more be got rid of.

By this time, it must be remembered, the Catholics had largely increased in numbers. It is disputed whether, in 1800, there was any increase at all in the numbers of the Protestants in Ireland during the preceding half-century; and it is certain that, from two to one, the Catholics had then become four to one. The penal laws had tended to banish the Catholics from the towns, and drive them into a rural life—too often sordid as their hopes, and wild as their despair. There in their recklessness, and under the influence of their priests—who always promote marriage to the utmost—the population had increased at an unusually rapid rate. The wise saw, at the end of the last century, that the Catholic question had become, in fact, a physical-force question. It had long been said, by a succession of writers and speakers, that the Catholics would obtain their liberties only by the fears and the wants of their oppressors; and now it began to be clear, with their numbers thickening on the Irish soil, and foes gathering against England on the continent, that the time was coming for the fears of government to act. The rebellion of 1798 showed, to every man living at the time, what cause the government had for fear, and what its fears led it to do. Those fears led to the Act of Union in 1800, which act was agreed to by the people of Ireland on a virtual pledge from Mr. Pitt that the Catholic disabilities should be removed. There is no doubt that Mr. Pitt purposed what he was held to have promised; but he pledged himself to more than he could accomplish. He promised more, on behalf both of king and parliament, than either was willing to perform. The king scrupled about the coronation oath, with regard to which he declared that his mind had been made up ever since he came to the throne in 1760. As he had done his part in repealing penal laws in 1778 and 1793, it was hardly to be supposed that he

would make a stand in his course of concession at the point
now reached; but Mr. Pitt had not formally ascertained
that he would not; and a vigorous stand indeed was now
made.

With regard to the coronation oath, the fact is, that it
was framed at a time when Catholics sat in both Houses of
parliament in Ireland, and when they were eligible to all
offices, civil and military.   The oath was taken by King
William two years before the disqualifying statutes of his
reign were passed.   Much more might be said about the
intent, scope, and terms of the coronation oath, showing
that it did not bear upon the question of the exclusion of
the Catholics; but the fact of the date is enough.   The
king, George III., however, was not one to discern things
that differ, or to admit facts which opposed his opinions.
So, when Lord Melville endeavoured to show him that his
oath did not disqualify him for improving the legislation
of the country, the king stopped him with the words:
'None of your Scotch metaphysics!'   According to his
own notion, he settled the matter by the well-known
declaration, which went to Pitt's heart, that he should
consider any man his personal enemy who proposed any
measure of relaxation of the Catholic disabilities.   He was
not enlightened enough to know that the affairs of nations
cannot wait on the ignorance of kings.   There were too
many who helped to keep him in the dark, by applauses of
his conscientiousness, and pleas on behalf of his perverted
sense of responsibility.   There were too many who, finding
every ground of reasoning, political and religious, cut from
under them, by the advance of time and enlightenment,
clung to the one remaining plea—that the king must not
be vexed.   Pitt was too wise to class himself with any of
these; but yet he could not follow what he clearly saw to
be the right.   He had, by some carelessness, brought himself into a difficulty which was too strong for him.   Even
he, who took upon himself more responsibilities than any
other man of his day would have ventured to assume, was
overcome by the force of the dilemma in which he found
himself placed.   The king's tendency to insanity formed
the peculiarity of the case.   The man who saw the case so
clearly—the pressing nature of the Catholic claims, and

the requisitions of his own honour in regard to them—
writhed under the anguish of having driven the king into
madness, and shrank from the risk of causing a repetition
of the calamity, though millions of wronged subjects were
waiting for their promised rights, and his own honour was
importunate for satisfaction. It was a cruel position; and
any man may be freely pitied who finds himself in it, however he came there. 'The king,' says Lord Malmesbury
(March 7, 1801), 'in directing Willis to speak or write to
Pitt, said: "Tell him I am now QUITE recovered from my
illness; but what has *he* not to answer for, who is the
cause of my having been ill at all?" This, on being
repeated, affected Pitt so deeply, that it immediately produced the letter mentioned above, and brought from him
the declaration of his readiness to give way on the Catholic
question.' Pitt's letter 'was most dutiful, humble, and
contrite.' Here was one side of his difficulty. The other
was, in Lord Malmesbury's words: 'While all these arrangements are making at home, all public business is at
a stand; we forget the host of enemies close upon us, and
everybody's mind thinks on one object only, unmindful
that all they are contending about may vanish and disappear, if we are subdued by France.'

The danger was imminent of the Irish uniting with the
French against that throne which the king declared would
become the right of the House of Savoy, if he violated the
coronation oath; and imminent the danger remained when
Mr. Pitt came in again in 1804. But he had had too
terrible a fright ever to recover his courage; and he
avoided the question during the short remainder of his
life. In 1807, there was much stir about it, and the
subject was brought forward in parliament, in the belief,
authorised by some of the ministers, that the king had
become apathetic about this, as about other public affairs;
but, when appealed to for his opinion, by the enemies of
emancipation, he showed himself as determined and as
anxious as ever; and Lord Camden intimated to Lord
Malmesbury that he conceived himself to have given a
sort of pledge to Pitt, 'that the question should not be
mooted during the king's life.' Lord Camden himself
was, 'like many others, not so much against the principle

of emancipation, as because the king had declared himself.'
Foolish and wrong as such a reason was, it was one which
tended to keep the Catholics from rebellion. If they could
really believe that their emancipation was awaiting the
death of an infirm man of sixty-eight, they might well
have patience, in the hope of obtaining what they wanted
by law, instead of by violence. And their condition was
no longer one which it was difficult to endure from day to
day, though it was such as they could not acquiesce in as
permanent. At that time, in 1807, their disabilities were
these.

The Catholics of Ireland could not sit in either House
of parliament. No Catholic could be a guardian to a
Protestant; and no priest could be a guardian at all. No
Catholic could present to an ecclesiastical living, though
Protestant Dissenters, and even Jews, could do so. Catholics
were allowed to have arms only under certain restrictions;
and no Catholic could be employed as a fowler, or keep
any arms or warlike stores, for sale or otherwise. The
pecuniary qualification of Catholic was higher than that of
Protestant jurors. The list of offices, state and municipal,
to which Catholics were ineligible, is long; and they were
practically excluded from the public service. They were
also liable to the penalties of the severest of the old laws,
if they did not punctually exempt themselves by taking
the oath and declaration prescribed by 13 and 14 George
III. c. 3. Their legal disabilities occasioned incalculable
suffering in their social relations—legal degradation being
always an invitation to the baser part of society to inflict
insult and privation which cannot be retaliated. There
was a systematic exclusion of Catholics from juries in
Ireland; and in some districts absolutely a banishment of
them from the soil. Every Catholic was so effectually
excommunicated, in certain parts of Ireland, that he could
not preserve his property, or remain on the spot; and if he
happened to die before he could effect his removal, the
passing-bell was jerked into a merry measure. Some
wretched facts of this nature were related, not only at a
general meeting of Catholics held in April 1807, but by
Protestant noblemen and magistrates residing in Ireland;
one of whom, Lord Gosford, chief-magistrate of the county

of Armagh, published a statement whose date alone could make us believe that it belongs to the present century. Still, as there appeared to be hope after the death of a man of sixty-eight, the Catholics did not rebel.

In 1808, both Houses of parliament refused to entertain the subject of Catholic emancipation, under existing circumstances. On that occasion, Mr. Grattan first introduced the proposition of the veto, afterwards so much discussed; according to which the king was to have power to put his veto upon the nomination of Catholic bishops. Mr. Grattan spoke as by authority; but a large portion of the Catholic body disapproved of the offer, and it occasioned much dissension among them. During Mr. Perceval's administration, broken up by his death in 1812, it had been a principle of his cabinet to resist the Catholic claims; but the resistance was based on no ground of principle, but only on the plea of unfavourable circumstances. Still, therefore, the Catholics might wait. But they were disposed to prepare for a change of circumstances, and, if possible, to hasten matters a little; so they enlarged the numbers, powers, and scope of their Catholic committee, which met, debated, issued circulars, and originated action, and then dissolved itself, from year to year. A vain war was waged against this committee in 1811 and 1812, by the Irish government, on the ground of the Convention Act of 1793. But the Catholics continued to carry through their meetings, and carry out their objects; and parliament refused to interfere against them, while declining to act in favour of the body they represented.

The time was now past for constructing cabinets on the principle of opposition to the Catholic claims. From this time it became an open question; and it proved as troublesome and unmanageable as open questions of pressing importance always are. Mr. Canning directly spoke out, and obtained a majority on his motion, that early in the next session the House should take the subject into its most serious consideration, with a view to a practical settlement. But before the next session, there was a new parliament, and the pledge of the old one was lost.

Now that the subject had obtained admission to parliament, arose the difficulties which were sure to spring up

about the details of any measure of emancipation. The
dissensions and discussions now began about how to
proceed, about the securities which were offered or
required, the safeguards which must be provided against
foreign influence, the limitations as to office and function
necessary at home, and all those matters of arrangement
which indicated to men of business that some years must
probably yet elapse before any effectual measure could be
obtained, while they indicated to men of sagacity that this
was the beginning of the end—that the final stage of the
struggle was entered upon.   The scruples of the sovereign
were no longer in the way: it was supposed, rightly or
wrongly, that no difficulty would be found with the
prince-regent: almost as soon as Lord Liverpool entered
office, he became convinced that concessions must be made
in no long time; and before his health failed, he is known
to have contemplated the necessity of retiring, to enable
Mr. Canning to carry Catholic emancipation.   Every one
saw that the shuffling expedient of sending over to Ireland
administrations composed half and half of pro and anti-
Catholic men could not answer for any length of time.   It
was clear that the crisis was coming; but the interval was
painful and dangerous—painful for the delay of right-
doing, and the obstinate clinging to wrongful power; and
dangerous to the political character of all concerned.
Lord Castlereagh and Mr. Canning went on, session after
session, moving the hearts and minds of the House and
the country with pictures of the state of Ireland and of
the Catholic mind; but nothing seemed to come of it.
Men grew weary of so much talk with so little deed.   By
the time they had arrived at the session of 1820, accusations were all abroad against these two statesmen;
accusations of insincerity and of cowardice; because it was
believed that if they chose to make this a cabinet
question, it could be carried at once.   They were accused
of being bought off by the blandishments of the court, and
the amenities of the other section of the cabinet.   Lord
Castlereagh soon after slipped away beyond the reach of
human censure.   How it told upon Mr. Canning was
indicated by the extraordinary quarrel between him and
Mr. Brougham in the session of 1823.   In 1824, the aspect

of the affairs of the Catholics was this, to a liberal and
enlightened Churchman : ' We are sorry we have nothing
for which to praise administration on the subject of the
Catholic question. . . . . Looking to the sense and reason
of the thing, and to the ordinary working of humanity
and justice, when assisted, as they are here, by self-interest
and worldly policy, it might seem absurd to doubt of the
result. But looking to the facts and the persons by which
we are now surrounded, we are constrained to say that we
greatly fear that these incapacities never will be removed,
till they are removed by fear. What else, indeed, can we
expect when we see them opposed by such enlightened
men as Mr. Peel, faintly assisted by men of such admirable
genius as Mr. Canning ; when royal dukes consider it as a
compliment to the memory of their fathers to continue
this miserable system of bigotry and exclusion ; when men
act ignominiously and contemptuously on this question,
who do so on no other question. . . . . We repeat again,
that the measure never will be effected but by fear. In
the midst of one of our just and necessary wars, the Irish
Catholics will compel this country to grant them a great
deal more than they at present require, or even contemplate. We regret most severely the protraction of the
disease, and the danger of the remedy ; but in this way it
is that human affairs are carried on.'

And what was it that was in the way of the emancipation of the Catholics ? This was the question of all others
that it was, at the time, the most difficult to get answered.
Was it the political or religious ground that was taken
now ? There could be no fear, in 1824, that the Irish
wanted to bring in the French, or to bring in the Stuarts,
or to dethrone the House of Brunswick in favour of any
royal house designated by the pope. There could be no
idea, in this century, of massacres for the faith, or of
gunpowder-plots, or of Smithfield fires, or of an inquisition
in England. And surely there could not be, in our day,
any notion of converting five or six millions of Catholics
from a false to a true faith by a system of exclusion and
insult. How was it ? What was the avowed ground of
the opponents of the Catholic claims ?

This is a case in which we see in what ' way it is that

human affairs are carried on.' The reality was all gone out of the question on one side, and had left merely a residuum of words. The newer generations did not, and could not feel the fierce political hatred and fear which instigated the early repression of the Catholics; and they showed no signs of religious proselytism. The truth was, there was no longer any common ground on which the opposition was conducted. Every opponent had his own plea; and the pleas were, for the most part, mere words. One talked of the coronation oath, following the lead of the Duke of York; though it was known that the king did not recognise that impediment. Another spoke of the compact with Ireland, according to which the Protestant Church was to be exclusively favoured by the state. Another had no confidence in the Catholics. Others dreaded letting in the influence of the pope. Others talked of 'the mysterious and sublimed union of Church and State being a sacred subject, that soars above the ken of worldly policy;' and of its being 'an ethereal essence, that sanctifies and gives a character of perpetuity to our state.' All these difficulties, misty and unsubstantial, were sure to be wafted away by the first strong breeze of danger. And so were the impediments which were, in fact, the most real—those arising from habit. The habit of considering the Catholics excluded, inferior, dangerous, kept under by the wisdom of our ancestors, was in fact the main obstacle to their emancipation. That which was afterwards ascertained and avowed was true now—that the real difficulty lay, not with kings, princes, and cabinets, but with the people of England, before whom the question had never yet been fairly brought. Nothing was so likely to bring the question before them as danger; and therefore it was that the advocates of the Catholics were justified in predicting, as they did from century to century, that fear would prove at last the emancipating power. Another means of presenting the matter fully to the popular mind began now, however, to come into full operation. The press was brought into action in a curious manner, on behalf of the struggling party. While the sons of Catholic gentry in Ireland were excluded from many lines by which eminence might be reached, they naturally flocked to the

career of the law.   While in London, training for the bar,
many of them were glad to eke out their scanty resources
by such profitable employment as they could find for their
leisure hours, which was not incompatible with their
business and their station; and a large proportion of
reporters for the London press at this time consisted of
young Irish barristers.   Those who reported the parliamentary debates naturally gave prominence to such as
affected the Catholic question; and for some years before
that question was settled, they indefatigably reported
whatever was said upon it, excluding for its sake, when
there was not room for everything, any other subject
whatever.   Those who are at present familiar with Irish
newspapers are amused to see how many columns of
parliamentary intelligence are filled with Irish affairs,
while those of England, Scotland, and the colonies are
crowded into a corner; and thus it was when the Catholic
question was approaching its crisis.   By this accident or
method, the British people were led to suppose that Catholic
affairs occupied much more of the time and attention of
the two Houses than they really did; and were brought,
accordingly, to devote more thought and feeling to the
great Catholic subject than they otherwise would.   Everything being thus in train, the events of 1825 began their
march, in the eyes of an attentive and anxious nation.

The king's speech, delivered by commission on the 3rd
of February, after congratulating parliament on the prosperity of the country, expressed gratification that this
prosperity extended to Ireland, and that the outrages
which had formerly prevailed had of late almost ceased.
'It is therefore,' continued the speech, 'the more to be
regretted that associations should exist in Ireland, which
have adopted proceedings irreconcilable with the spirit of
the constitution, and calculated, by exciting alarm, and
by exasperating animosities, to endanger the peace of
society, and to retard the course of national improvement.
His majesty relies upon your wisdom to consider, without
delay, the means of applying a remedy to this evil.'

This is the speech of which Lord Eldon wrote: 'To-day
we have cabinet in Downing Street, and council at Carlton
House, to try if we can make a good speech for the king.

But there are too many hands at work to make a good thing of it, and so you will think, I believe, when you read it. . . . I don't much admire the composition or the matter of the speech. My old master, the late king, would have said that it required to be set off by good reading. It falls to my lot to read it, and I should read it better if I liked it better.'

A part of this speech, a very small part, caused long and vehement debate in parliament. That small part was the letter 's' affixed to the word association. The question was, whether the reprobation expressed related to the great new Catholic association just arisen in Ireland, and was therefore a blow aimed expressly at the Catholics, or whether it included the Orange clubs which were in great force at that time. The Catholic Association claimed the credit of having quieted the outrages of Ireland, and asserted their right to honour accordingly; while their enemies clamoured for their suppression, on the ground of the adjuration by which they had quieted Ireland. This adjuration was: 'By the hate they bore the Orangemen, who were their natural enemies, and by the confidence they reposed in the Catholic Association, who were their natural and zealous friends, to abstain from all secret and illegal associations and Whiteboy disturbances and outrages.' Whether that letter 's' was a gloss or a reality, it is certain that the Catholic Association filled a space in the view of the ministry and the country which left little room for clubs of inferior magnitude. 'Let the proposed measures be carried,' said Mr. Brougham, 'and the Catholic Association will be put down with one hand, while the Orange societies will receive only a gentle tap with the other.'

The Catholic Association had held its first open meeting in January of the preceding year; and in the following May, Mr. Plunket had declared, on being questioned in the House, that the government was closely watching its proceedings. The great avowed object of the association was the preparation of petitions to parliament; but, during a course of months, no petitions were forthcoming, while other kinds of business proceeded briskly. The association held regular sessions in Dublin, nominated committees, received petitions, referred them to its committee of grievances, ordered a census of the population to be taken, and levied a tribute which was called the Catholic rent. This tribute was declared to be voluntary, but it can hardly be said that the payments of the poor in Ireland, collected on the requisition of the priests, are voluntary; and the weekly collection was generally regarded as a tax. The avowed objects to which the money was to be applied were the supply of a Catholic priesthood to America; the supply of more priests to England; and the purchase of as much as could be had of the influence of the press. Into what other channels the money might flow, there was ample room for conjecture. It was believed that the amount often reached fifty pounds in a day; and government and parliament soon thought it time to be watching how it was spent.

Among those who feared and disliked this association were the English Catholics generally. Lord Redesdale writes to the lord chancellor, on the last day of 1824: 'I learn that Lord Fingall and others, Catholics of English blood, are alarmed at the present state of things; and they may well be alarmed. If a revolution were to happen in Ireland, it would be in the end an Irish revolution, and no Catholic of English blood would fare better than a Protestant of English blood. So said Lord Castlehaven, an Irish Catholic general of English blood, 170 years ago; and so said a Roman Catholic of Irish blood, confidentially to me, above twenty years ago. The question is not simply Protestant and Catholic, but English and Irish; and the great motive of action will be hatred of the Sasenagh, inflamed by the priests.' Here was the old quarrel again; and here was the danger which made wise men believe that the day of emancipation was drawing on.

For a little while, the fear excited by this body caused an unusual jealousy on the part of the king about any favour being shown to English Catholics. He who had, after his accession, cordially offered religious equality to his Hanoverian subjects, cavilled at parliament, and grew stiff with his chancellor, in the summer of 1824, because the Catholic Duke of Norfolk was enabled, by a bill which passed both Houses, to exercise his office of earl-marshal of

England, by taking the oath of allegiance, without that of supremacy, or the declaration against transubstantiation. The dread was lest, by beginning to give anything, it should become necessary to give, first more, and then everything which the Catholics demanded.   As the chancellor himself bowed to the declared will of the Lords, the king yielded; and the earl-marshal appeared in his robes in the House which he could not yet enter as a peer of parliament: and the sky did not fall.

A deputation of Catholic lords and gentlemen, sent by the association, was sitting in London, to watch over the interests of their body, under the approaching attack upon it in parliament, and to be ready to afford information to friendly legislators of either House, in answer to whatever charges might be brought.   On the 10th of February, the Irish secretary, Mr Goulburn, brought in a bill 'to amend the acts relating to unlawful societies in Ireland;' the object of which was to put down the Catholic Association. Through Mr. Brougham, the deputation made known their desire to be heard at the bar of the House, in justification of their body from certain allegations made against them in parliament.   Of course, this could not be granted, as the association was not a recognised body, but one whose unconstitutional character was admitted on every hand. The only question really was, whether there existed a crisis which could be held to justify the formation of such an organisation?   Some spoke of the volunteers of 1780, and reminded each other that those volunteers had repeatedly received the thanks of parliament; but the parallel between the two cases failed in the important particular, that the volunteers did not unite for political purposes, but for the military defence of the country. They made use of their organisation at length for political purposes, and achieved them; but there was nothing in their case which could be allowed as a precedent in any but warlike or revolutionary times.   While the Catholic claims were an open question in the cabinet, and any one cabinet minister was pledged in its favour, there could be no excuse for any kind of revolutionary institution or movement.   Mr. Goulburn obtained his bill by a majority of 278 to 123, and it became law on the 9th of March.   It apparently annihilated the Catholic Association; but the dissolution was a mere form. To lay a finger upon it was merely to scatter a globule of quicksilver; it was sure to run together again. Justice was the only true amalgamating power; and every endeavour to delay its application only proved its necessity the more.

The parliamentary advocates of the cause mourned at length and aloud the formation of the association, and its adjuration: 'By the hate you bear to Orangemen.' Mr. Canning, to whom it was owing that the king was converted and the cabinet liberalised, declared that the procedure 'resembled the scheme of an enemy, who had devised this as the best invention for throwing back and thwarting the further progress of the question of emancipation.' So thought the friends of the Catholics, very sincerely. But they stood outside the cause; and those who were within it believed them wrong; and so the event proved them to be. The subjects of a great cause always move in it differently from the way that their friends outside would have them; and the sufferers usually show in the end that they understand their business best. They were satisfied now with their own method of proceeding. They knew that their association would be put down; and they were, no doubt, aware that it ought to be put down. The leaders were sagacious lawyers, as was shown by the curious care with which the addresses and proceedings of the body were kept within the letter of the existing law; so that it was necessary for the administration to come to parliament for a new law to suppress them. This necessity was the crowning success, for this year, of the association. The leaders were satisfied when they saw the House of Commons sitting night after night, adjourning late in the morning for successive mornings, filling the eye and ear of the nation with the acts and appeals of the Catholic body. This was victory for the time—the completest victory that the time would admit. They knew that the real obstacle to their emancipation was now the indifference of the English nation. They knew that the king was near the point of yielding; thanks to the influence of Mr. Canning. They knew that the cabinet was vacillating; thanks to the influence of Mr. Canning. They knew that if Mr.

Canning was called up, even to reprobate them and their proceedings, they would have an all-sufficient advocacy; for his very reprobation must be the strongest possible testimony to the pressure of the time.   They obtained all they could have contemplated, and perhaps more than they anticipated, in the avowal and narrative which the pressure of the time elicited from him, of his own experience, and that of all the statesmen of his day, in relation to this cause. Perhaps no single manifestation so aided the Catholic cause, in its whole career, as the memorable speech of February 15th, in which Mr. Canning delivered to the world the history of the Catholic question for the preceding century, and his own history in connection with it.   The narrative came to the ear of the nation as a decree of fate; and his political autobiography went far to win over the nation's heart.   Having shown how he took his stand upon the Catholic question when the most insuperable obstacle was removed by the withdrawal of George III. from political life, and how he refused office at the most tempting moment, rather than enter a cabinet decided against the Catholic claims, he went on : ' Sir, I have always refused to act in obedience to the dictates of the Catholic leaders; I would never put myself into their hands, and I never will. . . . . Much as I have wished to serve the Catholic cause, I have seen that the service of the Catholic leaders is no easy service.   They are hard taskmasters; and the advocate who would satisfy them must deliver himself up to them bound hand and foot. . . . . But to be taunted with a want of feeling for the Catholics, to be accused of compromising their interests, conscious as I am—as I cannot but be—of being entitled to their gratitude for a long course of active services, and for the sacrifice to their cause of interests of my own—this is a sort of treatment which would rouse even tameness itself to assert its honour, and vindicate its claims.   I have shown that in the year 1812 I refused office, rather than enter into an administration pledged against the Catholic question.   I did this at a time when office would have been dearer to me than at any other period of my political life; when I would have given ten years of life for two years of office; not for any sordid or selfish purpose of personal aggrandisement, but for far other and higher views. But, is this the only sacrifice which I have made to the Catholic cause? The House will perhaps bear with me a little longer, while I answer this question by another fact. From the earliest dawn of my public life—ay, from the first visions of youthful ambition—that ambition had been directed to one object above all others. Before that object all others vanished into comparative insignificance; it was desirable to me beyond all the blandishments of power, beyond all the rewards and favours of the crown. That object was to represent, in this House, the university in which I was educated. I had a fair chance of accomplishing this object when the Catholic question crossed my way. I was warned—fairly and kindly warned—that my adoption of that cause would blast my prospect. I adhered to the Catholic cause, and forfeited all my long-cherished hopes and expectations. And yet I am told that I have made no sacrifice! that I have postponed the cause of the Catholics to views and interests of my own! Sir, the representation of the university has fallen into worthier hands. I rejoice with my right honourable friend near me (Mr. Peel), in the high honour which he has obtained. Long may he enjoy the distinction; and long may it prove a source of reciprocal pride, to our parent university and to himself! Never till this hour have I stated, either in public or in private, the extent of this irretrievable sacrifice; but I have not felt it the less deeply. It is past, and I shall speak of it no more.'

Nothing could be a stronger testimony to the urgency of the cause than that the foremost of British statesmen should be subject to compulsion like this, forced to avowals like these, while separated by deep distrust and dislike from the Catholic leaders. But even yet, the degree of the urgency was not understood. Mr. Peel sat by Mr. Canning's side, and received his congratulations on his relation to the University of Oxford, and heard his hopes that the relation might subsist long and happily. But even then there were stirrings in the heart of the listener; there were doubts beginning to move in his mind which already put that relation in jeopardy, and were soon to exclude him, in his turn, from the representation of his university.

When his turn arrived, he confessed that the events of the
session of 1825 had made such an impression upon him
that he went to Lord Liverpool, desiring to resign his
office, because the opinion of the House was declared
against him on the Catholic question, and avowing to the
premier that he believed the time was come when 'something ought to be done about the Catholics.' Lord Liverpool's threat of retiring also induced Mr. Peel to wait for
another manifestation of the feelings of the country; but
this was the time when the hook caught the chain which
bound him to follow the destiny of Canning in his sacrifices for the Catholic question.

Mr. Canning called the Catholic leaders 'hard taskmasters,' whose advocates must submit to be bound hand
and foot. Nothing could please them better than such a
description. The reputation of a strong will is, in itself,
an unlimited power. These men had ceased to be sup-
pliants, and had become taskmasters, whoever might be
their servants. The description was true; for there was a
man among them who was about to become a power in the
state. Daniel O'Connell had been an active agitator on
behalf of the Catholic claims for so many years now, as to
be known by name through the length and breadth of the
kingdom. He had been a chief mover in the committees
in Dublin; he was the organiser of the association, and
was now reputed to hold three millions of the Irish people
in his hand, ready with a touch to be turned to good or
evil. He came up as a delegate invested in a kind of
glory; for in Dublin he had been indicted for sedition in
the January just past, and the grand jury had thrown out
the bills. He who had evaded the law in the formation
and procedure of successive Catholic committees—he who
had defied the law in the late prosecution for sedition—he
who held three millions of the Irish people in his hand,
and the peace of Ireland at his bidding, might think himself entitled to be a 'hard taskmaster.' And he who was
not only idolised by the multitude among whom he had
lived, and adored by his own family, but who so attached
his personal friends by his charms of intellect and temper,
as that they could not sit in the room while he was found
fault with, might well suppose himself authorised to issue

his commands, and have them readily obeyed, whatever
they might be. But there was one attribute of his which
made him too hard a taskmaster for men who chose to
retain their manhood—his incapacity for truth. The un-
truthfulness of O'Connell must be regarded as a constitutional attribute. He was so devoid of all compunction
and all shame in regard to the random character of his
representations, that the only supposition is, that he had
not the ordinary perception of truth and falsehood; and
this became at last so general an impression, that the rest
of his character was judged of, apart from this, in a way
which, perhaps, was never tried in the case of any other
man. If he could not obtain respect, he obtained admiration and enthusiasm, even from many who hold, with the
rest of the world, that the qualities he was deficient in—
veracity and high courage—are precisely the first requisites
of political honour, the most essential attributes of the
political hero. Nature now and then sets aside, with a
haughty movement, all rules—even of morals; and in this
case she so overruled matters, as that a man whom every
one knew to be neither brave, nor veracious, nor of thorough
disinterestedness, should obtain, not merely the influence,
but the deference which is usually accorded to high character only. Of course, he had qualities which must
account for this; moral as well as intellectual qualities.
His domestic use of power was very beautiful—genial and
benevolent. His ardour was captivating, and thoroughly
respectable, when thrown into the great cause. His
buoyancy and gaiety of spirit were as attractive and
attaching as his sagacity, energy, and perseverance were
animating to his coadjutors. When we consider, in connection with these things, what it must have been to the
Irish Catholics to have a champion and leader who was
really able to manage their cause, and determined to carry
it through—how much of ancient expectation and new
hope settled upon his head—we cannot wonder that he
was regarded by multitudes as a heaven-sent king, and
that he received homage accordingly, though some of the
highest kingly qualities were wanting. The truth appears
to have been, that in O'Connell two sets of characteristics
were united, which are usually supposed to be incom-

patible.   He was genuinely impetuous, ardent, open-
hearted, patriotic, and devoted; and then again, he was
genuinely cautious and astute; calculating, sly, untruthful;
grasping, selfish, and hypocritical.   He was profuse, and
he was sordid; he was rash, and he was unfathomably
politic; now he was flowing out, and now he was circum-
venting.   Among all his changes, however, he never was
brave, he never was reliable or accurate; and he never
kept his eye off the money-boxes which supplied his
annual income from the scrapings of the earnings of the
poor.   There was no reasonable objection to O'Connell's
being supported by his country.   There was every reason
why he should be, and none why he should not.   He had
a large family, and was sure to rise to great eminence in
his profession, if he had devoted himself to it as professional
men usually do.   If, because he was the man to redeem
the Irish cause, he was withdrawn from his profession and
its emoluments, it was merely just that he should be com-
pensated by the Irish people.   But nothing could be worse
than the way in which it was done; nothing could be
worse for his character, his mind, and the reputation of
the cause.   Instead of a single effort made vigorously and
once by the wealthy of his clients, and all who chose to
give, whether little or much, so that means might be
raised equal to the utmost which Mr. O'Connell could have
made by his profession, to set him free to serve his country
for life, the subscription was made an annual affair, and
levied under the compulsion of the priests.   There is no
need to dwell on this.   The consequences may be easily
inferred.   It made his very enemies blush to see how the
affair went on, in the latter years of his life, when the
begging season came round.   Great allowance must be
made for a man placed in such circumstances of precariousness.   But a review of his character on all sides,
with every allowance that justice and mercy require, must
leave an impression that he must indeed have been the
chief of the 'hard taskmasters,' with whom statesmen could
come into no alliance, because true alliance was not
possible, but only fettered service, such as cannot be
rendered by honourable men.

The sending of the delegates to London, and the necessity

of bringing the Catholic Association under the notice of parliament, were very welcome to the liberal section of the cabinet. Till now, their position had been painful, as a position of compromise must ever be. The administration in Ireland had been carefully composed, half and half, of favourers and opponents of the Catholic cause; and, of course, there had existed the consequent evil of an unsound and unsteady government in that disturbed quarter. The enforced silence upon Irish subjects in the cabinet must have been irksome; and the awaiting of some inevitable change not a little fearful. All were set free now; for they were all united in reprobating the Catholic Association as unlawful machinery which could not be allowed to work; and the occasion brought freedom of speech and hope of a good issue to the friends of the Catholics. They spoke out, and emptied their full hearts and minds; and they saw that the protracted debates on the Catholic subject, which succeeded one another for some months of this session, were aiding the cause more than any transactions of all previous years.

By the bill which put down the Catholic Association, it was declared unlawful for all political associations to continue their sittings, by adjournment or otherwise, or whether in full sittings or by committee, or officers, for more than fourteen days; or to levy contributions from his majesty's subjects, or from any descriptions of them; or for any such societies to have different branches, or to correspond with other societies, or to exclude members on the ground of religious faith, or to require oaths or declarations otherwise than as required by law. As soon as the parliament rose—that is, in July—a new Catholic committee offered a plan of a new association, and a recommendation to the Catholic body to push to the utmost their practice of petitioning and other political action, by methods independent of the association, as the law now forbade such action within it. Suggestion like this was, in fact, action; and nothing was gained by the new law but an excellent opportunity for setting forth the strength of the Catholic cause.

During March, Sir F. Burdett introduced, first, a debate on the general petition of the Catholics; next, a set of resolutions which were passed as the foundation of a relief bill, which went through the stage of debate in the Commons on the 21st of April. Mr. O'Connell declared, in a letter which found its way into the newspapers, that the preparation of the draft of the bill had been committed to him. This damaging declaration being noticed by the adverse members of the cabinet, was emphatically denied by the committee, who pledged themselves that no person out of the committee had had the smallest share in the preparation of the bill.

This bill was an immediate consequence of the avowal which the friends of the Catholics had found themselves bound to make in the preceding debate—that they were ready to support the Catholic claims when severed from their connection with the association. They were immediately taken at their word; and brilliant was the result. The debating was magnificent, or rather the outpouring of eloquence on one side; for all the strength was in one direction; and the majority by which the bill passed the Commons was 268 to 241. The bill proposed the repeal of disabilities; the enactment of a state provision for the Catholic clergy; and the raising of the Irish franchise qualification from 40s. to £10. It was supposed that by placing the first of these propositions between the other two—the advantage to the Catholics between an advantage to the state and one to the Protestant minority, who complained of being swamped by the Catholic majority at elections—the bill might be floated through parliament. The two latter provisions were called the wings of the bill; but they proved to be leaden wings. There was an outcry against both provisions too strong for even the popular O'Connell, who held the peace of Ireland in his hand. After having boasted that the bill was of his preparation, he could not deny his agreement to the obnoxious propositions. He made a recantation, and asked pardon of God and his country. Such an error and recantation may pass for once; and O'Connell's passed for this time.

After the division on the second reading of the bill in the Commons, the heir-presumptive made a bold stroke in he Lords to obtain its rejection there. In presenting a petition from the dean and canons of Windsor against the

Catholic claims, the Duke of York took occasion to declare
his own opinion on the subject, and his own intentions in
case of his succeeding to the crown. He laid before the
House the case of the late king—'the severe illness, and
ten years of misery which had clouded the existence of his
illustrious and beloved father,' on account of the scruples
of his conscience about the coronation oath: he declared
that his principles were the same; 'and that these were
the principles to which he would adhere, and which he
would maintain and act up to, to the latest moment of his
existence, whatever might be his situation of life—so help
him God!' The lord chancellor listened with delight, and
wrote out the speech in his anecdote-book before he slept.
The bigots on his side got it printed in gold letters, and
framed it for their drawing-room walls, and circulated it
through the country. The effect produced was somewhat
different from what was intended and expected. It showed
that an effort must be made to secure Catholic emancipation during the life of the present king; and exertion was
stimulated accordingly. It happened, too, that some words
had been spoken on the other side, which took great hold
of the public mind, and perhaps spread as widely as the
declaration of the heir-presumptive. On the 28th of
February, Mr. Plunket had said, in the debate on Sir F.
Burdett's motion, that the danger to be looked in the face
was not the danger of the days of James II., but of the
present time; the danger of exasperating millions of fellow-
subjects excluded from their rights. The bigot plea was
of the danger of innovation; but, said the speaker: 'Time
was the greatest innovator of all. While man would sleep
or stop in his career, the course of time was rapidly changing the aspect of all human affairs. All that a wise government could do was to keep as close as possible to the wings
of time, to watch his progress, and accommodate his motion
to their flight. Arrest his course they could not; but they
might vary the forms and aspects of their institutions, so
as to reflect his varying aspects and forms. If this were
not the spirit which animated them, philosophy would be
impertinent, and history no better than an old almanac.
The riches of knowledge would serve them no better than
the false money of a swindler, put upon them at a value

which once circulated, but had long since ceased. Prudence and experience would be no better for protection than dotage and error.' Lord Eldon was persuaded that these words, everlastingly true, were aimed at a speech of his about the Catholics of the time of Henry VIII., 'thinking it proper to treat this as a sort of speech which an almanac-maker, reciting past events, might make; and which, there-fore, might deserve no answer.' But the sentiment of Mr. Plunket's words made its way. 'Never,' says the chan-cellor, 'was anything like the sensation the Duke of York's speech has made. . . . I hear that "the Duke of York and No Popery" is to be seen in various parts. The Bishop of London declared that he believed—speaking when he delivered a petition yesterday—"that he was satisfied nine people in ten in the city were determinedly adverse to the claims of the Roman Catholics."' Yet the sentiment of Mr. Plunket's words made its way. 'I forgot to mention,' writes the chancellor, 'in my last, that the Commons stared me very impudently in the face, when they delivered to me the Catholic bill at the bar of the House. *This* bill, however, I think those gentlemen will never see again.' The Lords threw out the bill at a little before six in the morning of the 18th of May, by a majority of 48 in a House of 308. 'Lady Warwick and Lady Braybrooke,' writes the chancellor, 'would not let their husbands go to the House to vote for the Catholics; so we Protestants drink daily, as our favourite toast: "The ladies who locked up their husbands."' 'The glorious forty-eight' were toasted in bumpers, and the victors 'were becoming com-posed after their triumphs;' and still the sentiment of Mr. Plunket's words was making its way. The temporary defeat took place on Wednesday, May 18th. On the Thursday, 'Mr. O'Connell,' writes the chancellor, 'pleaded as a barrister before me in the House of Lords. His demeanour was very proper, but he did not strike me as shining so much in argument as might be expected from a man who has made so much noise in his harangues in a seditious association.' The chancellor forgot that a cause in the House of Lords could hardly be so inspiring to a barrister as the cause of his country to its champion; and that Mr. O'Connell might easily hold himself calm and

commonplace in another sphere, while in his own the
sentiment of Mr. Plunket's words was making its way.

During the next session, that of 1826, nothing was done
in parliament on the Catholic question beyond the presentation of petitions.   The Lords had declared their
opinion decisively enough, for the present; and in the
Commons, it was understood that the session would be
short, in view of the approaching dissolution, and that the
great questions of the time had better stand over for the
consideration of the new parliament.   The Catholic
petitions were chiefly directed to meet the objection of the
supposed divided allegiance of the Catholics.   It was in
vain attempting to meet this objection by the declaration,
however extensively confirmed, that Catholics held an
undivided allegiance to their king in civil affairs: no one
doubted this.   The objection was, that their spiritual
allegiance to the pope might at any time interfere with
their civil allegiance to their king.   The true way of
meeting this objection was to render them easy and
satisfied.   If the pope really wished to make mischief
between the Catholics and the British government, he
could do it very effectually already; and with the more
excuse the more they were wronged.   To keep them in a
state of exasperation by political exclusion was not the
way to render them loyal, but rather to make the pope
their partisan against their sovereign.   The petitions of
this session were therefore of little use.   They did not truly
meet the objection of one party, and were not needed by
the other.

A new enmity became manifest this year. The Catholics
and the Dissenters drew off from each other.   The
Dissenters were themselves suffering under disabilities
which might naturally dispose them to sympathise with
the Catholics, and to work in their behalf.   But they
were, generally speaking, lukewarm in the cause.   It is
not difficult to understand this, though the fact is not an
agreeable one to contemplate.   Like too large a majority
of mankind, the English Dissenters could feel deeply and
argue clearly about the rights of conscience, when their
own consciences were interfered with, but be too much
affected by fear to see the full force of their abstract

reasonings when their own experience was not concerned. They were Protestants; they feared the pope and the ravages of superstition as much as their Protestant brethren within the Church pale; and the annual Indemnity Bill, which gave them practical freedom, saved them from sharing the exasperation of the Catholics under their legal disabilities. And they were not united with the Catholics in any hope from the influence of Mr. Canning; for Mr. Canning was as openly and fixedly their adversary as he was the advocate of the Catholics. Mr. Canning's opposition to the repeal of the Test Act remains a rebuke to the pride of human reason and to the confidence of hero-worship. Those who exulted in his clear view of the case of the Catholics, and his soundly principled advocacy of their claims, were perplexed and abashed by his indefensible and unaccountable refusal to apply the same sagacity and the same principles to the case of the disqualified Dissenters. And it was not for Mr. Canning to complain of the judgment which his inconsistency was sure to bring upon him; nor for his friends to wonder and lament if, after his death, such speculations as that of Lord Rossmore, in his *Letter on Catholic Emancipation*, dishonoured his memory, as far as the matter went. ' Is there no satisfactory reason,' says Lord Rossmore, ' why a mind like that of Mr. Canning should depart from his own general principles in the case of the Dissenters alone? May he not have reasoned thus? If I concede the wishes of the Dissenters separately, may I not weaken the common cause—the Dissenters not having much sympathy with the claims of the Catholics? But if I carry emancipation, I secure the repeal of the Test and Corporation Acts; for, if the former succeeds, the latter follows.' This is not like Canning—such a method of coercing one set of people, under false pretences, to further the emancipation of another. But, if this was not his reason, there is no saying what was. It remains a painful mystery.

There is much that is painful in the survey of the time and persons under our present notice. The Catholics were putting forth all their powers in preparation for the elections; and the full force of the influence of the priesthood was brought to bear upon the forty-shilling freeholders, in a manner which made as complete a mockery of the representative system as was ever made by the Irish landlords, who had covered their domains with small freeholds for their political convenience. Some of this class of Irish landlords were ejecting their tenants by wholesale, for their obedience to the priests in the elections; and the new Catholic Association was voting funds for the relief of the people thus left homeless. The Dissenters were holding off from aiding the Catholics; and the Catholic leaders were reviling the Dissenters. Mr. Canning was doing wrong by the one body, by the very act of doing right by the other. The Duke of York was endeavouring, by a proceeding of extraordinary audacity, to achieve the dismissal of Mr. Canning from the cabinet. He was naturally animated by the effect his speech had produced; and he saw, as every one else did, what its operation was in stimulating the friends of the Catholics to obtain their emancipation during the life of the king. He took upon him now, in the autumn of 1826, to address the king on the subject of obtaining unity of opinion in the cabinet on the Catholic question. In this he was not likely to succeed, after his attempt on the royal feelings in his late speech. The king had observed on that speech, in a good-humoured way, that the duke might have left out his reference to his possible accession to the throne, as its present occupant did not mean to quit it. Preserving his good-humour he still would hardly relish the duke's interference with the opinions and constitution of his cabinet. But it was unnecessary to do more than keep quiet, in relation to the duke; for it was becoming clear that he would never more influence the politics of England, or any other human affairs. To complete the circle of wrong-doers, Mr. O'Connell was treating the illness of the Duke of York in the following style: 'I wish no physical ill to the royal duke; but if he has thrown his oath in the way of our liberties, and that as long as he lives justice shall not be done to the people of Ireland, it is mockery to tell me that the people of Ireland have not an interest in his ceasing to live. Death is the corrector of human errors; it is said to be man's hour for repentance, and God's opportunity. If the royal duke should not become converted from his political errors, I am perfectly resigned to the will of God, and shall abide the result with the most Christian resignation.' This declaration was received with 'laughter and cheers.' To this pass were men brought—to such a state of principle and temper as this, all round, by the protraction of injury to one class of fellow-subjects. The consolation was in the moral certainty that an effectual change could not be far off. On the whole, the anti-Catholic interest seemed to have gained most in the elections; but some great single victories had been obtained on the side of emancipation; and the power of the Catholic Association had been so effectually proved, by the expulsion of the Beresfords from the representation of their own tenantry, and in some other instances, that it was clear that the struggle could not now end by any other means than being brought to an issue. It was becoming clear that the Duke of York would never reach the throne; and a general belief was arising that the cabinet was in process of conversion to the views of Mr. Canning. There was a persuasion, on the whole, prevalent in the country, that this new parliament was the last which would be occupied with the discussion of the Catholic question.

CHAPTER XI.

Chancery Reform—Government moves for Inquiry—Report of Commissioners—Lord Eldon—Bill proposed—Jurors in India—Finance—Close of Session and Dissolution—The Elections.

In the course of the last three sessions of this parliament, a reform was begun which the nation had for some time been peremptorily demanding; by its discontents, yet more than by its express petitions. The delay of justice in the Court of Chancery had become insufferable; and the time was come for proof whether the grievance could not be amended. Perhaps no narrative of a process of reform is more instructive than this, in showing how that

inexorable Fate—the spirit of reform, evoked by grievance
—compasses its end, through all obstructions of human
error and ignorance, human will, and even human conscience, when that conscience is deficient in enlightenment.   Among the movers against the evils of the Court
of Chancery were some men who were not lawyers, and
who therefore naturally stated their case ignorantly; and
there were some who were trained and practised in a
different department of the law, and who were therefore
ridiculed by equity lawyers for errors in the object and
expression of their complaint.   The strong, united will of
the cabinet and of the equity lawyers was opposed to all
entrance upon the subject.   And the conscience of the
chancellor was so satisfied with the existing state of
things, that it resented any question of them; and, at the
same time, so tender, that it winced under any inquiry
into the discharge of business, as under a personal injury.
Yet the inquiry went on, because it had become necessary.
The chancellor's friends laughed at the complaint of the
locking up of large funds in Chancery for half a century
together, alleging the cases in which property was truly
in ward, and the dividends punctually paid; but there
were cases in which no proceeds could be obtained.   The
chancellor and his friends scorned the complaints of the
expenses of the court, showing that his income had never
exceeded a certain amount; but the expenses were intolerable notwithstanding.   The government clearly proved an
enormous increase of Chancery business within a certain
term, and avouched the industry of Lord Eldon; but it remained true, and unendurable, that suitors could not get their
business settled.   The chancellor and his friends called
the complaints 'ignorant fellows' and 'malicious rascals;'
and the complainants called the lord chancellor 'a curse
to the country;' yet, amidst their alienation, they worked
together, under that inexorable Fate—the spirit of
reform, evoked by grievance.   Thus it always happens,
and must happen; and it would be well if we could learn
from such histories to assume the certainty of reform, after
any manifestation of grievance, and to see the absurdity
of all violence, all loss of temper on any hand, in the
prosecution of a work which pays no heed to our infirmities.

On the 4th of June, 1823, Mr. John Williams, afterwards one of the judges of the Queen's Bench, moved for
an inquiry into the arrear of business in the Court of
Chancery, and the appellate jurisdiction of the House of
Lords, and the causes thereof. 'It now seemed to be conceded on all hands,' the mover declared, 'that evils of no
ordinary magnitude existed, and that the present system
could no longer go on without some amendment or improvement.'   It appears that the chancellor himself was of
the same mind with other people, as to the necessity of
inquiry; for, within a month of Mr. Williams's motion, he
communicated to the House of Lords his purpose of having
a commission to inquire whether any, and what improvements could be made in the administration of the Court of
Chancery.   Yet, his wrath against the inquirers in the
House of Commons seems to show that he would hardly
have stirred at this time, if they had not stimulated him to
do so.   Throughout the whole affair, which extended over
several years, he appears to have been unable, for a single
moment, to regard it as anything but a personal matter.
The complainants divided their informations into two parts;
those which regarded the faulty constitution or arrangements of the courts, and those which related to the quality
of the chancellor's mind, in which the tendency to doubt
had become so strong as to overbear the fine faculties and
attainments which otherwise fitted him eminently for his
office.   The debate on Mr. Williams's motion continued for
two nights, and brought out enough of fact and opinion to
assure the ministers that the subject would not drop till
something was done.   Their plea of the vast increase of
Chancery business availed only to prove that matters could
not go on as they were; and a broad hint to this effect was
given in the introduction of a discussion about separating
the judicial and political functions of the lord chancellor.

In the House of Lords it had been suggested in the preceding April to alter the method of hearing appeals there;
and it was proposed by Lord Liverpool, on the 26th of
June, that a deputy-speaker of the House of Lords should
be appointed, and that five days in the week, instead of
three, should be devoted to the hearing of appeals.   The
arrangement was made; but the chancellor could not let

the occasion pass without entering upon an exhibition of
self-assertion and self-defence, which not only lowered his
dignity, and engaged the compassion of parliament, but
proved to the movers in the question of Chancery reform
that it must inevitably be made a personal matter, as the
chancellor chose to regard it so; and the bickerings and
evil-speaking which hence arose became very painful, and
damaging alike to the character of the court and the progress of the question.

As the next session (of 1824) approached, the chancellor
grew uneasy, in apprehension of the renewal of the subject; and he applied to Mr. Peel for the full support and
protection of the cabinet.   Mr. Williams's motion was
brought forward on the 24th of February.   Lord Eldon
observes upon it that every moment of negligence in an
official course of twenty-two years was noted; and that
many of the complaints were perfectly new to him and his
friends—an evident benefit already arising from the discussion, and a clear reason for prosecuting the inquiry.
In answer to the motion for a committee, Mr. Peel moved
for a commission, such as the chancellor had proposed after
the debate of the previous summer.   This was what was
wanted, or something very like it; and Mr. Williams
therefore withdrew his motion.   The chancellor's own
account of the matter is curious.   'At my instance, therefore, Mr. Peel, in a most admirable speech, moved for such
a commission, as a great merit on my part in aiming at
improvement, instead of this committee of vengeance; and
this threw Mr. Williams, etc., upon their backs, and they
did not venture to divide.   So, for the present, *this* storm
is over, and matters will be tolerable till the next begins
to rage.'

Here was his mistake, in thinking himself at liberty to
stand still as soon as his enemies, as he called them, were
quieted by the pledges of his friends.   As soon as the
results were called for, he considered it a new onslaught of
the foe, and fortified himself in obstinacy accordingly, so
as to place his colleagues in a situation of great difficulty.
He gives his view in a letter of the date of February 28,
1824.   'The fact is, from year to year, party is attempting
to drive me out of the chancellorship. God knows I should

be very happy if I had nothing to do with it. If these malignant attacks had not been made against me, year after year, I should have been in retirement; but to hatred, malice, and uncharitableness, I will not give way. I will not gratify those who revile me. My rule through life has been to do what I think right, and to leave the consequences to God.' Strange words these last—given in the same breath with the declaration that he remained in office only because others wished him out of it! And this pettishness and self-will become nothing less than shocking when we consider on whom the eyes and minds of the movers in parliament were really fixed: not on an aged judge, whom they wished to insult and displace from gratuitous malice; but on the impoverished orphan, the sunken widow, the broken-spirited gentleman, whose lives were passed in vain hope, or listless despair, of getting justice from the court which assumed to be their protector. It was impossible to think much of Lord Eldon's complacencies, or tears, or self-pity, while vast estates lay waste and weed-grown, and whole tenantries sank down into pauperism under the blight of the Court of Chancery.

In the session of 1825, it had become apparent that the stir had not been without its use. It was now admitted on all hands that improvement was needed. The commission of the preceding year had collected a vast amount of evidence, but had not reported. There was a demand in the Commons that the evidence should be printed, without waiting for the report—a demand which was, of course, unacceptable to the lord chancellor and the other members of the government. The correspondence between the premier and the chancellor on this occasion shows how urgent the demand for Chancery reform had become, and how much more important it was than it could have been rendered by any mere enmity against the judge of the court. Meantime, that judge was strengthening himself against his enemies, instead of making them friends by working with them in a good cause. 'Lord Stowell,' he says, 'called on Wednesday very kindly to express his hope that Williams and Co. had not on Tuesday disturbed my peace of mind. They certainly did not. . . . . But,

thank God, I am well in health, and in mind I grow more
easy and callous.' The correspondence with the premier
took place on occasion of an order recorded in the journal
of the Commons, on the 30th of June, 'that there be laid
before this House a list of all causes that have been heard
by the lord chancellor, during the last eighteen years,
wherein judgment has not yet been given, specifying the
time when heard; comprising all petitions in cases of bankruptcy, already heard, but not decided.' The chancellor
was highly incensed, and applied to the ministers for information why such an order should have been permitted
to pass, and whether or not he was to be protected by his
colleagues. His colleagues advised him to despise his
enemies, and to keep quiet. But he could do neither; as he
avowed in a letter to Lord Liverpool in the following
November, in which he repeated his complaints and demands, concluding with a threat of retiring on the meeting
of parliament. Lord Liverpool's reply advises the chancellor to wait at least till the obnoxious motions should be
renewed; declares the intention of the ministers to oppose
it, by the mouth of Mr. Peel; adding: 'But in order to
make it *possible* for him to carry his intention into effect,
the report of the commission of inquiry must be ready,
and be laid before parliament immediately upon its meeting. . . . Let me entreat you, therefore, to spare no effort
for the completion of this report without further delay.
It is really become a question of vital importance, and
there is *no inconvenience* that ought not to be incurred for
the attainment of this object. Independent of the complaint of *neglect*, and of the *suspicion*, which the very delay
in making the report occasions, the report is really necessary, in order to enable ministers in the House of Commons to resist effectually the unjustifiable attacks daily
made upon the Court of Chancery. . . . . I hope I do not
appear to press this matter with too much importunity; but
I am so *deeply sensible* of its importance, that I should not
do my duty if I did not urge it in the strongest manner.
Let us but have the report, and all other difficulties may
be fairly encountered; but without that, no person in the
present heated state of the public mind upon the subject,
can answer for the consequence.'

In truth, while the chancellor was thanking God that he was well in health, and growing more easy and callous in mind every day, the same was far from being the case with the imprisoned debtors, the impoverished widows and orphans, and the broken-spirited gentlemen who were suffering under the practical denial of justice by his court. The damp was spreading in the houses, and the weeds growing in the fields of the estates shut up by his delays; and the workhouses were receiving more and more of the paupers who ought to have been cheerful labourers on those estates. The introduction of the subject into parliament two years before had roused some hope; and with hope came restlessness, and the deferred hope was becoming as dangerous as the premier intimated in his letter.

On the 18th of April, a petition from one of the sufferers was presented to the House, and another on the 21st; and on both occasions the court and the judge were attacked with great vehemence. Instead of retiring, however, as Lord Eldon had declared his intention of doing, on occasion of the expected stir, he preferred keeping himself 'easy and callous.' 'The chancellor,' says his biographer, 'was now become so far familiar with these annoyances as to endure them with considerable good-humour'—a good-humour which was not reciprocated by the other parties in the case, in the jail and the workhouse, and among the damps and weeds of dilapidated mansions. There was hope for them, however. The commissioners' report was ready; and it not only declared that the Court of Chancery had faults, and was capable of great improvement, but offered 187 propositions, containing the alterations in the practice of the courts which might, in the opinion of the commissioners, be adopted with advantage. As it was known that the attorney-general was to introduce a bill founded on the report, the subject was dropped for a month, but not till the opinion of the public was effectually declared and recorded in the House, and in the reports of its debates. That opinion, at the date of its utterance, is an item of history which ought not to be passed over. It may be most briefly conveyed in the words of Mr. Grenfell, spoken on the 18th of April, after some clamour in the House against Mr. Hume, who had said that

he thought it the greatest curse that ever fell on any
nation to have such a chancellor, and such a Court of
Chancery, as this country was visited with. 'Mr. Grenfell
said that he was not in the House when the words which
caused this discussion were used. If his honourable friend
had stated that the lord chancellor was a curse to the
country, he had done that which was not altogether
becoming in him, or any other member, to do. If his
honourable friend had said that the Court of Chancery
was a curse to the country, he had stated that which no
man conversant with the subject could deny. It was only
stating the current opinion of ninety-nine men out of
every hundred. And he would tell the House the reason
he had for holding that sentiment. It was because, by
the practice of that court, a rich man was enabled to
oppress, injure, and ruin a poor man. It was a mere
engine of oppression; and, constituted as that court was,
it was not too much to say that it was a curse to the
country.' This being, in the general opinion, the state of
the case, the 187 propositions of the commissioners might
not be too many for the reforms needed. One of the hopeful and pleasant circumstances connected with the presentation of the report was the testimony which it brought
out to the conduct of the chancellor during the preparation
of the work. It showed what he could do when his mind
was turned from its self-regards to business of real interest
and importance. Dr. Lushington declared that, from the
beginning to the end of the investigation, the lord chancellor had afforded the most material assistance to the
commissioners. His connection with the commissioners
had left 'a most favourable impression with regard to the
learning, intelligence, and integrity of the noble lord. So
far from ever seeking to check inquiry, he had done everything to promote and forward it.'

The chief complaint made, in the House and out of it,
about the report was, that it passed over in silence the
causes of past delays of justice. This was believed by
some to be attributable to the chancellor's influence. There
is little doubt that it arose from the tacit agreement in all
minds, that these delays were caused by the peculiar quality
of Lord Eldon's mind; that hesitation and overcaution

which made him, in his own time, the popular personifica-
tion of doubt, and which made him, in his judicial capacity,
so strange a contrast with himself in his political function,
where he appeared rash in the extreme, in the obstinacy of
his dogmatism.   In his judicial function, where his business was to decide, he was ever doubtful and hesitating;
while, in his political function, wherein he was called upon
rather to confer than to decide, he was to the last degree
oracular and peremptory.   This was understood by everybody; and the commissioners relied upon that knowledge.
It was also understood by everybody, that it was too late
now to alter the quality of the chancellor's mind.   It was
known that he was seventy-four years of age, and that he
must soon surrender the seals either to the king or to the
King of kings; and it was hoped that a decorous silence
on this point might, without injury, be preserved, from
due respect to the grey hairs of the old judge.   Dr.
Lushington passed over this point as lightly as he could.
He observed, that 'any person who read the evidence
would see that every witness was asked what was the
cause of the delay, and also what were the best remedies
for it.   He was aware that some of them had felt great
reluctance to answer that question; but he contended that
the commissioners could not have gone further, unless they
had purposely sought for matter to criminate the lord
chancellor.   Having said thus much, he would proceed.'

It was on the 18th of May that the attorney-general
moved for leave to bring in his Chancery Reform Bill,
founded upon the report of the commissioners.   It was not
discussed, as the dissolution of parliament was known to
be at hand; and it was understood that the motion proposed merely to lay the subject before the country, and
recommend it to the succeeding parliament.   Some correspondence among the ministers in the course of the autumn
shows, not only their willingness to carry through such
reform as should be decided on by the new parliament,
but their anxiety to be ready for co-operation by having
the requisite funds provided, or offered for purposes of
compensation under the new arrangements which were
contemplated.   Thus was the great question of Chancery
reform not only stirred, in the course of these three years,

but brought up to the point of legislative action before the dissolution of the expiring parliament.

Little more was done than has been already shown, during the last session of this parliament. The session was shortened by the approaching dissolution; and men's minds had little liberty from the engrossing subjects of the commercial crisis and the Catholic question. Many topics were more or less fully discussed; but their issues lay in future years. One decision, however, was made, with regard to the administration of justice in India, which is important enough to be recorded. By the words of the law, all British subjects were competent to serve on juries in India; but, by a custom now become too deeply rooted to be overthrown but by an express law, the half-caste population of India, now very numerous, were held disqualified as jurors, under the idea that they were not British subjects. By a bill passed this session, all 'good and sufficient' residents were declared competent to serve on juries—with the one reservation, that only Christian jurors should sit on the trials of Christians. Prejudice is ever stronger than law; and time and enlightenment must be waited for before our dark-skinned fellow-subjects in India could enjoy their due equality in the administration of justice; but the law had now done what it could in declaring the rights of the half-caste population; and further benefit might be hoped for, from occasion being taken, by the introduction of the bill, to point attention to the good done in Ceylon, by the free admission of natives to serve on juries, under the administration of Sir Alexander Johnston.

With regard to matters of finance, there was rather more than the usual amount of variation between the pictures offered by the chancellor of the exchequer and opposition members. In the midst of the unquestionable and fearful distress of 1826, the chancellor of the exchequer continued to attract to himself his nickname of Prosperity Robinson. Every session—no matter whether the political weather was fair or foul—he came down to the House exulting in his budget; exulting that his most sanguine expectations had been surpassed, or that his calculations had been un-affected by the misfortunes of the times. The opposition

members answered him with words of lamentation and
foreboding; lamentation at the deteriorating condition of
the working-classes, and forebodings that they would sink
yet further, under the pressure of taxation. Superficial
readers and hearers were amazed at so wide a difference of
statement on what appeared to be a matter of figures. But
figures have no more chance of being right than the merest
conjectures, unless the premises on which they are to
operate are well ascertained and agreed upon; and the
chancellor of the exchequer and his critics proceeded from
different premises, and resorted to different tests to discover the real condition of the country. Mr. Robinson
had taken off taxes: all agreed that this was well. He
had found that the reduced taxes had yielded more revenue
just in proportion to their reduction: wise men agreed
that this was natural and right. He gloried in the excess
of revenue above his calculations, and proceeded to take
off more taxes: wise men agreed to his proceeding, but
questioned the grounds of his exultation. He argued,
from the increase in the revenue, a vast improvement in
the condition of the people—an improvement commensu-
rate with the increase of revenue: and here wise men
thought him wrong. The difference was, that Mr. Robinson compared the yield of the revenue merely with its
yield in former years. His opponents considered also the
great increase in the number of consumers. And a wide
difference it was that there was room for here. All who
took this element into their calculations, thought Mr.
Robinson wrong: some believed that the condition of the
people was, on the whole, actually deteriorating; some
that it was only not improving; some that it was improving more slowly than it ought to do; and nowhere
was any party found to sympathise fully in the exultation
of the chancellor of the exchequer at this time. After the
census of 1831, it was found that, taking the nation all
round, each person consumed one-seventh more of the
necessaries and comforts of life which come under the
heads of taxation, than at the beginning of the century;
this small improvement having taken place chiefly during
the latter years of this period. Such a fact is full of
promise and satisfaction in itself; but the proportion of it

which was true in 1826 would have been grievously dis-
appointing to the chancellor of the exchequer—disappoint-
ing to his benevolence, even more than to his pride.

The reductions which the chancellor of the exchequer
found himself enabled to propose in 1825 were on hemp,
coffee, wine, spirits, and cider, and some of the assessed
taxes which pressed on industry, and on the comfort of the
working-classes; among which, the most important were
the house-tax on inhabited houses under £10 rent, and the
window-duty on houses not having more than seven
windows. An effort was made by Mr. Hobhouse to get
the whole window-duty repealed; but this pernicious and
most indefensible tax still subsists. These taxes together
amounted to a little more than a million and a half. In
1826, March 13, when the country was in a very suffering
state, and when parliament was about to be dissolved, the
chancellor of the exchequer passed in review our whole
financial system for the preceding ten years, declaring
that there had been a reduction of taxation to the amount
of twenty-seven millions and a half since the peace. Some
opposition members—Mr. Maberley, Mr. Hume, and Mr.
Hobhouse the foremost—protested against the statement
that there had been any reduction at all; the increase in
the number of tax-payers so far exceeding the relief, as
that multitudes had been deprived of the use of articles of
comfort and luxury who had formerly enjoyed them.
Thus, though the yield of the duties on comforts and
luxuries had so increased as to occasion the reduction of
some of them, the enjoyment of these comforts by individuals had considerably lessened; and the country was
therefore, if judged of by its consumption, in a declining
state. The object of this opposition was to obtain a revision of government expenditure, and a reduction in
many national establishments. The object was not obtained; the House of Commons throwing out by a large
majority the forty-seven resolutions offered by Mr. Hume,
and the motion founded upon them. The sum of the
resolutions was: 'That the continued pressure of taxation
has greatly increased the privations and distress of the
productive, industrious, and labouring classes of the community;' and the resulting motion was for an address to

the crown, praying that his majesty 'would be graciously pleased to take into his consideration the present alarming state of the country, and to direct an immediate inquiry to be made into the causes of the existing distress, and the adoption of measures calculated to bring it to as speedy a termination as possible, and to prevent its further spreading.' The motion was lost by a majority of 152 to 51, on the 4th of May, within a month of the dissolution of parliament. A more curious instance can scarcely be found than in the addresses of Prosperity Robinson and Adversity Hume, of the opposite conclusions which may be drawn from a view of a statistical subject, where the figures were indisputable on both sides—as far as they went. The discrepancy lay in the want of a common ground on which to base their calculations. The existing parliament, it is clear, thought the chancellor of the exchequer altogether in the right. In the poor-law inquiry of subsequent years, it came out that all who had congratulated the nation on a pervading spread and increase of material prosperity had been widely mistaken.

On the 31st of May, the session was closed by commission, the speech declaring 'that, the state of the public business enabling his majesty to close the session at a period of the year the most convenient for a general election, it is his majesty's intention to dissolve, without delay, the present parliament, and to direct the issue of writs for the calling of a new one.' The speech announced peace with the Burmese; declared that every endeavour had been used to preserve peace among the nations in both hemispheres; and expressed deep concern at the distresses of the manufacturing classes at home, admiration at the patience with which those distresses had been generally borne, and a hope that the pressure was gradually giving way.

Thus was dismissed the seventh parliament of the United Kingdom, after a duration of six sessions. It had done some great things. The Commons had not had the opportunity of protecting the queen further than by announcing that they were ready to protect her, for her case had never reached them; but such indications as they had been able to give were on the right side. The great work of parliamentary reform had begun with the enlargement of the representation of Yorkshire; and that of the abolition of slavery with the issue of the celebrated circular to the West India colonies. Our country had been ennobled in the eyes of the world by the foreign policy of Mr. Canning, enthusiastically sanctioned by parliament; and broad foundations had been laid for friendship with mankind at large, and prosperity at home, by a practical admission of the principles of free-trade. There had been a reduction of taxation, considerable, though less than men of a later time would have achieved during ten years of peace. These were things actually done. A considerable, but indefinite progress had been made towards other great achievements, which were sure to be effected in time. Nothing was done for national education, for Catholic emancipation, for emigration, for Chancery reform, for the repeal of the corn-laws, or for general parliamentary reform; but these great topics had been discussed, and some of them diligently studied; and all clear-sighted men knew that they were ripening for fruition, through all the gales of passion and frosts of indifference which retarded their growth. There could be no doubt that the country was in an advancing state, however severe the visitations of distress under which it was labouring at the end of the six years' term; and however fearful the turbulence of some districts and classes from the withholding of political rights on the ground of religion. Much as there was yet to be done and undone, the improvement in our political state since 1820 was very striking. The cabinet was liberalised, and still liberalising; and, in the train of the cabinet, the king. The House of Commons had grown wiser by its six years' experience, and under the influence of the genius of Mr. Canning—imperfect as was that statesman's fidelity to his own genius in some points of high importance. And now, there was every reason to hope that the new parliament would be an improvement upon its predecessor; and that the light which had been shed abroad in the diffusion of improved principles of policy would appear with some effectual concentration in the people's House, arranging their present affairs, and decreeing their future destiny, with a clearer and more comprehensive knowledge than hitherto.

The principal topics set up for tests at the elections were the corn-laws and Catholic emancipation; and, more partially, the abolition of slavery. The anti-Catholic strength rather gained than lost by the perturbation of the time. The uncompromised candidates said, with regard to the corn-laws, what was usually said in those days—that they would agree to what should be best for both grower and consumer; and the anti-slavery test did not obtain much support. There was an opposition talked of to Mr. Huskisson at Liverpool; but the enemies of free-trade could not find a candidate. Lord Howick and Mr. Beaumont failed in Northumberland; and Mr. Brougham in Westmoreland, where the Lowther interest put forth its strength. Some of the Radical demagogues tried their chance; or rather, as Cobbett avowed, did their best to empty the purses of certain of the aristocracy. Cobbett himself stood for Preston, and polled nearly 1000 votes; and Hunt opposed Sir Thomas Lethbridge in Somersetshire; of course, unsuccessfully. Lord John Russell failed in Huntingdonshire; and the Bedford interest altogether succumbed for the time to the anti-Catholic spirit. As has been mentioned, the priests were active in Ireland, and wrought wonders—overpowering the Beresford interest in Waterford.

One circumstance which makes the elections of 1826 memorable to those engaged in them was the excessive heat of the season. Deaths from sun-stroke were not confined to labourers in the field and on the road, but extended to persons engaged in the elections. There was difficulty in obtaining grass for horses, and even water for thirsty agents and electors. The effect of the drought upon the crops and the markets has been mentioned; and the consequent early summoning of the new parliament, in order to confirm the necessary alteration in the duties, and to grant an indemnity to ministers for that alteration. As there was an average crop of wheat, and a very abundant one of potatoes, the alarm and inconvenience caused by the drought of the summer were not of long duration.

CHAPTER XII.

Crimes and Punishments—Education—Emigration—Arts and Dis-
covery—Remarkable Seasons—Art and Literature—Necrology—
Politicians—Men of Science—Travellers—Artists—Authors—Poets:
Byron, Keats, Shelley—Close of the Period.

In casting the eye over the chronicles of these years,
nothing is so painfully impressive as the frequent records
of capital punishments. Even in these recent days, men
were brought out upon the scaffold in batches, and hanged
in rows. Boys of seventeen, hired for the adventure of
stealing sheep, or to pass forged notes, were hanged with
the strong-bodied burglar, and the hoary old coiner. The
day before an execution, the jail was crowded with the
families of the doomed men, come to bid them farewell.
Six or eight wives together, who are to be widows to-
morrow; fifteen or twenty children, who are to be orphans
to-morrow; these were the moaning and weeping reprovers
of our law, so barbarous at so late a day! Some ameliorations in the law had, as we know, taken place; but still,
men were brought out in batches, and hanged in rows.
The number of executions was fearfully on the increase;
and yet it was universally known that so much impunity
was allowed, on account of the severity of the law, as
materially to weaken the authority of law, and encourage
crime.

In 1826, a discovery was made of a gang of banditti
who led a romantic life in Gloucestershire. In the neighbourhood of Wickwar, the inhabitants had suffered cruelly
for seven years under incessant depredations, and the
consequent pains of insecurity. The thefts were so
various and vast as to indicate the co-operation of a large
number of persons; but none of the stolen property was
ever traced, nor any thief ever recognised. The police at
last were set to arrest, almost at a venture, a family of
the name of Mills—an old man and his wife, and their four

sons; and the confession of these people revealed the whole. The gang consisted of forty or fifty thieves, of whom thirty-one were immediately arrested. They had found or made a subterranean cavern of some extent, which was entered by a hole behind the fireplace in Mills' cottage—the large pot concealing the aperture. Nearly fifty pounds' worth of half-crowns was found there; no less than twenty flitches of bacon, and furniture, cloth, and farm produce in plenty.

The romance of smuggling was expiring at the close of the period we have traversed. From the date of Mr. Huskisson's measures coming into operation, such tales of adventure began to decline. The plain prose of the matter is, that smuggling does not answer when duties are reduced to 30 per cent. *ad valorem;* and the poetry of the case was henceforth to be found in fictions of a preceding time, and in the traditionary tales which haunt the Christmas hearth. The mournful romance of the game-laws remained, however. In that direction, men might still look for midnight murder, the raging of base passions, the filling of the jails, and the corruption of the peasant's home.

Within this period, the last remaining stocks in London —those belonging to St. Clement Danes in Portugal Street —were removed. This ancient instrument of punishment was henceforth to be looked for only in the by-places of England—in some nook of a village, or under some old park-paling—green with lichens, and splintering away under rain and wind, or the pranks of children, playing with we boards and the holes which were once so awful. A new instrument of punishment had been previously introduced in jails—the tread-wheel, the very name of which was presently rendered detestable by the abuse of the invention. New inventions are usually stretched beyond due bounds; and this was the case with the tread-weel. Not only men who had been unaccustomed to such muscular exertion as is necessary for ascending an interminable flight of stairs—which the work of the tread-wheel in fact is—were condemned to the same amount of treading as the most hardy, but women were put upon the wheel, long after the time which afforded ample proof that this was work totally unfit for women.

It might appear to a stranger from another hemisphere a strange thing that we should boast of our Christian civilisation, while we had such a spectacle to show as was seen even at a later time than this. An elderly lady, of good station and fortune, might be seen on the tread-wheel in Coldbath Fields prison, in the jail-dress, and with her hair cut close—for the offence of shoplifting. It is difficult to write this fact; and it must be painful to read it; but the truths of the time must be told. During this period, the tread-wheel was in high repute; and the punishment might be applied at the discretion of the justices of the peace connected with each prison; and it was some time before many of them had the discretion to see and admit the gross inequality of the punishment, and therefore its essential badness when applied indiscriminately. It was employed chiefly for raising water and grinding corn; and sometimes the convicts were punished over and above their sentence, by the mockery of being compelled to turn the wheel, to no purpose whatever.

In Ireland, the crimes of the early part of this period were as savage and atrocious as in any portion of the history of that unhappy country. It was in 1821 that the murder of the Shea family took place, on the borders of Tipperary, when the whole farmhouse and offices were burned, and seventeen persons thrust back into the flames, as often as they attempted to escape. The seventeen were the farmer himself and his wife, seven children, three female servants, and five labourers. The only offence alleged was, that Shea had brought labourers from a neighbouring village to dig his potatoes, when his own tenants would neither pay their rent nor work it out. After the formation of the Catholic Association, there was a rapid diminution of crimes of outrage; and the leaders of the association were no doubt justified in claiming the credit of the improvement. There is no ground for disputing their claim to have pacified the Catholic peasant population of Ireland for the time.

In England, evidences of popular ignorance abound during this period. In one place or another, from time to time, there was a demolition of machinery; sometimes power-looms, and sometimes thrashing-machines; and we meet with one or two instances of the stack-burning which became a rage some years afterwards. Instances of fanaticism abound: the Holy-Land Pilgrims—a sect of men who gave up their industry, and sold their property, to go to Jerusalem to meet the Lord; the followers of Joanna Southcote; the flying serpent of Dorsetshire and Devonshire, which, in the shape of a black blight, poisoned the air; the sorcerer, Isaac Stebbings, who was ducked in a Suffolk village, in the presence of thousands; the drowning of children, 'to put the fairy out of them;' and the desertion of Carmarthen fair, on the ground of the ancient prophecy of Merlin, that the town should be destroyed on the 12th of August, 1824; the cutting and carving of a witch at Taunton; and, above all, the sensation about the miracles of Prince Hohenlohe. It is observable, however, that a large proportion of such popular delusion lies at the door of scientific and professional men, who ignore a class of facts which demand their serious attention; which stand out clearly as facts under the cognizance of society; and which, till scientifically investigated, will continue to afford material for popular fanaticism. The sympathies and operations of Prince Hohenlohe have never been explained away, to the satisfaction of philosophical minds, by the common talk of imposture and the influence of imagination; and they never can be, any more than the phenomena of somnambulism, second-sight, prevision, and presentiments, which are found in all ages of the world, and all states of society. One of the greatest of physical inquirers, who died soon after this period, has left behind him a testimony which should be taken home as a lesson by those whose business it is to explore the mysteries of the human frame. Sir Humphry Davy says, in his *Dialogue on Omens:* 'In my opinion, profound minds are the most likely to think lightly of the resources of human reason; and it is the pert superficial thinker who is generally strongest in every kind of unbelief. The deep philosopher sees chains of causes and effects so wonderfully and strangely linked together, that he is usually the last person to decide upon the impossibility of any two series of events being independent of each other; and in science, so many natural miracles, as it were, have been brought to

light . . . . that the physical inquirer is seldom disposed
to assert confidently on any abstruse subjects belonging to
the order of natural things, and still less so on those
relating to the more mysterious relations of moral events
and intellectual natures.' When scientific men, and those
whose profession pledges them to the pursuit of physiological science, are open-minded and earnest enough to
admit and study mysterious facts which occur before their
eyes, popular fanaticism about sorcery and inspiration
may give way; but, till this happens, not even the
widest spread of popular education will give more than a
check to the cruel follies of superstition.

One class of the violences of this period arose from the
practice of body-snatching. No sufficient provision was
as yet made by law for the practice of dissection; a practice necessitated by the demands of science. Before it
could be foreseen what this necessity must become, an unfortunate arrangement had been made, by which disgrace
and horror were associated with the process of examining
the human body after death. The bodies of criminals
were devoted for this purpose; and much time, and
vigorous effort on the part of individuals, were required to
overcome the prejudice thus originated. Meantime, as
bodies must be had, there was nothing for it but taking
them from the churchyards by night; a painful fear was
spread over the whole class of survivors of those who were
buried in the ordinary way; and affrays and police-cases
in consequence, appear frequently in the records of the
time.

The period under review was far behind our own in
regard to liberty of thought, speech, and the press. The
influence which had deprived the poet Shelley of the
guardianship of his own children, and the state of public
opinion which had countenanced that outrage upon nature,
were still paramount; and we find a multitude of prosecutions for blasphemy, as well as for sedition, taking place;
and the law refusing its protection to literary property, on
account of opinions, statements, or merely representations
therein contained. In 1822, Lord Byron's publisher was
refused an injunction in Chancery to protect a poem of
Lord Byron's from being pirated, on the ground of its

appearing to contain blasphemous matter. This was not precisely the way to restrict the circulation of the poem; and thus it was bad as a matter of policy. Moreover, as the author wrote to the publisher : ' Cain is nothing more than a drama, not a piece of argument.' We of the present day should add, that the law acts with tyranny and impolicy when it suppresses 'argument' on any subject whatever. In the same year, protection against piracy was refused by the lord chancellor to the *Lectures* of Mr. Lawrence, the eminent surgeon, a work of 600 pages on physiological subjects. The author was debarred from the fruits of his labour on the ground that some passages of the book discountenanced the doctrine of the immortality of the soul. The lord chancellor thus did what he could to promote the circulation of cheap copies of a book which he considered dangerous. In the opinion of a subsequent time, he did a more dangerous thing, in discouraging freedom of research and of speech among men of science, who cannot work well in their function under the pressure of foregone conclusions and the threat of outlawry. As Messrs. Shadwell and Wilbraham observed, in their pleading on the case, the liberty of the press was materially involved in the question ; but as the event proved, the liberty of the press must give way before the force of the chancellor's 'conscience' on matters of opinion.

In the next year, Susanna Wright was brought up for judgment, for having been instrumental in publishing a libel on the Christian religion. 'She was neatly dressed, but appeared to have suffered in health from the imprisonment she had undergone.' She was sentenced to eighteen months' imprisonment in Coldbath Fields prison, to pay a fine of £100, and find sureties at the end of the term, under pain of a longer imprisonment.

In the next year, eight shopmen of Richard Carlile were sentenced to various terms of imprisonment, and to fines, for selling, in their employer's shop, Paine's *Age of Reason*, and three other works termed 'irreligious.' The results of this course of action soon proved to reasonable people that prosecutions like these did not tend to ennoble and endear Christianity to the very classes which were likely to be reached by these proscribed books. The Christianity of the state appeared in a tyrannical and most unlovable aspect, when it impoverished and imprisoned the needy and hard-working for offences against itself; and thus a new stimulus was given to the appetite for libel against Christianity. The courts of law, thus employed, were doing more for the dishonour of religion than was ever done by the contempt of the ignorant, and the invectives of the discontented, who had no knowledge of Christianity but in its abuses, and could not, therefore, influence any who had. Mr. Cobbett had reckoned on a greater prevalence of admiration for Thomas Paine than he found in England. He imported the bones of his favourite writer, in the expectation that they would be run after by sightseers and purchasers who regarded Christianity as Paine did, and would receive his bones as saintly relics. But nothing came of it. The public laughed, and a niece of Paine's was naturally very angry; but Cobbett was made a bankrupt about that time: the bones were not exhibited, nor heard of again.

The London Mechanics' Institute was founded in 1823; and in the next year was laid the first stone of the lecture-theatre. In 1825, the number of regular subscribers was 1185. In this year, there was a meeting of 120 gentlemen, who desired the formation of a university in London, to meet the wants of students who were precluded, either by religious opinion or mediocrity of fortune, from attending the existing universities. 'The object of the institution is,' said the prospectus, 'to bring the means of a complete scientific and literary education home to the doors of the inhabitants of the metropolis, so that they may be enabled to educate their sons at a very moderate expense, and under their own immediate and constant superintendence.' There are no incidents of the period under notice more cheering than these. It is true, neither of these institutions meets the great want of all—the education of the absolutely ignorant, who form the largest proportion of society in England; but both aid in preparing the way to this all-important object. The London University educates a host of young men of the middle class, who, from generation to generation, must exalt the standard of education among the great body of Dissenters, hitherto but half educated at the best; and who become the moving spirits of large classes which had hitherto lain below the surface of the prevalent learning of the time. And the value of mechanics' institutes in exciting and training the intellects of the fathers of the next generation of artisans and operatives can hardly be over-estimated. It is impossible but that the members of these institutes must be more anxious to procure education for their children, than if the advantages and charms of museums, libraries, lectures, and reading-rooms had not been opened to themselves. At the time of the establishment of these institutes, the chief advantage contemplated was the most obvious one—of opening means of knowledge to working-men who desired it; but we, of a somewhat later time, see a yet more important result accruing, in the exaltation of the idea of education in the popular mind, and the quickening of parental as well as personal desires for knowledge. The honour of originating these institutions belongs to Dr. Birkbeck more than to any other man; and to Mr. Brougham also great gratitude was throughout felt to be due. Dr. Birkbeck had been preparing for the great event of 1823 from the beginning of the century, by bringing together classes and audiences of working-men for instruction by lectures and mutual communication. His influence, and that of his coadjutors, always went to rouse the people to do the work for themselves, and not to wait for patronage or aid from the state. The response he met was hearty. Men of influence and high character presented themselves as leaders; and master mechanics and operatives flocked to the movement. Two-thirds of the committee of the London Mechanics' Institute were working-men; and a continually larger proportion of that class became directors, till, in eleven years from its formation, the directors were chosen altogether by and from the general body, with no other restriction than certain conditions of membership. In a short time, many large towns—Manchester, Liverpool, Sheffield, Coventry, &c.—opened mechanics' institutes; and then they spread into the central settlements of rural districts, where, by the establishment of branches, the circulation of

books could be carried on. At Chichester, an institute
numbered 400 members, and had two branches—at Bognor
and Selsey; and at Lewes there were 200 subscribers.
The men of the present generation may well distinguish
the year 1823 with a mark of honour in the catalogue of
their years.

After the close of the war, and two deficient harvests in
succession, government had taken alarm at the number of
unemployed labourers who burdened the country, and
made a feeble attempt to relieve society at home by encouraging emigration. They conveyed a small number of
settlers to South Africa, and established them there. By
the custom-house returns, which are not very reliable, but
the only data we have relative to that time, it appears
that the sufferers took the matter very much into their
own hands—the number of emigrants to South Africa
falling very short of that to our North American colonies,
and soon appearing far below that to Australia. In 1820,
according to these returns, nearly 18,000 persons emigrated
to our North American colonies, while 1063 were conveyed
to the Cape. As for the Australian settlements, the number
of emigrants to them increased nearly threefold between
1821 and 1826. The total amount of emigration is seen
to correspond with the state of affairs at home. In the
sad years of 1820 and 1821, it was—leaving out the odd
numbers—19,000 and 13,000; in the prosperous years of
1824 and 1825, it sank to 8000 and 9000; and in the disastrous year 1826, it suddenly rose to nearly 14,000, of
whom nearly 13,000 went to our North American settlements. These are facts which clearly point out the duty
of the state. There is evidently no question about whether
emigration shall proceed; no use in arguing now about
whether it is a good thing or not. It proceeds; and its
rate of procedure corresponds with the state of affairs at
home. The question is, whether it shall go on well or ill;
under kindly or cruel circumstances. In those days it
was common, we might say usual, in the bad years, for
the labourer to land on the distant shore with nothing but
his empty hands, and his tribe of hungry children at his
heels. We shall see hereafter what has been done in
regard to the question, whether such shall continue to be

the method of British emigration, or whether every one who goes out shall set forth with an assurance of finding, at the end of his voyage, wherewithal to make a home— land or employment, food, and a place in society. As we have seen, a committee of parliament was inquiring on this great question, at the expiration of the period under review.

A foreigner might point to the state of the chief in- surance office in England at this time, as a curious illustra- tion of the prudential character of the English mind. The Equitable Insurance Office, though the chief, is only one among many in London; and the number in the country has been perpetually on the increase. In 1825, the vested capital of the Equitable was upwards of eleven millions; and of this amount, nearly nine millions had accumulated in twenty-one years. In 1821, the sums insured against fire, in the United Kingdom, amounted to more than £400,000,000. There are no means of knowing precisely the amount of money on life-insurance in the hands of the offices of the kingdom; but it is believed to amount to forty millions. In looking at these facts as an indication of national character, we must bear in mind that the amount of insurance of life and from fire would un- doubtedly have been much larger throughout, but for the indefensible tax which has ever acted as a discouragement to this wise method of saving.

The progress of the arts of life during this period was such as to answer to all reasonable expectation. In May 1820, a young lady under age received by her trustees a sum of between £26,000 and £27,000, as compensation for the loss of custom at Bangor Ferry; which ferry had, up to this time, yielded the young lady £900 a year. This was in preparation for the erection of the Menai Bridge, which was opened on the 30th of January, 1826, at half- past one in the morning. The resident engineer undertook to conduct the mail across; and he had for his staff as many persons as could hang upon the coach. 'Amidst the blaze of lamps, the cheers of those assembled, and the roaring of a heavy gale of wind, the gates were thrown open, and the mail passed triumphantly across.' There was a throng on the bridge throughout the next day; and

truly it was a work worthy of admiration. The height
from the high-water line was 100 feet; and the length of
the chains was 1600 feet.

The first chain-bridge in Great Britain, however, had
been completed nearly six years before. It was the work
of Captain S. Brown, R.N., and was thrown across the
Tweed where the width of the river was 437 feet from
bank to bank. In 1822, the Caledonian Canal was opened,
after the labour of twenty years, and the sum of £900,000
had been spent upon it. The canal might or might not
turn out a good speculation; but there could be no doubt
of the character of the population of the wastes along its
course having changed remarkably in the progress of the
work. Regular and well-paid employment, and intercourse with able workmen brought from a distance, had
roused them from a state of torpor and ignorance, and
given them habits of industry and pleasures of intelligence, never dreamed of before.

On the 12th of September, 1823, the Bridge-house committee, in contemplation of a new London Bridge, met at
Guildhall to consult, and adjourned to the top of Fish-
mongers' Hall, to look about them, and determine where
they would put their new bridge. It was to be as near to
the old one as possible; and the old bridge was to stand
till the new one was completed. The first stone was laid
in June 1825, by the lord mayor, in the presence of the
Duke of York. Mr. Rennie, the architect, was the true
hero of the day. At the close of our period the works
were in great forwardness, and the first stone on the South-
wark side had been laid at the beginning of January 1826.

In 1823, we find that the length of streets lighted with
gas in the metropolis was 215 miles; and that nearly
40,000 public gas-lamps were lighted by the three principal
companies.

In 1826, the Thames Tunnel was fairly begun—the first
shaft having been actually united with the commencement
of the tunnel.

Cambridge University was henceforth to have an ob-
servatory; the senate having decreed, in 1820, that one
should be built, and furnished with instruments—voting
on the spot £5000 towards the cost.

The Faculty of Advocates at Edinburgh purchased, in 1825, a fine Danish library from Copenhagen; and in the next year, the Astorga library, the finest collection of Spanish books of law, chronicles, and romance, existing out of Spain.   This library, founded by the Marquis Astorga, Viceroy of Portugal under the administration of Olivarez, consisted of 8000 volumes, and was purchased for £3000.

In 1821 arrived the first Egyptian obelisk seen in this country.   It was one of the pair standing at the entrance of the avenue to the temple at Philæ, the Holy Island of the Nile, on the borders of Nubia.   It is of great value, from the curious matter contained in its inscriptions, which could not be read in London at the time it was brought over; and the privilege of possessing it seems to be enhanced by its having been very nearly lost in the act of removal.   A pier on the river-bank gave way under its weight, and it slipped into the Nile; but Belzoni, the traveller, recovered it very skilfully; and we next hear of it lying at Deptford, surrounded by artists who were eagerly making drawings from it, for engraving purposes. The old priests of the Holy Island, whose petition to Ptolemy it bears engraved, would have been astonished and dismayed if they could have foreseen how far it was destined to travel.

The art of lithographic printing was beginning to spread at this period; so that we read of patents being taken out for lithographic presses.   The importance of the invention may have been exaggerated in the enthusiasm of its first introduction; but there can be no question of its having wrought well in presenting to the popular eye works of art, of a quality, and in a multitude, which could never have been enjoyed without the discovery of such a method of cheap engraving.   The utility of the art in other ways —in multiplying copies of manuscript, &c.—is so great as to entitle the first popular use of the art of lithography to notice in a history of the time.

In 1824, the most eminent men in London and Edinburgh—including the members of the government—met to do honour to the memory of James Watt, as the bene-factor of his country and his kind.   The prime-minister,

who opened the business at the London meeting, declared
himself charged with a message from the king, that if it
should be determined on to erect a monument to James
Watt, his majesty would head the list with a subscription
of £500.   The Edinburgh meeting was led by Sir Walter
Scott and Lord Jeffrey.   Everywhere, the foremost men
seemed eager to honour the great benefactor who has done
so much for the material interests of society.   His statue
now graces Westminster Abbey, where he may, by some,
be thought to hold a middle rank between the Edwards
and Henries who lie there glorious in their regality, and
the higher sovereigns—the kings of mind whose memorials
sanctify the Poets' Corner.

In every period of modern history there seems to be
something to record of our increased knowledge of the
globe on which we live.   Now that we were at peace,
there was leisure and energy disposable for projects of
geographical discovery.

In 1820, some naval officers on the coast of South
America reported home that an antarctic continent, or
long series of islands, of whose existence an ancient rumour
is reported, had been discovered by the master of a
Northumberland trading-vessel—by name Smith.   It had
always been the custom for our trading-vessels, and, as it
appears, for those of other nations, to keep as near as
possible to Cape Horn in passing into the Pacific.   Mr.
Smith, in command of the *William*, traversed a higher
latitude, and fell in with a line of coast, which he followed
for two or three hundred miles, and which he named New
South Shetland—landing to take possession in the name
of his country.   He found the climate temperate, the coast
mountainous, and bearing an occasional growth of firs and
pines.   He passed large bays which abounded with the
spermaceti whale and seals.   A party of naval officers
afterwards accompanied him in his vessel, to verify and
certify his discovery; and New South Shetland has since
appeared in the maps of the world.   This discovery was
accidental at first, however well followed up: but our
North Polar knowledge was the result of express research.
In 1820, Captain Parry reported his discovery that Baffin's
Bay was no bay at all; he having found in its western

coast a passage into the Polar sea. Upon this, an expedition was fitted out for purposes of further exploration of the Arctic Circle; and rewards were offered by government—£5000 to the first ship which should reach 130° west long.; £5000 more to the first ship which should reach 150° west long.; and a further sum of £10,000 to the first ship which should reach the Pacific by the North-west Passage. Smaller rewards were offered for the attainment of high degrees of latitude. The result of this expedition was the discovery of the Strait of the Fury and Hecla, and the ascertainment generally that the land in those regions consists of a vast archipelago—one of the largest on the globe, of which Greenland may be considered the mainland. An overland expedition was sent at the same time, under the command of Captain Franklin, to explore the Coppermine River, and the coasts extending east and west of its mouth. In 1824, Captain Parry was sent again. From these and subsequent expeditions the northern coast of the American continent has become clearly defined, and the existence of a passage from ocean to ocean satisfactorily made out, though it is not yet known to have been traversed by any one person.

Considerable additions were made, during these years, to our knowledge of the interior of Africa. In 1823, Lieutenant Clapperton was employed, with Major Denham and Dr. Oudney, to explore a part of the African interior by proceeding south from the Mediterranean shore. Dr. Oudney soon died; but his two companions penetrated more than 1500 miles, in a measured straight line to Lake Tchad and the town of Soccatoo. In the great fresh-water Lake Tchad they saw huge hippopotami and elephants, and other mighty beasts on its banks. At Soccatoo, they found crockery and other ware with the names of English makers upon them. They offer a much more favourable picture of African civilisation in the interior than had been looked for. Besides this important piece of knowledge—important as affecting the destinies of the African race all over the globe—these travellers have given to the world much information about the territory round Lake Tchad, and south and west of it. On this occasion, the results repaid their hardships—which were great; but

their attempts to discover the course and rise of the Niger
were unsuccessful. In 1825, Clapperton, being raised to
the rank of commander, set forth again with several companions and servants, to explore the same region from the
southern side; but this expedition terminated disastrously,
the whole party dying except Richard Landêr, the faithful
servant of Captain Clapperton. The master might have
survived with his servant, but for his detention at Soccatoo for many months by the king, his old acquaintance.
He died within four miles of Soccatoo, in April 1827.

It is impossible to read the records of these years without being struck by the number of earthquakes, storms,
eclipses, and volcanic eruptions, and the recurrence of extraordinary drought. Some causes, unknown to science—
unknown, that is, in their mutual relations—appear to
have been at work, to produce remarkable effects in earth,
air, and sea. In 1820, a new crater opened on Mount
Vesuvius; and there were earthquakes in various parts of
the globe. In England, and throughout Europe, the
summer was intensely hot. On the 7th of September
happened the great eclipse—the greatest in the memory
of the existing generation—which drew away the peers
and listeners in the House of Lords, while the queen's trial
was proceeding. In the next year there were rains so
heavy as to cause floods in many districts of the kingdom.
That at Westminster rose four inches above the great
flood of 1774. On the 26th of April of this year, the
thermometer (at Cambridge), in the shade, with a north-
east aspect, stood at the extraordinary height of 73
degrees. Earthquakes occurred in the south of England;
and two in the west of Ireland were followed by landslips,
very disastrous to the residents. In the next year, there
was an earthquake in Yorkshire, and also at Lisbon and
Ancona; but the distinguishing calamity of the year was
the destruction of Aleppo, by successive shocks which
lasted for three days. Many other towns in the neighbouring regions were destroyed also; but at Aleppo the
immediate destruction was reckoned at upwards of 25,000
lives. Two rocks rose up in the Mediterranean, making
islets near Cyprus. In the autumn, Naples was threatened
by an eruption of Vesuvius, of extraordinary violence—

four rivers of lava flowing out from old and new craters. A volcano in Iceland began to stir, twice in the same year, coating large districts with layers of ashes. It was the turn of the western world the next year. On the coast of Chili, the sea suddenly sank twelve feet, and by the trembling of the earth, for a succession of many hours, the city of Valparaiso was destroyed. In 1834, Persia was the scene. Many towns, of which Shiraz was the chief, were swallowed up or overthrown, with the greater number of their inhabitants. After some extraordinary storms which seemed to spring up about the coasts of England and Holland during the summer, the disasters of the year were closed by a hurricane which swept over the North Sea, wrecking all the ships on the coast of Jutland, and then traversed Sweden, mowing down the forests which opposed its course. The waters of the Baltic were swept into the Gulf of Finland; and St. Petersburg was almost drowned in the rise of the Neva. The destruction of life, lands, houses, and goods, was beyond all estimate. Earthquakes continued through the two following years; and the heat of the summer in Europe was such as to cause much conjecture as to the reasons of the changes in the temperature of the seasons. Horses dropped dead in the streets of our towns, and men in the fields. Upon the heat followed, as usual, storms, and the fatal fires which it is so difficult to check after long drought. On the side of one of the Grampians, a spark caught the dried moss, and the fire spread for above a fortnight. At one time, the mass of fire was from five to seven feet deep in the moss, extending over an area of seven miles by five. On account of the heat, no one could approach to take measures for extinguishing it; and it burned itself out at last. During these years of elemental turmoil, men felt as singular a sense of precariousness—with the globe groaning and heaving under their feet, and meteors flashing and storms rushing about their heads—as we may suppose a race of ants to feel, when man comes with his candle and his gunpowder to blow up their settlement. Amidst the conflicting forces of nature, man felt as powerless as they.

One incident of the new reign, not quite unimportant, was that Windsor Terrace was once more opened to the

public, as a consequence of the death of the old king.
There, in the days of the last century, he used to walk,
with his young family around him, in the presence of a
crowd of gazing subjects. There, in his latter days, he
walked, blind, secluded, and with benighted mind; so that
for him the sun seemed not to shine, and the glorious
landscape stretching below might as well have been blotted
out. Now, the place was again opened to the public; but
not, as formerly, for loyal subjects to greet their king.
George IV. could not submit to the observances of royalty
which required his meeting his people. He secluded himself more and more, from morbid feelings of indolence and
self-indulgence. From a letter of Lord Eldon's we learn
how his ministers disliked and disapproved of this growing
indolence: 'There was what is called a grand review in
Hyde Park yesterday (July 10, 1824). The Duke of York
was, I hear, very popular, and prodigiously cheered. My
royal master was in Carlton House—that is, within half a
mile of this scene—but did not approach it. It is astonishing what is lost by this sort of dealing, and it is grievous
that popularity, which might be so easily earned, and
acquired at so small an expenditure of time and trouble,
should not only not be secured, but a feeling of disgust
and reproach be engendered towards a person with respect
to whom a very different feeling most easily might and
ought to be created.' While the king was thus negligent
of his personal popularity, his ministers and parliament
did an act which secured, among some eminent families, a
grateful attachment towards the House of Brunswick. By
a reversal of attainders, five families were, in 1824, restored to their ancestral honours, forfeited by rebellion in
the last century—the Jerninghams, Erskines, Gordons,
Drummonds, and Nairns; and in 1826, acts were passed
restoring the peerages of Earl of Carnwath, Earl of Airlie,
Lord Duff, Lord Elcho, and the baronetcy of Threipland
of Fingask.

It was during the period under notice that musical
festivals expanded into their full dimensions, though
Birmingham has for some time exhibited them as an institution. This expansion, and every other signal advance
in the love and practice of art may be regarded as direct

consequences of the peace. The opening of the continent
gave a vast stimulus to the artistic mind of England; and
the choral music of Germany was as striking a revelation
of the power of art to qualified travellers, as the picture-
galleries of that country, France, and Italy. By the
festivals of York, Norwich, Birmingham, and Worcester,
music of a high order was offered to multitudes of the
middle classes, some time before London could yield music
which, in the mass, could be compared to it; and subsequent times have shown that thus was awakened in the
English people a dormant faculty, whose training is a
most important auxiliary to true civilisation. If we now
observe anywhere among our people a tendency to musical
pursuit, stimulating the intellect, and softening the
manners, like the musical faculty of the Germans, we must
date its rise from the multiplication of musical festivals
after the peace—though these could never, of themselves,
have effected what has been done since by efforts of
another kind, for the popular musical education of England. The funds raised by these gatherings for the support
of charities are an important benefit; but it is perhaps
a greater that music of an elevating character has been
carried into thousands of English homes.

The king, on his accession, favoured the institution of a
Royal Society of Literature, to serve 'as a rallying-point
for concentrating and diffusing information, by a union of
persons of similar tastes and pursuits;' and for purposes
of literary patronage. The king declared his intention
of devoting a thousand guineas a year to pension ten
associates of the society; and the society agreed to contribute a similar sum to pension ten more. These associates
were to be men of eminent literary ability and good
character, the poverty of whose circumstances would
make the allowance of one hundred guineas a year acceptable to them. The society was also to promote the
publication of inedited remains of ancient literature, and
of works of a valuable but not popular character; to
reward literary merit by honorary tokens; to establish a
correspondence with men of letters abroad; and in every
way to promote the character and progress of literature.
The scheme advanced slowly; so that it was June 1823

before the first general meeting of the society was held, when its objects and constitution were declared to the world by some of the first men of the day.

Two curious discoveries were made in the State-paper Office in the years 1824 and 1826. It appears that while Milton was secretary to Cromwell, he must have deposited or left in this office the MS. of his Latin treatise on Christian Doctrine, which had been known to exist, but could never be found. It was now brought to light by Mr. Lemon of that office. It was contained in an envelope, addressed to Cyriac Skinner, merchant. Of course, it immediately fixed the attention of the learned, and it was soon published; but its contents, set forth in the great poet's bold and free style, were too heterodox for the taste of the learned of the modern time; and on account of the Arianism of the doctrine, and some startling views on divorce and other subjects, it was consigned, as far as was possible, to neglect. The other discovery was of some autograph MSS. of Queen Elizabeth, and of her secretary. These consisted of an entire translation of Boethius, and poetical versions of Horace, by the queen. With these came to light a mass of documents relating to the reign of Henry VIII.; and especially his proceedings in regard to his divorced wives.

While a new work of Milton was presented to his countrymen, his great poems were introduced to the homes of a far-distant people—the dwellers in a remote island, 'far, far amid the melancholy main.' The long winters of Iceland are cheered by literary enjoyments, like the milder seasons of southern lands; and at this time, while the new volcano was pouring out flames, and covering the reeking plains of Iceland with ashes, the harmless and genial flame of Milton's genius was beginning to kindle hearts within a thousand households. This, indeed, is fame! The translator of *Paradise Lost* into the Icelandic tongue was Thorlakson, a native poet, who died at Copenhagen in 1820.

The losses of our country by death were very great during the seven years of this period. Besides the statesmen whom we have seen to disappear in the course of our history, there were others who dropped quietly away, from being at the time not engaged in the public view. The old Lord Malmesbury, who has told us so much of the events and details of British policy during the last century, and who wooed the unfortunate Caroline of Brunswick for the Prince of Wales, died towards the close of 1820.   Lord Erskine died in 1823, leaving behind him the remembrance and tradition of an eloquence which his admirers believed to be absolutely singular.   In the same year departed an old admiral, whose mere name seems to carry us back to the naval warfare of a preceding century—Earl St. Vincent, who nearly reached the age of ninety.

Of philosophers, there died the great Herschel, who in middle life passed over from his passionate love of music to attend to the finer harmonies of the stars in their courses.   He learned many secrets of the heavens, and made them known to men; and in acknowledgment his name is written in light in the heavens themselves.   One of the remotest known planets of our system is symbolised by the initial of his name.   He left us not only his knowledge, but the means of gaining more.   His great telescope at Slough was the wonder of his time; and it will continue to be so, however science and art may enable men to improve the powers of the instrument.   He died in 1822, in his eighty-fourth year.—Sir Joseph Banks, president of the Royal Society, died in 1820, after a long and useful life spent in seeking and diffusing the knowledge of nature, and in encouraging in others the pursuit of natural science.—In the same year died one whose pursuits class him at once among the philosophers and the travellers—Arthur Young, the great master in agriculture.   His researches in agriculture led him to observe much of the political and social condition of the people of every country in which he travelled; and it is remarkable that he published, in 1769, a work on the expediency of a free importation of corn.   Whatever he said was attended to by some of the sovereigns of Europe, as well as peers and commoners; and his power was great, in his day, over the practice of agriculture, from Russia to Spain, and over the imposition of taxes at home which are in any way related to agriculture.   While he was burned in effigy in one place, he was receiving honorary medals in another.   He

might be sometimes mistaken, and somewhat apt to
exaggerate methods and advantages which presented themselves strongly to his mind; but no one questioned his
influence, or his innocent ardour in a most important
pursuit. He held, at the time of his death, the office of
secretary to the Board of Agriculture, though he
had been blind for ten years. He was in his eightieth
year.

The country had a great loss in the death of David
Ricardo, who died, not in the ripe old age of the philosophers we have been registering, but in his fifty-sixth
year; and just at a time (1823) when his influence in
parliament was beginning to manifest itself in the changed
spirit of legislation on economical subjects; and when,
moreover, the new men who had entered the cabinet were
those who could give wide practical effect to his philosophy.
He did all that an independent member could do, and
more than it could have been anticipated that any independent member could do, to accelerate the progress
of enlightened legislation during his short parliamentary
career; and his writings effected even more outside the
walls of parliament than his influence within. He was
missed and lamented for many years, by ministers, parliamentary comrades, and the public; and especially during
the bank follies and crash of the years immediately
succeeding his death. If any one could have made sound
doctrine heard, and have checked the madness of the
time, by keeping the House of Commons in its senses, it
was he; but he was gone, and our world was sorely the
worse.

The travels of Dr. Edward D. Clarke were read with
avidity in their day; and they answered some good
purposes in arousing the curiosity and stimulating the
imagination of the English reading public, whose faculties
had been kept too much at home by the long protraction
of the war. These books opened new regions to the fancy,
and acted in some degree as works of the imagination do.
And so they might; for they were truly works of fiction
to a considerable extent. Since those days, scientific
travelling has become something which the world was not
then dreaming of; and certainly Dr. Clarke never dreamed

of painstaking in research, or care in relating his adventures. He travelled because he was too restless to keep still; and he had been too indolent as a student to be qualified to use the best privileges of foreign travel. His observation was superficial, and his representations inaccurate. Therefore, his works are now neglected, if other travellers have been over the same ground; though they were, in their day, attractive and popular enough to make for him a considerable reputation. He died in 1822, in the fifty-fourth year of his age.—Another traveller, Belzoni, who died in the next year, may be considered English enough to be classed among the national losses, though he was born at Padua, and died in Africa. He lived much in England, regarded our country as his home more than any other, and enriched it with some precious fruits of his Egyptian researches. To him we owe a great part of the Egyptian discoveries made in recent years—the opening of the precious rock-temple of Aboo Simbel, and of the tomb of Osirei at Thebes; and of many monuments which, but for him, would have been buried still in the sands of the desert. He was a man of mighty stature and great strength, courage, and hardihood. He was himself reliable, while he believed few other people to be so; for his temper was suspicious and jealous. He had no scholarship. His business lay in another direction. It was for him to discover and bring to hand what scholars were to attest and reason upon; and his function was no mean one, as will be agreed by all who are aware what it is to have to deal with wild Arabs in wildernesses of rock and sand. Such a man will always be felt to have departed too soon, while any part of the ancient world remains to be uncovered to modern eyes. His age is not known; but he was about to make a youthful sacrifice of himself to the monastic life at Rome, when the entrance of the French, in 1798, compelled a change of purpose. He was thus, probably, only a little above fifty when he died in December 1823.—Another Egyptian traveller, Sir Frederick Henniker, died at an early age in 1825. He was only thirty-one. Among his adventures abroad was one which befell him on the road going down from Jerusalem to Jericho, when robbers stripped and wounded him, and left him for dead. He published a volume of notes of his travels, after his return, settling down as lord-lieutenant of the county of Essex, and colonel of the local militia. His book of travels is accurate and interesting.—Sir Stamford Raffles died in 1826. He was only forty-seven years of age; but he had done great things during his too short life. He it was who acquired Java for us, and governed it during the time that it belonged to Great Britain. He abolished slavery there, advanced in every way the welfare of the native population, and gave us a great amount of knowledge of those parts of the world; though his collections and journals, and all that he had, was lost by shipwreck on his return home. He did almost as much for Sumatra as for Java, especially by abolishing slavery; and we owe to him the establishment of one of the most important commercial settlements in the world—that of Singapore, which may be considered the key of the great far-eastern world. His last service to his country was establishing the British Zoological Society.—The geographer Arrowsmith, who visits all English households in the shape of the best maps of the time, died in 1823, in a good old age.—And in the same year we lost the great Jenner, who waged war against disease with greater success, as we believe, than any other physician who ever lived. Lady Mary Wortley Montagu supposed she was rendering a great service to humanity, and was long supposed by all to have done so, by introducing the practice of inoculation for the small-pox; and this was true, in as far as she communicated the idea of inoculation in any mode. But the ravages of small-pox became incalculably greater in consequence of her method, from the infection being always kept up, and spread abroad, to seize upon all who were predisposed to the disease. Dr. Jenner put together the facts of in-oculation and of the exemption from small-pox of the Gloucestershire milkers who had taken the cow-pox from their cows, and tried the experiment of inoculation for cow-pox, which has banished all dangerous degrees of small-pox wherever it has extended. He freely gave to the world his discovery of vaccination, and thus made himself one of the greatest of human benefactors. He reached the age of seventy-five.

Of actors, we lost, in this period, John Kemble, the emperor of his art; and Incledon, whose ballad-singing was singularly suited to the English taste of the last century.

Of artists, we lost some whom it grieved the heart of the nation to part with. The noble-hearted and gentle Flaxman died in 1826, at the age of seventy-one. Among his great benefits to his kind, it was one of the greatest— though he was wholly unconscious of it—that he showed in his whole life what the happiness of genius is, when allowed its full and free action. He had all the genuine attributes of genius—its purity, its generosity, its benevolence, its candour, its industry, its patience under God and towards man; and he was one of the happiest of men— joyous in his labours, blessed in his marriage, and serene in the contentment of his mind, and the simplicity of his life. His friends loved him almost to a point of idolatry. He brought to the general English mind, through the eye, the conceptions of Homer, Æschylus, and Dante; and presented in fresh nobleness and beauty, many a sacred image from the Scriptures. Working alone and in silence, in a spirit of monastic holiness, he was the effectual preacher of a wider church than walls can contain, or than can be reached by any other voice than that which appeals to the soul.—The sculptor Nollekens died in 1823, having attained the objects of his life in a greater degree than is usual. These objects were, first, money, and then fame; and he also desired long life. He lived to the age of eighty-six, left more than £200,000 behind him, and enjoyed a considerable reputation. His great natural powers had no fair chance against the drawbacks of a defective education, and an overwhelming tendency to acquisitiveness. He pursued a lower style of art than his powers would have fitted him for, if he had been morally wiser; and his latter days were passed among the unsatisfactory attentions of suspected legacy-hunters. He knew that he was admired by many; and, for some qualities, truly, though partially esteemed; but he must have known that he was not loved. Thus, while occupied through a long course of years with the ideas and labours, he missed the best privileges, of the artist life.—Another eccentric man and artist who died during this period, was Fuseli, the *protégé* of Reynolds, the beloved of Mary Wollstonecraft, the friend of Lavater and Bonnycastle. It was his earnestness which made his power and his fame. Exhibited in familiar subjects, and those which should be simply natural, it was grotesque enough; and the more so from the imperfection of both his drawing and his colouring; but when infused into his preternatural subjects—his 'Nightmare,' and 'Sin pursued by Death'—it is very impressive. His great service to society was in presenting to it his own originality, and in rousing attention to the arts of design and invention, at a time when our insular seclusion was unusually close, and the inferior departments of art naturally engrossed a disproportionate attention over the higher. He was as eccentric in his mind generally as in his art; but he had friends about him all his life, who thought it worth while to bear with his strange temper, for the sake of his goodness in other respects. His domestic life was happy and this peace at home, together with his habits of industry and temperance, had, no doubt, great effect in procuring him excellent health and long life. He was eighty-seven when he died in 1825.— Benjamin West was an American by birth; but he died (1820) president of our Royal Academy. As an historical painter he stood very high, if not unrivalled in this country, from his inventive power; though he was as feeble in expression as in colouring. Like so many of his brethren in art, he was simple and virtuous in his life, of devoted industry; and he lived to a great age—eighty-two years. He painted or sketched about 400 pictures; and when we consider how large some of these are, and how thronged with figures, we shall see that his life must have been spent chiefly in his painting-room. His greatest works are from Scriptural subjects. 'Christ Healing the Sick,' 'Christ Rejected,' and 'Death on the Pale Horse.'— One of the most eminent of our portrait-painters, Sir Henry Raeburn, died in 1823. His portraits are full of life, vigour, and prominence; and they are admirable as likenesses. He received his knighthood on the visit of George IV. to Edinburgh, and was appointed his portrait-painter for Scotland; but he died the following year.— William Sharp, the eminent line-engraver, died in 1824, in

a good old age. He was mainly self-taught, and was wont
to declare that his first attempts at engraving were made
on a pewter pot. To him we owe the practice of illustra-
ting, in a worthy manner, the eminent authors of our
literature. Sharp was a great Radical; and, in Horne
Tooke's time, was repeatedly brought before the privy-
council. He was a man not easily frightened, however;
and he used his opportunity to canvass Mr. Pitt and others
of the council for subscriptions to his forthcoming engraving of Kosciuszko's portrait. They could not command
their countenances to deal severely with him after this;
and they let him go. He was, with all his jocularity of
temper, ardour in his profession, and good sense on most
subjects, singularly superstitious—believing that the end
of the world was at hand, and bringing up Joanna Southcote to London, and maintaining her there. In middle
life, he might have become an associate of the Royal
Academy; but he took up the cause of some other eminent
engravers, less favoured than himself, in a manner which
offended Sir Joshua Reynolds, who dropped his claims and
his acquaintance.

Some lovers and patrons of art, who were, on that
ground, benefactors of society, died during this period.
Mr. Angerstein was born in Russia, but, from the age of
fourteen, spent his life in England, and was a most useful
citizen, in other ways besides accumulating his splendid
collection of pictures. He is believed to have saved the
credit of the country in the commercial crisis of 1793, by
his proposal of an issue of exchequer bills; and it was
through him that the discovery of the life-boat was established and rewarded. His collection of pictures was purchased by government for £57,000, to be the foundation of
a National Gallery of Paintings. Mr. Angerstein died in
1823, at the age of ninety-one.—Mr. Payne Knight died
in the next year, bequeathing his collection of medals,
drawings, and bronzes—worth £30,000—to the British
Museum. Mr. Knight was an eminent Greek scholar, and
of high cultivation in every way; and his accomplishments were ennobled by a magnificent public spirit.—The
Duchess of Devonshire, who died in the same year, devoted
her whole fortune to the promotion of the arts. She

caused excavations to be made at Rome, which restored to light many precious relics of antiquity that might otherwise have lain buried for ever.—In another way, the Duchess of Rutland—who died in 1825, in middle life—was a benefactress of the arts and of society; she built Belvoir Castle, superintending its erection for twenty-five years with a vigilant interest and taste. All the neighbouring villages and lands were in a constant state of improvement through her care; and she obtained many premiums from the Society for the Promotion of Arts and Manufactures, for her agricultural improvements and skill in planting. It is no wonder that a multitude of weeping mourners followed in her funeral train.

There were women among the authors who died during this period, whom the world was sorry to part with. The venerable Mrs. Barbauld, whose writings were small in bulk, but eminent in beauty, died, very old, in 1825. Her father had permitted her to share the classical education of her brother; and the result was seen in the mature richness of her mind, and the remarkable beauty of her style. Charles James Fox declared her *Essay on the Inconsistency of Human Expectations* to be the finest essay in our language; and her *Plea for the Repeal of the Corporation and Test Acts* was like a trumpet-call to the whole host of English Dissenters. Her private life was full of honour and of charm.—Then there was Jane Taylor, who wrote the delightful *Contributions of Q. Q.*, which are to be found in thousands of homes; and Mrs. Radcliffe, the mother of modern English romance; and Sophia Lee, one of the writers of the *Canterbury Tales;* and Mrs. Piozzi, once Mrs. Thrale, the hostess and friend of Dr. Johnson, and the recorder of much that we know of him: all these passed away within this period.—And also the busy, complacent, useful Richard Lovell Edgeworth, who put us upon improving our principles and methods of education, and was full of mechanical projects which set other people thinking and inventing and maturing; and the pompous Dr. Parr, who believed himself a second Johnson, when Johnson was more thought of than he is now; Parr, of whom Porson said that 'he would have been a great man but for three things—his trade, his wife, and his politics.'

His trade was school-keeping, for which he was unfit; his
wife was, as she took no pains to conceal, anything but
amiable; and his politics were ultra-liberal—a great
offence to the ministry when he dined with the queen, and
said grace at Alderman Wood's table.   He had acted with
a firmness and moderation which gained him respect at
the time of the Birmingham riots in 1791, when his house
and library were threatened with the same fate as those of
his friend, Dr. Priestley; and his reputation stood high on
account, not only of his scholarship, but of some sermons
and tracts which he had published; so that, though his
fame at the time can now be hardly understood, he was in
truth by no means beneath the notice of those who were
bound to watch the proceedings of the queen, and who
were scandalised at her choice of her domestic chaplain.—
The virtuous Lindley Murray died in 1826, at an advanced
age.   While learning our grammar of him, in our young
days, and growing tired of his name, as associated with
dull lessons, we little knew to how good a man that name
belonged.   Lindley Murray was an American; and he
came over to England in middle life, and remained with
us solely for the sake of the mildness of our climate, which
was rendered necessary to him by the loss of health.
Under a condition of muscular weakness which prevented
his walking for the rest of his days, he contentedly gave
up the usual objects and amusements of life, and humbly
devoted himself to be as useful as he could from his invalid
chair.   His school-books spread by tens of thousands over
both his native and his adopted country; and the proceeds
might have made him very rich.   But he thought he had
enough already for his simple tastes and moderate desires;
and he gave away, to those who were in need, the entire
profits of his works.   Thus, much as we have learned from
his books, we may learn something better from his life.—
A great public benefactor, who died in 1821, was Mr.
James Perry, of the *Morning Chronicle*, who gave a new
and elevated character and influence to the newspaper
press.   He was a scholar and a gentleman; and his attainments and character could not have wrought in a more
important direction than in that which he chose.   The
press is now called the fourth power in the state; and just

when the need of this power arose, the right man came to regulate, refine, and elevate it.

Of those whose divine office it is to refine and elevate the whole mass of society—the poets—we lost some of great name within a few years.

The good and accomplished Bishop Heber—more known and valued, perhaps, by the beauty of his hymns than by any other of his many qualifications—was suddenly snatched away in the midst of his usefulness in India. He was found dead in his bath—it was believed from apoplexy—in April 1826. His religious fervour gave a freshness of expression to his devotional poetry, which, if it does not stand in the stead of originality of thought, supplies us with what is always revered by all minds —originality of feeling. The hymns of Bishop Heber have therefore made their way among Christians of all denominations, and caused him to be ranked among the poets of his time. His age was only forty-three.—In the last century, the poems of Robert Bloomfield, the farmer's boy, were brought into notice by Mr. Capel Lofft—a man of letters and something of a poet himself. The protector and protected died within a year of each other—the poet in August 1823; the man of letters in May 1824.—And Hayley, the friend of Cowper, and author of some poems which had a good deal of popularity in their day, was gone.—A deeper cause for mourning, however, than any we have mentioned—perhaps the deepest of the period— was in the untimely loss of three great poets—Byron, Shelley, and Keats. At the time, the mourning for Byron was infinitely the widest and loudest; but it is not so now, and it can never be so again. His extraordinary popularity during his life, and for some time afterwards, and even now among survivors of his own generation, was justified by the fact of its existence. Such a popularity never arises, much less endures, without some reason; but the reason was of a temporary nature; and the fame must be temporary accordingly. Byron's power, which was great, employed itself in uttering, from his own conscious-ness, the discontents of his time. He was unaware of this, and always believed himself an isolated being, doomed to live and die without sympathy; whereas he was the mouthpiece of the needs and troubles of men in a transition state of society. When men found their troubles told, and their discontents avowed, in verse of a high order, by a man of high rank, youthful, proud, and egotistical, they rushed into a frantic sympathy with him, and received from him as true, noble, and beautiful, much that will not stand a comparison with nature, morality, and the everlasting principles of taste. Lord Byron could not produce, except by snatches, what was permanently true, because the eye of his soul was perplexed and dimmed by troubles which prevented his seeing things as they are; he could not produce what was inherently noble, because he was almost wholly engrossed by suffering moods of his own mind; he could not produce what must be lastingly beautiful, because he strove after affectations. As a greater than himself said of his irony and affectations: 'It is a paltry originality which makes solemn things gay, and gay things solemn; yet it will fascinate thousands, by the very diabolical outrage of their sympathies.' So said Keats, in pain and disgust at the levity of a passage of Byron, though no man could relish humour more keenly. Thousands were fascinated, and from the cause assigned. Unless it were Scott's, Byron's was the greatest literary fame of our own times. It was kept up by the interest universally taken, and pointedly invited by the poet himself, in his private misfortunes. His life was cursed by misfortune from his birth; and his earlier griefs so injured him as to make him himself the creator of his later ones. His life was not pure, nor his heart affectionate, nor his temper disciplined. There was good enough in him by starts, and by virtue of his genius, to suggest what he might have been, if reared under good influences. He wandered about the world during the latter years of his short life; and finally repaired to Greece, to give what aid he could against the Turks. There he died of fever, under a steady refusal to accept of timely medical aid, on the 19th of April, 1824.—In Keats, the world lost a poet of infinite promise. He was little more than a youth when he died; but he had made so vigorous and rapid a growth in power and wisdom, and was learning so to wield his magnificent faculties, that those who have studied his life and writings are dazzled at the mere conception of what he might have become. The world did not recognise his quality while he lived—indeed there was scarcely time for them to do so—and some few ignorantly denied and scoffed at its pretension; but year by year his name is oftener mentioned, and more and more minds are kindled at the scattered flames of his young genius, which would, if death had spared him, have shone like a lofty beacon above the ordinary level of human intellect. Men are often least conscious of their greatest losses; and in this, generations are like individuals. Keats died at Rome in February 1821, in the twenty-fifth year of his age; and when the news arrived in England, few heard, and fewer still regarded it. After the lapse of a quarter of a century, his fame is rising.—He was soon—in a year and a half—followed by his friend Shelley, who was drowned at the age of twenty-nine, off the coast of Italy. Shelley was a man of a noble and exquisite nature. He 'was the most truthful of men,' and of the most godlike benevolence. 'His aspect had a certain seraphical character,' we are told; and in that, it was a fair manifestation of himself. He was idolatrously beloved by those who knew him face to face; but his age and he were not on the best terms. There might be fault on both sides—some defect of prudence and patience on his; and, of course, a great want of enlightenment on the other: of course, because the greatest poets, as indeed the loftiest men of every order, have to educate their followers up to the power of appreciation of themselves. Thus Shelley was persecuted for his opinions; tortured in his domestic affections by Lord Eldon, who, with all his law, had no knowledge of the rights of opinion; and society not only looked on quietly, but a multitude applauded. So it was in his own day; and moreover, every act of his life—a life of singular purity and disinterestedness, when some crudenesses of youth were gone by—was criticised and mocked by little minds which could hardly open to receive the least of his thoughts. Yet, unpopular as he was, and young when he died, he did more than any other man to direct and vivify the poetical aspiration of our time. Shelley still lives to us, not only in his own writings, as yet but partially diffused, but in the whole body and spirit of our recent poetry, and existing poetical life.

We have presented and summed up the gains and losses of a seven years' period. We have now to enter upon another, shorter, but not less alive with incident and the spirit of progress.

BOOK III.

—◆◆—

CHAPTER I.

Opening of New Parliament—Death of the Duke of York—Grant to the Duke of Clarence—Illness of Lord Liverpool—Lord Liverpool and Mr. Canning—Lord Liverpool as Minister—The Corn Bill—Catholic Question—New Administration—Mr. Canning consulted—Mr. Peel—Resignation of Cabinet Ministers—Mr. Canning, Premier——New Cabinet—Retirement of Lord Eldon.

THE period on which we are now entering—the last years of the reign of George IV.—is one of remarkable interest and importance in the retrospect, though the complaint of the time was of stagnation of public business. It is true that, for three sessions, scarcely anything was done of what is commonly called public business. In regard to variety of subject, the records of parliament perhaps were never before so meagre, for three consecutive sessions. At the same time, the registers of the period are full of ministerial correspondence, ministerial explanations, and ministerial difficulties: for this there was ample reason; and in this lay the deep importance and interest of the period.

It is common for society to complain of loss of the public time, and postponement of public business, when a change of ministry, or other event, induces explanation of their personal conduct on the part of public men. It is common to complain of such explanations, as if statesmen were obtruding their personal concerns upon a public which does not care for them, but wants to be about its own business. But this is, wherever held, a vulgar error, and a most pernicious one. Every true statesman knows that his personal honour is a national interest; and every enlightened citizen knows that the highest distinction of a nation is the rectitude of its rulers; and that no devotion of time, thought, patience, and energy, can be too great for the object of upholding the standard of political honour among statesmen. In the most ordinary times, therefore, the enlightened citizen will eagerly receive, and earnestly weigh, the statements of public men with regard to their official conduct, aware that the postponement of legislative acts is a less evil than that of failing to discharge every conscience, to decide upon every reputation, as it comes into question; and thus to ascertain that the moral ground is firm and secure, before proceeding to political action. If it be thus in ordinary times, much stronger was the obligation to prove the conduct and reputation of statesmen at the period we are now entering upon. If, during the next three years, ministerial difficulties and explanations seem to be endless, there must be some cause; the embarrassment must be, in fact, a characteristic of the time.

We have witnessed the admission into the cabinet of two men who were called 'political adventurers'; and we have recognised in this event the sign that a new time had arrived, requiring for its administration a new order of men. Though the new men had acted and succeeded in their function, the struggles and perplexities of the transition from one state of society and government to another had yet to be gone through; and the beginning of these struggles and perplexities is what we have now to contemplate. We shall see ministry after ministry formed and dissolved. We shall see that the difficulty lay, not in finding competent men—for able men abounded at that time—but in determining what great principle, of those afloat, should so preponderate as to determine the government of the country. In the trial of this all-important point, the next three years cannot now be said to have been wasted, though at the time the vexation was severe, of seeing great questions standing still, ordinary legislative business thrust aside, and a temper and language of political bitterness rising up, such as could never have been anticipated among men of rational capacities and gentlemanly education.

The king opened the new parliament in person on the 21st of November, declaring in his speech that he called the Houses together for the special purpose of declaring

and accounting for the measures taken by government in
opening the ports to some kinds of grain and pulse, in consequence of the scarcity produced by the drought of the
summer.   In answer to various complaints in both Houses
about the scanty revelations of the speech, Lord Liverpool
and Mr. Canning pleaded the special nature of the business which occasioned the present sitting, and promised
the regular supply of information and suggestion at the
regular time—after the Christmas recess.   Ministers obtained the indemnity they sought for opening the ports
during the recess; and, with one exception, little else was
done before Christmas.   But that exception was a brilliant
and most significant one.   Mr. Canning accounted to
parliament, and obtained its enthusiastic sanction, for
sending troops to Portugal.

The sanction of parliament was indeed most enthusiastic; and so was the response from the country.   But it
is believed by those who ought to know, that this speech
was fatal to Mr. Canning.   His earnestness and eloquence
were taken by the Tories as a demonstration in favour of
liberalism.   They well knew that he was in fact, though
not in name, the leader of the government.   They knew
that the Duke of York so clearly considered him so, that
he had just made an audacious attempt, by addressing the
king, to get him dismissed from the cabinet.   They gave
all their strength to bear him down, and wrought against
him with a new exasperation, from the date of his
announcement of his having despatched the troops to
Portugal.   They could not bear him down in intention
and in act.   They could not bear him down in the
estimation of the country, in which he was indeed rising
from day to day.   But there was a way in which he was
in their power; they enfeebled his health.   They could
not bow his noble head, or tame his princely eye, by
reproach or threat; but they could and did, without
design or consideration, by the poison of disease.   There
are few men whose nerves are not more or less in the
power of other men's judgments and tempers; and of those
few, Canning was certainly not one.   His magnificent
organisation, adequate to the production of everything
that can ennoble the human being—absolutely teeming

with genius—had the one imperfection of being too sensitive. This was so clear—so evident on the merest glance at his face—that those have much to answer for who failed in the consideration thus bespoken by nature herself. Canning needed no indulgence. In the depth of illness, his high courage would have spurned it. He never deprecated; never, we may be sure, in the innermost breathings of his soul. He provoked much, dared everything, and endured till nature broke down. But nature was breaking down all the time that his enemies were most merciless; and they never saw it. It was visible in the weakening brow, the deepening eye, the quivering lip, the heavy and uncertain step. His enemies did not mark these signs which grieved his friends; and when, in reply to their rancour, the eye flashed again as it was wont, and the cheek flushed, and the voice rang from the roof, they were sure that they had done him no harm. From the time of his speech on sending aid to Portugal, the contest between Canning and his policy, and his foes and their policy, became deadly. It was indeed death that now interposed, and finally settled the conflict.

The Duke of York was the first who was withdrawn. The lord chancellor saw much of him for some weeks before his death; and the chancellor's opinion was, that his thoughts were almost exclusively occupied by the Catholic question, and the dread, in regard to that question, of the ascendency of Mr. Canning. In Lord Eldon's own opinion, his existence was essential to the effectual counter-action of Mr. Canning's influence, and to his displacement from the councils of the king. 'His death,' declares Lord Eldon, 'must affect every man's political situation—perhaps nobody's more than my own. It may shorten, it may prolong, my stay in office.' Of course, Mr. Canning himself must have known as well as other people the importance of the life that had gone—the significance of the death that had arrived. It must have been with a singular mixture of feelings that a man of his patriotism and power of will, and of his magnanimity and sensibility, must have bent over the vault in St. George's Chapel, into whose darkness, amidst the blaze of torches, the body of his arch-enemy was descending. It was then and there that he took his own death; perhaps at the moment when he was thinking how quiet is that resting-place at the goal of every human career, where the small and great lie down together, and 'princes and counsellors of the earth' —like his foe and himself—are quiet, and sleep after their warfare.

If those who attended that funeral could have seen their own position between the past and the future as we see it now, it would have so absorbed all their thoughts as that the body might have been lowered into its vault unseen, and the funeral anthems have been unheard. A more singular assemblage than the doomed group about the mouth of that vault has seldom been seen. In virtue of our survivorship, we can observe them now, each one with his fate hovering over his uncovered head. He who was next to be lowered into that vault was not there. He was in his palace, weak in health and spirits—relieved and yet perplexed that the course of government was simplified by the removal of his remonstrant brother, whose plea of nearness to the throne—now so solemnly set aside—had made his interference at once irksome and difficult to disregard. There would be no more interference now; no more painful audiences; no more letters brought in with that familiar superscription. The way was clear now; but to what? Liverpool and Canning must settle that. If they felt that the Catholic question must be settled, they must show how it was to be done; and they must do it. Liverpool and Canning! By that day twelvemonths, how was it with them? Lord Liverpool was not at Windsor that night. He laid down his careworn head to rest unaware that but a few more days of life—as he considered life—remained to him. The body breathed for some months; but in a few days after this the mind was dead. As for Canning, his heart and mind were full as his noble brow shone in the torchlight. He well knew that it was not only his chief personal enemy who was here laid low, but the only insurmountable barrier to his policy! He saw an open course before him, or one which he himself could clear. He saw the foul fiend Revolution descend into that vault, to be sealed down in it with that coffin. He saw beyond that torch-lit chapel a sunny vision of Ireland tranquilised; and the hope rose within him that he might achieve a peace at home—the sound peace of freedom—as blessed as the peace which he had spread over the world abroad.   And all the time, the chill and the damps of that chapel, dim amidst the yellow glare with the night-fog of January, were poisoning his vitals, and shortening his allowance of life to a mere span.   Beside him stood his friend and comrade, Huskisson.   They were born in the same spring; they were neither of them to know another moment of health after this chilly night-service; and their deaths were to be not far apart.   What remained for both was the bitter last drops of the cup of life; sickness, toil, perplexity, some humiliation, and infinite anguish.   Here, if they had known their future, they would have laid down all self-regards, all ambition, all hope and mirth, all thoughts of finished work and a serene old age, and have gone forth to do and suffer the last stage of their service, before dropping into their untimely rest.   These two had made no professions of grief about the death of the prince; they did not vaunt their feelings; yet here they were, sad and solemn; while beside them stood one whose woes about the loss of his royal friend, and about the irreparable loss to the empire, were paraded before all men's eyes, and dinned into the ears of all who would listen.   Here stood Lord Chancellor Eldon, beside the open grave in which he declared that the hopes of his country were being buried. Was he lost in grief?—his ready tears in fuller flow than ever?—his soul absorbed in patriotic meditation? 'Lord Eldon, recollecting'—what?—that he might catch cold— stood upon his hat, to avoid chill from the flags; 'and his precaution was completely successful.'   If it had but occurred to Canning to stand upon his hat!—but he was thinking of other things.   There were others for whom death was in waiting; and some for whom great labours and deeds were preparing in life.   The troublesome opponent of ministers, Mr. Tierney, who was to be found dead in his study before the next royal funeral; and Lord Graves, who was to die by his own hand, under the provocation of royal vice or levity.   And what tasks lay before those who were yet to live and work!   Among the

six dukes who bore the pall, was he who was to succeed to
the highest military office now thus vacated ; and Wellington himself no doubt thought this night that he was of
one mind in the great political questions of the day with
the prince whose pall he bore.   No doubt he believed that
he should, in his proper place, do what he could to exclude
the Catholics, and to keep the conscience of the sovereign
fixed upon the coronation oath, and his duty to Protestantism : in his proper place, we say, because the duke
spurned the idea of a military chief like himself taking
civil office, and openly declared, with indignation at an unfounded rumour, that he should be mad if he dreamed of
the premiership.   Yet, before this royal vault should
again be opened, Wellington was to be premier, and use
his office to repeal the disabilities of the Catholics.   Truly,
pledges and prophecies are dangerous things for statesmen
to meddle with in times of transition ; and it would seem
to be a main feature in the mission of the honest and
resolute Wellington—honest and resolute beyond all cavil
—to prove the presumption of pledges and prophecies in
times of transition.   Then there was Peel, with the same
work before him, and much more, of which he had not yet
begun to dream ; and with the fate before him of losing
his best-beloved honour—the representation of his university—and gaining several others, any one of which
would suffice to make an immortality.   And there was
Hardinge, the friend of both the deceased and the incoming commander-in-chief, who was to signalise his age in
the history of India by his administration and achievements both of peace and war.   And there was, as chief-
mourner, he who was to be the next king, and in whose
reign was to occur that vital renovation of our representative system, which will be to thoughtful students of a
thousand years hence what Magna Charta is to us.   What
a group was here collected, within the curtain of the
future, seeing nothing but the vault at their feet, and the
banners of the past waving above their heads ; and,
wherever they thought they saw some way into the coming
time, seeing wrongly—mistaking their own fancy-painting
on that curtain for discernment of what was behind it !
And behind that veil, agents work unheard—death at his

grave-digging; and the people with their demands and
their acclamations; and the trumpet-voice of conviction
summoning prejudice to the surrender. But what they
saw not, we, as survivors, see; and what they heard not,
we hear; for now that curtain of futurity is hung up over
our heads as banners of the past; and the summons of
death, and of the popular will, and of individual conscience,
are still audible to us; not in their first stunning crash,
but as funereal echoes to which those banners float.

The Duke of York went to his grave sincerely mourned
by many, and partially honoured by many more who could
not honestly grieve that he did not reach the throne. In
his youth, he had shown valour and an earnest aspiration
to good generalship in the campaigns in Flanders. During
the thirty-two years that he held the office of commander-
in-chief, he did eminent service to the state in his
administration of the army—instituting and carrying
through such reforms and new discipline as made his
management in fact a re-creation of that national force.
His nature was frank and honourable, if only he had done
justice to it. It endeared him to his friends, even to the
point of inducing them to overlook, and almost to justify
his vices. The loyal cant of the day was that in his vices
'there was nothing un-English—nothing unprincely;'
but the princes and people of England could not be
expected to admit among their characteristics recklessness
in sensual vice and pecuniary extravagance. His dissoluteness was, if not 'unprincely,' vulgar, as all selfish
passion is; and his recklessness about debt was, we may
surely say, eminently 'un-English.' We cannot give up
probity in money-transactions as an English characteristic.
As for his high Toryism, when all danger from it was
past, men remembered that he was ill educated, and, by
his position, precluded from the enlightenment which was
flowing in upon men in humbler stations. It was the
subject of grave apprehension, very reasonably, while he
lived, with his foot upon the steps of the throne, and his
eye upon the crown; but as soon as he was let down into
the grave, it was remembered with a sort of respectful
compassion as a delusion troublesome to himself, and a
weakness which would, in a former age, have been regarded

as a grace of royalty. His statue stands conspicuous on
its pillar within sight of the Horse Guards, where so much
of his business lay. It might be that some debtors,
ruined by his cruel extravagance, might sigh in their
prison when they heard of its erection; and some, whose
domestic honour and peace had been tainted by his
passions, might wonder at the strange distribution of
homage in a state which professes the purity of Christianity; but it was pretty generally admitted that he had
done his country better service than princes often do, and
that to his labours were partly owing the successes of our
wars, and the high character of our military forces. His
death took place on the 5th of January, 1827, and his
funeral on the 20th.

The Duke of Wellington succeeded, as has been said, to
his office of commander-in-chief; and his sailor-brother,
the Duke of Clarence, to his prospect of the throne. On
the 15th of February, a message from the king was presented to both houses of parliament, recommending an
addition to the income of the Duke and Duchess of
Clarence, in view of the increased expenses which would
be occasioned to them by the duke's proximity to the
throne. A good deal of objection was made to this in the
Commons, but none in the Lords. The great distress of
the people, whose condition had just been made the subject
of a royal letter to the bishops, and the inconvenience of
the precedent, were the grounds of opposition, and these
were met by the plea that the maintenance of royal dignity
was an object which must not give way to temporary
pressure, and that the sum proposed was only a portion of
what would be saved to the country by the death of the
Duke of York. Up to this time, the income of the Duke
and Duchess of Clarence had been £26,500. By the death
of the elder brother, an addition of £3000 a year would
now accrue; and it was proposed that parliament should
grant £9000 more—namely, £3000 to the duke, and £6000
to the duchess; by which their joint income would be
raised to £38,500. After much opposition and debating,
it was thus settled.

It was on Thursday, the 15th of February, that this
royal message was presented; and it was taken into con-

sideration the next evening—Friday. Lord Liverpool
brought forward the subject in the Upper House, and
spoke upon it. He was never seen to be better or more
cheerful. The next morning, Saturday, his servant was
surprised at not hearing the bell, as usual, after breakfast,
and went into his master's study, where he found Lord
Liverpool lying on the floor in an apoplectic fit. Whether
he would live was for some time doubtful; but it was
quite certain that his political career was ended. His
colleagues wrote in their private letters: 'Heaven knows
who will succeed him.' Some felt it 'a tremendous blow
under present circumstances.' The principal of these circumstances was the universal expectation—a state of
doubtful expectation—about the proposed Corn Bill, and
some legislation about the Catholics. The king was at
Brighton; and Mr. Peel went down to inform him of the
event. Mr. Canning was at Brighton, confined to his bed
by the illness caught at the funeral; and Mr. Huskisson
was confined to the house in London from the same cause.
Mr. Canning had charge of the Corn Bill, and he was
awaiting with extreme anxiety the approaching discussion
of the Catholic question. At such a moment as this the
premier was struck down; and the two friends could
neither meet nor wait upon the king. We have the lord
chancellor's first impressions on the occasion: 'If other
things made it certain that he would otherwise succeed
him, I should *suppose* Canning's health would not let him
undertake the labour of the situation. But,' he adds, in
his usual temper towards Canning, 'ambition will attempt
anything.' Two days after, the chancellor became very
oracular, as was natural, when it was certain that there
was nothing to be known. 'This, at any time,' he says,
'would be an event of importance; so immediately after
the Duke of York's death, and upon the eve of the days
when the great questions of the corn-trade and Catholic
emancipation are to be discussed and decided, it is of importance so great, that nobody can be certain whether it
is not of so much importance as to render almost certain
wrong decisions upon these vital questions.' If we can
make out any meaning here, it is that Lord Eldon now
supposed a liberal policy sure to prevail, and believed that

Lord Liverpool had been the only security against the
dreaded 'changes in our institutions.' The letter proceeds: 'Nobody knows, and nobody can conjecture with
probability, how soon the illness of the minister will, as it
seemingly must, dissolve the administration, or how
another is to be formed and composed. Speculation as to
this is very busy, and politicians are all at work. The
opposition are in high spirits, and confidently expecting
to enjoy the loaves and the fishes. They may—but they
also may not—be disappointed.'

The first thing decided upon was to wait awhile, for
the chance of Lord Liverpool recovering sufficiently to
send in his resignation. Week after week, as it passed
away, showed this to be less and less probable; and by
the end of March it was found necessary to set about appointing his successor. Setting aside their political relations, the loss of Lord Liverpool was very affecting to Mr.
Canning. Through life, the two had been close personal
friends, from the time of their first meeting at college.
They were born in the same year; they were inseparable
at Christ Church, where they laughed at one another's
whims—Jenkinson's brown coat, with buttons bearing the
initials of the great orators, and Canning's gloriously
nonsensical verses; and where, in the intervals of their
mirth, they discussed the gravest subjects of human interest, with the earnestness belonging to the genius of the
one, and the integrity of the other. They entered parliament at the same time, under Mr. Pitt, and were never
separated in their private regards by the differences on
public matters which occasionally arose. This is highly
honourable to them both. It must be a strong friendship
which could enable the man of the world to bear with the
views of the man of genius, when those views were too
large for his comprehension; and which would enable the
man of genius to bear with the negative qualities of the
mediocre man of the world, in times which demanded all
the energies of every statesman. In political life, each
was largely indebted to the other; as is more apparent to
us now than perhaps it ever was to them. Lord Liverpool
was not, apparently, fully aware that it was Canning who
had of late years made his government illustrious in the

eyes of the world; but every one now knows that it was
so.   And Canning could hardly estimate at the time the
influence of Lord Liverpool's presence in securing him a
field for the exercise of his statesmanship.   If he had
entered the cabinet he could hardly have remained there,
during the last four years, under any other premier of the
same politics as Lord Liverpool.   It was no time for
weighing these considerations, when the news of his
friend's seizure came to him as he lay fevered in his bed.
He had but just returned from visiting Lord Liverpool at
Bath, where he had gone, after the duke's funeral,
to improve his health.   He had come back worse than he
went; and in the depth of his illness, this news reached
him.   The effects of grief, anxiety, and sickness, were
visible enough when he appeared in the House to bring
forward the measures he had in charge, and to encounter
the onslaught of persecution, which was never mitigated
by any touch of reverence, sympathy, or even common
humanity, till it had laid him low.

The country was not the worse for the loss of Lord
Liverpool, though his official life had been useful in its
way, at certain periods of his career.   He was a good
balance-wheel when the movements of parties might otherwise be going too fast.   He had no striking ability, either
in action, or in speech.   He was diligent, upright, exceedingly heavy, and, as his friends well knew, extremely
anxious under his sense of responsibility.   He could not
throw off his cares for a day or an hour—either in the free
air of Wimbledon, or in his trips to Bath ; and it ended in
his cares throwing off his life.   He declared in private,
that on no one day for twenty-five years of official life had
he seen his heap of letters on the table, without a sharp
pang of apprehension, and a sense of reluctance to break
the seals—so strong did he feel the probability to be every
day that something was going wrong in some part of the
world.   It appears strange that a man of his cast, merely
respectable in abilities and characteristics, should have
held office so long—the premiership for fifteen years—in
times of such stir and convulsion; but the fact was, his
highest ability was that of choosing and conciliating able
men, and keeping them together in sufficient harmony to

get through their work, if nothing more. Nobody quarrelled with him; and he set his whole weight against his
colleagues quarrelling with each other; so that the Eldons
and the Cannings, the Bexleys and the Huskissons, met in
council, week after week, for years together, inwardly
despising and disliking each other, but outwardly on
decent terms, and all working in their own way in their
own offices. This could not go on for ever; and, as we
have seen, Lord Liverpool himself knew it could not go
on much longer. He meant to retire presently, to leave
the way open for some settlement of the Catholic question.
Thus, the nation did not sustain much loss by the brief
shortening of his term; nor was there the affectation of
mourning a great political loss. There was decorous
regret that such a penalty on toil and conscientiousness
should have overtaken so meritorious a public servant;
and then ensued extreme eagerness to know what influence
would next be in the ascendant. This could not be ascertained till the following April.

In the meantime, the Corn Bill must first be brought
forward. It was committed to Mr. Canning's care, as
leader in the Commons. He was extremely anxious about
it, as it was the elaborate work of his two friends, Lord
Liverpool and Mr. Huskisson; and the subject was not
one that he felt at home in. His diffidence was aggravated
by the misfortune that he and Mr. Huskisson were kept
apart by illness, in London and Brighton, and were thus
precluded from personal conference about the bill. The
only thing that could be done was to send a confidential
friend backwards and forwards, till each minister was in
possession of the mind of the other. If the conclusion of
the matter could have been foreseen, or the causes of that
ending have been made known as they ought to have been,
the trouble and anxiety might have been, in great part,
spared. The Duke of Wellington made an end of the
measure, by heading the opposition in the House of Lords,
and carrying an amendment which vitiated the bill too
seriously to allow it to be proceeded with; the very bill
which had been prepared by the premier, and fully sanctioned by the cabinet of which the duke was, at the time,
a member. It was not till the 1st of March that Mr.

Canning was well enough to bring forward the measure; which he did in the form of a set of resolutions, intended to be the foundation of a new corn-law. According to the resolutions, foreign corn might always be imported, free of duty, to be warehoused; and it might always be let in for home consumption on payment of certain duties; for instance, the duty on wheat was to be 1s. when wheat was at 70s., and to increase 2s. with every decrease of 1s. in price; and so on, in different proportions, with other kinds of grain. The resolutions were well received and supported —the House rejecting, by a majority of three to one, on an average, the amendments proposed on behalf of the landed interest. A bill—the new corn-law, as it was supposed to be—was brought in on the 2nd of April, and passed on the 12th, before the House adjourned for the Easter holidays. When parliament reassembled, Mr. Canning was premier, and the conduct of the bill in the Upper House devolved upon Lord Goderich (Mr. Robinson under his new title). Under some extraordinary misconception, the Duke of Wellington declared that he believed the amendment he had to propose would be acceptable to the government; whereas it went to establish the principle of prohibition, which it was the main object of the measure to cast aside. His amendment proposed that 'foreign corn in bond should not be taken out of bond until the average price of corn should have reached 66s.' The government was left in a minority of eleven in the vote on this clause on the 12th of June; and the bill was therefore abandoned.

The debate on the Catholic question came on on the 5th of March, and continued two days. The anti-Catholic speakers, who mustered strong in this new parliament, wandered away from the consideration of the motion before the House into the whole set of old topics—back to the Treaty of Limerick, and wide among the doings of the priests at the late elections; and Mr. Canning had to bring them back to the question of the night, which was: 'That this House is deeply impressed with the expediency of taking into consideration the laws imposing civil disabilities on his majesty's Roman Catholic subjects.' Mr. Canning's speech was deeply impressive to the House; but it would have been more so, and have been received as an oracle by the Catholics, if it could have been known that these were his last words on the subject which he had at heart during the whole of his career. The danger of neglect, of letting things alone in such a crisis as had arrived, was his last topic on this last occasion. After stating that 'one bugbear was fairly disposed of'—the coronation oath—he said : 'What are the other dangers which exist at this eleventh hour, I have yet to learn ; but a singular fate has attended this question. The question is : "Will you do as we propose? or will you do nothing? or what will you do?" And, secondly : "What dangers do you apprehend?" Now, to the question : "Will you do as we propose? or will you do nothing? or will you do something else?" the answer is clear enough : "We will not do as you propose." But to the two remaining branches of the question, no answer is given. And when we ask : "What dangers do you apprehend from the passing of a bill similar to that of 1813?" we are also unable to get any answer. . . . . I conjure the House to reflect that the motion is merely a declaration on the part of the House, that the state of Ireland and of the Roman Catholic population is such as to demand the consideration of the House. To this proposition it is intended to oppose a direct negative, importing that the House does not think the state of Ireland, or the laws affecting the Roman Catholics, deserve consideration. That is the issue upon which the House is now going to divide. The resolution goes no further than that the House should adopt the opinion of its predecessors, who sent three bills up to the House of Lords, of relief to the Roman Catholics. . . . . On the other hand, if this resolution should be negatived —if the House of Commons should decide that the consideration of the state of Ireland is not worthy to be entered upon—then is the House of Commons changed indeed ; and it would be more easy to imagine, than it would be safe for me to express, the consequence that may ensue from such a change.'

It was now just five years since Mr. Canning uttered in the House what he supposed would be his last appeal on behalf of the Catholics—in 1822, previous to his intended departure for India. He was then mistaken ; and now,

when really uttering his last appeal, he was unconscious
that it would be so. Never could he have been more
earnest than now; for any retrogression of the Commons on
this subject would be, at the moment, a most untoward
circumstance for the cause and for himself. It was the
moment when a new administration was about to be
formed; when its determining principle—whether avowed
or not—was to be concession or opposition to the Catholic
claims; and when the king himself was falling back, on
the removal of the rivalry of the Duke of York. The loss
of the Commons from the cause must be most disastrous at
such a crisis. This loss, however, had to be sustained.
The division took place a little before five in the morning of the 7th of March, in a House of 548 members; and
there was a majority of four against the motion. The
anti-Catholic party *had* gained by the elections. The
Marquis of Lansdowne had given notice in the Lords of a
motion grounded on the petitions sent up by the Catholics;
but on this decision of the Commons, he withdrew it,
fairly avowing that he dared not go forward, nor brave the
consequences of the disappointment to the Catholics, if
both Houses should display a majority against them. This
was an anxious season for the friends of the Catholics, to
whom it appeared that the question had gone back, and
who scarcely dared to reckon on the patience of their
wronged fellow-subjects. But men rarely know what
circumstances are really prosperous or adverse. This was
but the step back, before the spring. It was too late now
for the Catholics to be disheartened, when they had just
seen what they could do in the field of the elections.
They roused themselves for the struggle which was to
prove the final one.

First, this question broke up another cabinet. Of the
existing cabinet, the Duke of Wellington and Mr. Peel
were the strong men on the one side, and Mr. Canning
and Mr. Huskisson on the other. Lord Liverpool had kept
them together hitherto—he having been openly of the
anti-Catholic party all his life, but being well known
among his colleagues to have arrived at the conviction,
and to be about to act upon it, that the friends of the
Catholics must soon carry their point. The repressive

and combining influence of Lord Liverpool being now removed, the diverse elements of the government parted off and rose up against each other; so that it became immediately necessary to decide which should have the ascendency. It was not yet considered indispensable that there should be an undivided cabinet on this question. The question might be left open; but whether the premier should be of the one way of thinking or the other was the particular which could not but bring this all-important matter to an issue.

Mr. Canning could not be dispensed with. The public showed that it thought so; the king certainly thought so; and the members of the administration and their friends betrayed in their correspondence, and by their methods of consultation, that, if they themselves did not think so, they feared that everybody else did. Mr. Canning also held the second place in the cabinet, and had the first right to look to the premiership, and to be consulted upon it. He it was, therefore, whom the king summoned, on the 27th of March, when it was found to be in vain to wait for any amendment in the state of Lord Liverpool, and when the restlessness of the country and of political parties showed that there must be no more delay in forming an administration. The interview was long, and embarrassing to both. The king requested Mr. Canning's opinion on the practicability of placing at the head of the cabinet a statesman who held Lord Liverpool's avowed opinions on the Catholic question. Mr. Canning declared that it might, he believed, be done, and a wholly anti-Catholic government be formed; in which case, of course, he must retire; and he plainly intimated that he could not remain in the government except as prime-minister. This could have been no surprise to the king; for there was no statesman of Mr. Canning's way of thinking to whom he could, with any propriety, have been made subordinate. Yet the king could not bring himself at once to the point of nominating Mr. Canning; and this first negotiation was at an end.

What might have been the next step if the king had been let alone, there is no saying; but some anti-Catholic members of the aristocracy, alarmed at the strength of the popular expectation in favour of Mr. Canning, took a step of greater boldness than the sovereign was disposed to endure, and ruined their own cause by an attempt at intimidation which roused the royal resentment. A Tory peer, a duke and privy-councillor, requested an audience of the king, and told his majesty that he came as the express representative of eight peers—all, like himself, holding great electoral influence—to declare that if Mr. Canning was placed at the head of the cabinet, they would all withdraw their support from the government. This took place on the fourth day after the abortive interview. The effect of this disrespectful and corrupt proceeding was to determine the king on the instant to send for Mr. Canning.

By this time, Mr. Canning was aware that if he became premier, the government must lose the services of Mr. Peel; for Mr. Peel had told him so on the 29th of March. Between these two statesmen there was, with all their differences of opinion, and much clashing of interests at this crisis, no ill-will. Private letters of Mr. Canning's are in existence which declare that Mr. Peel was the only seceding member of the government who behaved well to him at this time; and it is known that he declared Mr. Peel to be his rightful political heir and successor.

Mr. Peel's difficulty in this instance was a peculiar one. It arose from his being responsible in his office for the administration of the affairs of Ireland. He was disposed for a cabinet divided on this question, as the House of Commons had just shown itself so very equally divided; and on almost every other question of importance, he was of the same mind with those of his colleagues who sat with him in the Commons. But he felt that he could not fill his place in the House as Irish minister with any satisfaction under a premier who advocated a policy in regard to the Catholics opposite to his own. Such were his reasons, assigned by himself in a frank and admirable letter to Lord Eldon, of the date of the 9th of April. He made no difficulty that could be helped, and caused no embarrassment. He spoke to no one but the king and Mr. Canning on the subject; and his intentions and feelings became known only by the king's mention of them to the chan-

cellor. It is a curious circumstance that while Mr·
Canning was telling the king that he believed an anti-
Catholic cabinet could be formed, and offering in that case
to retire, Mr. Peel was telling his majesty that he 'could
not advise the attempt to form an exclusive Protestant
government;' and that he could not be a party even to
the attempt, if it should be contemplated. He was confident that the king was of the same opinion. And so it
appears by the result. This letter of Mr. Peel's was
written on the 9th of April, and it was on the 10th that
the king sent for Mr. Canning; not now, as before, merely
in his character of privy-councillor, to consult and advise,
but to receive the charge of forming an administration.
The *animus* with which this result was anticipated by his
anti-Catholic colleagues is shown in various of Lord
Eldon's letters. 'I think—who could have thought it?—
that Mr. Canning will have his own way. I *guess* that I,
Wellington, Peel, Bathurst, Westmoreland, &c., will be
out.' Some occasional notices in the old chancellor's
letters of the temper of the times unveil to us something
of what the 'political adventurer' had to go through, on
taking possession of the highest political seat in the
empire, and make but too natural his rapid descent to the
grave. 'The whole conversation in this town,' writes
Lord Eldon from London, 'is made up of abusive, bitterly
abusive talk, of people about each other—all fire and
flame. I have known nothing like it.' 'I think political
enmity runs higher, and waxes warmer, than I ever knew
it.' Thus it was in private, before and during the Easter
recess; and after that recess, no one needed any other information than the reports of the debates to learn how
far the spirit of persecution, and the language of personality, could go among noblemen and gentlemen who were
charged with the gravest of all trusts, but could neither
discern the greatness of the man whose heart they were
breaking, nor the needs of the time which he was summoned to rule. Doubtless it was the needs of the time,
the political transition, that they quarrelled with, though
they themselves believed, as did their victim, that it was
the man; but if this goes to palliate their conduct in any
degree, it did not to him lessen the smart of the wounds

they inflicted in every possible mode, and at every possible opportunity.

We have seen that Mr. Canning received the king's commands on the 10th of April. He immediately applied to all his late colleagues, inviting them to remain in their offices. Of the replies that he received, the most extraordinary appears to be that of the Duke of Wellington, who requested to know, before signifying his intentions, who was to be at the head of the government. Mr. Canning's answer of course was that it is usually understood that the individual charged with the construction of a government is to be at the head of it; and then the duke resigned. 'It was on the 11th of April,' to adopt Mr. Canning's own statement of the affair, 'that he received the resignation of Lord Westmoreland. Of the résignation of Mr. Peel he was aware some days before. He received the resignation of the Duke of Wellington on the 12th, at half past ten A.M. Lord Bexley sent in his shortly after. With these, and the verbal resignation of Mr. Peel, he went to St. James's. Those of Lord Eldon and Lord Bathurst arrived during his absence, and did not reach him till he was in the king's closet, having been sent after him, according to his directions, in case of their arrival. He would state further that, so far were they from anticipating the resignation of Lord Eldon, that the king and himself were both under the delusion that there were the best reasons to expect the support of his services in the new arrangements. . . . . It was bare justice to Lord Eldon to say that his conduct was that of a man of the highest feelings of honour, and that throughout it had been above all exception.' Mr. Canning presented this handful of resignations to the king, saying: "Here, sire, is that which disables me from executing the orders I have received from you, respecting the formation of a new administration. It is now open to your majesty to adopt a new course, for no step has yet been taken in the execution of those orders that is irrecoverable; but it becomes my duty fairly to state to your majesty that, if I am to go on in the position where you have been pleased to place me, my writ must be moved for to-day'—it was the last day before the Easter recess, and orders for the moving of the writ had been given—'for if we wait till the holidays, without adopting any definitive steps, I see that it is quite hopeless for me to attempt to persevere in the objects I have undertaken.'   The king, in reply, gave him his hand to kiss, and confirmed him in his appointment: declaring, however, according to some accounts, that he himself was resolved to oppose any further concessions to the Catholics. In two hours after this interview in the royal closet, the House of Commons was ringing with acclamations—Mr. Wynn moving: 'That a new writ be issued for the borough of Newport, in consequence of the Right Hon. George Canning having accepted the office of first lord-commissioner of the treasury.'

The minister had now the Easter recess before him for constructing his cabinet; but there were more resignations to come in.   The Duke of Wellington gave up his office in the ordnance, as well as that of commander-in-chief. Lord Melville, though agreeing with Mr. Canning on the Catholic question, declined holding office with some whom he believed Mr. Canning about to solicit.   The master of the Mint, Mr. Wallace—the attorney-general, Sir Charles Wetherell—and the judge-advocate, Sir J. Beckett, next resigned; and even four of the king's household officers. There must have been among these personages an expectation of a new time—of a transition to what they called Radicalism or revolution, under a minister of liberal politics; for it is difficult to see how some of them could be affected by Mr. Canning's becoming the head of a cabinet in which the Catholic question was still to remain open, the king's resolution to oppose further concession being understood.

It was this which made Mr. Canning's task a very difficult one, it being impossible for him to fill up the vacant offices with men of his own opinions on the great question of the day.   The task was achieved, however, by the 27th of April.   On that day every office in the government was declared to be filled up.   Lord Bexley returned to office; the heir-presumptive became lord high admiral the day after Lord Melville's resignation of his office at the head of the admiralty; Sir John Copley, created Lord Lyndhurst, became chancellor; Lord Anglesey went to the

ordnance, Lord Dudley to the foreign and Mr. Sturges
Bourne to the home office.   Mr. Robinson, who had remained, was removed to the Upper House, with the title
of Lord Goderich, in order to lead the business there.
Mr. Canning himself assumed the chancellorship of the
exchequer, uniting it with that of first lord of the
treasury, in order that Mr. Huskisson and he might work
with the fuller effect together in matters of finance.
Thus the minister was prepared with a complete government to meet the House of Commons on its assembling on
the 1st of May, to the surprise of not a few of both friends
and foes, who had believed it impossible that he could
surmount such a mass of impediments as had been thrown
in the way of his entrance into the highest office of the
state.   The curiosity was now intense to see how he would
proceed.

The times were so busy and exciting that men had hardly
leisure to note, as they would have done at any former
period, the retirement of the aged chancellor.   Perhaps
there was in their minds, perhaps there was in his own, a
doubt whether he had retired, never to return—he who
had talked of it so often and so long, and had yet adhered
to office for a longer time than any other chancellor, lay or
clerical, from the Norman conquest downwards. His tenure
of office had been but once interrupted, and had extended
over within a few weeks of a quarter of a century.   He
felt sensibly the calmness with which his resignation was
received by the political world and the country at large,
though he was ready to be at least invited back to office
under future ministers. He has left on record one really
painful fact in connection with his retirement—a fact so
painful as to enable us partly to account for his low estimate of persons beyond his own set of acquaintances.   He
writes, on the eve of his retirement: 'If I had all the
livings in the kingdom vacant when I communicated my
resignation—for what, *since that*, falls vacant I have nothing
to do with—and they were cut each into threescore livings,
I could not do what is asked of me by letters received
every five minutes, full of eulogies upon my virtues, all
which will depart when my resignation actually takes
place, and all concluding with: "Pray, give me a living

before you go out." ' He delivered up the seals on the 30th
of April, the day before the reassembling of parliament.
His usual self-gratulation did not fail him on this great
occasion of his life. By the heartiness with which
Lord Eldon is always found rejoicing in his own conscientiousness, as in a special gift of Providence, it seems as if
he could not suppose that other men could ordinarily desire
and endeavour to do their duty. He writes: 'I have now
taken my farewell of office. . . . . I bless God that He has
enabled me to look back to a period of nearly half a century,
spent in professional and judicial situations and stations,
with a conviction that the remembrance of the past will
gild the future years which His providence may allow to
me, not merely with content, but with that satisfaction and
comfort, and with much happiness, of which the world
cannot deprive me.' This is characteristic; and the old
chancellor might be partly right in his special self-gratulation. We hope that most public men are at least as conscientious as he; but there are probably few who are so
confident and exulting in their own righteousness. The
enjoyment of his special prerogative seems, however, to
have been far from sufficient for his peace. It was necessary
to him that others should value him as highly as he
valued himself; and it is not long before we find him sore
and irritated at that diminution of his political importance
which was the natural and inevitable consequence of his
retirement into private life.

CHAPTER II.

Enmity to Mr. Canning—Business of Parliament—The Corn Bill—
Close of the Session—Mr. Canning's Health—His Death—Funeral
and Honours—Character of Mr. Canning.

THE session lasted two months after the reassembling of
parliament on the 1st of May. It was a season of turbulence and rancour, which it is painful and humbling to
look back upon. The only consolation is in the reflection
that the disorder, though it took the appearance of hatred
between individual men, was in fact a feature of the state
of political transition. The minister was the professed
object of the rancour, and it was he who sank under it;
but not even he, with all his powers, and all his attributes
of offence, could have caused such perturbation at another
time, and in another position. The real conflict was
between old and new principles of policy, and the wounds
which men received were as representatives of those principles. In as far as Mr. Canning could keep this truth
before him, he was able to bear what was inflicted; but
he could not always keep it in full view. Perhaps no
man of any temperament could have done so; and it was
not to be expected of one so sensitive as he. Yet he might
have got through if he had had any fair chance of health;
but he had been ill ever since the funeral in that cold
January night which had been nearly fatal to many
besides himself. Now, feeble and exhausted, he was to experience no mercy. Those who had differed from his
former politics, and those who detested his present aims;
all who had suffered under his sarcastic wit; all who were
disappointed that he had overcome his late difficulties; all
who were jealous of a 'political adventurer' having risen
over the heads of the aristocracies both of birth and of
political administration, stimulated one another to insult,
and overpower, if they could, the minister who stood exposed to all attacks— incapable of aid, because himself so

immeasurably greater than all who would have aided, as
than all who attacked him.   During the remainder of the
session he was a lion at bay.   The lion may turn a flashing
eye upon his hunters, and shake the woods with his roar;
but a sufficiency of wounds must prostrate him at last; and
so it was here.   Here was the flashing eye, the indomitable valour, and the thundering utterance, under which the
assailants quailed for the moment.   But the powers of life
gave way; and, in a little while, only the silent ghost
remained in the old haunts, to call up the awe and remorse
which were now too late.   It is universally agreed that
personality and insult were never before so rank in any
assembly of English gentlemen as now, during the two
months following Mr. Canning's accession to the premiership.

The most tangible complaint of his adversaries was
about ' coalition;' and this fact is warrant enough for the
supposition that the discontent was with the time, though
the complainers themselves believed it was with the man.
The minister was supported by the Whigs; and the reason
why was that he and they agreed upon most subjects of
importance.   About reform of parliament they differed;
but, as Canning's arch-foe, Lord Grey, declared, there was
no near prospect of carrying this question; and it was, in
his opinion, no reason for separating men who could unite
to carry points of more pressing urgency.   They differed
about the repeal of the Corporation and Test Acts; and
this was nearly all.   They were agreed upon the leading
question of the times—the Catholic disabilities; and on
all matters of foreign and commercial policy and finance,
by which Mr. Canning was most eminently distinguished.
The attendants at Pitt dinners, the Tories who professed
to worship the statesman who desired Catholic emancipation and parliamentary reform, were not exactly qualified
to cry out upon the union between Mr. Canning and the
Whigs, whose differences might be called almost nominal,
in comparison with those which should have divided the
Tories from Mr. Pitt.   The fact was that names, and
recollections, and insignia, connected the Tories with Mr.
Pitt, while political principles separated them; and political principles united the Whigs and Mr. Canning, while

names, recollections, and insignia, severed them. Some were wise enough to see that principles are of more importance than badges and names; and we should be lenient towards those who are less enlightened, remembering how, in ordinary times, these names and badges serve as safeguards of political honour and consistency, and that it is not every one who can see the moment when they cease to be true, and ought therefore to be discarded. All the wisest people—and Mr. Canning assuredly for one—would have been thus lenient, if the offended persons had kept within the bounds of temper and courtesy. For the prevailing rancour, however, there could be no excuse.

The enmity appeared not only in connection with the explanations which necessarily took place on all sides after the reassembling of parliament. No one subject of the few brought forward during these two months could be debated, or even touched upon, without occasion being taken to cavil at the new administration, and especially its head. But of all the shafts which were aimed at him, it is believed that none struck so deep as one—or rather a quiverful—from the hands of Lord Grey. In a speech of apparent calmness, of deep melancholy, of affecting unconsciousness of the destiny awaiting himself and his victim, and of the most intense personal animosity against Mr. Canning, Lord Grey opened his views in the House of Lords on the 10th of May. He believed his own political life to be closed; and he declared in pathetic terms his sense of loneliness in this latter stage of his life. He did not blame his brother Whigs for their coalition with Mr. Canning, if their personal feelings did not forbid it; but his did. He avowed his want of confidence in the minister, and gave his reasons for it. A more striking and mournful instance can hardly be found than this speech, of the effect of prejudice, in blinding one great man to the merits—even to the most familiar attributes—of another. Lord Grey had soon occasion to show how well he could bear misconstruction and rancour; but if anything could have shaken his firmness in his own hour of the ordeal, it must have been the remembrance of this fatal attack on Canning —so insolent, hard, and cold; so insulting, and so cruel! As might be expected, from the state of mind which produced it, the speech was full of misconstructions and mistakes. As far as its matter was concerned, nothing could have been easier than to answer it; but the question was how? The practice of answering in one House the personal attacks made in another is radically objectionable; and Mr. Canning had the greatest reluctance to have recourse to this apparently only method; and besides, he was not in a state of health which would have borne him through such an exertion. He believed that ere long he should be able to reply to Lord Grey in person; but they never met more. Lord Grey's political friends, now the allies of the minister, did full justice to Mr. Canning's character in the Upper House; but this particular speech was never efficiently answered, and the thought of it rankled in the breast of the victim to the last.

When the Commons proceeded to business, there was something almost as perplexing as strange in the aspect of the House—Mr. Brougham and Sir Francis Burdett, Mr. Tierney and Sir Robert Wilson, sitting on the ministerial benches; and some who had till now scarcely known any other seat, finding themselves on the opposite side. The one point in which all parties appeared to agree was in wishing the session over. In the present state of men's minds, no great question could be discussed with due calmness; and the ministerial members especially wished that their relations with the cabinet should become more assured and consolidated before they exposed the greatest questions of the time to the passionate treatment of the legislature. Thus, not only were notices of motions on parliamentary reform, and repeal of the Corporation and Test Acts—Mr. Canning's great points of difference with his new allies—withdrawn, but also two on the Catholic question, which was too serious a matter now to be committed to the forces of such a tempest as at present perturbed the world of politics.

A motion tending to take bankruptcy matters from under the jurisdiction of the Court of Chancery was negatived by a large majority.—Mr. Hume failed in his endeavour to get repealed that one of the Six Acts of 1819 which imposed a stamp on cheap periodical publications.— On the ground of petitions from some of the ports, a

committee was asked for to inquire into the state of the
shipping interest; and this called up Mr. Huskisson to
justify his policy by such clear proofs of the increased
employment of British shipping, both absolutely and in
relation to foreign shipping, that the mover, General
Gascoyne, Mr. Huskisson's colleague in the representation
of Liverpool, abstained from pressing for a division.—Two
bills, attacking some of the worst evils of the game-laws,
those incessant rebukes to our pride of progress and
civilisation, reached the third reading, and then were
thrown out—Lord Wharncliffe's by a majority of one; the
Marquis of Salisbury's by a majority of sixteen.   Lord
Suffield, however, obtained the legal prohibition of man-
traps and spring-guns, and other such barbarous defences
of game at the expense of men.—Mr. Peel obtained some
important improvements in the criminal law.   Five acts
were passed under his management, by which a great
simplification of the law was effected, much old rubbish
got rid of, and a way prepared for further reforms.—Some
corrupt boroughs were doomed to disfranchisement; but
the session closed before the necessary steps were taken.—
The new chancellor of the exchequer proposed to move for
a finance committee in the next session; and there was
therefore little discussion of the budget of the present,
which was brought forward on the 1st of June.   The view
which he presented of the affairs of the country was dark
enough.   The people were hardly yet beginning to recover
from the depression of 1826.   All were so far satisfied that
it was better to leave the country to itself than to attempt
at present any financial innovations, that Mr. Canning's
resolutions with regard to supply met with no opposition,
and all financial discussion was deferred till the committee
of next session should be moved for.—Mr. Canning moved
and carried an amendment on a motion of Mr. Western's
respecting the corn-laws; the amendment being grounded
on the bill which had passed the House in the spring, and
been thrown out by the mistake of the Duke of Wellington.
The last words of the last speech of Mr. Canning in
parliament related to the conduct of the Duke of Wellington in this matter, and pledged the government to bring
forward another Corn Bill in the next session, of the same

bearing as that which had been lost. Great offence was given in the Upper House by his declaration that he believed the duke to have been, while meaning no harm, 'made the instrument of others for their own particular views.' At the moment, some few voices cried 'Order;' 'but they were instantly lost in loud and continued shouts of "Hear, hear."' This speech was the last of the oratory which has become a tradition, and will continue to be so for an age to come. Except to answer a trifling question, on the 29th of June, Mr. Canning never spoke again in parliament.

We have seen how meagre were the legislative results of the session. All were glad when it closed. Mr. Canning's enemies felt powerless in the face of his administration—the strongest, it was believed, since the days of Pitt; while his adherents desired repose from parliamentary conflict in order to consolidate their combination, while their leader sorely needed it for the strengthening of his exhausted frame. On the 2nd of July, the session was closed by commission, with a speech which noticed little but the gradual revival of manufacturing employment, and the royal hope that the corn-laws would be a subject of attention in the next session.

The time was now come for repose to many who greatly needed it after the excitement of a most stormy session, during which, if there was little done, there was more felt and said than some had strength of body and mind to bear. Mr. Canning and Mr. Huskisson were both very ill. Mr. Huskisson was ordered abroad by his physicians. Mr. Canning could not, of course, leave his post; and those who watched him with the almost idolatrous affection which he inspired in all who were near to him saw that no outward repose could be sufficient for his needs. Time was the only healer that could avail him, for his oppression was of the mind. He keenly felt the loneliness of his position—estranged from those who had always been his comrades, and whom he loved with all the capacity of his large heart; obliged to bear with their misconstruction, more painful to him than the insults of their followers; and prevented by former passages of his life, and by many ghosts of departed sarcasms of his own, from throwing himself into intimacy with his new coadjutors. He had a bitter sense of loneliness on the pinnacle of his power; and bitter was it to bear alone the remembrance of the usage he had met with during the last few weeks. Time and success would set all right. Of success he was certain; for he was not one who failed in his enterprises. Whether time would aid him depended on whether his bodily forces would hold out. Those who looked at his care-worn face and enfeebled frame trembled and doubted; but there were some months before him of the finest season of the year; and it would be seen what they could do for him. A week after the dispersion of parliament, he dined with Lord Lyndhurst at Wimbledon, and sat down under a tree while warm with walking; and upon this followed a feverish cold and rheumatism. On the 18th, Mr. Huskisson called to take leave before his continental journey, and found him in bed. He looked so ill that his friend observed that he seemed the most in need of change and relaxation; to which Mr. Canning replied: ' Oh, it is only the reflection of the yellow linings of the curtains.' Mr. Huskisson went abroad the next day, to be brought back by the news of his friend's death. Two days after this last interview, Mr. Canning removed to the Duke of Devonshire's villa at Chiswick, where Fox died, and inhabited the very room. He did not gain strength, though he attended to business, and on the 25th dined with Lord Clanricarde. He complained of weakness, and went home early. On the 30th, he waited upon the king, who was so alarmed at his appearance that he sent his own physician to him. Some friends dined with him the next day. He retired early, and never left his bed again. His illness—internal inflammation—was torturing, dread-ful to witness; but there was yet much strength left, for he lived till the 8th of August. On the 5th, the Sunday before his death, he desired his daughter to read prayers, according to his custom when he could not attend church. His agony ceased some time before his death, when mortification had set in. It was a little before four in the morning of Wednesday, the 8th of August, when he breathed his last.

For some few days before, the nation had been on the

watch in fearful apprehension of the news; but yet the
consternation was as great as if this man had been
supposed immortal. Multitudes felt that the life most
important to the world of the whole existing generation
had passed away. It was a life in which men had put
their trust—more trust than should perhaps be put in any
life—from the isles of Greece to the ridges of the Andes.
When those who had, by their persecution, sapped that
life now awoke to a sense of its importance, they must
have been amazed at themselves that they could have
indulged spleen and passion in such a case, and have
gratified their own prejudices and tempers at so fatal a
cost. But thus it is when men serve, instead of mastering,
their prejudices and passions: they know not what they
do; and if they discover what they have done, it is
because it is too late. All the honour that could be given
now was given. All the political coteries, the whole
country, the whole continent, the whole world, echoed
with eulogy of the departed statesman. From the most
superficial and narrow-minded of his critics, who could
comprehend nothing beyond the charm which invested
the man, to the worthiest of his appreciators who were
sensible of the grandeur of his intellect and the nobility
of his soul, all now joined in grief and in praise; and
none with a more painful wringing of the heart than those
who had but lately learned his greatness, and the promise
that it bore. Of his near friends, one sat unmoved and
insensible in the midst of the universal lamentation—Lord
Liverpool, whose mind had died first, but whose frame
remained after the grave had closed over his comrade and
successor; and another, Mr. Huskisson, received, among
the Styrian Alps, a report of Canning's convalescence,
three days after he was actually dead. The mournful
news soon followed; and in a few days, Mr. Huskisson
was on his way homewards, heart-stricken for the loss of
his friend, and convinced, as he repeatedly and earnestly
said, that his own political career was over.

Mr. Canning was fifty-six years of age. He was borne
to his grave in the Abbey on the 16th of August. His
family wished his funeral to be as private as the funeral
of such a man could be; and they declined the attendance

of several public bodies, and a multitude of individuals; but yet the streets were so thronged, in a deluge of rain, that a way was made with difficulty; and the Abbey was filled; and the grief of the mourners next the coffin hardly exceeded that which was evident in the vast crowd outside. The next morning, the king bestowed a peerage on Mr. Canning's widow. Statues of the departed statesman, and monuments, exist in many places in the world; and it is well; but the niche in history where the world holds the mind of the man enshrined for ever, is his only worthy monument.

It would be a curious speculation—but it is one not in our way at present—what Mr. Canning would finally have been and have done, if the great European war had lasted to the end of his life. His glory in our eyes is mainly that he was the minister of the peace; his immortality lies in his foreign policy, by which peace was preserved and freedom established, in a manner and to an extent which the potentate of the world of mind is alone competent to achieve. Czars, emperors, kings, and popes, may make peace one with another, in a mechanical, and therefore precarious manner; and this is all that, as the princes of the earth, they can do. The princes of the wider and higher realm of mind can do what Canning did—spread peace over continents, and the great globe itself, vitally, and therefore permanently, by diffusing and establishing the principles of peace. Of a history of the peace, he must be the hero. In a state of war, he must have been something great and beneficent; for his greatness was inherent, and his soul was—like the souls of all the greatest of men—benign; and his power—the prerogative of genius— was paramount as often as he was moved to put it forth. Without being able to divine what he would have done in a state of continuous war—without daring to say that he would have calmed the tempest in its wrath as effectually as he forbade it to rise again—we may be assured that he would have chosen to do great things, and have done what he chose.

One of the strongest evidences of Mr. Canning's power is the different light in which he appeared to the men about him and to us. His accomplishments were so brilliant, his graces so exquisite, his wit so dazzling, that all observers were completely occupied by these, so as to be almost insensible to the qualities of mind which are most impressive to us who never saw his face. To us he is, as Lord Holland called him, 'the first logician in Europe.' To us he is the thoughtful, calm, earnest, quiet statesman, sending forth from his office the most simple and business-like dispatches, as free from pomp and noise as if they were a message from some pure intelligence. We believe and know all that can be told of his sensibility, his mirth, and the passion of his nature; and we see no reason for doubting it, as, in genius of a high order—in Fox, for instance—the logic and the sensibility are so intimately united, that in proportion as the emotions kindle and glow, the reason distils a purer and a yet purer truth. But to us, to whom the fire is out, there remains the essence; and by that we judge him. We hear of his enthusiasms, kindling easily at all times, but especially on the apprehension of great ideas; but what we see is, that no favourite ideas led him away from a steady regard to the realities of his time. We hear of his unquenchable fancy; but we see that it never beguiled him from taking a statesmanlike view of the society spread out below him, and waiting upon his administration of the powers of the government. He was one of the most practical of states-men; and herein lay one of the most indisputable evidences of his genius. His genius, however, never was questioned. There might be, and there were, men who disparaged genius itself in its application to politics; but there were none who doubted Canning's having it, whatever it might be worth.

His faults were, not only unworthy of his genius, as all faults are, but of a nature which it is not easy to reconcile with genius of so high an order as his. Some of them, at least, were so. We may be able to allow for the confidence, and the spirit of enterprise—of adventure—which helped to obtain for him the name of 'adventurer;' the spirit which sprang into the political amphitheatre, ready for the combat on all hands, and thinking at first more of the combat than the cause; we can allow for this, because time showed how, when he knew life and its seriousness better, the cause of any principle became everything to him, and the combat a thing not to be sought, however joyfully it may be met.   The name of 'adventurer' can never be given to him who resigned office rather than take part against the queen, and gave up his darling hope of representing his university in order to befriend the Catholic cause.   He was truly adventurous in these acts, but with the self-denial of the true hero.

We may allow, again, for the spirit of contempt, which was another of his attributes least worthy of his genius. It was but partial; for no man was more capable of reverence; and much of his ridicule regarded fashions and follies, and affectations of virtue and vice; but still, there was too much of it.   It did visit persons; and it did wound honest or innocent feeling. as well as exasperate some whose weakness was a plea for generous treatment. For this fault, however, he paid a high penalty—he underwent an ample retribution.   Again, we may allow for some of his political acts—such as countenancing restrictions on the press—from the consideration of the temper and character of the times, and of his political comrades; but they necessarily detract from our estimate of his statesmanship.

The same may be said about parliamentary reform.   It is exactly those who most highly honour the advocates of reform of parliament who can most easily see into the difficulties, and understand the opposition, of the anti-reformers in parliament.   But there is no knowing what to say about Mr. Canning's opposition to the repeal of the Corporation and Test Acts.   He knew the facts of the case, of course; his advocacy of the Catholic claims shows that he knew the principle of it.   His inconsistency in this case must be regarded as one of the waywardnesses— one of the faults, at once intellectual and moral—for he alleged no reasons, no plea which he himself would call reasonable—which are the links that bind down even the greatest to their condition of human frailty.   As for all the rest of him, he was worthy of his endowments and his great function in life.   He was an excellent son to his humble mother, who died, happily for herself, before him —in March of the same year.   He was nearly as large an

object in the mental vision of all the leading men of his
time as in that of his proud mother, or of his adoring
family and private friends. His mind and his name did
indeed occupy a great space in the world, from the year
1822 till his death; and when he was gone, there was a
general sensation of forlornness throughout the nation,
which made the thoughtful ponder how such dismay could
be caused by the withdrawal of one from amidst its multitude of men.

CHAPTER III.

Lord Goderich, Premier—His Colleagues—Affairs of Greece—Treaty
of London—The Porte—The Egyptian Fleet—Battle of Navarino—
Ambassadors leave Constantinople—Greek Pirates—Troubles in
the Cabinet—Dissolution of the Ministry—Duke of Wellington,
Premier.

The Catholics were now eager to learn their fate; and the
nation—indeed many nations—had the strongest interest
in knowing whether Mr. Canning's principles were still
to reign by the administration of his friends, or whether
the old Tories were to return to power. It was soon
known that there was still to be a mixed cabinet, under
the premiership of Lord Goderich.

Mr. Huskisson, feeble in health, and cast down by the
loss of his life-long friend, wished to leave office. He had
turned homewards on hearing the bad news, and remained
a few days at Paris, partly to await the arrival of the
dispatches which were travelling after him, and partly for
needful rest. If the Tories should come into power, or if
a successor of his own views could be found, he intended
to winter in the south of Europe. When his letters arrived,
however, he found that he had no choice. The new premier
earnestly pressed him to take the colonial office; and the
king had emphatically expressed his desire that Mr.
Huskisson would return to enter upon his function as soon
as possible. Thus, then, it was clear that Mr. Canning's
policy was to be in the main pursued, and this was not the

less believed for the Duke of Wellington's returning to the command of the army; for he made an open declaration that he did so for the sake of the public service, and by no means from any sympathy with the proceedings of the cabinet, of whose mixed character he disapproved as much as he had done five months before. He desired to be considered as standing aloof from the policy of the cabinet. Of course, people asked why he could not have held his command in the same way during Mr. Canning's administration; to which he replied by an intimation that there were personal reasons for his secession at that time. The great difficulty was what to do about the office of chancellor of the exchequer, filled by the departed premier. It was declined by two members of the administration, and by Mr. Tierney; and at last it was given—unfortunately as it turned out—to Mr. Herries, who had been secretary of the treasury under Lord Liverpool. If there were before too many conflicting elements in the government to be securely controlled by any hand less masterly than Mr. Canning's, matters were pretty sure to go wrong now, after the admission of a functionary so little powerful in himself, and so little congenial with his colleagues, as Mr. Herries. The Whigs were very near going out at once; but they were persuaded to stay and make a trial. Lord Harrowby yielded his place to the Duke of Portland, Mr. Canning's brother-in-law, who had been lord privy seal; and Lord Carlisle, an excellent moderator and pacificator, succeeded to the Duke of Portland.

This was the third administration which had existed within seven months, and it had no great promise of stability. The recess, however, was before it—the greatest advantage to a new cabinet; and the nation supposed that by the end of the year it would be seen what it was worth; whether it could hold together, and what it proposed to do. By the end of the year the case was indeed plain enough—that it was about the weakest administration on record. Difficulties occurred in several departments; but the most confounding were in that of foreign policy. The foreign secretary, Lord Dudley, raised to an earldom in September of this year, was a man of great ability, and much earnestness in his work; and he was fully possessed

with Mr. Canning's views. At a former period, he had
suffered under a nervous depression which too clearly
indicated the probability of that insanity which ultimately
prostrated him; but at this time, he appeared to be capable
of business, and to be eccentric in manner only, and not in
ways of thinking. Some inconveniences occurred from his
singularities, which made it rather a relief when he retired,
in May of the next year; but they did not occasion any
serious difficulties. He was in the habit of thinking aloud;
and, amusing as this might be in cabinet-council, it was
dangerous anywhere else; and it is believed that in the
autumn we have now arrived at, he directed to the Russian
ambassador a letter intended for the French—to Prince
Lieven a letter intended for Prince Polignac. Prince
Lieven took this for a *ruse*, and boasted of his penetration
in being aware of the trick. It was the state of a portion
of our foreign affairs which might have made this accident
a most disastrous one. The truth is, the difficulty was
great enough, without any aggravation from carelessness
and unfortunate accidents.

The aspect of the Greek cause was much altered by the
part the ruler of Egypt had been for some time taking in
the war. Mohammed Ali, the Pacha of Egypt, a tributary
and vassal of the Porte, had brought all his energy, and
all his resources, to the aid of his sovereign. Before he
did this, the war dragged on, as it might have done for
ever, if the parties had been left to their rivalship of weakness. But when the pacha sent his son Ibrahim with
ships, troops, money, and valour, to fight against the
Greeks, everything was changed. By the end of 1826, the
whole of Western Greece was recovered by the Turks; and
the Greek government had transferred itself to the islands.
Men who find it at all times difficult to agree, are sure to
fall out under the provocations of adversity; and the dissensions of the Greek leaders ran higher now than ever.
Each was sure that the disasters of the country were owing
to some one else. It was this quarrelling which prevented
the Greeks from taking advantage of some successes of
their brave general Karaiskaki, to attempt the relief of
Athens—closely pressed by the Turks. The Turkish force
was soon to be strengthened by troops already on their

march; and now, before their arrival, was the time to attempt to relieve Athens. Some aid was sent; and some fighting went on—on the whole with advantage to the Greeks; but nothing decisive was done till Lord Cochrane arrived among them, rated them soundly for their quarrels, and took the command of their vessels—the Greek admiral, Miaulis, being the first and the most willing to put himself under the command of the British officer. In a little while, Count Capo d'Istria, an official esteemed by the Russian government, was appointed president of Greece for seven years. The Turkish reinforcements had arrived, absolutely unopposed, before Athens; and this rendered necessary the strongest effort that could be made for the deliverance of the place. General Church brought up forces by land, and Lord Cochrane by sea; and by the 1st of May, the flower of the Greek troops, to the number of ten thousand, were assembled before the walls of Athens. It was soon too clear to the British commanders that nothing was to be done with forces so undisciplined and in every way unreliable. The troops of Karaiskaki lost their leader, and incurred disaster by fighting without orders; and then, through a series of mistakes and follies, the issue became hopeless. Between eight and ten o'clock in the morning of the 6th, all was ruined. The killed and wounded of the Greeks amounted to 2500; and the rest were dispersed, like chaff before the wind. Of those who escaped, the greater number took refuge in the mountains. Lord Cochrane was compelled to throw himself into the sea, and swim to his ship. General Church strove hard to maintain his fortified camp at the Phalerus, with 3000 men whom he had collected; but when he found that some of the Greek officers were selling his provisions to the enemy, he gave up, and retired to Egina—sorely grieved, but not in despair. Lord Cochrane kept the sea —generally with his single frigate, the *Hellas*, contributed to the cause by the United States—and now and then with a few Greek vessels, when their commanders had nothing better to do than to obey orders. He was alone when he took his station off Navarino, to watch the fleet of the Egyptian Ibrahim; and he had better have been alone when he went on to Alexandria, to look after the fleet

which the pacha was preparing there; for, when the
Egyptians came out to offer battle, the Greeks made all
sail homewards.

The Turks now supposed they had everything in their
own hands. On the intervention of the French admiral,
De Rigny, they spared the lives of the garrison of the
Acropolis, permitting them to march out, without their
arms, and go whither they would. Then, all seemed to
be over. The Greeks held no strong places but Corinth
and Napoli, and had no army; while the Turks held all
the strong places but Corinth and Napoli, and had two
armies at liberty—that of the Egyptian leader in the
west, and of the Turkish seraskier in the east—to put
down any attempted rising within the bounds of Greece.
But at this moment of extreme humiliation for Greece,
aid was preparing; and hope was soon to arise out of
despair. While Mr. Canning was fighting his own battles
in parliament, he had his eye on what was passing in
Greece; and the fall of Athens, and the dispersion of the
Greek forces, only strengthened his resolution that the
powers of Europe should hasten the interposition he had
planned long before.

It was important to Russia that Turkey should be
weakened in every possible way; and Russia was therefore
on the side of the Greeks. The sympathies of France and
England were on the side of the Greeks; but they must
also see that Greece should be freed in reality, and that
Turkey should not be destroyed; so they were willing to
enter into alliance with Russia to part the combatants,
preserve both, impose terms upon both, and see that the
terms were observed. The Duke of Wellington had gone
to St. Petersburg to settle all this; and the ministers of
the three courts laid before the government of the Porte
at Constantinople, the requisitions of the allies. The
great object was to separate the Turks and Greeks—the
faithful and the infidels—who could never meet without
fighting; and it was proposed, or, we may rather say,
ordained by the allies, that all the Turks should leave
Greece, receiving compensation, in some way to be devised,
for the property they must forsake. The Greeks were to
pay a tribute to the Porte, and to be nominally its sub-

jects; and the Turkish government was to have some sort of veto on the appointment of officials; but substantially the choice of officers, and the enjoyment of their own modes of living, were to be left to the Greeks. As might be expected, the victorious Turk was amazed at this interference between himself and his rebellious subjects; and if he would not listen to dictation before the fall of Athens, much less would he afterwards. There was threat as well as dictation; threat of enforcing the prescribed conditions; but the Porte braved the threat as loftily as it rejected the interference.

The rejection was too natural and reasonable not to be received as final; and the three powers therefore proceeded to their acts of enforcement. It may be remembered that Mr. Canning, ill and wearied, after the close of the session, exerted himself to transact some public business. The chief item of this business was causing to be signed the treaty with France and Russia, concerning the affairs of Greece, which was finished off in London, and immediately despatched to Constantinople. In this treaty, the alliance and its purposes were justified on the ground of 'the necessity of putting an end to the sanguinary contest, which, by delivering up the Greek provinces, and the isles of the Archipelago, to the disorders of anarchy, produces daily fresh impediments to the commerce of the European states, and gives occasion to piracies which not only expose the subjects of the contracting powers to considerable losses, but render necessary burdensome measures of suppression and protection.' England and France moreover, pleaded the appeals they had received from the Greeks. The treaty concluded with a declaration and pledge of disinterestedness: of desiring nothing which the whole world besides was not at liberty to obtain.

A month from the date of the arrival of the instructions to the ambassadors at Constantinople was the time allowed to the Porte for consideration. If the terms of the three powers were not by that time acceded to, they must proceed to the threatened enforcement, with every intention to preserve their own pacific relations with Turkey. The work of mediation was to be carried on by force, in such a case, under the plea that such a proceeding would be best for the interests of the contending powers, and necessary for the peace and comfort of the rest of the world. There were squadrons of all the three powers ready in the Levant; that of Russia being commanded by Admiral Heiden; that of France by Admiral De Rigny; and that of England by Sir Edward Codrington.

The formal note of the ambassadors at Constantinople was delivered in on the 16th of August, with a notification that an answer would be expected in fifteen days. On the 30th of August, no reply having been volunteered, it was asked for, and given only verbally. Again the Porte declined recognising any interference between itself and its rebellious subjects; and when the consequent notice of enforcement was given, the Turkish government became, as any other government would, in like circumstances, bolder in its declaration of persistence in its own rights. Then began a season of activity at Constantinople such as had seldom been witnessed there; horses and provisions pouring in from the country, and sent off with ammunition, arms, and stores, to occupy the posts along the Bosphorus and the Dardanelles. There was an incessant training of troops, under the eye of the Sultan or his vizier; and the capital seemed in the way to be turned into a camp. There is something striking in the only words the Turkish minister would utter, in the final interview of the 14th of September: 'God and my right,' said he, in the calmest manner. 'Such is the motto of England. What better answer can we give, when you intend to attack us?'

Meantime, the Egyptian fleet, strongly reinforced, had arrived in the Morea; and the English commander had no right to interpose any obstacle; the time being the end of August, and the answer of the Porte not being yet delivered. Sir Edward Codrington, however, hailed Ibrahim, informed him of what was going on at Constantinople and offered him a safe-conduct, if he wished to return to Egypt. But if he chose to enter the harbour of Navarino, to join the Turkish fleet there, he must clearly understand that any of his vessels attempting to get out would be driven back. Ibrahim chose to enter. There now lay the ninety-two Egyptian vessels, and the Turkish fleet, crowded in the harbour; and off its mouth lay the British squadron on the watch. For some time, Ibrahim occupied himself in preparing his troops for action against the Greeks; but on the 19th of September he determined to try an experiment. He sent out a division of the Turkish fleet, to see if the English would let them pass. Sir Edward Codrington warned them back; but the Turkish commander replied that he was under no other orders than those of Ibrahim. The Egyptian prince, being referred to by both parties, and afterwards by the French admiral, who had come up with his squadron, and the danger of the case amply explained to him, declared that he would recall the Turkish ships, and wait the return of couriers whom he would send to Constantinople and to Alexandria; but that as soon as he received orders to sail, his whole combined fleet would come out, and brave all opposition. A sort of armistice was agreed on, verbally, for twenty days, during a long conference between the Egyptian, French, and English commanders, on the 25th of September. The two latter trusted to Ibrahim's word that his ships would not leave the harbour for the twenty days—ample facilities having been allowed by them for the victualling of his troops; and they sailed for Zante to obtain fresh provisions for their fleet. As soon as they were gone, only five days after the conference, Ibrahim put out to sea, to sail to Patras. On the 2nd of October, an armed brig brought notice to Sir E. Codrington of this violation of the treaty. The admiral immediately returned with a very small force, met successively two divisions of the Turkish fleet, and turned them back to Navarino. In his wrath, Ibrahim carried war inland, slaughtering and burning, and driving the people to starvation, and even uprooting the trees wherever he went, that no resource might be left to the wretched inhabitants. As the spirit of the Treaty of London was thus broken through, the three admirals concluded to compel an adherence to the terms agreed upon at the conference, by entering the harbour, and placing themselves, ship by ship, in guard over the imprisoned fleets. The strictest orders were given that not a musket should be fired, unless firing should begin on the other side. They were permitted to pass the batteries, and take up their position; but a boat was fired upon by the Turks, probably under the impression that she was sent to board one of their vessels. A lieutenant and several of the crew were killed. There was a discharge of musketry in return by an English and a French vessel; and then a cannon-shot was received by the French admiral's ship which was answered by a broadside. The action, probably intended by none of the parties, was now fairly begun; and when it ended, there was nothing left of the Turkish and Egyptian fleets but fragments of wreck strewing the waters. As the crews left their disabled vessels, they set them on fire; and among the dangers of the day to the allied squadrons, not the least was from these floating furnaces drifting about among a crowd of ships. The battle, which took place on the 20th of October, lasted four hours. The Turkish and Egyptian forces suffered cruelly. Of the allies, the English suffered the most; but with them the loss was only seventy-five killed, and the wounded were under two hundred. The three British line-of-battle ships had to be sent home, after being patched up at Malta for the voyage.

The anxiety of mind of the three admirals is said to have been great, both on account of the calamity itself, and the doubt about how their conduct of the affair would be viewed at home. One reasonable apprehension was, that there would be a slaughter of the Christians at Constantinople. But things were now conducted there in a more cautious and deliberate manner than of old. An embargo was laid on all the vessels in the harbour; but the mob of the faithful were kept in check. There were curious negotiations between the government and the ambassadors, while each party was in possession of the news, and wanted to learn how much the other knew. The sultan himself wished to declare war at once; but his counsellors desired to gain time; and there were doubts, fluctuations, and bootless negotiations, in which neither party would concede anything, for several weeks. The Turks would yield nothing about Greece; and the allies would yield neither compensation nor apology for the affair of Navarino. On the 8th of December, however, it being clear that nothing could be gained by negotiation the ambassadors left Constantinople. The Christian merchants might have embarked with them; but they must have left their property behind; and some preferred remaining. The Turkish authorities went to great lengths in encouraging them to do so; but whether this was from pacific inclinations, or from a sense of their value as hostages, could not be certainly known; and the greater number did not relish trusting themselves to conjecture in such a case. The day before the ambassadors left, an offer was made of a general amnesty to the Greeks. But this was not what was required. As they sailed out of the harbour, the sultan must have felt that he was left, deprived of his fleet, at war with Russia, England, and France. But the coolness and ability shown by his government, in circumstances so extremely embarrassing as those of this autumn, were evidence that there were minds about him very well able to see that if Russia desired to crush him, England and France would take care that she did not succeed. As for the Greeks, their government was thankful to accept the mediation of the allies; but so weak as to be unable to enforce any of their requisitions. Piracy, under the Greek flag, reached such a pass in the Levant, that Great Britain had to take the matter into her own hands. In the month of November, it was decreed, by an order in council, that the British ships in the Mediterranean should seize every vessel they saw under the Greek flag, or armed and fitted out at a Greek port, except such as were under the immediate orders of the Greek government. Thus we were carrying matters with a high hand in regard to both parties concerned in the unhappy Greek war. It is a case on which so much is to be said on every side, that it is impossible to help sympathising with all parties in the transactions preceding and following the battle of Navarino; with the Greeks, for reasons which the heart apprehends more rapidly than tongue or hand can state them; with the Porte, under the provocation of the interference of strangers between her and her rebellious subjects; with the Egyptians, in their duty of vassalage, however wrongly it might be performed; with the allied powers, in their sense of the intolerableness of a warfare so cruel and so hopeless going on amidst the haunts of commerce, and to the disturbance of a world otherwise at peace; and with two of those three allies, in their apprehension of Turkey being destroyed, and Greece probably once more enslaved, by the power and arts of the third.

If the case appears to us now, so many years after the event, perplexing, and in every way painful, what must have been the sensation in the cabinet of Lord Goderich on the arrival of the news of the battle of Navarino? The cabinet was already torn by dissensions of its own, so serious and unmanageable that the premier was meditating his resignation. At a moment when the members of the government were feeling that no one of them was sure of his function for a week, and that it was certain that all could not remain in power, came this thunder-clap—this stroke of war in the midst of peace. They were the successors of the great peace-minister, whose fame as a pacificator had spread over the world; and here was a fierce belligerent act perpetrated on an ally, amidst declarations of peace, and probably a train of consequences to be met which there was no seeing the end of! Any power but Turkey would go to war with us on the instant. If Turkey did not, it would be only through her weakness; and the first consequence of that weakness would be that Russia would endeavour to devour her; and there again was danger of far more formidable war. While waiting to hear how the news would be received at Constantinople, it was necessary to decide at once on the countenance to be given to the admirals who had been driven to act on their own judgment. The countenance afforded them by their respective governments, in the first instance, was cordial and emphatic; and there can be little doubt that this was right. Theirs was a position of singular difficulty; not only they acted in good concert to the best of their judgment, but no one ventured to say what they could have done better, while all deplored the event. There was a degree of chance-medley about the catastrophe which seemed to exclude the event from the scope of human control; and in cases so out of the common course, the wisest method always is to uphold the reputation, and with it the nerve and confidence, of responsible public officers. So, from the existing government, Sir Edward Codrington received ample justice. The news of the battle arrived in London on the 10th of November; and on the 13th Sir Edward Codrington was gazetted as Knight-commander, and eleven of his officers as Companions of the Bath. From the Emperor of Russia and the King of France, the English admiral received thanks and high honours; and, whatever differences of opinion existed as to the treaty and the policy of the allies towards Turkey, there was nothing heard in parliament but praise of the officers whose charge it was to carry that policy into effect.

The difficulties which endangered the existence of the cabinet at this time were occasioned by a discordance of principle among its members, though they took the form of a personal quarrel. Mr. Herries was unacceptable to the liberal section of the ministry ; and, though he naturally supposed that, having acted with Lord Goderich before, he could act now in a cabinet of which Lord Goderich was the head, he found that the premier's connection with the Whigs had materially changed their relation to each other. The immediate cause of quarrel was about the finance committee, promised by Mr. Canning, and looked forward to in the approaching session. It was time to be making arrangements for this committee and to be agreeing upon a chairman. Lord Goderich left the affair in the hands of the ministers who sat in the Commons, concluding that the chancellor of the exchequer would take the lead, or at least be cognizant of whatever was done. But negotiations were entered into with Lord Spencer to secure Lord Althorp for chairman, without a word being said to Mr. Herries; and it was only by accident that he learned what proceedings had been taken in the business of his own office without his knowledge. It did not gratify his feelings to find that everybody, all round, supposed that he knew, or had forgotten to inquire whether he did or not. Either personal offence was intended, or he was too insignificant to have been the object of it; and in either case his position was intolerable. The nomination of Lord Althorp was disapproved by him, and he opposed it, stating his reasons. This was

on the 29th of November. Other difficulties, many and
serious, had now arisen; and from this time till the 19th
of December, the country can hardly be said to have had
a government at all. Lord Goderich had formally tendered
his resignation. It was clear that either Mr. Huskisson or
Mr. Herries must go out; but nothing could be settled for
want of a head to the cabinet ; for, of course, Lord
Goderich could not act as such among his colleagues after
having sent in his resignation. On or about the 20th of
December, Lord Goderich was induced to withdraw his
resignation; and then Mr. Herries, and immediately after
Mr. Huskisson, placed their offices at his disposal. But Mr
Herries was again forgotten or slighted. No one told him
of Mr. Huskisson's offer to resign, while the premier urged
him to retain his place. As soon as he heard of Mr. Huskisson's resolution to abide by the nomination of Lord
Althorp, and to go out if he could not carry that point,
Mr. Herries resigned. Lord Goderich, apparently believing both these gentlemen to be absolutely essential to his
government, and being unable to reconcile their differences, gave the matter up, and went to Windsor, on the
8th of January, to explain to the king that he could not go
on, and to resign his office.

These miserable dissensions had been occupying the
time and the minds of the ministers during the precious
weeks which should have been employed in preparing for
the approaching session of parliament. Parliament was
to have met at this very date; but, in order to afford time
for the formation of a ministry, it was further prorogued
to the 29th of January. During the interval of actual
dissolution, Mr. Huskisson had been desired by the king
to send Lord Harrowby to him. Lord Harrowby went to
Windsor, but was firm in declining the premiership, on
the ground of ill health. There is good reason to believe
that Mr. Huskisson might have risen into Canning's seat
at this time; but he was warned by his friend's fate, and
decided that he had not health for the office.

There had now been enough of mixed administrations,
or the king thought so. Lord Liverpool had kept one in
working-order by his weight of character, his business
faculty, and the power and dignity accruing from his

length of service.   Mr. Canning would have kept such an
administration together by the commanding power of his
mind.   But it was not to be supposed that any one else
could be found who could bring harmony out of elements
of discord; and the condition of public affairs was such as
unusually to require a strong and united government.   So
the king sent for the strongest and most peremptory man
of all; and, in spite of the Duke of Wellington's declaration not long before, that he should be mad if he ever
thought of undertaking an office for which he was so little
fit, he found himself, before the middle of January 1828,
prime minister of England.

CHAPTER IV.

The Wellington Cabinet—The King's Speech—The Porte—Finance
Committee—Repeal of Dissenters' Disabilities.

FOR a few days the old Tory party were happy.   All
would be well now.   The king would have no more
trouble about the Catholics, for they would be put down.
Lord Eldon would be the person consulted by the duke
about the formation of the new ministry, and would have
great influence in it, even if he should at length, at
seventy-seven years of age, think himself too old for office.
There would be no more talk of a balance of parties in the
cabinet; but the duke would have his political comrades
drilled into uniformity—'a perfect machine,' as he had
declared his Peninsular army to be.   So people thought;
but the strongest and most peremptory of men must bend
like a willow-wand before the force of opinion.   Opinion
was now too strong for even the Duke of Wellington; and
no one of these anticipations was fulfilled.

The day after the duke received his majesty's commands,
he wrote to Lord Eldon, declaring his intention of calling
on him the next day.   By Lord Eldon's account, the meeting was a somewhat awkward one; the ex-chancellor
evidently expecting the offer of some position in the

administration, though too old to resume his seat on the woolsack. 'From the moment of his quitting me,' writes Lord Eldon, 'to the appearance in the papers of all the appointments, I never saw his grace. I had no communication with him, either personally, by note, letter, by message through any other person, or in any manner whatever; and, for the whole fortnight, I heard no more of the matter than you did; some of my colleagues in office—and much obliged to me too—passing my door constantly on their way to Apsley House, without calling upon me. In the meantime, rumour was abroad that I had refused *all* office; and this was most industriously circulated, when it was found that there was, as there really does appear to me to have been, very great dissatisfaction among very important persons on my account, as neither included in office, nor at all, not in the least, consulted. . . . . However, there was a degree of discontent and anger among persons of consequence, which, I suppose, working together, with its having been somehow communicated that I was much hurt at this sort of treatment, brought the Duke of Wellington to me again; and the object of his visit seemed to be to account for all this. He stated, in substance, that he had found it impracticable to make any such administration as he was sure I would be satisfied with; and, therefore, he thought he should only be giving me unnecessary trouble in coming near me—or to that effect.' Then out came the old politician's soreness about not having been offered the office of president of the council; and about being considered impracticable, which he was sure nobody had any reason to suppose; and about having been neglected for a whole fortnight. The duke gave as a justification for having concluded that Lord Eldon would not have approved the composition of the ministry, that it seemed as if he did not like it, now the whole was complete; to which Lord Eldon replied, that he thought it a d——d bad one. 'We conversed together,' he continues, however, 'till, as it seemed to me, we both became a good deal affected.' They might well find themselves 'a good deal affected.' Perhaps we may feel something of it, in merely reading the record. It is sad to think of these old comrades parting off in the way they

were doing now, under a control which neither of them
liked, but to which the younger could wisely bend, while
the elder could only fret and be angry.   Agreeing in dislike of the changes in the times, they differed about how
to meet them ; and the elder called the younger incon-
sistent; and the younger called the elder impracticable.
The wedge was in, which was to split up policies, and
parties, and friendships.   It had been driven in some way
now; everybody having, by intention or mischance, lent a
hand to drive it further for some time past.   The duke
was the man to knock out the wedge, and make all whole
again; but lo! he found himself under a compulsion
which permitted him no choice but to drive the wedge
home, leaving our Protestant constitution, as Lord Eldon
believed, shivered to fragments.   Meantime, he was compelled, as others had been, to adjust a balance of political
forces in the cabinet, and to find, as if he had been a
weaker man, that it was not in the power of his will to
make them work.   As Lord Eldon classified them, pen in
hand, it came out clear before his eyes that Protestantism
was in as much danger as ever.   Of the thirteen, he marks
six as favourers of the Catholic claims, saying : 'The other
seven are as yet for Protestants, but some *very loose.*   You
will observe Dudley, Huskisson, Grant, Palmerston, and
Lyndhurst (five), were all *Canningites,* with whom the rest
were, three weeks ago, in most violent contest and opposition.   These things are to me quite marvellous.   How
they are all to deal with each other's conduct as to the late
treaty with Turkey, and the Navarino battle, is impossible
to conjecture. . . . .   Viscountess Canning has written a
strong letter, as Lord Ashley tells me, to Huskisson,
strongly reproaching him for joining—I use Ashley's own
expression—her husband's murderers.'   From Mr. Huskisson's own explanations of his position, it appears that this
statement concerning him is substantially true.   In the
first grief on his friend's loss, he uttered expressions which
were certainly received as a pledge that he would never
enter office in conjunction with those who had left Mr.
Canning in the lurch.   His words, as avowed by himself,
were, 'that his wounds were too green and too fresh to
admit of his serving in the same cabinet with those who

had deserted the service of the country, at the time his friend's administration was formed.' Yet here he was now, in office under the Duke of Wellington, and by the side of Mr. Peel! We cannot wonder at the irritation of Mr. Canning's family; and we are, judging by the event, sorry that Mr. Huskisson entered this cabinet; but we must remember the strangeness of the time, which confounded all calculations, and made sport of all consistencies. This, of itself, would guard us against a peremptory judgment; but we also know that Mr. Huskisson's acceptance of office was approved by the oldest and most valued friends of Mr. Canning. Still, the general feeling was that Mr. Huskisson passed at this time under a cloud from which he never again emerged in full brightness.

It was in his former office, the colonial, that he remained; and Lord Dudley remained in the foreign office. Mr. Grant was president of the Board of Trade, and treasurer of the navy; and Lord Palmerston, secretary at war. These were, what we may call, the semi-liberal members of the administration. Mr. Herries remained, but in an office—master of the Mint—which need not bring him again into collision with Mr. Huskisson; while Mr. Goulburn succeeded to the chancellorship of the exchequer. Mr. Peel succeeded Lord Lansdowne at the home office. Lord Lyndhurst remained chancellor, and Lord Bathurst held the office—president of the council—which Lord Eldon had hoped to be able to accept or refuse. One of the most important appointments was that of the Marquis of Anglesey to the viceroyalty of Ireland, in the place of Lord Wellesley.

This administration was nearly the same as that which had existed under Lord Liverpool; the only important changes being that Mr. Canning and Lord Eldon were absent, and Lord Lyndhurst and Lord Dudley present in their stead. But the men were altered. The spirit of the time had changed them; and it was no more the same government that had existed under Lord Liverpool than if it had been composed of other men.

There was great eagerness throughout the country to see how much would be said in the king's speech about the great existing subjects of interest, that men might know what to expect from the new government. There was not a syllable about Ireland or the Catholic Association, and nothing about corn. There were intimations of improving prosperity at home; a recommendation to inquire diligently into financial affairs—in other words, to appoint the proposed finance committee; a notification that the troops had returned from Portugal—their appearance there having answered the purposes for which they were sent; and about half the speech related to affairs in the east. One paragraph supplied matter of debate in both Houses, and of party offence, for some time after; and there are persons who have not got over it to this day. The paragraph was this: 'Notwithstanding the valour displayed by the combined fleet, his majesty deeply laments that this conflict [of Navarino] should have occurred with the naval force of an ancient ally; but he still entertains a confident hope that this untoward event will not be followed by further hostilities, and will not impede that amicable adjustment of the existing differences between the Porte and the Greeks, to which it is so manifestly their common interest to accede.' Few words have excited more debate or more passion in their time than this word 'untoward.' To us, after the lapse of years, it seems a simple affair enough—this application of the word 'untoward' to an event which, originating in a sort of accident, ought to have involved us in war with Turkey, and might have brought us into collision with Russia. But the word was hardly looked upon at all with simplicity, as in cases where no passion is concerned. The late administration regarded it as implying censure on their policy; and the officers in the Mediterranean, as impeaching their judgment; and the more on account of the compliment to their valour. According to some, Russia was made suspicious. According to others, France was made angry. In short, it was a season when all men were on the watch for symptoms, and when many were implicated in great public affairs on new and doubtful grounds; and in such circumstances, a single word may become the rallying-point of a whole rabble of passions. The observer of those times is curious to know whether the framers of the speech would have changed the word,

or the paragraph, if they could have foreseen the excitement that would ensue; and whether they could have
found any other expression that would have conveyed
their meaning with less offence.

At home, the whole affair ended in debate. There were
motions for explanations, and to obtain the thanks of
parliament for the British officers engaged at Navarino—
motions which were withdrawn when the objects of debate
were accomplished; but there was no war. Russia was
quite willing to undertake that part of the consequences of
the ' untoward event;' and the Porte had enough to do to
cope with Russia, without insisting on war with England
and France.

On the departure of the ambassadors from Constantinople on the 8th of December, the Turkish government
protested against the resident Christians being put under
the protection of the Netherlands ambassador, and claimed
the office of protector for itself. Four days after the departure of the Russian ambassador, the Turkish vizier
wrote to the Russian minister a remonstrance against the
act, as one apparently unauthorised by either government,
and likely to convey a false impression of the hostile disposition of the Porte. To this no answer was returned.
Three weeks afterwards—just at the time when Lord
Goderich was going out—a document sent by the vizier to
all the governors of provinces in the Turkish dominions
was made public, which revealed the whole state of the
case. The Turkish government made great complaint of
the publication of this document, and insisted upon its
being regarded as a mere letter of private instructions,
addressed to its own servants. The world had nothing to
do with the mode in which it had got abroad. The contents were what other powers had concern with; and
these were such as to put an end to all disguise, and
render further duplicity needless. This document declared
that the coming war was, under political pretences, a
religious war; that the Christian powers desired to place
the infidels over the heads of the faithful in all countries
where they lived intermingled, in order to overthrow the
institutions of the prophet; that all the negotiations which
had been entered into, all the humility towards the

Christian powers, all the apparent apathy about the loss of
the fleet at Navarino, had been merely for the purpose of
gaining time for military preparations; and that it was
needless to explain that in the cause of Islamism, there
was no obligation to keep faith with infidels; that it was
of the utmost consequence to defer the outbreak of war till
the summer approached; and that every art had been
employed, and would be employed, to protract the negotiations till that time; and that, meanwhile, every effort must
be used by the officers of the empire to make the people
understand that this was a holy war, in which failure was
a misfortune too great to be contemplated, as not only
would the faithful and the infidels be made to exchange
social positions, but the mosques would be converted into
churches, and perhaps profaned by the sound of bells.
'Let the faithful then,' this document concluded, 'have no
thought of their arrears, or of pay of any kind. Let us
sacrifice willingly our properties and our persons, and
struggle, body and soul, for the support of our religion.
The worshippers of the prophet have no other means of
working out their salvation in this world and the next.'
After this, there could be no doubt of what would happen;
and preparations for war went on in both countries. In
this same month of January, lists were made of the
Christians resident in Constantinople, and they were
ordered off, with very few exceptions. Even the Ar-
menians, subjects of the Porte, were treated like the
foreign merchants, or worse. Some of the most respectable were put into prison, and about twelve thousand were
banished. The Bosphorus was closed; and the corn in the
vessels of any nation, then in harbour, was seized. Reinforcements were sent to the fortresses on the Danube;
and a great camp was formed near Adrianople. The loss
of the fleet was a terrible misfortune, as it left Russia
mistress of the Black Sea; but all that could be done was
done, in the interval before April, when the emperor
formally declared war against the Porte. Thus stood
matters six months after the battle of Navarino. No
terms had been obtained for the Greeks; and if there was
some respite and impunity for them, it was obtained only
by the approach of that Russian war with the Porte which

it had been a chief object with England and France to control, by joining in the Treaty of London.

The finance committee, which had been the occasion of the misunderstandings in Lord Goderich's cabinet, was moved for by Mr. Peel on the 15th of February, and voted for almost unanimously. It consisted of twenty-three members, of whom two were Mr. Herries and Mr. Huskisson. The latter begged at first to be excused, on account of the pressure of business in his own office; but the wish for his presence in committee was so strong and general, that he yielded. The report of this committee was delivered in too late to admit of many of its recommendations being immediately adopted; but one discovery which it made very early caused the speedy passage of a short bill, to suspend the act for granting government life-annuities till a better basis should have been found for the calculations of the duration of life. When Mr. Perceval brought in, in 1808, his bill authorising the sale of these annuities, the calculations were based on Dr. Price's tables. Whether these tables were originally inaccurate, or whether the duration of human life had improved since they were framed, they were certainly now causing the government annuities to be sold too low. There was also some curious speculation going forward, against which no minister could be expected to be on his guard, till warned by experience. Speculators bought annuities on the lives of persons whose chances of longevity were unusually strong. On careful inquiry, it appeared to these speculators that the most long-lived class of men is that of Scotch gardeners; and many were the hale Scotch gardeners picked out, and, for a consideration, made government annuitants. It had occurred to Mr. Finlaison that some national loss was sustained through these annuities; and he entered into calculations which proved to him that the loss was great. He went to Lord Bexley in 1819, and told him his views; and he was directed to prosecute his inquiries. Now, on looking to the outstanding annuities, Mr. Finlaison calculated that the rate of mortality, instead of being one in forty was only one in fifty-six, and that the average of female life especially was much longer than had been supposed. The loss to the public was estimated at £95,000 a year; nearly £8000 a month. Nothing could be done with the sales which had been actually made; but by the act now quickly passed, the process was to be stopped till better terms were provided.

When the estimates were brought forward, it was proposed to grant a pension of £3000 a year to Mr. Canning's family, in the person of one of his sons. Mr. Canning had as every one knew, no private fortune. He would have become wealthy in India; and, if he was kept at home for the public service, it was clearly the duty of the public whom he served, to the sacrifice of wealth, to see that his family did not suffer from poverty. He had held no sinecures; and had received nothing but the salary of the offices he filled. There had been no time to lay by a provision for his family, even if his income had admittted of such accumulation; and his death was sudden and untimely. It appears a clear case enough; one in which there could be but one opinion and one voice. The sum proposed to be granted to Mr. Canning's son was from a special fund, to which his father would have become entitled, if he had lived to the expiration of two years from his entrance upon his last office. Reasonable as the claim and the method appear to be, and as they appeared to most persons at the time, so strong an opposition was raised that the matter was twice debated at great length. The objections were, some on the score of economy; some on that of the mischief of the precedent; and many more on that of dissatisfaction with Mr. Canning's policy. It is impossible to avoid supposing that the opposition arose mainly from the feelings which, a year ago, had been brought to bear upon Mr. Canning himself, and which the events of the interval had not calmed down or chastened. There was but too little improvement visible in the tone of some who might have learned moderation from the affecting lessons of the preceding months. The opposition consisted of 54 in a House of 216. Mr. Bankes perhaps went further than any one else, when he proposed to charge to Mr. Canning the expenses of the battle of Navarino, and of the Mediterranean fleet in connection with it. The ministers were eager to promote the grant —one and all—and the more eager, perhaps, for the

doubtful or hostile terms on which they had been latterly
with the departed statesman; and the economists among
them could be as hearty as the rest, without drawback, as
they could show that this pension would involve no charge
to the country. It was merely the transference of a sum
from an existing fund to Mr. Canning's son, in lieu of his
father, who must have had it, if he had lived. It was for
the lives of both sons that the pension was granted, as the
elder was in the navy, and thereby exposed to many
casualties. Five months afterwards, he was drowned in
bathing at Madeira—died in the reservoir into which he
plunged after being extremely heated by exercise. He
was a post-captain in the navy; and fresh sympathy was
awakened towards the family when its new representative
came to this mournful and untimely end.

The great interest of the session was the debate and
division on the proposed repeal of the Corporation and
Test Acts. Lord John Russell moved, on the 26th of
February, that there should be a committee of the whole
House to consider of these acts. In his speech, he gave
the history of the acts, clearly showing that they bore no
relation to present times and circumstances, but to some
long past and widely different. The Dissenters might be,
or appear, dangerous to the House of Stuart; but they
were certainly loyal subjects of the House of Hanover,
and did not deserve to be excluded from civil office by the
Corporation Act; and, as to the Test Act, it was originally
intended as a barrier to the Church against the king, who
was a converted papist. The circumstances were antiquated,
and so were the restrictions; and it was time, for the credit
of English understandings, that they should be repealed.
The disqualifications of Dissenters were presented very
forcibly to the House, by a succession of speakers, and
seen at once to be both disgraceful, and in other ways
injurious. The government opposition was conducted by
Mr. Peel and Mr. Huskisson. It was not surprising in
those days, however it might be now, that Mr. Peel was
on the side of old fashion and orthodox assumption; but
that Mr. Huskisson should appear in behalf of intolerance
and injury for opinion, was mortifying to those who
appreciated him most. Both, however, were as feeble as

the friends of religious liberty could desire; their ground
was the narrowest and the most temporary that could be
held; and it was taken solely because there was no other.
Both admitted the principles involved in Lord John
Russell's motion and speech; but Mr. Peel argued that the
Dissenters did not really suffer, as they were incessantly
relieved by Indemnity Bills; and Mr. Huskisson feared
injury to the Catholic cause by releasing the Dissenters
from a condition of disability which kept them vigilant
on the subject of the rights of conscience, and from the
insult that it would be to the Catholics to release others
from disabilities while theirs remained.   The House
decided in favour of the committee by a majority of 44 in
a House of 430.   Mr. Peel had, happily, declared his
belief that the existence of the Church of England was
not bound up with these restrictions; so he could give up
the contest, and .bow to the will of parliament, without
such struggles and agonies as those of Lord Eldon and
others, who believed that all was over now with the true
Protestant religion in our country.

The question arising what was the government now to
do? it was a matter of importance to decide whether the
rejection of the expected bill should be secured in the
Upper House, or whether government should provide such
securities, to be attached to the bill, as might make it least
objectionable.   This last course was decided on—the will
of the Commons being so declared as to make the thought
of opposition too hazardous.   After the bill had been read
twice and when the House was about to go into committee,
Mr. Sturges Bourne proposed the substitution of a declaration for the sacramental test; a declaration of the person
entering upon office, that he would not use any of the
powers or influence of his office for the subversion of the
Established Church.   And, as there would be some absurdity in requiring such a declaration from officials in the
service of the crown, another clause was proposed, which
rendered it optional with the crown to require or omit the
declaration.   There was nothing in the first of these proposals to which the Dissenters could object so seriously, as
to endanger the bill; as they had no thought of taking
office for the purpose of injuring the Church, but only for

the sake of doing the duties and enjoying the rights of
equal citizenship; and they were pleased at the second
clause, because it left open a probability that the declaration itself—the last badge of difference on account of their
religious opinions—would fall into disuse. They therefore
contented themselves with protesting through their advocates in the House, against the imposition of any badge
whatever; and pushed their bill. When it arrived in the
Upper House, the Duke of Wellington spoke in its favour,
saying that the only reason why the government had at
first opposed it in the Commons was that the system had
appeared to work well hitherto; but, as it was clear that
the Commons thought the time was come for a change,
and as the principle of the old exclusion or opprobrium
was not in itself defensible, he now thought it the duty of
the peers to pass the bill, if they were satisfied, as he was,
that the declaration afforded sufficient security against
injury to the Established Church. Thus was it regarded
by government, and by some of the spiritual peers; the
Archbishop of York, and the Bishops of Lincoln, Durham,
and Chester, speaking in favour of the bill. 'We who
oppose,' says Lord Eldon, 'shall be in but a wretched
minority, though the individuals who compose it will, as
to several, I think, be of the most respectable class of
peers; but the administration have—to their shame be it
said—got the archbishops and most of the bishops to support this revolutionary bill.' Again: 'All the Whig lords
will be against us; as government began in the Commons
by opposition, and then ran away like a parcel of cowards,
I suppose government also will be against us; but what
is most calamitous of all is, that the archbishops and
several bishops are also against us. What they can mean,
they best know, for nobody else can tell; and, sooner or
later, perhaps in this very year—almost certainly in the
next—the concessions to the Dissenters must be followed
by the like concessions to the Roman Catholics. That
seems unavoidable; though, at present, the policy is to
conceal this additional purpose.' We should like now to
know how many influential members of both Houses entertained this expectation, at this date of April 1828. On
the 12th of the month, the chancellor again writes: 'We,

as we think ourselves, sincere friends of the Church of England, mean to fight, as well as we can, on Thursday next, against this most shameful bill in favour of the Dissenters, which has been sent up to us from the Commons—a bill which Peel's declaration in the House as to the probability of its passing in the Lords, has made it impossible to resist with effect. . . . . If the Lords won't at least alter it, which I don't believe they will, I don't see how, if the Commons act consistently with themselves, Sir F. Burdett can fail in his motion on the 29th, in favour of the Roman Catholics. The state of minds and feelings in the Tory part, and aristocratical part, of the friends of Liverpool's administration is, at present, excessively feverish, and they support ministers, because they know not where to look for others. It is obvious that the ministers who were Canning's followers, to use a vulgar phrase, rule the roast, or at least have too much influence.' In his speeches Lord Eldon declared his principle broadly; and he was so angry with the bishops, and so pertinacious with his amendments, that it is clear 'that he considered this measure of the last importance, from its involving release from all religious disabilities, as well as those of Protestant Dissenters. He said : ' The constitution required that the Church of England should be supported; and the best way of affording that support to her was to admit only her own members to offices of trust and emolument.' Most people thought, by this time, that Lord Eldon's method was likely to be fatal to the Church, by inflicting injury and indignity on nearly half the population of Great Britain and Ireland; for to that number did Protestant Dissenters, Catholics, and Jews, now amount. Lord Eldon declared, 'that if he stood alone, he would go below the bar, and vote against the bill; and were he called that night to render his account before heaven, he would go with the consoling reflection that he had never advocated anything mischievous to his country.' The Lords would not receive his proposed amendments; and he was very unhappy—'hurt, distressed, and fatigued,' he declares, 'by what has lately been passing in the House of Lords. I have fought like a lion, but my talons have been cut off.'

Such amendments as the Lords did pass were called

'poor things' by the old earl; but there was one whose
practical bearing would have gratified his bigotry, if he
could have foreseen it.   It would have solaced him to
know that the principle of exclusion from offices of citizenship for religious opinion was to be extended and perpetuated by a sort of accident.   The Bishop of Llandaff
proposed to add to the declaration a few words expressive
of belief in Christianity.   This was in consequence of a
hint from Lord Harewood; not because he supposed it
necessary but merely decorous.   He proposed it 'for the
credit of parliament.'   These words were : 'On the true
faith of a Christian.'   By the carrying of this clause, the
Jews have since been excluded from offices which they were
before competent to hold.   This was not the first time that
the Jews were unintentionally wronged by measures proposed to affect a different party.   As Lord Holland informed
the House, there was nothing to keep Jews out of parliament since the reign of Charles II., except the abjuration
oath, which was introduced into the Toleration Act—the act
brought in against the adherents of the House of Stuart.
And now they were again excluded—freshly wronged—by
words which were imposed, not for any purpose of necessity, but for the credit of parliament!   However much a
subject of regret, it is not one of surprise to those who
have experimental knowledge of the operation of laws
restrictive on opinion.   The principle of mutual judgment
for matters of opinion, and of legislative partiality for
opinion, is so radically unjust and mischievous, that it
ought to be no matter of surprise if the injury spread
beyond its designed bounds, and the tyranny works out
retributive consequences.   Lord Holland entered his protest against these words on the journals of the House:
'Because the introduction of the words "upon the true
faith of a Christian" implies an opinion in which I cannot
conscientiously concur—namely, that a particular faith in
matters of religion is necessary to the proper discharge of
duties purely political or temporal.'   And also because it
had been found, in preceding cases, that a suspension of
this clause had taken place in regard to persons not contemplated in the imposition of the declaration.   The
amendments of the Lords were agreed to by the Commons;

and in the beginning of May, the bill which, in its finished state, Lord Eldon characterised as being, in his 'poor judgment, as bad, as mischievous, and as revolutionary as the most captious Dissenter would wish it to be,' received the royal assent.   Lord Eldon's only idea of a Dissenter was, that he was a captious and revolutionary man, always bent upon the destruction of the Church of England; and this being the image in his eye, we may pity him for the terror of his soul.   A wiser man, who knew something of Dissenters, and of their strong resemblance to other men, felt happier on the occasion.   Lord Holland said, that in performing the pleasing duty of moving ' that this bill do pass,' he could not refrain from expressing his feelings in language both of gratitude and congratulation—gratitude to the House, for the manner in which it had discharged its duty to the country; and congratulation to the country upon the achievement of so glorious a result.

This was universally considered the great measure of the session—the great achievement of the year; and it was no small achievement to have obtained an equal position of citizenship for as loyal, and peaceable, and principled a set of men as any in the kingdom.   The credit is due, not to either the aristocratic or the liberal section of rulers and their adherents, but to the liberal members of each House unconnected with government.   Government yielded only when it could not resist.   And now, men looked anxiously to see what would be done about the Catholics, after this practical protest against exclusion from office on account of religious opinion.

CHAPTER V.

Dissensions in the Cabinet—Mr. Huskisson's Resignation—Changes in the Administration—Catholic Question—Clare Election—State of Ireland—Brunswick Clubs—Forty-shilling Freeholders—The Viceroy—His Recall—Aspect of the Question—Close of the Session of 1828.

MORE dissensions in the cabinet! There had been rumours about hidden troubles there as early as March; and when the Corn Bill was brought forward on the 31st of that month, it became clear that there had been difficulties among its framers. It could hardly be otherwise when Mr. Huskisson was necessarily the chief authority in the matter, and the Duke of Wellington, who had thrown out the bill of the preceding year, was the head of the government. His principle of prohibition was disavowed by the government in regard to the present bill. The measure was declared to be in principle exactly that of last session; but the duties proposed were higher. It was generally understood that the premier had met with a firmer adherence to Mr. Canning's measure than he expected among his colleagues; and he yielded—as he had now become practised in doing. He had yielded to the expediency of taking the premiership, after openly declaring that he should be mad if he ever did such a thing. He had yielded to the necessity of forming a mixed cabinet, when the king had hoped to have a united one by placing him at the head. He had yielded the emancipation of the Dissenters, and he now yielded his own particular objection to the Corn Bill. Truly, it was now evidently too late to look for the old fashioned 'consistency' which had been formerly the first requisite in statesmanship. If it was not to be found in the honest, resolute, imperious Wellington, it need not be looked for anywhere; or rather, it must be admitted that consistency meant now something different from what it used to mean. The duke went, with a good grace, through the process of bringing forward the government Corn Bill, destitute of the provision which he had thought indispensable a year before, and of any substitute for it; and his liberal colleagues did not pretend to approve of the higher rate of duties. It was a compromise throughout. The agricultural interest complained of the absence of all prohibitory provisions; and other interests complained of the duties, and of the point at which they were fixed—the pivot-point from which ascent and descent of duties began; which they conceived to be virtually raised from 60*s*. to 64*s*. by the increased duties charged on the intervening prices. But the bill passed on the 26th of June. Mr. Huskisson made no secret of his opinions on the corn-laws. He condemned them in themselves, but thought they could not be abolished in the existing state of affairs. 'However expedient to prevent other evils, in the present state of the country,' he said, 'they are in themselves a burden and a restraint upon its manufacturing and commercial industry.' The cabinet compromise appearing to be successful as far as this bill was concerned, it was supposed that the disagreements in the government were surmounted, and that all might now go on smoothly. But it was not to be.

There had been in February a serious call for explanations from the Duke of Wellington and Mr. Huskisson about some expressions of the latter, uttered to his constituents at Liverpool on his late re-election; and both made these explanations in parliament. Mr. Huskisson was reported to have said on the hustings that he did not enter upon office under the duke without having obtained from him guarantees that Mr. Canning's policy would be followed out. The duke, of course, rejected with scorn the idea that any gentleman would propose to him any guarantee of the sort; or that he could for an instant listen to such a proposal. 'Is it to be supposed,' said the duke, 'that the right honourable gentleman to whom I suppose the noble earl to allude, could have used the expressions ascribed to him at the Liverpool election? If my right honourable friend had entered into any such corrupt bargain as he was represented to describe, he would have tarnished his own fame, as much as I should have disgraced mine. It is much more probable—though I have not thought it worth my while to ask for **any**

VOL. II.

explanation on the subject—that my right honourable friend stated, not that he had concluded any wholesale bargain with me, but that the men of whom the government is now composed are in themselves a guarantee to the public, that their measures will be such as will be conducive to his majesty's honour and interests, and to the happiness of the people.' And Mr. Huskisson, supported by abundance of needless testimony, declared that this was nearly what he did mean and say—namely, that in the composition of the cabinet would be found a sufficient guarantee for the carrying out of a liberal policy. Still, though this matter was cleared up, affairs did not work easily; and a disruption of the cabinet took place in May —the immediate occasion being a misunderstanding between the same two members of the government.

Mr. Huskisson's popularity was somewhat declining. He had lost some of the sympathy of the country by re-entering office with Mr. Canning's enemies; and when it was seen with what different ministries he could sit in cabinet, and how, among many changes, he, the bosom friend of Canning, could abide in office, the old sneer—of his being a 'political adventurer'—was revived, with perhaps greater effect than in a more aristocratic time. The events of this month of May damaged his reputation seriously; and he never, during the short remainder of his life, got over it. Those who knew him well, and those who, not knowing him, were duly sensible of the compass and value of his policy, understood his feelings so as to acquit him of everything morally wrong—of everything in the least questionable about personal honour—of everything but uncertainty and error of judgment; but they could not complain of the world in general for forming a somewhat severer judgment. Those who knew the man understood his sensitiveness about responsibility—his timidity about breaking up the government of the country on account of difficulties of his own. And those who appreciated the importance of his free-trade policy—the charge of which he could not depute to any one till some were educated up to his point—could well understand that he would bear with much, and hesitate long, before he would vacate a position in which alone he could effectually promote that policy. He seems indeed to have lingered too long; and to have mismanaged his method of retiring, so as to have made his secession look too much like an expulsion from the cabinet; but those who knew his state of health, his need and desire of rest and travel, and his suffering in public life since the death of his friend, were well aware that his self-regards would have led him into private life long before. We cannot doubt that he often wished that he had followed his inclinations. Many and many a time within the last eight months must he have wished that he had resisted the desire of the king and Lord Goderich, and, seeing more clearly than they, remained abroad; and from this time—this May, 1828— he could have had few but bitter thoughts connected with the last stages of his public career. His final ministerial struggle is a strange instance of strong impulse followed by infirmity of purpose.

Bills were brought into parliament to disfranchise the boroughs of Penryn and East Retford; the movers—Lord John Russell and Mr. Tennyson—proposing to transfer the franchise to Manchester and Birmingham. About the disposal of the franchise there were two opinions; one, that it should be given to the neighbouring hundreds; the other, that it should be transferred to populous towns. Mr. Peel, whose opinion was the most important in the House, had declared that, if there were two boroughs to dispose of, he should advocate the transference in one case to a town, and in the other to the neighbouring hundreds. Mr. Huskisson had declared that if there were but one, he should be for giving it to a town. The Penryn case was first sent up to the Lords, and the East Retford case was discussed in the Commons, on the 19th of May, under a persuasion on the part of the government that the Penryn bill would be thrown out by the Lords; so that there would be only one borough to deal with. Here arose the ministerial difficulty. The government opposed, through Mr. Peel, the transference of the franchise to Birmingham, while Mr. Huskisson felt himself bound by his previous declaration to vote for that transference. Lord Sandon expressly claimed his vote on this ground; and he did not see how he could refuse it; though some suggested that he might avoid voting against his colleagues, on the pretext that the House of Lords had not yet decided on the Penryn bill. Mr. Huskisson himself earnestly wished for an adjournment of the subject, that Mr. Peel and himself might have an opportunity of coming to some understanding; but he could not carry this point; and he voted against his colleagues. At the moment, he did not see that he could remain in office; or, at least, that he could avoid offering to resign. He went home, at two o'clock in the morning, with the buzz of the excited House in his ears, and the significant countenances of colleagues and opponents before his eyes; exhausted with fatigue after sixteen hours' attention to business; feeble in health and sick at heart; and, instead of waiting for the morrow to consider, when refreshed and composed, what he should do, he sat down, and wrote to the Duke of Wellington, a letter which was intended by Mr. Huskisson to be an offer to resign, but understood by the duke to be an actual and formal resignation. The duke received the letter before ten the next morning—was surprised—did not think the superscription, 'private and confidential,' had any bearing on the purport of the letter, and made all haste to lay it before the king as a formal resignation. Friend after friend went to him on Mr. Huskisson's behalf; but the duke would acknowledge no mistake or undue haste on his own part. Mr. Huskisson wrote one explanatory letter after another; but still the duke declared the resignation to have been positive; and if so, and if the duke wished it to be irrevocable, it was irrevocable. The truth plainly was, that Mr. Huskisson was first mistaken in his estimate of the fatal character of his vote; next, hasty in writing to the duke under exhaustion and perturbation, though his impulse was worthy and honourable; and, finally, too slow to accept the consequences of his own act. The duke was clearly less anxious about a disruption of his cabinet than pleased at the occurrence of a fair opportunity to dismiss 'the Canningites.' He offered one option to Mr. Huskisson—to withdraw his letter; but, as that act would have stultified the writer in regard to all his subsequent explanations, it could not, of course, be thought of. After a miserable series of negotiations, explanations, remon-

strances, accidents, and mistakes, so many as to suggest
an idea of fatality, Mr. Huskisson's office was filled up on
the 25th of May. Painfully as he had shrunk from the
risk of disturbing the government, lest the country should
lose the benefit of a continuance of Mr. Canning's policy,
Mr. Huskisson was now compelled to witness, as a consequence of that little letter of his, the retirement of all
'the Canningites.' Lord Palmerston, Lord Dudley, Mr.
Lamb (afterwards Lord Melbourne), and Mr. Grant resigned; and were succeeded by Sir Henry Hardinge, Lord
Aberdeen, Lord Francis Egerton, and Mr. Vesey Fitzgerald.
Mr. Huskisson's place was filled by Sir George Murray.

At last, here was a cabinet such as the king desired,
and had hoped to have in January—a cabinet in which the
affairs of the country could be managed as in old days, and
on good old principles. Were the king and the duke
happy at last?

The king could not much enjoy anything at present.
In the preceding year, Lord Eldon had remarked a serious
decline in his health; and he did not seem to be rallying.
His state of health and nerve, of temper and spirits,
enhanced the difficulties of his ministers, which were
serious enough without that addition.   Lord Eldon
declared, a few days after Mr. Huskisson's retirement:
'The minister will have great difficulties to struggle with.
The Whigs, the Canningites, and the Huskissonites, will
join and be very strong.   With the exception of Lord
Lonsdale, the great Tory parliamentary lords are not
propitiated by the new arrangements and many of them
will be either neuter or adverse.'   But a more serious
difficulty was arising than any caused by this phalanx of
foes.

In the debate on the Dissenters' bill, the duke had said,
while showing how unconnected he conceived this bill to
be with the Catholic cause: 'There is no person in this
House whose feelings and sentiments, after long consideration, are more decided than mine are with regard to the
subject of the Roman Catholic claims; and until I see a
great change in that question, I certainly shall oppose it.'
Recently as this had been said, there was already 'a great
change.' The duke had not yet, perhaps, done yielding.

It was a pity he had not yet learned to refrain from engaging for future states of his mind.

On the 8th of May, after the passing of the Dissenters' bills, and before the resignation of Mr. Huskisson and his liberal colleagues, the Catholic question was brought forward by Sir. F. Burdett. The debate, which occupied three evenings, ended with the adoption of a resolution, that it was expedient to consider the state of the laws affecting Roman Caaholics, in order to such an adjustment as might be satisfactory to all parties. There was now a majority of six, where in the preceding session there had been a minority of four. It was thought advisable, considering the excitement caused by every movement on this question, to learn, before going further, what the Lords were likely to do; and a conference took place on the 19th, when the managers for the peers received the resolution of the Commons. The 9th of June was the day appointed for the consideration of the resolution. Before that day arrived, a 'great change' took place, which produced an immediate effect on the tone of the Duke of Wellington.

During Mr. Canning's short administration, the Catholics had been very quiet. The premier was their friend, and a powerful one. During Lord Goderich's short administration, they had been suspicious and restless. The premier was their friend, but he was a powerless one. When the Duke of Wellington assumed office, they became violent; for then the premier was their enemy. O'Connell boasted that no law should or could put down the Catholic Association; and it was, in fact, as active as ever. Their success in such of the elections as they had carried—a great success following upon a sudden thought, without any preparation or previous consultation—had taught them what to do next, by showing them what a vast electoral power they held in their command of 'the forties,' as O'Connell called the forty-shilling freeholders. Vigorous preparations were made for the next general election. Missionaries were sent out to rouse and instruct the forties throughout Ireland; the priests gave all their influence to the cause; and O'Connell spent his days in abusing the Duke of Wellington, and exciting hatred towards England.

The exasperation of the landlords of the forties was extreme. They found the priests and the great Catholic leader everywhere, interfering with their tenantry, and rousing the ignorant population of their estates to what they called insubordination. Till now, it was a thing unheard of that the tenantry of a landed proprietor should not vote as his landlord desired. To obtain their votes, the proprietors had cut up their lands into forty-shilling freeholds, and had covered their estates with an indigent population; and now, this political power, for which they had sacrificed everything—including the welfare of the indigent tenantry themselves—was turned against them by the priests and the agents of the association. The enmity was so fierce, and the mutual injuries so exasperating, that it seemed as if a dissolution of society must take place. While the Tory peers were fearing for the Church and the purity of the constitution if the Catholics were emancipated, men of wider views saw that society itself must fall to pieces in Ireland if they were not. It was in the midst of this state of things, and before the Lords had debated the Catholic question for this year, that Mr. Huskisson and his colleagues went out, and some new elections must take place on the assumption of office by their successors.

Mr. Vesey Fitzgerald, who represented the county of Clare, was the successor of Mr. Grant, as President of the Board of Trade. He was in favour of the Catholic claims; and neither he, nor any one else in England, doubted his being returned, as a matter of course, with the hearty good-will of the Catholics. But the Catholics seized the opportunity of bringing their cause to a crisis. Their leaders resolved that Mr. O'Connell should be elected; and the thing was done with a high hand. The Catholics in London held a meeting, and subscribed funds; and the Catholic rent in Ireland yielded what else was wanted. The Irish people, though extremely docile to their leaders, were, to the lowest of the forties, too acute not to see that there was little use in electing a representative who could not sit; and it was not enough for them that O'Connell declared, on his reputation as a lawyer, that there was nothing in the existing law which prevented his being elected. This was clear, of course, but not sufficient; so he proceeded to pronounce that he could sit in parliament and vote, without taking the oaths. The acute Irish naturally wondered what, in that case, became of their grievance of being unrepresented, and why O'Connell had not been there all this time. But Mr. O'Connell was not the only lawyer who avowed that opinion. Mr. Butler, an English Catholic barrister, published at this time a similar opinion, with the grounds assigned. So the electors thought they would try.

The excitement was prodigious. In every corner of the county of Clare there was such preaching and haranguing, that to a spectator it looked more like a crusade than an election. As one of their patriots, Mr. Shiel, afterwards said: 'Every altar was a tribune.' If an orator arrived in the dead of the night, he had a crowd about him in five minutes. It was not all joyous excitement. There was misery enough in the midst of it; for the people were between two fires. They had their religion on the one hand, with all its awful threats, and their landlords on the other; for almost every landlord in the county exerted himself for Mr. Fitzgerald, and strove to engage his tenantry on the same side. In a position of such difficulty, the people had, naturally, recourse to their priests for guidance; and this decided the struggle, and left the landlords powerless.

The 30th of June was the day fixed for the polling; and in the meantime, while this extraordinary electioneering was fixing the attention of all men, the Catholic debate came on in the Lords. By a shrewd and quiet passage in a speech of Lord Eldon's, we learn that the electioneering of the Catholics was in the minds of the peers during the debate. What Lord Eldon 'wished particularly to notice on this occasion was, a recent proscription, by their chief orator, of twenty-eight county and borough members. From the tone of confidence in which the speaker calculated on removing those obnoxious representatives, it appeared that the Roman Catholics had already sufficient elective power in their hands, and ought not to require that it should be increased.' The interest of the debate lay in the speech of the Duke of Wellington. Amidst declarations of his sense of the difficulty and danger of making alterations, he impressed almost everybody with the idea that he saw yet more danger in making no changes. His complaints of the present agitation of the subject were chiefly on the ground that it prevented such consultation and mutual understanding as might take place if people's minds were at rest. The concluding words are remarkable now, as showing how a man, who considered himself eminently practical, could set his mind, and well-nigh stake his statesmanship, on impossibilities; and they were felt to be so remarkable at the time for what they foreboded, that they were repeated everywhere as a cause for either hope or dread. He said:

'There is also one fact respecting the state of things in Ireland, to which I should wish to call your lordships' attention. From 1781 to 1791, during which many troublesome questions with respect to that country were discussed, the Roman Catholic question was in fact never heard of; and so little was the question thought about, that when my noble and learned friend (Lord Redesdale) brought into the House of Commons, at that period, a bill respecting the Roman Catholics of England, it is a remarkable fact that the then lord-lieutenant of Ireland was not only not consulted on the subject, but actually did not know of it until the bill was brought into parliament. So little did the Catholics of Ireland disturb the public mind at that moment, that the question was allowed to pass quietly by, almost without comment. If the public mind was now suffered to be thus tranquil—if the agitators of Ireland would only leave the public mind at rest—the people would become more satisfied, and I certainly think it would then be possible to do something.'

This, if not very wise, appeared significant. People smiled at the idea of going back now, voluntarily, into the indifference of a past time—of pouring back the lava streams into the crater of the volcano; but they saw that the more this was found to be out of the question, the more inevitably would the ruling powers discover it to be 'possible to do something.' We find, accordingly, in a letter of Lord Eldon's, written soon afterwards: 'O'Connell's proceedings in Ireland, which you will see in the

papers, and the supposed or real ambiguity which marked
the Duke of Wellington's speech, have led to a very
general persuasion that the ministry intend, or at least that
the duke intends, next session, to emancipate the Roman
Catholics, as he has the Dissenters; and the world is uneasy.'

The Clare election came on. Bands of the forties were
marched into Ennis, the county-town, under the leadership
of priests, and with the watchword: 'For God and
O'Connell!' the most intelligible expression to them of
the adjuration: 'For God and our right!' Mr. Fitzgerald
reasoned; Mr. O'Connell declaimed and bullied, using on
the hustings language so insufferable, as to make the
gentry of the county wonder what sort of an appearance
he would make in parliament, if he should really ever get
there.   After a few days' polling, it was evident that Mr.
Fitzgerald had no chance; and he withdrew. A protest
against Mr. O'Connell's election, as illegal, was offered;
and the matter was argued by counsel before the sheriff
and his assessor. It was, of course, decided that the election was legal, the difficulty of admission to parliament
consisting only in the nature of the oaths to be tendered
to the representative on his presenting himself in the
House. No one could take upon himself to say beforehand that any man would not take the oaths. Mr.
O'Connell was therefore returned, as elected by a majority
of qualified freeholders; but the circumstances of the contest—a notification of the religion of each candidate, and
of the presentation of the protest—were stated on the face
of the return. A petition against his return was immediately presented to the House of Commons; but the
session was nearly over, and nothing was done in regard to
it. O'Connell was well pleased at this, as the recess was
before him, for agitation in his new character of member
of parliament; for as such he was extensively regarded in
Ireland. He now gave out that Catholic representatives
must be elected, as occasion offered, for all the counties of
Ireland. The Catholic Association pushed its preparations
for this great effort; and it began by taking under its
protection such of the forties as had been ejected, or dis-
trained upon for rent by their landlords, in consequence of

their votes at the late election. Thus far the association had acted in wary evasion of the Suppression Act. That act expired in July; and the association immediately afterwards met, with an ostentation of defiance, to discuss and push their measures. They could not be touched now till the next session; and the intervening months were diligently used. Many of the English Dissenters took part with them, subscribing funds for the Clare election, and preparing to aid them further by the use of their nonconformist organisation.

Mr. O'Connell did not bring the question of his eligibility for parliament to an issue this session. His enemies said it was 'manifest that he could do more mischief by prolonging his existence as a pretended M.P., than he could do if he was now to appear, and be turned out of the House of Commons.' His party justified his absence on the ground that much might happen before the next session, to improve his chances of admission—some crisis was evidently near at hand, which it might be well to await— some new elections might possibly occur which might bring a group of Catholic representatives, instead of a single one, to the table of the House, and make the attempt much more imposing. Whatever were his reasons, Mr. O'Connell did not offer himself for admission to the House during the three weeks of the session which remained after his return as member for Clare.

'Nothing is talked of now which interests anybody the least in the world,' writes Lord Eldon on the 9th of July, 'except the election of Mr. O'Connell, and the mischief that it will produce among debaters in the House of Commons, and the more serious mischief which it will, in all human probability, excite in Ireland. As O'Connell will not, though elected, be allowed to take his seat in the House of Commons, unless he will take the oaths, etc.— and that he won't do, unless he can get absolution—his rejection from the Commons may excite rebellion in Ireland. At all events, this business must bring the Roman Catholic question, which has been so often discussed, to a crisis and a conclusion. The nature of that conclusion I don't think likely to be favourable to Protestantism. . . . We shall see whether our present rulers

have the courage with which a Mr. Pitt would have acted
under present circumstances.   I don't expect it of them.'
It is clear that the Clare election had already done some
good.   It had opened the eyes of the most haughty of the
anti-Catholics to the fact, that the question was approaching its crisis and conclusion.

The next obvious effect was a singular one—the conversion of some of the county members of Ireland who were
strong in the Protestant interest.   It has been seen that
the association was threatening and preparing to carry all
the other Irish counties as it had carried Clare; and one
part of its preparations was, composing pledges which the
Catholic candidates should be required to take.   Even if
the system of pledging had not been objectionable, these
pledges must have been considered so in themselves, by every
man of strict principle and independent mind; and every
candidate who would not agree to them was to be opposed
by the whole power of the Catholic Association.   Already
the old relations of landlord and tenant were broken up;
and the landed proprietors who had fallen under the
machinery of the association, were humbled and disabled.
Here was another mode of operation, threatened, under
which the political power of the Protestants was to be
utterly crushed.   The counties would be lost; or, if an
existing member here and there held his position, it would
be in a sort of vassalage to the association, and at its
mercy.   The alarm operated very quickly in producing
conversions among the Irish county representatives and
their friends.   So early as the 12th of August—ten days
after the moving of the pledges in the association, we find
Mr. Dawson, brother-in-law of Mr. Peel, and hitherto a
vehement anti-Catholic, publicly avowing a change of
opinions which induced him now to desire and advocate
Catholic emancipation.   Mr. Dawson was the head of the
anti-Catholic party in the Commons, and was in the service
of the crown; and whatever he said publicly was of consequence, not only to his party, but to the administration.
What he now said, at a public dinner in Londonderry,
was that the Catholic Association must clearly be either
crushed or conciliated, or society must dissolve into its
elements in Ireland.   He did not pretend to suppose it

could now be crushed; and he avowed his wish that it might be conciliated. An example like this was sure to be eagerly imitated by many of the sufferers under the present evils of society in Ireland; and the conversions went on rapidly. The association cared little about them; for they were confident that they should soon have the government avowedly on their side. Notwithstanding all the disgrace with which Mr. Dawson was visited by the ministry, and all the disavowals of his relatives of any participation in what he had said, and all his protestations that he spoke for himself alone, the Catholic Association felt secure. He would not have said anything, they were certain, that could put him into radical opposition with the ruling powers, in whose immediate service he was. He might have been rash in speaking so soon and so broadly; but there could be no doubt that what he had said might be taken as a prophecy of good times to come. So the association went on gaily and boastfully—promising speedy victory, but neglecting no preparations for carrying on a long conflict, if need should be.

We find in a speech of Mr. Shiel's at this time, an account of the state of society in Ireland, which probably all parties, from Lord Eldon to Mr. O'Connell, would agree to be a fair representation. At one of the aggregate meetings, of which several were held during the parliamentary recess—at the great Munster meeting—Mr. Shiel said: 'What has government to dread from our resentment in peace? An answer is supplied by what we actually behold. Does not a tremendous organisation extend over the whole island! Have not all the natural bonds by which men are tied together, been broken and burst asunder? Are not all the relations of society, which exist elsewhere, gone? Has not property lost its influence—has not rank been stripped of the respect which should belong to it? and has not an internal government grown up which, gradually superseding the legitimate authorities, has armed itself with a complete domination? Is it nothing that the whole body of the clergy are alienated from the State, and that the Catholic gentry, and peasantry, and priesthood, are all combined in one vast confederacy? So much for Catholic indignation

while we are at peace; and when England shall be involved in war——. I pause; it is not necessary that I
should discuss that branch of the division, or point to the
cloud which, charged with thunder, is hanging over our
heads.'

No feature of Irish society alarmed government and all
reflecting men more at that time than the sudden and
almost total cessation of Irish crime. That which, if it
had come about gradually, and as a consequence of improved education or prosperity, would have been hailed as
the greatest of encouragements and blessings, was now
ominous and most alarming, as showing the power of the
Catholic leaders, and the strength of their organisation.
At the bidding of these leaders, feuds were suspended;
factions met and acted as brethren; and men mastered
their strongest propensities, in order to become a vast
soldiery for the achievement of political objects. In almost
every county, the judges on circuit congratulated the
magistrates on the disappearance of atrocious crimes, and
the paucity of even the lighter offences. The government
would rather have had to deal with the average amount of
Irish outrage than to witness a lull which boded a coming
hurricane. Ireland was governed now by a power greater
than their own.

On the expiration of the suppression law in July, when
the Catholic Association resumed its primitive form, the
Orange Clubs sprang up again, affording a new cause of
alarm. New Orange Associations were formed, under the
name of Brunswick Clubs, which collected a Protestant
rent, and in every way imitated the Catholic organisation.
The strength of the Brunswick Clubs lay in the north;
that of the Catholics in the south; but they did not, as
the magistracy hoped, lie apart, railing at each other, without attempting collision. A rash and foolish Catholic
agitator, Mr. Lawless, declared his intention of braving
the British lion in its den—its Irish den. He would visit
'all the strongholds of the Orangemen.' And he went,
with tens of thousands at his heels, for no other purpose,
as far as appears, than rousing the antagonism of the
Orangemen. He advertised, for some time previously, his
intention of entering such and such a town, attended by so

many thousand Catholics; and, naturally enough, the town
was entered, early on the appointed morning, by troops of
Orangemen—many or most of them armed This was not
to be endured. The magistrates warned the people against
attending these assemblages. The soldiery were kept on
the alert. On one occasion, when the agitator himself was
prevailed on by the magistrates and military commander to
turn back, his followers got into a scuffle with the Protestant mob, and one man, a Catholic, was killed. The
Catholic Association saw that this would never do. Their
policy was one of peaceful parade; and they would enter
into no competition of force with the Orange party. They
put forth all their influence at once to stop the assemblages
of their own body, to induce them to lay aside all uniforms,
flags, and military music, and abstain from all provoking
demonstrations. It was wonderful how promptly and
thoroughly the leaders were obeyed. Bodies of men, in
one case amounting to fifty thousand, marching on with
flags, music, and uniform, were met on the road by a
hortatory address of O'Connell's and at once turned back
and disbanded themselves, making no complaint of the loss
of their pleasure, or of the money they had spent in their
decorations. Throughout these perilous weeks, the legality
and peaceableness were certainly on the side of the
Catholics—the rashness and vanity of some of their leaders
being kept in check by the good sense and earnest
patriotism of others; while, of the Orangemen—of the
Brunswick Clubs—even the old Tory, Lord Eldon, could
find nothing more approbative to say than this, in answer
to a request for his opinion on the subject of forming a
Brunswick Club in England: 'Already very inconvenient
questions seem to have been stated, whether the calls upon
the people of the country have not, some of them, been expressed in such terms as make it questionable whether those
who, in such terms, make such calls, act as legally as they
ought.' This is put so very delicately, that we may see
how reluctantly the admission is made. He goes on: 'It
is true, those who may so complain may most justly be
told that they have not so objected to the shamefully
illegal proceedings of the Roman Catholic Association;
and I think it not impossible that we may hear some

abusing in parliament the proceedings of Protestant Associations, who have mainly encouraged the proceedings of the Roman Catholic Association ; but this is an example not to be followed.' It is curious to see how utterly blind Lord Eldon was, even at this time, and with all his fears of the Liberals, and his distrust of the government, to the real pressure of the case. No man talked more loudly of his terrors, or of expected apostasy in high places; yet what he anticipated was this and no more : ' I look on the Roman Catholic question as, bit by bit, here a little and there a little, to be ultimately, and at no distant day, carried. I have no conception that even Oxford will struggle effectually against the great Church interests which will patronise that question, and those who support it in parliament.' It was too late for giving liberty ' bit by bit, here a little and there a little.'

The Protestant Clubs in England did not succeed very well. The people generally were disposed to leave the matter to the government. There was a meeting of twenty thousand people on Pennenden Heath in Kent, convened by Protestant leaders, and attended by some advocates of the Catholic cause. The petition to parliament proposed by the conveners was merely to declare attachment to our Protestant constitution, and to pray that it might be preserved inviolate. Some noblemen present moved that the business of dealing with the Catholics should be left to the government; but the petition was adopted by a large majority. This was the only demonstration of any importance in England.

O'Connell now found himself strong enough to declare his pleasure as to the legislation which should take place in regard to his cause; and he even dared a schism in the Catholic body. The English Catholics parted off from the Irish on the question of securities. They were willing to negotiate with government on the subject of securities: O'Connell scorned them, feeling, as he said, that it was better to receive a part of the Catholic claims, without being fettered with securities, and in full certainty that the rest of the demand must soon be granted, than to receive political equality on terms which might occasion future difficulty. He would not entertain the 'paltry

question of political discount;' he would have full emancipation, either at once or by instalments; but he would
give nothing in return for clear political rights.   But on
no subject were his asseverations so emphatic as on that of
the disfranchisement of 'the forties.'   He well knew that
his former agreement to sacrifice the forties had never
been forgotten; and he now doubled and redoubled his
protestations, given in the strongest terms the language
affords, that he would never permit their franchise to
be touched.   On the 16th of December, the association
unanimously passed a resolution, 'that they would deem
any attempt to deprive the forty-shilling freeholders of
their franchise a direct violation of the constitution.'
Mr. O'Connell 'would rather die' than yield that franchise;
'would say that if any man dared to bring in a bill for the
disfranchisement of the forty-shilling freeholders, the people
ought to rebel, if they cannot otherwise succeed.'   Again:
'Sooner than give up the forty-shilling freeholders, I
would rather go back to the penal code.   They form part
of the constitution; their right is as sacred as that of the
king to his throne; and it would be treason against the
people to attempt to disfranchise them. . . . . I would
conceive it just to resist that attempt with force; and in
such resistance I would be ready to perish in the field, or
on the scaffold.'   So said O'Connell up to the end of the
year.   As for Mr. Shiel, he said, in anticipating the policy
of the Duke of Wellington: 'I trust he will not pursue
this course; but if he should, I tell him, we would rather
submit for ever to the pressure of the parricidal code,
which crushed our fathers to the grave, than assent to this
robbery of a generous peasantry.'   These declarations were
made in public, at the Clare election, and at the meetings
of the association, and printed in the newspapers, at a
time when all men's ears were open, and every word of
the Catholic leaders echoed from end to end of the empire;
and by them the leaders must be judged.

During these important months, nothing seems to have
been seen and heard of the Irish government, till, on the
1st of October, it issued a proclamation against such
assemblages as had already been put down by the influence
of the association.   All was again still and mute till a

strange incident, which occurred in the last month of the year, fixed attention on the two friends—the Duke of Wellington and the Marquis of Anglesey, who governed England and Ireland.

Dr. Curtis, the titular Catholic Primate of Ireland, had been intimate with the Duke of Wellington ever since the Peninsular war, when Dr. Curtis held a high office in the University of Salamanca, and was able to render important services to the British army. The Catholic primate wrote to the premier on the state of Ireland, on the 4th of December of this year; and on the 11th the duke wrote in reply—as friend to friend, and without any idea of a political use being made of what he said. There was nothing in the letter which would have fixed attention, if it had been from any other man; and it now appears natural and reasonable enough, and little or nothing more than he had said in parliament half a year before. He reciprocates his correspondent's desire to see the question settled; sees no prospect of it; laments the existing party-spirit and violence; thinks, if men could bury the subject in oblivion for a short time, during which difficulties might be pondered—a curious method, by the way, of burying a subject in oblivion—' it might be possible to discover a satisfactory remedy.'

A copy of this letter was presently in Mr. O'Connell's hands. Mr. O'Connell carried it to the association, and read it aloud; the association received it with cheers, and recorded it on their minutes, as a decisive declaration of the prime-minister in favour of Catholic emancipation. This was not, perhaps, so audacious a stretch of interpretation as some persons—probably including the writer of the letter himself—supposed; for the impediments were now clearly only external and circumstantial; and the association might reasonably feel equal to the conquest of all such. Meantime, Dr. Curtis had replied to the duke, in a long letter in which he set forth his reasons for thinking that the burying the subject in oblivion was wholly out of the question; and that every attempt to get rid of it would be extremely dangerous. He sent copies of the duke's letter and his own reply to the lord-lieutenant; and the lord-lieutenant in return explained his own view to be that the Catholic agitation should be continued. No doubt, this was not intended in contradiction or opposition to the premier; but under the idea that the Catholic agitation was the surest means of overpowering the difficulties which embarrassed the premier, and thus of aiding the government. Its effect, however, was strange, from its appearance of being in direct opposition to the views of the head of the government. Not less strange was the following sentence of Lord Anglesey's reply: 'Your letter gives me information on a subject of the highest interest. I did not know the precise sentiments of the Duke of Wellington upon the present state of the Catholic question.' What were men to think of this? They must conclude one of two things—both highly injurious to government; either that there was such indifference about the Catholics as that their cause had not been discussed with the lord-lieutenant among other subjects of Irish policy; or that the lord-lieutenant was not in the confidence of government at home. It was impossible not to entertain the last of these suppositions; especially as the viceroy proceeds to say that he must acknowledge his disappointment at finding—still from the duke's letter merely—that there was no prospect of Catholic emancipation being effected during the approaching session of parliament. This was on the 23rd of December; only six weeks before the opening of the session. These are curious disclosures of the way in which one of the most important events in British history, and in the history of civil and religious liberty everywhere, was first awaited, and then brought to pass.

This letter, too was immediately carried to the Catholic Association, and read aloud amidst plaudits, like the other. In this case the applause was natural enough; for the letter recommended a strenuous pushing of the Catholic cause, by peaceable means: 'The question should not be for a moment lost sight of;' but 'let the Catholic trust to the justice of his cause,' and use none but unexceptionable means, that his plea might 'be met by the parliament under the most favourable circumstances.' Such encouragement from the ruler of Ireland and a privy councillor of the king, might well be received with

cheers. A large tribute of admiration was voted to him
for his 'manliness and political sagacity.' His sagacity
seems to have failed him in regard to his own interests,
however; his reputation for prudence and even political
honour. If he was surprised, no one else was, when the
next English packet brought his recall. He left Ireland
in January, and was succeeded in the viceroyalty by the
Duke of Northumberland.

One cannot but see some comic intermixture with the
very serious aspect of the times, at the close of 1828.
There were the Duke of Wellington and the Marquis of
Anglesey made the two pets of the Catholic Association—
their letters treasured in the minutes, and themselves
assumed to be both friends of Catholic objects; while, at
the same time, and in consequence of these very proceedings, the duke was recalling the marquis, because the
marquis had brought the duke into an irremediable difficulty. The Catholic Association was pledging itself to
send seventy county members into the House, while its
very existence was for the purpose of obtaining an admission to parliament at all. While the Catholic leaders were
assuming that they should have all they wanted very
soon, and the Brunswick Clubmen were certain that they
would never obtain anything at all, as long as there were
true Britons who would make their dead bodies a barrier
between the Catholics and the privileges of Protestantism,
the English Tories, through the mouth of Lord Eldon,
lamented that, 'bit by bit,' emancipation would be granted;
and the Liberals were certain that the duke meant to
yield everything in the course of the next session; while
the duke himself certainly was not aware, in the middle
of the closing month of the year, that he meant anything
at all. He might appropriate the saying of the sage: 'All
I know is that I know nothing.'

Mr. Shiel has left us a picture of the time, in a speech
at the association: 'The minister folds his arms, as if he
were a mere indifferent observer, and the terrific contest
only afforded him a spectacle for the amusement of his
official leisure. He sits as if two gladiators were crossing
their swords for his recreation. The cabinet seems to be
little better than a box in an amphitheatre, from whence

his majesty's ministers may survey the business of blood.'
The viceroy was recalled for desiring and promoting what
the head of the government was about to do.　As for the
great Catholic leader, the most noticeable particular about
him was his having pledged himself to perdition, if ever
again he would compromise the franchise of 'the forties.'
Times seem to have become too hard for men's wits—for
their endowments of sagacity and judgment, and of that
prudence which, in affairs so momentous as this, should go
by the name of conscience.

CHAPTER VI.

Affairs of Portugal—Don Miguel in England—His Usurpation—
Queen of Portugal in England—Death of Lord Liverpool.

In the speech with which the king, by commission, dismissed parliament on the 28th of July, the first point of
interest was a declaration of the reviving prosperity of the
people.　After the dreadful shocks of 1825 and 1826, it
was some time before any revival of trade was apparent,
at all adequate to the wants of the working-classes.　But
now the immense stocks of every species of manufacture
which had been prepared under the mania of speculation
were pretty well cleared off; money and commodities had
resumed an ascertained and natural value; and the state
of the revenue and the general contentment indicated that
a condition of prosperity had returned.　One advantage of
this was, that many statesmen, and whole classes of
'interests,' became convinced that free-trade—as the very
partial relaxations of former commercial restriction were
then called—was not the cause of the late distresses—was
certainly enhancing the prosperity—was, in short, found
to be a very good thing.

The king's speech carefully indicated that the war which
had been declared between Russia and the Porte was
wholly unconnected with the Treaty of London; and
promised to continue the efforts which had been made, in
concert with the King of France, to promote peace between
Russia and Turkey.　Meantime, the emperor had been

induced not to carry war into the Mediterranean, where so many interests were involved; and had actually recalled his warlike instructions to the commanders of his fleet in the Levant.

It was announced that great disappointment had occurred with regard to Portugal; and that it had been found necessary by all the powers of Europe to withdraw their representatives from Lisbon.

The mistake with regard to Portugal had been in ever appointing as regent such a man as Don Miguel. It might be evident enough that difficulties would be reconciled, and the future would be provided for, by uniting the interests of the different branches of the royal family, in his regency, and his marriage with the yet childish queen; but all political arrangements proceed on the supposition that more or less reliance is to be placed on the acting paties—that some obligations of conscience, or at least of reputation, exist in each party that enters into a contract. But the conduct of Don Miguel in regard to his father, and in other instances, had shown him to be not only untrustworthy, but a sort of moral monster who cannot be treated with as men usually are. Yet his brother, the Emperor of Brazil, thought he had arranged everything, and settled adverse claims, by appointing him Regent of Portugal, and promising him marriage with the young queen.

At the beginning of this year, Don Miguel had been in England. He spent nearly two months in London; and it was regarded as a good sign that he went there, and associated with the rulers and statesmen of a free country, rather than visit the courts of despotic sovereigns. He had taken the oath to preserve the new constitution of Portugal, and had written to his sister—his predecessor in the regency—from Vienna, that he was determined to maintain inviolate the laws of the kingdom, and the institutions legally granted by Don Pedro, and to cause them to be observed, and by them to govern the kingdom. And before he left England, he had, according to the universal belief, written a letter, voluntarily, to George IV., in which he said that 'if he overthrew the constitution, he should be a wretch, a breaker of his oath, and a usurper

of his brother's throne.' There was never any question of
his being bound by the strongest obligations to administer
constitutional government in Portugal, if he had been one
who could be bound by any obligations whatever. But,
as it was proved that he was not such a one, he should not
have been trusted with any political powers whatever.

The princess-regent took leave of the cortes in January;
and on the 22nd of February, Don Miguel landed at
Lisbon. Among the acclamations which greeted him—the
cries of 'Long live the Infant!'—a few voices were heard
shouting 'Long live Don Miguel, the absolute king!'
Neither on this occasion, nor when he went in procession
to the cathedral, and heard more of the same shouts, did
the prince take any notice of them. They passed as the
cries of a few discontented men among the rabble; and it
was never clear whether Don Miguel had at this time any
intention of usurping the throne, or whether he was afterwards instigated to it by his mother. From the moment
when he fell on his knees before his mother, he showed
himself her slave, and wrought out her wicked pleasure
most zealously, whatever might have been his previous
intentions. He was to swear to the constitution, four
days after his arrival, in the presence of the two chambers
and of the court. There was something strange about the
ceremony, which excited the suspicions of the bystanders.
The prince was ill at ease, hurried and confused; and he
spoke too low to be heard by those nearest to him. The
Archbishop of Lisbon who administered the oath stood
directly in front of the prince, with his priestly garments
spread wide, so that the regent was little better seen than
heard. He is declared not to have touched the book of
the gospels, and to have said, when the show was over:
'Well, I have gone through the ceremony of swearing to
the charter; but I have sworn nothing.' One significant
circumstance is that there was no register, or legal record
of any kind, of the event. The next day the new ministry
was announced; and the announcement spread dismay
among the constitutionalists. The funds fell; the bank,
which was to have set off on a new score that day, feared
a run, and postponed its payments indefinitely—all business was at a stand in Lisbon. The mob assembled under

the windows of the queen-mother shouting for absolutism;
and the prime-minister distributed money among them.
During the month of March the proceedings of the regent
were so open and shameless in insulting and displacing
liberals and favouring the absolutists, that many hundreds
of the best families in Lisbon left the capital. Just at
this time, the British troops sent by Mr. Canning were
embarking for their return; and a large amount of money
—a loan from M. Rothschild to the prince—was arriving.
The new British ambassador at Lisbon, Sir Frederick
Lamb, decided, on his own responsibility, to detain the
troops, and send the money back to London; that the
usurper—for it was now no secret that the prince was about
to assume the title of king—might be awed by the presence
of British troops, and unaided in his treasonable purposes
by British gold. This was in the middle of March;
and it was the beginning of April before the British
ambassador could receive instructions how to proceed.

On the 14th of March the prince dissolved the chambers,
to evade the passing of a vote of thanks to the British
commanders, and some troublesome inquiries into state
abuses. On the 2nd of April the British troops were
embarked for home, in pursuance of orders received by the
ambassador. Before this, the prince had been declared in
several provincial towns to be absolute king, Don Miguel I.
When the British troops were gone, and with them all the
respectable liberals who could get away, there was no
further impediment to the proclamation taking place in
the capital; and the thing was done on the birthday of
the queen-mother, on the 25th of April. The scene was
opened by the commandant of police with his guard, before
the hall of the municipality, between eight and nine in
the morning. Baring their heads, and drawing their
sabres, they cried aloud: 'Long live Don Miguel the
First! Long live the empress-mother!' Thereupon the
national flag was slung up on the roof of the hall, and the
municipal authorities appeared in the balcony, to proclaim
the new king. The proclamation was repeated at noon
through the city; and all citizens were invited to sign a
memorial, imploring Don Miguel to assume the function
of king. This memorial was presented in the evening;

but the paucity and doubtful character of the signatures—according to some authorities—annoyed and alarmed the prince. According to others, the signatures were wonderfully numerous; but the prince dared not proceed to extremities at once, because all the foreign ambassadors had notified that they should leave Lisbon immediately on his assumption of the title of king. He desired the memorialists to wait, and see what he would do.

A note was sent round the next morning from the foreign minister to these representatives, regretting the popular manifestation of the preceding day, and assuring them that everything possible had been done by government to keep the people quiet. The foreign ambassadors met to confer upon their reply; and they agreed upon a notification to the minister that they suspended all official intercourse with the government till they should receive fresh instructions from their respective courts.

All disguise was soon thrown off. On the 3rd of May, Don Miguel issued a summons to the ancient three estates of the kingdom, who had not been assembled for upwards of a hundred and thirty years. They were to meet to 'recognise the application of grave points of Portuguese right,' since the importunate demand of various bodies in the state, that the prince would assume empire, had become very perplexing to him. The difficulty was how to sign this document. The awkwardness of signing in Don Pedro's name an invitation to declare that Don Pedro had no rights in Portugal, was so great, that the prince actually signed it as Don Miguel I. As king, he summoned the estates who were to meet to invite him to become king.

The estates met on the 26th of June, and immediately declared Don Miguel to be lawfully King of Portugal. On the 28th, the new sovereign assumed his full name and title. He had not been left in peace and quiet in the interval. Oporto and other towns had risen against him; and many of the Portuguese refugees in England had returned to conduct the war. But they were delayed on the voyage; affairs had been mismanaged; and there was nothing left for them to do but to make the best retreat they could through Spain.

Of course, the ambassadors all took their departure at

the end of June. At first, the usurper did not conceal his
rage and mortification; but presently he gave out declarations that they had all been recalled by his express desire,
in order to be succeeded by others less addicted to free-
masonry—his word, and that of other despots, for liberalism.
From this time the course of the usurper became altogether
disgusting. His practices could only be—where it was
possible—denied by his flatterers; nobody vindicated them.
He filled the prisons; set aside the laws, in order to procure the sacrifice of his enemies; confiscated all the property he could lay hands on; and spread such ruin that,
with all his devices, he could not raise money enough for
his purposes. He actually asked for a loyal subscription;
and the names of the donors, advertised in the *Lisbon
Gazette*, looked grand in regard to rank and title; but the
sum produced was only £4000.

Don Pedro, meantime, had heard of his brother's dutiful
acceptance of the charge of the regency, and of his being
in London, where the Brazilian emperor hoped he would
learn some good lessons. Believing that the time was
now come for his final surrender of all authority in
Portugal, the emperor prepared his concluding act of
abdication on the 3rd of March. He little dreamed what
his unworthy brother was doing, or he would not have
yielded up his powers at such a time; and much less
would he have sent his young daughter to Europe. As
for the manifesto of abdication, the Brazilian ministers at
Vienna and London assumed the responsibility of keeping
it back, and preventing its being officially communicated
to any of the European powers. When the bad news from
Portugal reached the emperor, he issued a decree, on the
25th of July, reprobating the acts of the usurping government, but treating his brother with a leniency which
appeared strange; but which may perhaps be accounted
for on the supposition that he had fears for his daughter,
and might be uncertain about her probable fate. He
spoke of Don Miguel as doubtless a captive and a victim
in the hands of a party who compelled him to acts abhor-
rent to his nature. The government newspapers at Lisbon
retorted by assuring the world that Don Pedro could **not
have** prepared such a decree, except under the influence of

'the horrid sect of freemasons, who are the enemies of the throne and the altar.'

The little queen, Donna Maria, now nine years old, arrived at Gibraltar on the 2nd of September, on her way to Genoa, where she was to land, and proceed to Vienna, on a visit to her grandfather, the Emperor of Austria. The news which her conductors heard at Gibraltar, however, put them also upon considering their responsibilities; and they decided—as so many had before done, to the high honour of our country—that England was the safest retreat for a sufferer under political adversity. One of the frigates was immediately sent back to Brazil with the latest news of what had occurred; and the other brought Donna Maria to England. She arrived off Falmouth on the 24th of September. She was received with royal honours; and there was something very affecting in the sight of the eagerness with which the noble Portuguese refugees rushed on board, to devote themselves to her and the vindication of her rights. If she was too young to be duly touched with a sense of her situation, others felt it for her. He who had sworn to govern for her with fidelity during her tender years, had usurped her throne: he who was to have been her husband, had repelled her from the shores of her own kingdom, and cast her upon the mercy of the world. No wonder the refugees rushed to her feet; for every heart in England bled for her.

When the frigate arrived at Falmouth, the queen and her conductors were uncertain whether she would be received as Duchess of Oporto, or as a sovereign. Everything hung now on a few moments. But all was well. The royal salute came thundering over the waters from the forts and the ships, and up went the flags on every hand. Then up went the royal standard of Portugal, and the young girl and her retinue knew that she was acknowledged queen by Great Britain. On her way to London, she was greeted with addresses by the corporations of all the principal towns she passed through, and the people everywhere received her with cheers. In London, almost before the Portuguese residents could pay their duty to their sovereign, the prime-minister and foreign secretary arrived to welcome her majesty to our metropolis. They came in their state carriages, in military uniform, and covered with orders. The king sent messages. He was at his cottage at Windsor, living in almost utter seclusion, and, as his people now began to be aware, in feeble and declining health. On the 12th of October, the birthday of Don Pedro, an affecting ceremony took place at the residence of the Marquis Palmella. The whole of the Portuguese and Brazilian legations being present, and the Brazilian and Portuguese ministers at the courts of Vienna and the Netherlands, the Marquis Palmella told the whole story of Don Pedro's conduct and the young queen's position, read the decrees and the emperor's dispatches, and, in short, put his hearers in possession of the entire case, in a discourse of three-quarters of an hour. The marquis then, as the intended prime-minister of the queen, first took the oath of fealty to her; and his example was followed by all present—ambassadors, generals, peers of her realm, members of the cortes, and military and political officers of various ranks—in all, above two hundred. She had thus a little court about her while she remained in England; which was till the next year, when her father recalled her to Brazil. By that time it was explained that, while Great Britain acknowledged her sovereignty, discountenanced her usurping uncle, and desired to extend all due hospitality towards her, it was not possible to do more. Our treaties of alliance with Portugal, it was declared, bound us to aid her against foreign aggression, but not to interfere in her domestic struggles. We had sent troops to Portugal when Spain was invading her liberties; but we could not impose or depose her rulers.

Towards the close of the year—on the 15th of December—the funeral-train at last left the door of Lord Liverpool's abode at Wimbledon. Of those who had hourly looked for his death nearly two years before, and who had held the affairs of the country suspended in expectation of it, some had long been in their graves. He was now released at last; and his funeral-train was a long one; for his private life had won for him a gratitude and warm regard, which made him now more thought of as the kindly hearted man than as the respectable minister who had ostensibly governed the country for fifteen years.

CHAPTER VII.

Difficulties in the Cabinet—The King—Mr. Peel's Resignation of his
Seat in Parliament—King's Speech and the Address—Catholic
Relief Bill—Mr. Peel—The Duke of Wellington—Catholic Relief
Bill passed—The King's Vacillation—The Bill becomes Law—Irish
'Forties'—Clare Election—Prospects of Ireland.

THERE never was an instance in which men were more
universally blamed than the Wellington administration
were at the time of the removal of the Catholic disabilities. The public always will and must judge by what
they know; and those who knew only what was on the
face of things, could not but form an unfavourable judgment, in every light, of the conduct of the duke and his
colleagues. Their own party, of course, thought them
faithless, infirm, and cowardly. The fact was before all
eyes, that they had suddenly relinquished the declared
principles, and stultified the professions, of their whole
political lives, deceived and deserted their friends and
supporters, and offered to history a flagrant instance of
political apostasy. The opposition complained, with equal
appearance of reason, that, after having thwarted, in every
possible way, the efforts of Mr. Canning and the other
friends of the Catholics, they shamelessly carried the
measures which they would not hear of from Mr. Canning;
that, having damaged the liberal statesmen of their day
with all their influence, they stepped in at last to do the
work which had been laboriously prepared in spite of
them, and took the credit of it. Truly, their credit was
but little with even those who put the best construction
upon their conduct. By such, they were believed to have
yielded to an overwhelming necessity; and thus to deserve
no praise at all; while there was much that was inexplicable and unsatisfactory in their method of proceeding.
There was evidence, that up to the middle of December,
the prime-minister did not intend to remove the Catholic
disabilities, or that he chose the public to suppose it;

while on the 5th of February, the speech from the throne
recommended their removal. Time, however, clears up
many things. The conduct of the ministers was inexplicable; for their difficulties were of a nature which they
could not explain. They explained, as much as men of
honour and loyalty in their position could, the necessity
which existed for what they were doing; but about everything which most closely concerned themselves, everything
which was necessary to clear their political character, they
were compelled to keep silence. By others, however, bit
by bit, and in a course of nearly twenty years, disclosures
have been made, which appear to put us in full possession
of their case, and leave us with the conviction that their
fault lay in their preceding political course, and not in
their conduct at this juncture. Their anti-Catholic principles and policy had been mistaken, as the liberal party
had, of course, always declared. There was nothing new
in that. And a close study of the facts of their case, as
now known, seems to lead to their acquittal of all blame
in the great transactions of 1829.

The difficulty which embarrassed them, and compromised
their reputation, was in regard to the king. Lord Eldon
and others, who saw him from time to time, had been
struck by the change in his health in 1827, from which
period he continued to decline. By his mode of living
he had never given himself a chance for health; and when
the health breaks up under such circumstances, there can
hardly be any serenity of temper or tranquillity of mind
He was at this time truly wretched; and he made every
body about him miserable. He vacillated between de-
spondency and levity, irascibility and weak fondness; and
worst of all, not the slightest dependence was to be placed
upon his word. In unreliableness he was a match for
O'Connell himself. There is usually a tacit understanding
among us in favour of ministers, where any difficulty with
the sovereign is supposed to exist. It was so in the case
of the hovering insanity of George III., and there have
been times since when a generous aid has been afforded by
opposition in parliament to a minister who might be
supposed to be under embarrassments which a loyal subject and servant of the crown could not explain, or in any

way indicate.   But during the crisis under our notice, no
one could imagine the difficulties the administration were
under with the king; and the extreme seclusion in which
the king shut himself up, gave them no chance of his so
exposing himself to any eyes but their own, as to obtain
for them the allowance which their position required.   It
is all known now; or, at least, so much is revealed as
amply to vindicate the honour of the Wellington administration.

On the 28th of September, 1828, the Duke of Wellington
had written to the viceroy of Ireland that the Catholic
question was 'a subject of which the king never hears or
speaks without his mind being disturbed.'   On the 11th of
November, again, he wrote: 'I cannot express to you
adequately the extent of the difficulties which these and
other occurrences in Ireland create, in all discussions
with his majesty.'   We have already seen evidence that,
up to the middle of December, the ministers had no idea
that anything could be done towards conciliating the
Catholics.   The king's own account of what happened
next was this—given to Lord Eldon in conversation on
the 28th of the next March: 'That at the time the administration was formed, no reason was given him to
suppose that any measures for the relief of the Roman
Catholics were intended or thought of by ministers; that
he had frequently himself suggested the absolute necessity of putting down the Roman Catholic Association
—of suspending the Habeas Corpus Act, to destroy the
powers of the most seditious and rebellious proceedings
of the members of it, and particularly at the time that
Lawless made his march; that, instead of following what
he had so strongly recommended, after some time, not a
very long time before the present session, he was applied
to, to allow his ministers to propose to him, as a united
cabinet, the opening of parliament by sending such a
message as his speech contained ; that, after much
struggling against it, and after the measure had been
pressed upon him as an absolute necessity, he had consented that the Protestant members of his cabinet, if they
could so persuade themselves to act, might join in such
a representation to him, but that he would not then, nor

in his recommendation to parliament, pledge himself to anything. He repeatedly mentioned that he represented to his ministers the infinite pain it gave him to consent even so far as that.'

It was foolish to talk of refusing to pledge himself to anything, while permitting his ministers to request from him a message to parliament which he contemplated granting. In consenting to receive the proposed representation of his ministers, he pledged himself to their policy; and he must have known at the time that he did so, though in his anger and wretchedness afterwards he endeavoured to persuade himself and Lord Eldon that he had kept open a way of escape. Meantime, the case of his ministers was a hard one. Having once obtained the king's consent to bring forward a measure in relief of the Catholics, they should have had every encouragement and assistance from him. But he led them a terrible life at present, when they had quite enough to bear from other quarters, and when they were so completely committed that nothing could be gained by making them miserable.

When February came in, the best informed politicians began whispering to each other that the king's speech, which was to be read on the 5th, would contain large concessions to the Catholics. On the 4th, at the dinners held as usual at the houses of the two leaders of government in parliament, the speech was read, and found to contain all that had been rumoured, and more. After an allusion to the disorders in Ireland caused by the Catholic Association, and expressions of a determination to put them down, followed the recommendation of the king to parliament to consider whether the civil disabilities of the Catholics could not be removed, 'consistently with the full and permanent security of our establishments in Church and State.' On the same day, Mr. Peel addressed a letter to the vice-chancellor of Oxford, offering to resign his seat for the university, because he believed that his resistance to the Catholic claims had been one of the main grounds upon which the confidence of his constituents in him had been founded; and he could now resist those claims no longer, but, on the contrary, found himself impelled for the peace of the country, to advise the king to propose a settlement of the question. What Mr. Canning had foregone, Mr. Peel now resigned—the honour and the trust which he valued above all others.

Mr. Peel's resignation was accepted ; and the new election soon took place. There was an intention on the part of the anti-Catholic members of the University to bring forward Lord Encombe, the grandson of Lord Eldon, who consented to the nomination; but it was found that Mr. Peel was so strongly supported that it would be necessary to oppose to him a candidate of graver years and greater weight than the youthful Lord Encombe; and Sir Robert H. Inglis was the choice of the University. The contest was eager and close. During the three days that it lasted, 1364 voters polled; and the majority by which Sir Robert H. Inglis won his seat was only 146. Mr. Peel was returned for the borough of Westbury, in time to assume the management of the Catholic Relief Bill in the Commons.

No division took place in either House on the address in answer to the royal speech, which was, as usual now, delivered by commission. The king appeared averse to meeting his parliament, or seeing any one else whom he could avoid; and the present occasion was one the least likely to draw him forth from his retirement, though the sanction of his presence would at this time have been especially valuable to his ministers. The prime-minister expressed his desire that no discussion of the Catholic question should take place till the measure should be brought forward; explaining that the measure would be proposed in a substantial shape, without going through a committee; that its purport would be a removal of all the civil disabilities of the Catholics, with a few special exceptions; and that it would be accompanied by provisions rendered necessary by the removal of the disabilities.

Before the subject could be entered upon, it was essential to procure the dissolution of the Catholic Association. The preceding acts passed for the purpose had failed; and the difficulty was great of framing a law which could not be evaded as they had been. The present act was limited as to time, being proposed for only one year; and the penalties were not severe; but it gave large powers to the

viceroy of Ireland. It was not opposed by the friends of
the Catholics, who took it as a part of a series of measures,
and were well aware that there would be no need to put
it in force. And its powers were never put to the proof;
for the association dissolved itself before the bill became
law. The bill was brought forward by Mr. Peel, in the
Commons, on the 10th of February; and it passed the
Lords on the 24th of the same month. Already the association existed no longer; and the Houses and the
country were at liberty to go on with the great question
of all.

On the 5th of March, Mr. Peel brought forward the
measure for the relief of the Catholics. The tables of
both Houses had been loaded with petitions for and
against the bill, from the first possible day after its announcement. The strength of the anti-Catholic party, as
shown in petitions, was great; but in the House of
Commons it was not so. The same reasons which had
caused the conversion of the administration, caused that
of their adherents generally; and the power of argument
was all on one side.

The bill proposed an oath, in the place of the oath of
supremacy, by which a Catholic entering parliament
bound himself to support the existing institutions of the
state, and not to injure those of the Church. It admitted
Catholics to all corporate offices, and the enjoyment of all
municipal advantages; and to the administration of civil
and criminal justice. The army and navy were open to
them before. The only exclusions were from the offices of
regent, of lord chancellor of England and Ireland, and of
viceroy of Ireland. From all offices connected with the
Church, its universities and schools, and from all disposal
of church-patronage, they were of course excluded. Such
were the grants and exclusions. As for the securities and
restrictions proposed, the most important related to the
franchise; and of these, the chief was the substitution of
a ten-pound for a forty-shilling qualification, in Ireland.
The government refused to interfere, in one way or other,
with the Roman Catholic religion, but were willing to
leave it on the footing of dissent, neither proposing, on
the one hand, to endow the clergy, nor, on the other, to

pry into its relations with Rome; but the bill forbade the display of the insignia of office in any place of worship but those of the Established Church; the use of Episcopal titles and names by Roman Catholic clergy; the extension of monachism within the empire; and the introduction of more Jesuits than were already in the country, and who were henceforth to be subject to registration. Such were the securities and restrictions.

Mr. Peel's speech lasted four hours, during which time the House was alternately in a state of profound stillness and echoing with cheers. At times, the cheers were so loud as to be heard in Westminster Hall. The occasion united in itself two very strong interests—that which related to the settlement of the Catholic question, and that which regarded the principles and conduct of the leading statesmen of the time. In both directions, the speech was eminently satisfactory. The Catholic question might be considered as settled, as the exposition of the measure fell from the lips of the speaker; and in regard to the political character of Mr. Peel—the most important man in the country at that time and to this day—the case was clear to the eyes of the impartial and philosophical observer; and all subsequent events have been but illustrations of what was that night revealed. Mr. Canning was wont to say that Mr. Peel was his rightful successor in statesmanship; and so he has proved himself: but the method of his procedure has been as different from that of Canning as the nature of the man. Each has been an inestimable blessing to his country, in a singular and perilous period of transition—the one, in spite of the drawbacks which attend upon all human agency; the other, apparently in consequence of them. Mr. Canning had a glorious apprehension of the principles of freedom, clouded and intercepted by prejudices full of insolence and perverseness. He toiled and made sacrifices for the relief of the Catholics, and used all the influence of his office and his character for the promotion of political liberty abroad; but he opposed parliamentary reform and the relief of the Dissenters. Mr. Peel appears never to have had, in his youth and early manhood, any conception of popular freedom at all. What he has is the result of a political experience

which has emancipated him from the misfortunes of his
early political training and connections. If any man
could be said to have been born into a condition of
political opinion, it was he. He was born into con-
servatism, and reared in it, and stationed to watch over
and preserve it; and herein lies the misfortune which
probably alone has prevented his taking rank as a first-
rate statesman. But that which is his personal misfortune
has been, in the opinion of many of the wise, the saving
of our country from revolution in an age of revolutions.
He has been our bridge over the abyss in which the state
might, ere this, have been lost. A statesman who, setting
out on his course without high and definite aims, finds his
principles by the wayside as he proceeds, can never be the
highest of his order, however faithful and courageous he
may be in the application of the truths which he has appropriated; but in the absence of the loftiest statesmanship which can be conceived of, and which no reasonable
nation expects at any given time to enjoy, the greatest
blessing which can be desired is that of a statesman who
can understand and guide the time; that guiding—that
leading-on—supposing him ahead of the average wisdom
of his generation.

And this is what Mr. Peel has been to his country from
the day of his bringing in the Catholic Relief Bill. He
was not then what he has since proved himself capable of
being; but his explanation on that day showed to sagacious
observers precisely what he was, and what he might be
expected to become. At that time he was sorry that
changes on behalf of liberalism were required. It would
have pleased him better to have been able to go on in the
old ways which he believed to be safer for rulers, and
happier for the people, than the new methods which compelled their own adoption. But he saw the necessity; he
saw that to preserve the peace of society, and to respect
the convictions of the majority, was a higher duty than to
rule according to his own predilections. It was an irksome and a humiliating duty; but it was a clear one; and
he did it. He had much to bear from the rage and contempt of old connections, and from the jealousy and scorn
of the Liberals who had hitherto been his opponents; but

these visitations were penalties on his former and lower opinions—on his previous false position, and not on his new enlightenment. The enlightenment was not yet great; but when once the clouds begin to part, there is no saying how much sunshine may be let down; a rent was made in the educational prejudice which had hitherto canopied his mind; and such rents are never closed. The cry at the time was, about this speech, in the market-places and by firesides, that it was not the speech of a great man; that it assumed a tone no higher than that of reluctant yielding to an irresistible necessity. And this was quite true. Such was the tone of the speech; and it was this very characteristic which gave hope to the wise that the speaker would become, or would prove himself, a great man hereafter. They liked the simple truth of the explanation better than any sudden assumption of a higher ground. There was honesty and heart enough in it to afford an expectation that he would soon attain a higher ground, while there was an assurance that he would not pretend to any other ground than that which he actually held. From that time his expansion and advancement have been very remarkable. His mind and heart have kindled with an enthusiasm of which he was, twenty years ago, supposed unsusceptible; an enthusiasm of popular sympathy, and in favour of a pervasive justice. The union of this liberal sympathy with former habits of political conduct has made him a statesman precisely adapted to his age; to serve his country and his time, though not to reap the immediate rewards of popularity, or adequate gratitude. The mischief of his early false position has followed him throughout, and must ever follow him. Even such services as his, in themselves so unques-tionable, have been received, up to the latest period, with a certain degree of mistrust; and this is right; not because the man deserves it—for he has long shown that he merits, and from the most thoughtful he certainly enjoys, the fullest confidence that can be reposed in any man who has proved himself fallible in his vocation; but because it is inevitable that a man who has once been in a false posi-tion must forego the unhesitating trust which is reposed in a man of equal qualifications, who has always recog-

nised, taken, and held his own true position. We have
not, however, any other man of equal qualifications. We
cannot have one of a more unquestionable disinterestedness; and Mr. Peel stands pronounced, beyond all controversy, the greatest statesman of his age. To him we owe
our rescue or exemption from the political calamities which
perhaps no one else could have averted; and to him we
are indebted for so many homely and substantial benefits
of good government, and such brilliant renovations of our
national resources, that it seems impossible for the national
gratitude to overtake his deserts. If he was at first the
victim, he has since shown himself the conqueror, of time
and circumstance; and, for many years past, it has been
clear to the unprejudiced, that all fault-finding with Mr.
Peel's character and political conduct, as a whole, resolves
itself into a complaint that he was not made another sort
of man than he is. This glance into the future, of whose
events we have yet to treat, may be excused by the relation which that future bears to the occasion when Mr.
Peel first stood up a reformer on any controverted party
question. He was aware at the moment that he stood at
the most critical point of his political life; and after the
lapse of twenty eventful years, it is impossible to say that
he exaggerated, in the interest of the hour, its importance
to himself, while he was perhaps further than some other
people from being aware how serious was its significance
in relation to the welfare of his country.

The state of the question, and the position of the
ministry, were briefly presented in the speech. 'According to my heart and conscience,' said Mr. Peel, 'I believe
that the time is come when less danger is to be apprehended to the general interests of the empire, and to the
spiritual and temporal welfare of the Protestant establishment, in attempting to adjust the Catholic question, than
in allowing it to remain any longer in its present state.
. . . . Looking back upon the past, surveying the present, and forejudging the prospects of the future, again I
declare that the time has at length arrived when this
question must be adjusted. . . . . I have for years attempted to maintain the exclusion of Roman Catholics
from parliament and the high offices of the state. I do

not think it was an unnatural or unreasonable struggle.
I resign it in consequence of the conviction that it can be
no longer advantageously maintained; from believing that
there are not adequate materials or sufficient instruments
for its effectual and permanent continuance. I yield therefore to a moral necessity which I cannot control, unwilling
to push resistance to a point which might endanger the
establishments that I wish to defend. . . . . The outline
of my argument is this. We are placed in a position in
which we cannot remain. We cannot continue stationary.
There is an evil in divided cabinets and distracted councils
which can be no longer tolerated. . . . . Supposing this
established, and supposing it conceded that a united
government must be formed; in the next place, I say that
that government must choose one of two courses. They
must advance, or they must recede. They must grant
further political privileges to the Roman Catholics, or
they must retract those already given. They must remove
the barriers that obstruct the continued flow of relaxation
and indulgence, or they must roll back to its source the
mighty current which has been let in upon us, year after
year, by the gradual withdrawal of restraint. I am asked
what new light has broken in upon me? why I see a
necessity for concession now, which was not evident
before? . . . . I detailed, on a former occasion, that a
dreadful commotion had distracted the public mind in
Ireland—that a feverish agitation and unnatural excitement prevailed, to a degree scarcely credible, throughout
the entire country. I attempted to show that social intercourse was poisoned there in its very springs; that family
was divided against family, and man against his neighbour;
that, in a word, the bonds of social life were almost dis-
severed; that the fountains of public justice were corrupted; that the spirit of discord walked openly abroad;
and that an array of physical force was marshalled in
defiance of all law, and to the imminent danger of the
public peace. I ask, could this state of things be suffered
to exist, and what course were we to pursue? Perhaps I
shall be told, as I was on a former occasion, in forcible
though familiar language, that this is the old story! that
all this has been so for the last twenty years, and that

therefore there is no reason for change. Why, this is the very reason for a change. It is because the evil is not casual and temporary, but permanent and inveterate—it is because the detail of misery and outrage is nothing but the 'old story,' that I am contented to run the hazards of a change. We cannot determine upon remaining idle spectators of the discord and disturbance of Ireland. The universal voice of the country declares that something must be done. I am but echoing the sentiments of all reasonable men, when I repeat that something must be done. I wish, however, to take nothing for granted, but to found my argument, not upon general assent, but upon unquestionable facts. I ask you to go back to a remoter period than it is generally the habit to embrace in these discussions—I ask you to examine the state of his majesty's government for the last thirty-five years, and to remark the bearing of the Catholic question upon that government, the divisions it has created among our statesmen, the distraction it has occasioned among our councils, and the weakness it has consequently produced. I ask you then to observe what has been the course of parliament for the same period. And, lastly, what has been the consequence of the divisions in the councils of the king, and of disunion between the two Houses of parliament—the practical consequences as to Ireland.'

The narrative of these divisions is mournful enough, not only in its detail of the consequences to Ireland, but as proving how much evil men will cause and endure rather than surrender their prejudices and the power which they hold on the tenure of bigotry. In the time of Lord Liverpool, it appears that the prejudices had become scarcely tenable, and the power of tyranny very precarious. In 1825, Mr. Peel declared: 'I stated to the Earl of Liverpool, who was then at the head of the administration, that in consequence of the decision given against me in this House, it was my anxious wish to be relieved from office. It was, however, notified to me that my retirement would occasion the retirement of the Earl of Liverpool; and that such an event would at once produce a dissolution of the administration, the responsibility of which would rest with me. . . . . Lord Liverpool was then approaching the end of his career. I had entered public life under his auspices, and I shrank from the painful task of causing his retirement, and the dissolution of his majesty's existing government. If I had acted simply in obedience to my own wishes, I would have resigned. I was induced, however, to retain office, and to ascertain the result of another appeal to the country, by a general election. In 1826, there was a new parliament. In 1827, a majority in this House decided against the Catholic question. In 1828, however, the House took a different view of the matter, and though it did not pass a bill, it agreed to a resolution favourable to the principle of adjustment. That resolution being passed, I was again in the situation in which I had been placed in 1825, and I determined to retire from office. I intimated my fixed intention in this respect to the Duke of Wellington : but I felt it my duty to accompany that intimation with the declaration, not only that I would not, in a private capacity, any longer obstruct a settlement which appeared to me ultimately inevitable, but that I would advise and promote it. Circumstances occurred, as I have already explained, under which I was appealed to to remain in office ; under which I was told, that my retirement from office must prevent the adoption of the course which I was disposed to recommend. I resolved therefore, and without doubt or hesitation, not to abandon my post, but to take all the personal consequences of originating and enforcing, as a minister, the very measure which I had heretofore opposed.'

In the other House, the explanations were as characteristic, and almost as interesting, as in the Commons. The Duke of Wellington apologised at the outset for being about to make a longer speech than their lordships were accustomed to hear from him ; but he made shorter work of it than any other man would have done. It was in the course of this speech that he uttered the declaration which is, and will continue to be, more remembered than anything else he ever said. 'I am one of those,' said the great Captain, ' who have probably passed a longer period of my life engaged in war than most men, and principally, I may say, in civil war ; and I must say this, that if I could avoid, by any sacrifice whatever, even one month of civil

war in the country to which I am attached, I would
sacrifice my life in order to do it.' In order to do this
now, in his absolute conviction that Ireland was on the
verge of civil war, the hero of a hundred fights laid down
what he cared for much more than his life. Having made
up his mind to it, he did it well. His measure was
thorough; the grace it gave was almost free; so nearly
so, that the opposition made a great laugh out of the
securities and restrictions proposed. He said little in the
way of personal excuse, and he got the thing done quickly.
He would not listen to any plea for a dissolution of
parliament, to any remonstrance about not taking the
sense of the country once more. The mass of anti-Catholic
petitions showed him what might be the state of turmoil
into which the country would be thrown by the question
being referred to it; and the existing state of Ireland
rendered the times too critical for such an experiment.
The will of the Commons was plainly enough declared,
and that was constitutional warrant sufficient for him to
proceed upon; and, being resolved to carry the matter
through, he granted no delay. The opposition in the
Commons was swamped by the union of the liberal and
the ministerial members, and the majority on the first
division was 188 in a House of 508 members. This was
on the motion for going into committee on the 5th of
March. On the 10th, the bill was brought in by Mr.
Peel, and read a first time. The debate took place on the
second reading, which was fixed for the 17th; and the
majority the next night was 180 in favour of the bill. It
issued from the committee on the 27th, not one of the
many amendments proposed having been carried. There
was more debating on the 30th, on occasion of the third
reading, when the House did not adjourn till near four
o'clock in the morning. The majority was 178 in a House
of 462.

On the same evening, the premier brought forward the
bill in the Lords, had it read the first time, and fixed the
second reading for two days afterwards, in the midst of
great clamour about his precipitation. The debate lasted
three nights, and issued in a majority of 105 in favour of
the bill; the numbers being 217 for the second reading,

and 112 against it. It was but nine months since this same House had decided by a majority of 45 against entertaining the question at all—a proof how rapid and threatening had been the march of events in the meantime. As in the Commons, all the amendments proposed were rejected; and on the 10th of April the bill passed, by a majority of 213 to 109.

It was not yet law, however; and there were some who did not even now give up all hope that the bill and the administration would perish together. Of those who had struggled against the measure, Lord Eldon perhaps had toiled the hardest; and he had worked with a stout heart because he believed that he had private reasons for hoping that the king would overthrow the policy of his ministers at the very last. 'What a consistent career has Lord Eldon's been!' wrote a contemporary at this date, 'the ever-active principle of evil in our political world! In the history of the universe, no man has the praise of having effected so much good for his fellow-creatures as Lord Eldon has thwarted.' As he thought this 'the most dangerous measure that was ever brought before parliament,' and as he believed that it would inevitably occasion the destruction of the Church, the aristocracy, and the monarchy, it was natural that he should use every art of procrastination, and all possible emphasis of warning, while the measure was in progress; and that he should record his protest, comprehending ten grounds of dissent, on the journals, when all other means of opposition were exhausted; but those who observed him were surprised that he appeared to forget his misery at the last. He looked cheerful, and indulged in jocularity; insomuch that Lord Holland, taking up a proverb just quoted by Lord Eldon, said, that in opposition he had 'come in like a lion, and gone out like a lamb.' The secret of this was, that Lord Eldon had been admitted by the king, and after two very long conversations, was not without hope that the sovereign would, as he called it, do his duty at last—stand by the constitution, and disappoint the Catholics. We have learned, by the bringing to light of Lord Eldon's private papers, much of what passed in these two interviews; and it is well, for the truth of history, that we know thus

much of what the ministers had to struggle with, in their
dealings with a sovereign who, according to this record,
was as unscrupulous with regard to truth, as he was weak
and passionate.

The first interview took place on the 28th of March,
two days before the Relief Bill left the Commons; and it
lasted about four hours. The king seems to have opened
by a statement so manifestly untrue, that Lord Eldon,
who 'refuted this allegation of the king's' in his private
memorandum, must have seen how cautiously he ought to
receive the complaints of the present ministers which
followed. 'His majesty employed a very considerable
portion of time in stating all that he represented to have
passed when Mr. Canning was made minister, and expressly stated that Mr. Canning would never, and that he
had engaged that he would never, allow him to be troubled
about the Roman Catholic question. He blamed all the
ministers who had retired upon Canning's appointment;
represented, in substance, that their retirement, and not
he, had made Canning minister. He excepted from this
blame, in words, myself.' This is as foolish as it is clearly
false; but his majesty was not at this time affirming 'on
the word of a king,' but indulging in the fretfulness and
helpless anger of a child; in which state men will sometimes, like passionate children, say anything that their
passion suggests. , And this helpless being was he whom
his ministers, weighed down by responsibility, had to call
master, and to implicate in their work !

'He complained that he had never seen the bills; that
the condition of Ireland had not been taken into consideration; that the Association Bill had been passed through
both Houses before he had seen it; that it was a very
inefficient measure compared to those which he had in
vain himself recommended; that the other proposed
measures gave him the greatest possible pain and uneasi-
ness; that he was in the state of a person with a pistol
presented to his breast; that he had nothing to fall back
upon; that his ministers had threatened—I think he said
twice, at the time of my seeing him—to resign, if the
measures were not proceeded in, and that he had said to
them " Go on," when he knew not how to relieve himself

from the state in which he was placed; and that, in one of those meetings, when resignation was threatened, he was urged to the sort of consent he gave, by what passed in the interview between him and his ministers, till the interview and the talk had brought him into such a state, that he hardly knew what he was about when he, after several hours, said " Go on."   He then repeatedly expressed himself as in a state of the greatest misery, repeatedly saying : " What can I do?   I have nothing to fall back upon ;" and musing for some time, and then again repeating the same expression.'

It is clear that the king had given his ministers his formal sanction to proceed, on their presenting the alternative of their resigning.   It was mere childishness now to say that he was in such a state that he did not know what he was about ; and it is astonishing that he could for a moment think of drawing back, or suppose that Lord Eldon could suggest or sanction such a retractation.   This appears to be what he was aiming at throughout these two interviews ; but, well as the old Tory would have liked to see the measure destroyed, he could not assume the responsibility of encouraging the king to withdraw his royal word.   The whole demeanour of the king appears to convey the impression that he thought his ministers were doing something wilful and wanton in proposing relief to the Catholics.   Throughout the two interviews, he speaks as if the premier and Mr. Peel had taken it into their heads to gratify the Catholics, purely for the purpose of teasing their sovereign.   He thinks and speaks of no one but himself; dwells only on his own annoyance, never even alluding to the state of the Catholics, or of the kingdom at large.

' After a great deal of time spent,' Lord Eldon's account continues, ' in which his majesty was sometimes silent— apparently uneasy—occasionally stating his distress, the hard usage he had received, his wish to extricate himself —that he knew not what to look to, what to fall back upon—that he was miserable beyond what he could express—I asked him whether his majesty, so frequently thus expressing himself, meant either to enjoin me, or to forbid me, considering or trying whether anything could be found or arranged, upon which he *could* fall back. He said : " *I neither enjoin you to do so, nor forbid you to do so ;* but, for God's sake, take care that I am not exposed to the humiliation of being again placed in such circumstances, that I must submit again to pray of my present ministers that they will remain with me." He appeared to me to be exceedingly miserable, and intimated that he would see me again.'

Within a fortnight after, on the 9th of April, the day before the bill passed the Lords, the old earl went again to the king, with more addresses. The interview lasted three hours, the first portion of the time being occupied with complaints and expressions of misery uttered in almost the same words as before. At length Lord Eldon spoke, and courageously. He reports :

'I told him that his late majesty, when he did not mean that a measure proposed to him should pass, expressed his determination in the most early stage of the business; if it seemed to himself necessary to dissent, he asked no advice about dismissing his ministers. He made that his own act—he trusted to what he had to hope for from his subjects, who . . . . . could not leave him unsupported ; that, on the other hand, there could not but be great diffi culties in finding persons willing to embark in office, when matters had proceeded to the extent to which the present measure had been carried—as was supposed, and had been *represented—after full explanation of them to his majesty,* and he had so far assented. This led to his mentioning again what he had to say as to his assent. In the former inter- view it had been represented that, after much conversation, *twice* with his ministers, or such as had come down, he had said " Go on ; " and upon the latter of *those two* occasions, after many hours' fatigue, and exhausted by the fatigue of conversation, he had *said* "Go on." He now produced *two papers*, which he represented as copies of what he had written to them, *in which he assents to their proceeding and going on with the bill*, adding certainly in each, as he read them, very strong expressions of the pain and misery the proceedings gave him. It struck me at the time, that I should, if I had been in office, have felt considerable diffi- culty about going on after reading such expressions; but whatever might be fair observation as to giving, or not, effect to those expressions, *I told his majesty it was impossible to maintain that his assent had not been expressed,* or to cure the evils which were consequential, after the bill, in such circumstances, had been read a second time, and in the Lords' House with a majority of 105. This led him to much conversation on that fact, that he had, he said, been deserted by an aristocracy that had supported his father; that, instead of 45 against the measure, there were twice that number of peers for it; that everything was revolutionary—everything was tending to revolution—and the peers and the aristocracy were giving way to it. They, he said more than once or twice more, supported his father, but see what they had done to *him.* I took the liberty to say that I agreed that matters were tending rapidly to revolution. . . . . But I thought it only just to some of the peers who voted for the bill to suppose that they had been led, or misled, to believe that his majesty had agreed and consented to it. He then began to talk about the coronation oath.' It was rather late to be taking that matter to heart, after all the years that had passed, during which he had let it be understood that he should not, in the matter of the oath, follow the example of his father and the Duke of York. When this point was discussed, and it was settled that every man must do as he thinks right in taking any oath, without making any one else responsible :

'Little more passed, except occasional bursts of expression : "What can I do? What can I now fall back upon? What can I fall back upon? I am miserable, wretched, my situation is dreadful; nobody about me to advise with. If I do give my assent, I'll go to the baths abroad, and from thence to Hanover; I'll return no more to England— I'll make no Roman Catholic peers—I will not do what this bill will enable me to do—I'll return no more—let them get a Catholic king in Clarence." I think he also mentioned Sussex. "The people will see that I did not wish this." There were the strongest appearances, certainly, of misery. He, more than once, stopped my leaving him. When the time came that I was to go, he threw his arms round my neck, and expressed great misery.'

Though Lord Eldon told the king that it was impossible to draw back, he certainly entertained hopes that refusal, or at least delay, might yet be expected. He says : ' I certainly thought, when I left him, that he would express great difficulty when the bill was proposed for the royal assent—great, but which would be overcome—about giving it. I fear that it seemed to be given as matter of course.' It was with great horror that the old earl heard the conclusion of the business. ' April 14, 1829.—The fatal bills received the royal assent yesterday afternoon. After all I had heard in my visits, not a day's delay! God bless us, and His Church !'

What else could the helpless sovereign do, when even his friend, the late chancellor, told him that he could not draw back? Delay could have done no good, and might have cost him dear. The only thing he could now do was to exhibit his temper towards his ministers, and all friends of the Catholics. He particularly requested the attendance of Lord Eldon at his next levee; and he distinguished him by attentions which contrasted strongly with his coldness towards those who were 'in the high places of office.' This gracious reception, however, did not make Lord Eldon quite happy. 'I was grieved,' he says, 'that my visit was a visit of duty to a sovereign whose supremacy is shared by that Italian priest, as Shakspeare calls the pope. But I heard that he much wished it, and I understood that it would be a relief if I would go. . . . . He is certainly very wretched about the late business. It is a pity he has not the comfort of being free from blame himself.' The king's manner was observed, as he intended it should be. Two days afterwards, Lord Eldon writes : 'The universal talk here is about the manner in which the king, at the levee, received the voters for the Catholics—most uncivilly—markedly so towards the lords spiritual, the bishops who so voted—and the civility with which he received the anti-Catholic voters, particularly the bishops. It seems to be very general talk now, that his ministers went much beyond what they should have said in parliament, as to his consent to the measure. Consent, however, he certainly did; but with a language of reluctance, pain, and misery, which, if it had been represented, would have prevented a great deal of that ratting which carried the measure.'

Such was the monarch in whose name the ministers were compelled to act, and such the temper and conduct they had to bear with from him. Such was 'the first gentleman in England'—casting himself on the neck of his old adviser, bemoaning himself like a child, and indulging himself in persecuting the peers for their opinions, after having, by his message, demanded their opinions on Catholic relief, and led the way. His gentlemanliness might be very striking to those who were in his presence; but it is not very conceivable to us now, when we find it did not preserve him from agitation and passion, from such despotism as he could use, and from extreme personal rudeness. We hardly know which to wonder at most— his rebellion against a necessity of which he could not have been ignorant, or his reputation for good-manners.

On looking back to this time, nothing is more surprising than the quietness with which the disfranchisement of the forty-shilling freeholders took place. There were some few who saw and exposed the badness of the proceeding; but they were very few; and the very men who ought to have understood and been faithful to the principle of the case—the very men who, in the same session spoke and voted for parliamentary reform—helped to extinguish the political liberties of the 'forties.' Mr. Brougham regarded it as 'the almost extravagant price of the inestimable good' which would arise from Catholic emancipation. Sir J. Mackintosh declared it a tough morsel which he had found it hard to swallow. Lord Duncannon, Lord Palmerston, and Mr. Huskisson, tried another method. They did what argument could do to obtain the inestimable good, without paying the extravagant price which they did not conceive to be necessary. If they had been duly supported by all the friends of parliamentary reform, there is little doubt that the relief of the Catholics might have been obtained without the sacrifice of so vast an amount of political rights. But among the silent and idle was O'Connell, who threw overboard his beloved 'forties,' after pledging his life to destruction, and his soul to perdition, if he ever again slighted their liberties; and in a case where O'Connell so failed, we have little power of censure to spare for meaner offenders.

The two sides of the case were stated to be these. The Irish landlords had split up their estates into small properties for their own political purposes; and the long trains of adherents had followed their great man to the polling-booth, as obediently as sheep go to the water, till the recent period when the forties were secured by O'Connell and the priests on behalf of the Catholic cause. The landlords would now have been glad to be able to undo their work, to consolidate these small properties, and get rid of the forties. But this was a work which can never be undone. No earthquake came to swallow up the forties; no volcano overflowed to fuse their little properties into one. The landlords therefore desired that the men whom they had made freeholders should be disfranchised. They pleaded, and truly, that these multitudes were led by the priests, and that their numbers were so great as to swamp all the rest of the county constituency; so that the representation of the Irish counties would be wholly in the hands of the Catholic leaders. The wish of many landlords was that the franchise should be restricted within a twenty-pound qualification; but the government would not hear of any thing higher than a ten-pound franchise.

The pleas on the other side were of the iniquity of playing fast and loose in this manner with political liberties, and of treating a merely inconvenient constituency in the same manner as a corrupt one. No corruption, no moral disqualification, was alleged against the forties. They had at first been under the influence of the Protestant landlords, and they were now under that of the Catholic priests; but every principle of political morality taught that the true remedy for such dependence was, not in retrogression, but in promoting the freedom and enlightenment of the class so easily led. There was irreparable mischief in visiting with the same penalties the superstitious voters who were led by their priests, and the corrupt who were bought with gold. As for considerations of expediency, the worst dangers, the only appreciable dangers arising from this large constituency, would be over when the Catholic Relief Bill was passed. Formidable

as the action of this constituency might be when directed
towards objects not yet legalised, it could no longer be
mischievous when Catholics had free entrance into parliament. If every county in Ireland should send Catholic
members to parliament, where was the evil? It could
only happen through the real preponderance of Catholics
in the constituency, and would afford a fair representation,
while the Catholic element in the legislature would still
be small in the presence of the Protestantism of the rest of
the empire. It ought not to be forgotten, too, by the
friends of the Catholics, that their relief had been obtained
by this very constituency whom it was now proposed to
disfranchise. Those friends of the Catholics were bound
by every obligation of principle and feeling to resist such
a demolition of political rights as was proposed in return
for action so beneficial. But, admitting these things in
the main, and scarcely attempting to excuse themselves,
almost all the friends of the Catholics voted for the disfranchisement of the forties. The bill for that object
accompanied the Catholic Relief Bill through both Houses,
and received the royal assent at the same time. In each
House only seventeen voted in favour of the rights of the
forties, while the majority in favour of their disfranchisement was 122 in the Lords, and 206 in the Commons.
Among the voters, we do not find the names of Mr. Huskisson, and some others who spoke against the Disfranchisement Bill. They contented themselves with stating
the grounds of their disapprobation, and then stultified
their speeches by voting with the government or not at
all. The quietness with which the decision of parliament
was received in Ireland, was a remarkable evidence of the
importance of the great measure of relief. Every one was
engrossed with that. The association sat no longer, and
could not therefore remonstrate. O'Connell strove to turn
away attention from the wrongs of the forties whom he
had deserted, and to occupy all minds with the great boon
just obtained, and the spectacle of his attempt to take his
seat. No one could have believed beforehand that so
sweeping a disfranchisement of any class in society could
have taken place with so little remonstrance or threat of
retribution.

It was thought by many persons that the dignity of the Catholic Relief Bill was lowered by its containing a clause evidently intended to exclude Mr. O'Connell from parliament till he should have been re-elected. There was, perhaps, a strong temptation to show him up to his followers, to whom he had pledged his reputation as a lawyer that he could sit in parliament without taking the oaths. The point might have been regarded as still disputable if Mr. O'Connell had been allowed to take his seat, in any manner, without being re-elected; and therefore the admission to parliament, by means of the new oath, was limited to the case of 'any person professing the Roman Catholic religion, who shall after the commencement of this act be returned as a member of the House of Commons.' The matter was easily settled by this clause; but there were many who thought it a pity that justice should stoop from her height to humble and annoy an individual who was virtually triumphant. The discussion occasioned by Mr. O'Connell's claiming his seat without a new election was considered by the country an extraordinary spectacle; and not a little astonishment was expressed at the difficulty which the House seemed to find in settling the bearings of a law just passed by themselves.

Mr. O'Connell, supported by Lords Ebrington and Duncannon, presented himself to be sworn at the table of the House of Commons, on the 15th of May. He was not, after all, the first Catholic member who so presented himself; for Lord Surrey, the son of the Duke of Norfolk, had been elected for Horsham during the Easter recess, and had taken his seat; but the strongest interest naturally attached to the appearance of Mr. O'Connell. The clerk offered the oath which had been repealed by the late act; and Mr. O'Connell objected to it, on the ground that it was no longer in force, its repeal being distinctly declared in the new act. The clerk communicated the objection to the speaker, who had, of course, made up his mind what to do and say. He addressed the House, declaring his opinion that the election having taken place under the old law, the oaths imposed by the old law must be taken, to entitle any member to sit in that House. The House might be appealed to by petition from without, or by the question being raised within itself. Meantime, Mr. O'Connell must withdraw. As soon as Mr. O'Connell had withdrawn, Mr. Brougham moved that he should be recalled, in order to be heard in regard to his claim. Every one was aware that he must be heard. As it required some consideration whether he should be heard at the table or at the bar, the debate was adjourned from the present Friday to Monday the 18th. On that day, Mr. O'Connell spoke at length at the bar, and astonished some of his hearers as much by the gentlemanly moderation of his tone and manner as by the strength of his pleas. When he finished, opinion was very much divided as to his construction of his case; and some proposed that, as there appeared even to the lawyers to be doubt, Mr. O'Connell should have the benefit of the doubt, and be at once admitted on taking the new oath. There would, however, have been no real kindness to him and his constituents in so admitting him as to leave room for any question as to the legality of his position; and the true reason for the proposal probably was, the desire to avoid the excitement of a new Clare election at that time. The solicitor-general having moved that Mr. O'Connell was not entitled to sit without first taking the oath of supremacy, the question was pressed to a division, when the numbers were 190 to 116 in favour of Mr. O'Connell's exclusion.

When Mr. O'Connell appeared at the bar, the next day, to hear the decision of the House, he was asked whether he was ready to take the oath of supremacy. He requested permission to look at the oath; and, after considering it for a short time, observed: 'I see in this oath, one assertion, as to a matter of fact, which I know is not true; and I see in it another assertion, as to a matter of opinion, which I believe is not true. I therefore refuse to take this oath.' Then ensued some discussion as to whether a writ should be issued for a new election, or an act be passed for the relief of Mr. O'Connell, in order to avoid the excitement of a new election; but the issue of the writ was agreed to without a division.

Mr. O'Connell was elected without opposition; but not for this was the language of his addresses and speeches the less violent and outrageous. He left not a moment's

doubt in the mind of any one of his intention to keep up
agitation in Ireland, by means as indefensible in themselves as ever, while they had no longer the excuse of
being the resort of a man under persecution. The atrocity
of his language in regard to all English statesmen is
scarcely credible now, even when the speeches themselves
are before our eyes; and this incendiarism of course
appears worse after his having shown how mild and
moderate he could appear away from home, and among
persons too enlightened to be animated by violent language.
He pledged himself to obtain the repeal of everything
objectionable in the new act—the disfranchisement of the
forties, and the checks upon the increase of monachism in
Ireland. He promised everything the Irish would like
to have, if the county of Clare would return him now;
and among other things, the repeal of the union. From
this time the cry of repeal was Mr. O'Connell's tool for
cultivating the agitation by which, in regard to mind
fame, and fortune, he lived. From this time he was dishonoured in the eyes of all upright men. Up to this time
he had had a good cause, and was truly the hero of it
There was many another good cause yet to be advocated
for Ireland, of which he might have been the hero—of
which he must have been the hero, if he had had in him
anything of the heroic element. But from this time, his
true glory was extinguished. He rose in influence, power,
and notoriety, to an eminence such as no other individual
citizen has attained in modern times in our country; but
the higher he rose in these respects, the deeper he sank in
the esteem of those whose esteem is essential to the establishment of true fame. Up to this time, he might be a
patriot, though his methods were too much those of a
demagogue; up to this time, he had a clear, definite, and
virtuous aim before him, and he followed it to the point of
success; but henceforward he professed aims which were
not only unreal, but which he evidently did not expect
that rational people could suppose to be real. Henceforward there was no more stability, no more of the
dignity which is involved in a noble cause: he made men
fear him, court him, groan under him, admire him, and, as
regards the ignorant lower class of Irish, adore him; but

from this moment, no man respected him. After his addresses at the second Clare election, there could be no more mistake about O'Connell.

The Catholic Association assembled again, under the name of an 'aggregate meeting' of the Catholics, to promote the re-election of Mr. O'Connell. The rent was still in existence—a large balance of its funds being in the hands of the treasurers, and disposable only at the bidding of the body which had collected it. Five thousand pounds of this money were voted towards the expenses of the new elections. On the 30th of July, Mr. O'Connell was returned without opposition, nearly a month after parliament had risen; so that he did not take his seat till the opening of the next session—February, 1830.

Here, then, we have witnessed the close of one of the most important controversies which ever agitated society in any age or country. In significance it perhaps yields to no social controversy whatever; in importance it must of course yield to some few great organic questions which concern essential principles of government. It must be considered as of less importance, for instance, in a large view, than the question of reform of parliament. But it was practically, and on a near view, of more pressing urgency than any other, or than all others put together; and under the pressure of this urgency, men generally judged amiss of the issues—as men are wont to do in circumstances so critical. The No-Popery terrorists were scarcely more mistaken in their anticipations of woe and destruction from the emancipation of the Catholics than the liberal politicians of the time were in their expectations of the contentment and tranquillity which were to ensue in Ireland. The last reasonably laughed at the hobgoblin images of the pope and the Jesuits which the London Tories and Irish Orangemen conjured up, to frighten themselves and everybody else whom they could alarm; they reasonably insisted on the impossibility of doing anything for Ireland till this measure of relief should be granted; but they unreasonably went further in their expectations, and concluded that the tranquillity of Ireland would follow from the measure of relief. Mr. O'Connell had said that it would; but all who looked at the aspect

of affairs for themselves, setting at nought the word of Mr.
O'Connell as it deserved, saw that Mr. O'Connell never
meant that Ireland should be tranquillised; and that if
he had wished for her tranquillisation ever so earnestly,
he could not have effected it. A sudden change in the law
could not make a permanent change in the temper of a
nation—even of a nation which knew how to reverence
law. But by the Irish, the function and the value of law
had never been understood; and it was now Mr. O'Connell's daily and nightly care that the people should not be
the better disposed towards the law for its having become
favourable to them. In his popular addresses at this time,
we find the pervading thought and purpose to be inducing
the people to distrust and despise legislation. He told
them that he had got the new law for them, and could get
as much more as he liked; and he represented the whole
administration of law and justice in Ireland as purposely
hostile to them, and to be regarded only for the sake of
safety, whether in the form of obedience or evasion. He
advocated, both by precept and example, a wholly empirical method of political and social existence, instead of
using his efforts to bring society into a tranquil organic
state. Accordingly, the relief measure appeared to produce no effect whatever upon the temper and troubles of
Ireland. A multitude of Catholics found themselves
deprived of the franchise; and landlords, Protestant and
Catholic, found the value of their property much diminished
by the operation of the same provision. The Orangemen
became more furious and bigoted, through fear and jealousy
of their triumphant neighbours; and those triumphant
neighbours were urged on by their leaders to insufferable
insolence towards the government and sister-nation which
had granted them relief no longer possible to be withheld.
The list of Irish outrages, the pictures of Irish crime which
follow, in the registers of the time, the record of Catholic
emancipation, are very painful; but they show, not that
there was anything wrong in the procedure of relief, but
that it had been too long delayed. There could not have
been stronger evidence that a less generous measure would
have done no good, and much mischief. As it was, there
was no room for regret that the right thing had been done

at last, and done in the freest and amplest spirit and
manner. If there was any cause for regret, it was that it
had not been done long before; and also that even its
promoters should so little understand the operation of
tyrannical restrictions as to believe that their effects would
cease with their existence. Injury may be forgiven, and
even forgotten; insult may be forgiven, though perhaps
never forgotten; but the temper and character generated
under insult and injury cannot, by any process, be changed
at once into a healthful condition of trustfulness, integrity,
and good-humour. The emancipators of the Catholics
therefore had to put up with a different fate from that
which had been predicted for them by the true patriots
and best political prophets who had anticipated a brighter
coming time for Ireland. They had not grateful Ireland
at their feet, relieved from the raging demon—calm,
clothed, and right in mind; but, on the contrary, it could
scarcely be seen whether or no the demon was really cast
out. There was no gratitude, no peace, no trust, no inclination to alliance for great common objects. But then,
on the other hand, there was infinite relief in the sense of
the removal of wrong, in safety from revolution and civil
war, in consciousness that the way was now clear for the
regeneration of Ireland—clear as far as the political conscience of England was concerned. Ireland was not, under
her new emancipation, what her Grattans and Plunkets
had expected, nor what the Cannings and Broughams, and
Wellingtons and Peels, had hoped to see her; but it was
enough for support that the right act was done, and that
the grand obstruction of all was removed; though so many
more were found to exist, that, after a lapse of twenty
years, we see no end to them yet.

CHAPTER VIII.

Admission of Catholic Peers—Changes in the Cabinet—Parliamentary
Reform—Lord Blandford—Duel—Parliamentary Proceedings—
Relations with Portugal—King's Speech.

The Catholic question was so engrossing to the mind of
the whole nation, that the records of the year present few
notices of other subjects. In connection with it, however,
some incidents occurred which are worthy of note.

When the House of Lords assembled after the Easter
holidays, on the 28th of April, there was an unusually
full attendance, and many ladies were present, in expectation of a very interesting spectacle. On the entrance of
a group of persons who proceeded to the table, there was
a profound silence; amidst which, three Catholic peers—
the Duke of Norfolk, Lord Clifford, and Lord Dormer—
took the oaths. They had obtained entrance at last to the
legislative assembly where their fathers sat and ruled
when their faith was that of the whole land. In those
days, the cathedrals were theirs, and the universities, and
the crown, and the legislature; all the ' thrones, domina-
tions, princedoms, virtues, powers,' of the civilised world;
and now, here was a little remnant of the old Catholic
peerage re-entering upon the function of government under
a sad reduction of pomp and circumstance. To the student
of history and the antiquarian, the spectacle was one of
deep and somewhat melancholy interest; but the more
ignorant among the possessors of power looked upon these
peers of ancient lineage as a sort of intruders—as the
newest order of upstarts, whose admission vulgarised their
Protestant legislature, while endangering its Protestantism.
Here, however, was the hereditary earl-marshal of England
present once more as a peer of parliament; and he and his
companions were soon after joined by more of their own
faith. On the 1st of May, Lords Stafford, Petre, and Stour-
ton took the oaths and their seats. Soon after, Lord Eldon

paid a visit to two melancholy duchesses, who showed him their vast collections of Protestant speeches, protestations, and pledges—'some in gold letters'—which, in better days, the ladies had taken for an ample security that no Catholic would ever sit as a legislator; but their sympathising old friend told them they might now throw all those valued securities into the fire. One of these ladies was the wife of 'the young Duke of Richmond, who did very well in all he said during the debates' against the admission of the Catholics, and in opposition to the ministry. Though he failed in his object, he was not without his reward for his opposition. 'I hear,' writes Lord Eldon, 'that he is a great favourite with the king; which seems not to be the fortune, be it good or bad, at this moment, of those addicted to his ministers.'

In the same cause, Sir Charles Wetherell, the attorney general, had made sacrifices. The administration had hoped that he would at least have kept silence on their great measure, though he had refused to prepare the bill; but he held it dishonest to keep silence, threw his whole powers into opposition, and of course was immediately dismissed from his office, in which he was succeeded by Sir James Scarlett, who had been attorney-general under Mr. Canning. Another change was occasioned by the retirement of the lord high admiral, the Duke of Clarence, who was thought, by the straightforward and simple-mannered premier, to have mixed up too much of the popularity-seeking of the heir-presumptive with the business of his office. There had been a vast deal of jaunting and cruising about, presenting of colours, preparation of shows on sea and land, which appeared to the Duke of Wellington to be more expensive and foolish than in any way serviceable; and it is believed that the retirement of the lord high admiral was caused by a plain expression of the premier's opinion on this matter. It is said that on a long account for travelling expenses being sent into the treasury by the lord high admiral, the Duke of Wellington endorsed the paper: 'No travelling expenses allowed to the lord high admiral,' and dismissed it. The health of the Duke of Clarence was unsatisfactory at this time—enough so to justify his retirement without other cause. His office merged again into that of first lord of the admiralty, which was held by Lord Melville, who was succeeded at the Board of Control by Lord Ellenborough. It was believed at the time that the ministers would have liked to offer the privy seal to Lord Grey, but that the king could not be asked to approve of it. Lord Grey's time was approaching; but it was not quite yet. Meantime, the ministers 'took Lord Rosslyn, as another Whig.'

While waiting for Lord Grey, however, the subject of parliamentary reform was not dropped. It was brought forward on the 2nd of June in an extraordinary manner. The Marquis of Blandford declared himself unhappy in the thought that the 'borough-market' was now so thrown open to Catholics, as that there was no longer any security for the liberties of Englishmen, or for the prosperity of their manufactures and commerce. Such an influx of Catholics into parliament might be secured by the purchase of boroughs as that the voice of the nation might be silenced, and Protestantism extinguished. The mover brought forward two resolutions—one declaring that there existed boroughs and small constituencies which might be bought for money; and the other, that the continuance of such boroughs, and of such practices in them, was disgraceful and injurious in every way. The resolutions were negatived by a majority of 74 in a House of 184. The debate, and the occurrence which excited it, occasioned great amusement to the liberal party in the House; and Mr. William Smith observed, that 'one effect he was happy to find, had been produced by the Roman Catholic Relief Bill—an effect which its best friends had not anticipated; it appeared to have transformed a number of the highest Tories in the land to something very nearly resembling Radical reformers.'

A few days before the Relief Bill went up to the Lords, the whole country was electrified by the news that the prime-minister had fought a duel on account of the bill, or rather on the implication of his honour in the bill. These were days when foolish men were more foolish, and hasty men more hasty than usual; and a very foolish and hasty charge against the Duke of Wellington, of designs to overthrow the Church and constitution under **false** pretences, was put forth in the newspapers, in a letter from Lord Winchilsea to the secretary of the committee for establishing King's College, London. It is generally agreed that gentlemen must judge for themselves about the requisitions of their honour; but it certainly appeared to the great majority of the nation rather amusing that the Duke of Wellington should think it any more necessary to vindicate himself against a clumsy charge of secret conspiracy against the constitution, than to show his courage by fighting a duel. A graver question was whether it could be justifiable in the head of the government to risk his life, at a juncture so extraordinary, in a personal quarrel. The duke gives his own view in the letter to Lord Winchilsea which contains his challenge. Every effort had been used to induce the earl to make reparation for his calumnious expressions; which he refused to do, unless the duke would explain how long he had entertained his present political views—a requisition wholly absurd on the face of it. 'The question for me now to decide is this,' the duke wrote on the 20th of March: 'Is a gentleman who happens to be the king's minister to submit to be insulted by any gentleman who thinks proper to attribute to him disgraceful or criminal motives for his conduct as an individual? I cannot doubt of the decision which I ought to make on this question. Your lordship is alone responsible for the consequences.' The earl did not choose to be responsible for the death of the prime-minister of England, at a most critical time in the history of the country; and perhaps he was conscious of wrong. After receiving the duke's fire uninjured, he fired in the air; and then permitted his second to deliver to the second of the Duke of Wellington a declaration of regret and retractation, which he caused to be published in the news-papers. It was an absurd affair; but it might have cost the nation dear.

The distress among the silk-weavers being extreme this year, an attempt was made in parliament to procure a reversal of the free-trade policy of Mr. Huskisson. It was so plainly shown, however, that, whatever the distress might have been in any case, it was aggravated to excess by the ignorance and violence of the unhappy operatives, that the agitation of the subject produced an issue the reverse of that which had been hoped. It was shown that at Coventry the handloom-weavers were thrown out of work by the introduction of machinery, which, instead of learning to use, they attempted to destroy. The London silk-weavers struck for wages which could not be obtained, and destroyed by night the webs and material of workmen who would not join the strike. To revert to the old restrictive policy could be no remedy for evils like these. Instead of this, the duties on raw silk were again lowered, amidst prophecies of ruin within the House, and outside— in Bethnal Green and Spitalfields—scenes of fierce riot, which Mr. Peel declared that he knew to be intended to intimidate the House from lowering the duties.

The budget occupied little time and attention this session. The report of the chancellor of the exchequer was, on the whole, favourable; but the surplus was not greater than was required to be set apart for the reduction of the national debt; and there was therefore no diminution of taxation.

A bill passed the Commons this session for legalising the sale of game. It came up to the Lords supported by the unanimous suffrage of the Lower House. Lord Wharncliffe set before the peers such an array of facts in regard to the corrupting and disorganising effects of the game-laws, as must, one would have thought, have procured an unanimous vote for their modification or repeal from any body of men whatever. But Lord Westmoreland soon showed that there was to be an opposition. He declared that the bill ' would depopulate the country of gentlemen.' This sounded very fearful; for the worst that had been apprehended hitherto was that even the total repeal of the game-laws 'would depopulate the country of' hares and pheasants. His lordship 'was sure that the friends of liberty in the other House must have been asleep when this bill passed.' And now Lord Eldon seems to have thought that the friends of liberty—that is, of aristocratic sports —were napping in a little too much security in the Lords' House. He speaks of his own opposition to the measure, and says : ' The prime-minister opposed this bill also, and we old Tories thought ourselves safe in our views of defeat-

ing it; but many of the old Tories, being very much out
of humour, would not buckle to, and the Whigs, the old
opposition, all sticking together, and, I suppose, courting
popularity with the lower orders by their vote, let the
duke have something like a proof that they were mightier
than he; and so he was in a minority.' The bill was
read a second time by a majority of ten; but the peers
took more care of their 'liberty' next time; and the
majority—of two—was on the other side. The jail must
still be crowded with peasants sent to that school of crime
for catching wild animals; the life of a hare or a pheasant
must still be protected more carefully than the character
and liberty of a man; and still, while hundreds of
thousands of the working-classes were sinking into disease
and death from want of bread, the game of noblemen
was to be encouraged to eat and destroy food to the value
of £5,000,000 in a year. The bill would have done little
in comparison with the reform which was then, and is
still, needed; but that little was refused by the lords of
the soil, who could not have fully known what they were
doing, but who preferred liberty of sporting to the trouble
of inquiring. Lord Eldon's language shows that he was
aware that the game-laws were disliked by 'the lower
orders;' but he was notoriously fond of shooting; and it
seems not to have occurred to him, nor to some wiser and
better men than he, that it is dangerous to pursue an aristocratic amusement at the expense of disgusting the middle,
and corrupting and exasperating the 'lower orders' of their
countrymen. This subject comes up again and again in the
recent history of England; and even yet, the sportsmen
in parliament have not laid aside their tone of levity on
a matter which has in it all the seriousness that can attach
to any political topic whatever. While reviewing the
course and issue of other great questions, the mind occasionally reverts to this yet pending one, with some
wonder, whether in this case as in so many preceding,
there will be insolence, levity, and blindness, to the last
moment, to be succeeded by panic, rapid conversion, and
precipitate legislation. Such a speculation may be laughed
at by those who look at the game-law question as one of
liberty of sporting, regarding merely the pleasures and

privileges of gentlemen, and the lives of hares and birds; but there is another side to it, as we shall have occasion to see hereafter. The true and permanent aspect of the question is that in which it regards the feeding or robbing the hungry—the deterioration or improvement of the land—the filling or emptying of our prisons—the increase or diminution of crime—the oppression or redemption of a million of rural labourers ; one might say, the very existence of society as it is, and is to be. Of course, the game-laws will give way, sooner than our social organisation; but the two cannot much longer exist together ; and when the sportsmen in parliament attain to seeing this, the grave aspect of the question will present itself to them as it does now to those who foresee the end. Meantime, we have noted one of the first attacks on the aristocratic privileges of the gun, and the kind of thought, speech, and temper, which the attack called forth.

One of the most interesting debates of the session was on the subject of our relations with the Queen of Portugal. The conduct of England in preserving her neutrality as to the *de facto* government of Portugal had been apparently so strange as to cause eager and angry discussion, not only on the continent, and on the other side of the Atlantic, but in the British parliament. It is well that cases of such extreme nicety in regard to international honour occur now and then, embarrassing as they may be at the moment ; for so close an appeal to principles is good for the national conscience, and a noble exercise for the national rulers. Seldom has there been a case more trying to flesh and blood than the one before us, or more honourable to the conscience of the government. Thus, at least, is the matter regarded now, at a distance of twenty years; though at the time it was difficult for the majority to enter into the motives of a conduct apparently contradictory.

In August 1828, Lord Aberdeen had been applied to by the Portuguese refugees for permission to send a large quantity of arms and ammunition from England to Brazil. The minister replied that permission would be granted on a pledge from the applicants that the arms and ammunition should not be employed in the civil dissensions in Portugal, in which England was bound, as a neutral power, not to interfere. The pledge was offered; Count Itabayana declaring that he could give a clear and precise reply, that there was no intention of employing these stores in the civil dissensions of Portugal. Yet, the arms and powder were immediately conveyed, not to Brazil, but to Terceira. Terceira, the largest island of the Azores, which are under the dominion of Portugal, had declared in favour of the young queen, and driven off the troops of Don Miguel. The sending these arms there in such a mode awakened the suspicions of our government that men would soon be sent after them; and thus the island would be garrisoned and strengthened by England for war against the actual ruler of Portugal; a proceeding which would have been a direct breach of neutrality. In October, application was made for a conveyance for the Portuguese troops to Terceira. The reply of the Duke of Wellington was, that ' England was determined to maintain a neutrality in the civil dissensions of Portugal, and that the king, with that determination, could not permit the ports and arsenals of England to be made places of equipment for hostile armaments.' He intimated also that the 4000 Portuguese troops could not be allowed to remain in any English port, as a military body, ready for action. All needful hospitality should be shown them; but they must disband, and distribute themselves over the neighbouring towns and villages, or wherever they pleased, and not remain concentrated in Plymouth. The answer was, that sooner than separate and dissolve their military organisation, they would go to Brazil. The duke's reply was, that we did not wish to send them away, but that they could repair to Brazil if they chose; and a British convoy was offered to protect them from Portuguese cruisers. This convoy was declined. In the next December, application was made for permission and means of transport to send the refugees, unarmed, to Terceira; and this was refused on the ground of the former deception. The applicants were told: ' We have been already deceived; you profess to sail as unarmed men, but you will find arms on your arrival at Terceira.' The profession then, on the part of the Portuguese leaders, was that they were going to Brazil; but the government were aware that

they sailed with false clearances, which were obtained
at the custom-house as for Gibraltar, for Virginia, and for
other places. The expedition consisted of four vessels,
which carried 652 officers and men, under the command
of General Count Saldanha, who had been the Portuguese
war-minister under the constitution. Distinct notice had
been given to the heads of the expedition that any attempt
to land at Terceira would be prevented; and that a British
force would be found ready for the purpose stationed off
the island.

A small force of armed vessels had, in fact, been despatched under the command of Captain Walpole, of the
Ranger, with instructions to cruise off the island, and to
inform the Portuguese under Saldanha, if they appeared,
that he had authority to prevent their landing. 'And,'
continued the instructions, ' should they persist, notwithstanding such warning, in hovering about, or in making
any efforts to effect a landing, you are then to use force
to drive them away from that neighbourhood, and keep
sight of them until you shall be convinced by the course
they may steer, and the distance they may have proceeded,
that they have no intention of returning to the Western
Islands.' As Captain Walpole was keeping his watch, on
the 16th of January, off Port Praya, in Terceira, the
expedition appeared. The vessel which carried Saldanha
came first. It paid no attention to the two shots fired
by the *Ranger* to bring them to; and appeared resolved
to push into port at all hazards. Captain Walpole was
compelled to fire; and his shot killed one man and wounded
another. That single shot echoed round the world; and it
was years before the reverberation died away. Everybody
in all countries, who did not know what had passed unseen,
asked what this could mean. England had received the
young queen and her adherents with all hospitality and encouragement; had withdrawn her ambassador from Lisbon
on the avowal of Don Miguel's usurpation; and now was
firing upon the young queen's troops, when they were
entering the port of an island which had remained faithful
to her. The most mortifying comment was that of the
usurper. Don Miguel announced in the *Lisbon Gazette*,
that, ' the conduct of England towards Portugal, in such

circumstances, had been above all praise.' The steady
reply of the English government was that we were not at
war with Portugal; and we should not go to war with
Portugal while her conflicts were civil. Our obligations
were to defend her, on her own appeal, against foreign
aggression; and beyond these obligations we would not go.
Our immediate business was to preserve our neutrality.

Captain Walpole's shot compelled Saldanha to a conference, at the end of which he declared that he considered
the whole expedition prisoners to the English. Captain
Walpole took care not to indicate the direction in which
the Portuguese should depart; and he told them to go
where they pleased; only not to stay where they were.
They sailed westwards; and he followed them, Saldanha
keeping up the affectation of supposing him the captor of
the expedition. On the 24th, when the vessels were
within five hundred miles of Scilly, Captain Walpole
thought it time to put an end to this pretence, lest any
colour should be afforded, by their simultaneous arrival in
the Channel, to the charge that England had violated her
neutrality, to the injury of the constitutional cause. He
therefore sent to ask Saldanha where he was going.
Saldanha expressed astonishment at the question, and said
that prisoners of war always went wherever their captors
chose to lead them. Captain Walpole, declaring that
Saldanha's conduct determined him to escort the expedition
no further, turned back to Terceira, where he intercepted
another vessel charged with Portuguese officers, and fitted
out from London. The vessel was just about to enter
Port Praya. Captain Walpole supplied her with water and
provisions, and bade her go. The case of the Portuguese
does seem hard when viewed by itself; but their repeated
deceptions show their own consciousness that they had no
right to involve a neutral power, whose hospitality they
were receiving, in their political conflicts. If they had
brought their vessels and stores from Portugal or Brazil,
or from any country beyond the limit of Portuguese
alliance, it would have been well and good; but their
conduct, however palliated by the temptation and distress
of their circumstances, was not such as the English government could allow to pass unrebuked and unexplained.

Don Miguel's conduct was not such as to permit any reasonable person to suppose that the English government could have any partiality on his behalf. He set aside the sentences of the courts on political prisoners when they were not severe enough to please him; and actually caused death to be inflicted by his own mere order, when transportation had been decreed by the judges. He imprisoned multitudes, and confiscated their goods to himself without any pretence of law; and even attempted the life of his sister, the late regent, with his own hand. The princess was suspected by him of having sent a servant to England, with money and jewels, to save her property from his rapacious grasp. He rushed, armed, into her chamber, and demanded an account of the departure of this servant. When she did not reply, he rushed upon her with a bayonet which was fixed upon a pistol in his hand. She grappled with him, and actually threw him down. He sprang up, and again attacked her; but by this time her chamberlain was in the way. Don Miguel stabbed the chamberlain in the arm, and fired his pistol at the princess. The ball killed a servant by her side, but she was rescued by other servants, who came at the noise of the scuffle. Under such a sovereign, Portugal indeed deserved the pity expressed for her misfortunes in the king's speech, delivered by commission, at the close of the session of 1829, on the 24th of June: 'It is with increased regret that his majesty again adverts to the condition of the Portuguese monarchy. But his majesty commands us to repeat his determination to use every effort to reconcile conflicting interests, and to remove the evils which press so heavily upon a country, the prosperity of which must ever be an object of his majesty's solicitude.'

The speech announced, in decorous terms, that the war with Turkey was turned over to Russia. Ambassadors from France and England were on their way to Constantinople; and Russia had not, on account of her own quarrel with the Porte, withdrawn her name from the negotiations for the final pacification of Greece. The king thanked his parliament for their attention to the affairs of Ireland and the Catholics, which he had especially recommended to their deliberations; and sincerely hoped that the important measures they had passed would tranquillise Ireland, and draw closer the bonds of union between her and the rest of the empire.

The king was not gone to the German baths and Hanover, leaving 'Clarence' or 'Sussex' to be king of the Catholics. He remained in seclusion at Windsor, Brighton, or London. It was generally understood that he was ill, and universally suspected that he was very miserable. The close of his unhappy life was now not far off; and the state of certain foreign affairs troubled him almost as much as the achievements of his own ministers and parliament at home.

CHAPTER IX.

It was about the political state of France that the king and ministers of England were troubled at the close of the year 1829. By that time, indeed, their relations of sympathy with the government of France were becoming the cause of more reasonable anxiety than even feelings of mutual hostility could have been. To understand this, we must look back a little.

At the time when Mr. Canning sent British troops to Portugal to repel aggressions from Spain, which were supported by France, there were three parties in France by whom England was very differently regarded. In 1827, indeed, there was such disorder in the political state of France, that there was scarcely any subject on which the three great parties were not in bitter enmity against each other; and Mr. Canning's foreign policy was naturally a prominent topic.

The French king and his government justified England, in word, as well as by the act of recalling their own ambassadors from Madrid, on occasion of Ferdinand's interference with Portugal. But they had their cause of quarrel with Mr. Canning. They vehemently resented his expressions about the occupation of Spain by the French in 1823; about his method of baffling her policy by separating the South American colonies from Spain; and about the power which would be wielded by England in the event of a war of opinion in Europe. This ruling party, called the moderate royalist party, was, in 1827, supposed to be the strongest. The other two were the ultra-royalist, which would have supported Ferdinand through everything, would have placed and upheld Don Miguel on the throne of Portugal, would have made the Jesuits masters of education in France, and which hated England to the last extremity; and the liberal party, which justified Mr. Canning throughout, and sought to make their own liberties approximate to those of England.

Men could hardly tell, at the commencement of the session of 1827, how to account for the agitation and turbulence pervading society in France, of which every one was sensible. Everybody was expecting that something fearful would happen soon; yet no one seemed to know why. The minister Villèle was extremely unpopular; but this appeared to be rather on account of something he was expected to do, than from anything he had yet done. The financial statement of the session was very favourable. It came out afterwards that it was delusive, and that the condition of the people in the provinces was deplorable; but this was not yet understood in Paris. From some unknown cause, everything seemed thrown out of its course, so that events were no longer calculable, nor political bodies reliable. In the preceding session, the minister had been perplexed by the new Chamber of Peers, where he had supposed he might have altogether his own way. The peers had rejected his project of a kind of law of primogeniture, and had refused to tolerate the presence of the Jesuits in establishments of public instruction. The other chamber sank in the national estimation from day to day; and in proportion the liberal party within it rose into strength and influence. The newspaper press harassed the minister by its unremitting hostility; while the journals, which he held at his disposal, had scarcely any readers. The minister saw that he must either resign or put down the press. Unhappily for himself and his trust, he chose the latter course; and here was the first thunder-clap of the tempest whose distant mutterings had held the nation in dread.

During the preceding year, the bishops had been urgent with the government to restrain the licentiousness of the press, and the ministerial majority of the Chamber of Deputies had carried addresses for the same object; and now at the opening of the session, a bill was brought in, which must have gratified the expectations of the bishops and the Tory deputies to the utmost. This bill was the production of Peyronnet, keeper of the seals, and minister of justice. Hitherto the law had provided that five copies of every new work should be deposited in the appropriate government department. But this deposit was made at the moment of publication, allowing no time for revision by the police—a purpose never contemplated in the arrangement. Now, it was to be enacted, that no work of twenty sheets and under should be exposed for sale, or be allowed, in any portion, to leave the printing-office, till five complete days had elapsed from the period of deposit; nor any work of above twenty sheets, till after the expiration of ten days. The penalties were fines and confiscation of the edition. So much for works not periodical. As for periodicals, cheapness was to be done away with by the imposition of heavy stamps. The publication of the political journals was to be rendered almost impossible by restrictions as to proprietorship and editorship; and all proprietors whose case did not come within the conditions of the new law — all women, minors, and partners, beyond the number of five—were to find their property in journals extinguished within thirty days from the passing of the law unless they could previously accomplish a forced sale. Fines and other punishments, and stamp-duties, were heavily augmented. A fine of five

hundred francs (about £21) was ordained for every article
relating to the private life of any Frenchman living, or any
foreigner resident in France, without express permission
being obtained from the individual noticed; and, lest
there should be any remissness in such individuals, from
a dislike to bringing their private affairs under the notice
of the courts, it was provided that the public prosecutor
might take up the case if the aggrieved party did not.

It is worth while giving this brief sketch of Peyronnet's
atrocious law of the press, to show what the Bourbon
government of France was in its latter day. The wickedness of bringing forward such a law in the nineteenth
century can be equalled only by the folly and blindness
of the venture. The king and his ministers might as
reasonably and hopefully have proposed to put a padlock
on the tongue of every Frenchman.

The chamber would hardly listen to the description of
the law when it was proposed. One of the deputies, M.
Casimir Périer, quitting his seat, exclaimed: ' You might
as well propose a law for the suppression of printing in
France, for the benefit of Belgium.' Shouts of surprise
and indignation burst forth at intervals; and at the close
of Peyronnet's speech, there was too much confusion to
permit the continuance of business. Of course, the journals
all came out furiously the next day; all except the ministerial papers, which nobody read. At the earliest possible
moment, petitions began to pour in from the remotest of
the provinces. The most striking, however, of the myriad
of remonstrances called forth by the occasion was that of
the French Academy. It was particularly striking on
account of the undue subservience to royalty for which
that great society was notorious. But this law was too
obviously injurious to the interests of science and literature
to be allowed to pass without the strongest protest that
could be offered by the association which represented the
science and literature of France. Of the 28 members who
attended the discussion as to what should be done, 18
voted for the remonstrance, and 4 went away without
voting, leaving only 6 in favour of keeping quiet under
the infliction. M. Michaud was one of the speakers who
exposed the consequences of the law; and the three mem-

bers who were charged with the preparation of the remonstrance were MM. Chateaubriand, Lacratelle, and
Villemain. The next day, Villemain was deprived of his
office in the privy-council; and the government newspaper
announced that M. Michaud was no longer one of the
readers to the royal family, nor M. Lacratelle dramatic
censor. Crowds immediately assembled before the houses
of these three gentlemen, thus dismissed from office; and
subscriptions were set on foot for the publication of works
which it was known that they were preparing. The
director of the academy requested an audience of the king,
to present the memorial; and the king refused to see the
director of the academy. He could not yet, however,
prevent the French nation seeing the remonstrance; for
it was published, and spread far and wide.

Though the government was more powerful in the
Chamber of Deputies—of which it had controlled the
elections—than anywhere else, it had a severe struggle
to obtain a majority in the committee which was to
consider the bill; and, after all, the provisions of the law
were so altered and softened that the minister hardly
knew his own bill when it came forth from committee.
He obtained the restoration of some of its original clauses;
and the bill was sent up to the peers by a majority of 233
votes to 134. It was commonly said that, if it passed the
peers, not more than three or four journals would continue
to appear in Paris; and the ministers took no pains to
conceal that this was exactly what they wished.

While the peers were occupied with the bill, the deputies were invited to pass a measure to secure themselves
against newspaper reporters. Speech was to be repressed
in every direction. Men were not silenced yet, however;
and they made the king aware of their opinions. The
committee of the peers began their work by calling before
them the chief printers and booksellers of Paris, to give
evidence as to the probable operation of the law, if passed.
Putting this together with the fact that, of the seven who
composed the committee, four were of liberal politics, the
government must have seen pretty clearly what the result
was likely to be. Just at that time (April 16), the king
reviewed some of his troops and the National Guard; and

the ominous silence with which he was received seems to have struck upon his heart. He called his ministers to council the next day, and declared his will that the bill for the regulation of the press should be withdrawn. It is said that Peyronnet's appearance in the Chamber of Deputies on this 17th of April was really forlorn. He was embarrassed; his voice faltered; and the listening members could scarcely catch the words of the royal ordinance. They were immediately repeated loudly enough, however. The 30,000 journeymen who would have been deprived of bread by the passage of this law, caught up the news, and spread it over Paris; and the whole city was presently blazing with illuminations and fireworks. The rejoicings of the people were regarded by the ministers as manifestations of revolutionary tendencies; and no one member of the administration as yet offered to resign.

It had been arranged, before this issue, that the king should review the National Guard on the 29th of April, 'in token of his satisfaction at their zeal in his honour, on the anniversary of his return to Paris.' Some doubt had arisen in regard to the loyalty of a portion of this popular force; and there was a question whether the review should take place in the court of the Tuileries—which was not the most popular locality. The king, however, declined to alter the announcement given; and the occasion was prepared for, as a great fête-day. When the king appeared, surrounded by his brilliant staff, and followed by the whole royal family, none but loyal cries were heard; but, after a time, a voice here and there from the ranks shouted: 'Down with the ministers!' 'Down with the Jesuits!' The officers and comrades of those who thus shouted strove to silence them; but in vain. The king was heard to say, in a tone of great dignity: 'I came here to receive homage, and not admonitions.' Upon this arose a great shout of: 'Long live the king,' but the disloyal cries were renewed and multiplied. The king would have borne with them, as is known by his having formally signified his satisfaction with the state of the guard, and the ceremonial of the day; but his ministers could not forgive their share. The cries were uttered, with great rage, under their windows; they went to the king, to hold council, and sat late into the night. Before daylight, the royal and ministerial order for the disbanding of the National Guard was received by its commandant; and before seven in the morning, all the posts of the guard were occupied by troops of the line.

Two days after the close of the session, in June, the old censorship of 1820–21 was brought into action. Every one expected this; but nobody was the less angry. In August, government took offence at the orations and ceremonies which signalised the funeral of a deputy who had been expelled from the chamber in 1823, and prosecuted the printers and publishers of the report of the funeral. The speakers and reporters came forward to acknowledge their share in the matter. All the parties were prosecuted; and all authors, speakers, publishers, and printers, were acquitted, and the confiscated copies of the pamphlet ordered to be restored. Lafayette, who was one of these parties, made a kind of political progress through France; and he damaged the government, at every stage of his journey, by a plain narrative of its policy of the year. The king was travelling at the same time. He visited the camp at St. Omer; was loyally received; enjoyed the spectacle of the improved condition of his people—which was, in truth, very miserable—since he visited the same regions in his younger days; and returned to Paris, fancying that all was well.

The next proceeding of the government remains inexplicable. The Chamber of Deputies was more devoted to them than any future one could be expected to be; yet they dissolved it this autumn. They spared no effort to manage and control the elections; and their power of doing so was very great. But they had brought on a crisis which was too strong for them; and the new elections were fatal to the Villèle ministry. The ultra-royalists and liberals made a junction for the occasion, and returned a motley assemblage of deputies, whose only point of agreement seemed to be hostility to Villèle and his comrades. In Paris itself, every ministerial candidate was thrown out. At the moment of dissolving the Chamber of Deputies, the king had declared the creation of seventy-six new peers in a batch. The peers, having been unmanageable,

were now to be swamped.   In the new batch were found
the only archbishops (five) who were not peers before;
and the most slavish of the creatures of the government
who had been thrust into the late assemblage of deputies.

The king and his minister were among the last to perceive that these measures would not do—that they were
intolerable ; but they discovered it at last; and on the
4th of January, Villèle resigned.

The people of Paris were on the watch.   On occasion of
the election returns, towards the end of November, there
had been serious troubles in Paris; and it was at this
time, as far as we are aware, that the first mention of
barricades occurs.   Some of the rioters, we are told, pursued by the patrol, raised barricades by means of the
masons' tools and hewn stones which they found near the
church St. Leu, where some new houses were in process of
construction.   It is two years and a half after this that
we find, in our own *Annual Register*, the first mention of
barricades, and of something else : 'As a detachment advanced, it was stopped by a new obstacle, a barricade
formed across the street by one of those long coaches to
which the Parisians have given the name of *omnibus*.'

The people of Paris were, as has been said, on the watch.
The countenance of every minister was examined as he
came forth from royal audience, during the six weeks
between the close of the elections and the resignation of
Villèle; and during the whole of the next two years they
remained on the watch, while a weak and incompetent
ministry was kept in, only by consent of all parties,
because no party could put in a set of men of its own.
During this period, minds and affairs were ripening for
the great struggle to come; and everybody, unless it were
the royal family, was aware that though little appeared to
be done, the time was not lost.

The chief signs of the times were, first, the introduction
of an impeachment of Villèle, which was allowed to stand
over from the session of 1828 to the next, in order to prevent his return to office—a proceeding of which he and
his master could not complain, as the delay was reasonably
accounted for by their frustration of all attempts to obtain
the evidence required.   Next, the continually growing

proof of the impoverished condition of the people engaged
in labour and trade ; and, again, the introduction of more
liberals into office and the chamber ; a sure token of change :
and the more, because it was achieved by a coalition for
the crisis between the liberals and the ultra-royalists.

Among those who were on the watch during all this
time, was he by whom England was brought into relation
with this great French quarrel. Prince Jules de Polignac
has been mentioned as the French ambassador in London,
who was a party to the Treaty of London in regard to
Greece. Prince Polignac was one of those men about
whom neither the world at large, nor any one in it, knows
how to be moderate—the accomplished, narrow-minded,
strong-minded, conscientious oppressor, whom the oppressed hate with extremity of hatred, and whom his associates respect and regard as a man of sincerity, conscience,
and loyalty. The people of France lived in incessant mistrust of him, and dread lest he should not remain in
London. The King of England and the Duke of Wellington entertained a cordial admiration and a strong personal
friendship for him ; and his own sovereign was attached
to him as to a faithful and able adherent and champion.
At the beginning of 1829, the Count de Ferronay, the
French foreign minister, the most respected and trusted of
the weak ministry then existing, was compelled by illness
to retire from office; and immediately Prince Polignac
appeared in Paris. It was reported that he had been
secretly sent for; that, if he could be got into office, he
was gradually to restore the Villèle policy; and with one
intolerable aggravation—that he was to work out in
France the pleasure of the Tory ministry of England.
The hated Wellington, who had brought back the Bourbons, and in this had helped to impose the tyranny under
which the French nation groaned, was now about to impose a friend and fellow-conspirator of his own upon
France, and to rule the struggling nation with the rod of
the Holy Alliance. If the French king and ministry had
hoped to bring in Prince Polignac, they found it would
not do for this time. The ministers themselves threatened
to resign, if the prince came in as the nominee of the king.
So, Prince Polignac returned to London, after having made

a speech of self-defence in the chamber against the accusations of the newspapers. But he was not absent long. He
was seen in Paris in July, a few days before the ominous
close of the session of the chambers; and on the 8th of
August, the publication of some royal ordinances made
known to the world the formation of what will be for ever
called the Polignac ministry, though the prince's office was
at first only that of foreign minister. The transactions
from the time of his appointment to the stormy close of
the year, were such as might well disturb the feeble and
anxious mind of the King of England, sinking as he was,
daily deeper in disease, in his close retirement at Windsor.
The caricatures of the day, whose authors were probably
not aware how ill he was, represented him as going, under
pretence of fishing, to weep at Virginia Water, which
spread out, by means of that influx, to a lake of handsome
size. He certainly never was more reasonable than in his
apprehensions for Polignac and for France—his ideas of
the welfare of France being what they were.

It is not now easy to decide what were the principles
on which the Polignac ministry intended, in the first instance, to govern. When, in September, the people, indignant at the government practice of tampering with their
chamber, and thus procuring revenue by means of taxes
decreed by creatures of government, formed associations
for purposes of resistance to illegal taxation, the Polignac
ministry made bitter complaints of misconstruction and
unfair prejudgment. 'Judging by the newspapers,' said
the ministers, in the *Moniteur* of the 19th of September,
'the government dreams only of *coups d'état*, and contem-
plates the overthrow of the charter. . . . Those who say
such things know very well that the ministers, unless they
had lost all common sense, could not conceive the bare
idea of violating the charter, and substituting a government by ordinances for that of the laws. Such men know
also that if the ministers desired ever so much a method
of government like this, the king would, on the first hint
of such a system, thrust them out of power—out of that
power which he has confided to them, in his name and
under their responsibility, to govern according to the
laws.' The only question, with regard to these protesta-

tions, is whether they were weak or wicked. If Prince Polignac really intended in September to govern only according to law, and to cherish the charter, the king and prime-minister of England need not be ashamed of their friendship for him then; but they must have wholly cast him off from their respect and regard, when, in a few months, he had falsified all his professions. The French people believed nothing that he said. They expected from him exactly that which he did. The newspapers told their opinions and anticipations very plainly. While almost the whole journalist press of Paris reviled the ministry from day to day, that of London praised it and exulted in it, with a fervour so strange and so unanimous, that it was no wonder that the friendship of the two administrations became a subject of suspicion to the sensitive and unhappy people of France, and that they gave the name of 'the Wellington ministry' to the Polignac cabinet. One of the very few English journals which thought ill of the new French ministry from first to last, was the *Examiner;* and among its remarks at the time are these : ' There seems to be this peculiarity about the new French ministry—that those who know least of it approve it most. The London journals, with a few exceptions, have been in raptures with it, while the French are hurling upon it a storm of the bitterest displeasure. . . . Why the ministry should be found good in the eyes of the English Whigs and Radicals, is more strange than that it should be overcharged with ill in the representations of the French *liberaux.* Our neighbours, indeed, style it a Tory ministry; and because the Duke of Wellington's original Tory ministry has worked better than could have been expected for us, it is supposed that Tory ministers, all over the world, must have a similar operation. A Tory ministry cured our state of bigotry, but it may happen to kill the liberality of France. We cannot, also, but give our neighbours credit for knowing more of their own affairs than we do; and the common sentiment of the intelligent on the other side of the water, seems decidedly inimical to the new administration.'

The protestations of the ministry were scarcely issued before their authors began to show what they were worth. They renewed their war against the press. M. Bertin,

responsible editor of the *Journal des Débats*, was prosecuted
for the following words, which appeared in his paper on
the accession of the new ministry : ' The bond of affection
and confidence which united the monarch with the people
is broken.   Unhappy France! unhappy king !'   On these
words a charge was founded of offence against the king's
person and authority, on the ground that any impeachment of the king's judgment in choosing his ministers
was an attack on his authority; and any declaration
that there was no longer love between the king and his
people, or between the people and their king, was an
offence against his person.   The courts of Paris were
above trifling like this.   After a deliberation of three
hours as to the form of the judgment, the conclusion was
that M. Bertin was acquitted; because, ' however improper might be the expressions of the article complained
of, and however contrary to the moderation which should
be preserved in discussing the acts of the government,
they did not constitute actionable offences against the
royal person or dignity.'   Silence within the court had
been enjoined; but the acclamations with which the
judgment was received were deafening; and they were
caught up by the crowds outside, who soon, by their
shouts, let all Paris know the result of the trial.

Meantime, the cabinet was not strong in itself.   Hitherto,
the king or the dauphin had presided at council; but both
became weary of the dissensions and weakness which they
were compelled to witness; and Prince Polignac was made
president of the council.   Upon this, the best, in their
opinion—the most ultra-royalist of the ministers, Labour-
donnaye—withdrew.   And now, the consequences of a
bad season had to be met, in addition to other difficulties.
Wet and cold weather had materially injured all the crops
in the country ; the manufacturers' stocks were large, and
a multitude of people therefore unemployed, when the
winter set in early, and with great severity.   What would
Polignac, whose head was full of old feudal ideas, do for
the modern farming and manufacturing France?   What
would he do—and this was the most anxious question to
himself—with the chambers?   The Chamber of Deputies
was hostile ; but to resort to a new general election could

only make matters worse. It is believed that even now, on the eve of meeting the chambers, he was undecided as to whether he would satisfy himself by merely putting down journalism—not seeing that journalism was now an expression of the national will—or whether he would supersede the electoral laws by royal ordinances, in order to obtain a chamber which would work to his liking. Whatever might be in his mind, the fact of the case was, that the monarchy and the national liberties were now brought face to face for their decisive conflict, and that Prince Polignac was not aware of it.

Early in January 1830, the king issued a notice to the chambers to meet on the 2nd of March. From this it was supposed that the representative part of the state was safe for the present. But there was evidently no improvement in the temper of the royal and governing clique. When the president of the court which had acquitted M. Bertin went, according to custom, to offer to the king and royal family the usual wishes for the new year, he met with a reception which showed that, in France as in England, the first gentleman in the empire could lose his good-manners in personal pique. The upright judge, M. Seguier—who had asserted the function of his court in the memorable words: 'The court gives judgments and not services'—offered his congratulations to the king, with an expression of satisfaction in the privilege of a yearly audience to tender these wishes. The stern reply of the king, was, 'that he desired the magistrates of the court never to forget the important duties they had to fulfil, and to render themselves worthy of the marks of confidence they had received from their king.' As for the royal ladies, the only word they had to give in reply to similar congratulations, was: 'Pass on;' and all the courtiers behaved to the judges exactly after the manner of the royal family. Childish as this appears in the reading, it was of vast importance at the time, as showing that the government could not tolerate the independent administration of justice—the most fatal of all symptoms.

Throughout February the newspapers contained articles which hinted, or said plainly, that men were now driven to revive the old question, what France had gained by the

return of the Bourbons, and whether she could prosper
better under some other dynasty. Of course, the prosecutions of the journals were unremitting, and the sentences
were often severe; but the more fines were imposed, the
larger were the subscriptions to pay them; and the more
men went to prison, the more volunteers appeared to carry
on their work outside.

On the 2nd of March, the king, surrounded by the
royal family, met the chambers. There was more than
ordinary pomp and gravity observable in the proceedings.
It was remarked, and afterwards told, in every home in
France, that when the king set his foot on the step of
the throne, he dropped his hat, which was picked up by the
Duke of Orleans, and presented by him, kneeling on one
knee. The speech was listened to with breathless eagerness; and up to the last paragraph it gave nothing but
satisfaction. It told of peace abroad, of a good state of
the finances, of fidelity to the charter; but the last paragraph ruined everything. In it the king called upon the
peers to aid him in governing the country well; expressed
his trust in them to repudiate wicked insinuations; and
declared that if obstacles to his government should arise
which he could not, and did not choose to foresee, he
should find strength to overcome them in the loyalty of his
people. The surprise and dismay caused on the instant
by these words were evident enough through all the usual
loyal demonstrations of the occasion.

The peers replied coldly to this direct appeal, assuring
his majesty that there was indeed nothing to fear from the
obstacles of faction, as the government would have the
support of both chambers, and of the great majority of the
nation; as the crown and the charter—the rights of royalty
and the liberties of the people—were inseparably connected, and must be transmitted undivided. This was
pretty strong in the way of admonition and rebuke; but
the ministry dared not object, for fear of bringing upon
themselves something worse, in the form of direct censure.
The king, to whom the address was presented on the 9th
of March, ventured to congratulate himself on the substance of his sentiments having been so perfectly apprehended.

The tug of war was in the other chamber, where, from the first day of the session, the ministers found themselves overpowered by the liberals, who carried all the appointments of the chamber. The attendance was very full during the days employed in the preparation of the address. Some paragraphs of this address declared that the charter supposed, in order to its working, a concurrence between the mind of the sovereign and the interests of his people; that it was the painful duty of the deputies to declare that that concurrence existed no longer, the present administration ordering all its acts on the supposition of the disaffection of the people—a supposition which the nation had a right to complain of, as injurious to its character, and threatening to its liberties. It was not supposed that the king entertained this distrust. His heart was too noble to admit it. But he could not be further from desiring despotism than his people from desiring anarchy; and he was implored to have the same faith in the loyalty of the nation as the nation had in the sincerity of his promises. Finally, his majesty was appealed to, to choose between his faithful and confiding parliament, and the parties who misapprehended the calm and enlightened mind of the people of France.

There was doubt as to whether the king would receive this address, though it passed by a majority of 221 to 181. He received it, however, on the 18th of March, at noon. The attendance was more numerous than usual. The president of the chamber read the address—the last the unhappy monarch was ever to receive from his parliament —with a grave and firm voice, which, however, faltered towards the close. The king listened with gravity; but, when he delivered the reply which had previously been agreed upon in council, strong emotion was evident in his voice, through the constrained calmness of his manner. His reply—for which the King of England was earnestly listening in his retreat at Windsor, and the British ministry, because the peace of our country might depend upon it—was this: 'Sir, I have heard the address which you present to me in the name of the Chamber of Deputies. I was justified in relying on the concurrence of the two chambers, in accomplishing all the good which I con-

templated. I am grieved to find that the deputies declare
that, on their part, such concurrence exists no longer.
Gentlemen, I announced my intentions in my speech at
the opening of the session. These intentions are immu-
table. The interest of my people forbids my receding
from them. My ministers will make my further purposes
known to you.'

The next day the chambers were prorogued to the 1st
of September. And where was the king on the next 1st
of September? 'Long live the king!' cried some on the
ministerial side. 'Long live the charter!' cried some on
the opposite side. 'Long live the constitution!' shouted a
voice from one of the galleries, where the citizens of
Paris had crowded in, to see what would happen. The
royalists set up the cry: 'Down with faction!' and called
upon the president to order the departure of strangers;
but the president's authority was at an end now that the
session was closed, and the whole assemblage broke up in
disorder. There were many heavy hearts in both chambers,
and in every street in Paris. It had not been supposed
that the king would stand out to such a point as this.
It was the first time that the sovereign had used the
power of thus untimely dispersing his parliament. The
budget was not brought forward, nor any provision made
for some extraordinary expenses of the time. Every one
saw that a dissolution might next be expected, and that
this was a rupture which could not be healed. The
liberals, who were virtually conquerors, were sure of their
ground; but they were full of solicitude about what was
to happen next. The royalists were merry and confident,
looking upon the present crisis as the emancipation of
royalty from tutelage.

After a grand expedition had been sent off to Algiers,
which, it was hoped, would divert the attention of the people
from politics, and fix it upon military glory, the chambers
were dissolved, on the 16th of May; new elections
ordered for June and July; and the new parliament
directed to meet on the 3rd of August. And where was
the king on that 3rd of August?

In the elections, the government was beaten at all points.
The nation was fond of military glory, as hitherto; and

multitudes enjoyed the spectacle and the news of the imposing departure of the Algerine expedition. But the political crisis had gone too far to be lost sight of. Finding this, the ministry not only employed their whole power and influence in endeavouring to carry the elections, but actually instigated the king himself to canvass for votes in a proclamation which was issued on the 14th of June, and which began with the words : ' The elections are about to take place throughout the kingdom. Listen to the voice of your king !' The voice of the king proceeds to extol the charter and the national institutions; but declares that, in order to make them available, the royal prerogative must remain unassailed. The concluding words are interesting, as the last which this wretched sovereign addressed to his subjects. ' Electors ! hasten to the place of voting. Let not guilty negligence induce you to absent yourselves ! Let one sentiment animate you— one banner be your rallying-point ! It is your king who requires this of you; it is a father who summons you. Do your duty, and I will do mine.' Characteristic last words !

The government being beaten at all points, what was to be done next? Either the ministry must resign, and open the way to a new course of policy, or they must choose one of two desperate methods of governing the country— dispensing with a parliament altogether, or setting aside the electoral laws, and ordaining new ones, in order to obtain an obedient Chamber of Deputies. The government newspapers put out feelers about these latter courses, or audaciously advocated them; but everybody supposed that the administration would not venture upon them, but would resign. Up to the 26th of July, however, there was no appearance of an intention to do anything but simply meet the new chambers. The letters of summons to the peers had been transmitted, and the deputies were travelling towards Paris from all parts of the kingdom. They did not know—and the people along the roads, who were rejoicing in the capture of Algiers, little suspected—what was taking place between the Polignac ministry and the king.

Up to the last moment, the proposed plan of the ministry had been to bring forward in the chambers a

popular budget, in which many and great economical
reforms would be recommended. Then, they were to excite
to the utmost the patriotic pride of the members about the
Algerine victories ; and they hoped that through the blaze
of those glories, they might carry, almost unobserved, the
restrictive laws of the press which they were resolved to
obtain. Except their actual conduct, nothing could be
more blind and foolish than this plan of procedure, nor
more insulting to the French nation, who were thus to be
treated like children—bribed to suffer restraint by the
exhibition of a glittering toy. Their actual conduct was,
however, even worse. Finding it out of the question to
meet the chambers, they still did not think of resigning,
but addressed a memorial to the king, petitioning and recommending him to set aside the charter. They had their
own sense of duty ; and, mistaken, utterly foolish, as it
was, they resolved to abide by it. They believed that the
monarchical principle was now to be surrendered or
snatched from destruction by a bold hand. They despised
the cowardly suggestion of retiring from the contest, and,
as they viewed the matter, deserting the king; so they
remained beside him, and urged him on to destruction. In
ruining their king, and outraging his people, they never
felt the smallest doubt that they were discharging a sublime duty. Whatever the King of England might think of
this, the British premier had shown that his sympathy
could not go this length. His measures of the preceding
year were a practical and most powerful protest against
the policy which was unjustly supposed to be instigated,
or at least countenanced, by him, because a personal friend
of his was responsible for it. Prince Polignac was known
to be inaccessible to counsel. It is probable that if he
had ever obtained any opinion at all from the Duke of
Wellington, or had guided himself by the policy of England in her last great crisis, he would not have been the
one to overthrow the monarchy of France.

The ministers had discussed, in some of their meetings,
a plan of three ordinances, which, being issued by the
king, might free the government at once from its two
great difficulties—the press and the chambers. These
ordinances were laid before the king in council, on the 21st

of July, together with a memorial which explained their object and their necessity. This memorial declared that there was no provision in the charter for the protection of the periodical press, which had at all times been, from its very nature, nothing but an instrument of disorder and sedition; that it had established a despotism in the Chamber of Deputies, where every man who adhered to the side of order was sure to be insulted by the newspapers; that the Algerine expedition had been endangered by the disclosures and criticisms of the press; that the king's own words and sentiments had been disrespectfully discussed in the journals; that it was for his majesty to say whether such conduct should go unpunished; that government and the press could not coexist; and that the prolonged cry of indignation and terror from all parts of the kingdom against the journals of Paris showed which must give way. So much for the press. As for the other difficulty, the representation, the ministers suggested that the right of government to provide for its own security existed before any laws, and, being founded in the nature of things, must overbear all laws; that the time had arrived for the assertion of this primary right; that all legal resources had been exhausted in vain; and that, if the ordinances proposed were not in accordance with the letter of the laws, they were with the spirit of the charter; and that the administration did not hesitate to recommend to the king the issuing of the accompanying ordinances, convinced as they were that justice must always prevail. Such was the memorial which was published with the celebrated ordinances of Charles X. and his Polignac ministry.

These ordinances were three. By the first, the liberty of the periodical press was suspended; no journals were to be issued but by the express authorisation of government, which must be renewed every three months, and might be withdrawn at any time; and all writings of less than twenty pages of print were to lie under the same conditions. By the second ordinance, the Chamber of Deputies was dissolved, on the ground that means had been used, in various parts of the kingdom, to deceive and mislead the electors, during the late elections. By the third ordinance, means were taken to correct such abuses by setting aside those provisions of the charter which were found inconvenient in their operation; by the power conferred on the king by the charter to consult the security of the state, he lessened the number of deputies, reduced their term of office, and altered their qualification, and the methods of election.

It is scarcely credible, even now, that any government of our day should have conceived of doing such things as these by the mere will of the sovereign; and the question arises how the government could have gone on thus far, administered by men who now showed themselves destitute of all idea of nationality, law, and the purposes of social organisation. These three ordinances, together with some subordinate articles, recalling to the council some men odious to the people, were countersigned by the six ministers present in council, and kept profoundly secret till half an hour before midnight of the 25th of July, when they were communicated to the responsible editor of the *Moniteur* newspaper, for publication in the morning. So profoundly had the secret been kept, that neither the heads of the police nor the soldiery had the least idea that any extraordinary call was likely to be made upon their energies. The ministers had not made the slightest preparation for any awkward reception of their measures. There is no evidence that, amidst all their complaints of popular disobedience and violence, they dreamed of resistance to the ordinances. As for the public, though something of the sort had been predicted and vaguely expected, from the day of Polignac's accession to office, the amazement and dismay at last were as overwhelming as if no forebodings had been entertained.

The opposition journalists were the first to act on that memorable 26th of July. They obtained an opinion from the most eminent lawyers in Paris of the illegality of the ordinances; and then assembled, to the number of forty-four, in the office of the *National*, to prepare the celebrated protest which first gave direction to the bewildered mind of Paris. By this protest, they proved the illegality of the ordinances, declared their own intention of resisting them, and invited the deputies to meet on the properly appointed day—the 3rd of August. 'The government,' said the protest, 'has to-day forfeited that character of legality which makes obedience a duty. We, for our part, shall resist it. It is for the rest of the nation to determine how far its own resistance shall extend.' A legal sanction was given, in the course of the day, to such a method of proceeding as this, by the decision of a magistrate, M. Belleyme, who authorised the printer of the *Journal of Commerce* to continue the issue of that paper provisionally, as long as the ordinance of the 25th had not been promulgated according to the legal forms. At the Exchange the excitement was tremendous. Crowds assembled in all the avenues to it, long before the gates were opened; and then the hubbub was such as might have alarmed even Prince Polignac, if he had witnessed it; but his way was to see very little, and to believe nothing but what he saw. Every one wanted to sell, and nobody to buy; manufacturers declared that they should close their establishments, and dismiss their workmen; and the Exchange had not been seen in so stormy a state since the return of the Bourbons. Presently, the stir and excitement had spread to the remotest corners of Paris; and in the theatres the usual occasions were found or made for expressing the popular opinion. The day passed over, however, without actual insurrection; and the ministers agreed that the discontent would exhaust itself in harmless murmurs; that no struggle need be apprehended till the new elections should be entered upon; and that they need not send police or soldiery into the streets, to disperse the groups which began to form there. Even the usual leave of absence, asked by some military officers, was granted as on ordinary days. Marmont, Duke of Ragusa, who commanded the troops, held a most difficult position. He had no warning whatever of what was going to be done, though the ministry were as well aware as he was, that whole divisions of the soldiery were so full of popular sympathy as to be unreliable, in case of insurrection. As the event showed, there were only 6000 on whom he could depend: and of these nearly 2000 were needed for the supply of the regular posts in Paris, and about the king's palace at St. Cloud; so that the general had but little

more than 4000 men wherewith to defend Paris, and put
down revolt, if the citizens should be disposed to resist the
overthrow of the charter.

The most remarkable scene, on Tuesday the 27th, was
the conflict between the police and the newspaper corps.
The doors of the offices were closed, and the papers were
thrown out of the windows as fast as they could be
printed; and the eager mob handed them, by tens of
thousands, to every house, or to every reader who wished
to see the famous protest. The police, meantime, were
standing before the doors, unable to effect an entrance,
because nobody would give any aid. One blacksmith
after another was brought to the spot, with his tools; but
one after another folded his arms, and refused to force the
locks. When half Paris had witnessed the scene, so
damaging to the authority of the government, the doors
were at last broken in, the manuscripts and books seized,
the types thrown away, and the presses broken: a process
which did not make the temper of the government more
respected than its power had been. During this day, the
Tribunal of Commerce declared itself. The printer of the
Courier Français had been afraid to print the paper in
violation of the ordinance, and the editors sued him for
breach of contract. The tribunal, by the voice of its
president, Ganneron—a voice which sounded firm and clear
amidst the first roar of the revolutionary storm—pronounced that the ordinance, being contrary to the charter,
could not be binding on any one, from his majesty the king
to the remotest of his subjects; and that the printer must
act, in fulfilment of his contract, within twenty-four hours.

Before two o'clock, Marmont was posting his troops,
and bodies of men were arming themselves from the
gunsmiths' shops. Some thirty deputies had met to
consider whether or not they should assemble on the 3rd
of August; and the police and soldiery drew round their
place of meeting. They do not appear to have thought
of anything but legal resistance as yet; but in the
midst of their consultation, a deputation came to them
from the electors of Paris, to say that by the promulga-
tion of the ordinances, law was at an end, and that insurrection was the method open to the citizens, and that

which they were prepared to adopt. The deputation declared that assemblages were beginning in the streets; that they, the representatives of a multitude, like-minded with themselves, had cast themselves, 'body and goods,' into the enterprise; and that they now called upon the deputies to sanction and guide their proceedings. Next came a body of young men, messengers from a large association resolved on an immediate struggle, who offered a guard to the assembled deputies. These last could come to no immediate determination under these exciting visitations, with police and soldiers all about the neighbourhood, and shots multiplying in the streets, and at the very door. They appointed a place of meeting for the morrow, when some of them were to come prepared with a decisive protest, which should be immediately considered, and issued when agreed upon. The ministers met this afternoon at the foreign office; and though they knew everything that was going forward, saw with their own eyes the state of the streets and the armourers' shops, and had —Prince Polignac and M. de Montbel—been pelted with showers of stones, they could not yet perceive the seriousness of the occasion. They expected the people to become quiet, and talked of declaring Paris in a state of siege, as a threatening measure, and of bringing in troops from a distance, if matters were not right to-morrow morning. They had great faith in the power of soldiery against a mob; and thought little of the all-important circumstance that various bodies of the troops had shown disinclination to act against the citizens.

On Wednesday morning, the 28th, barricades were seen rising in all directions; paving-stones, powder, and lead, were carried into houses favourably placed for attacking troops in the streets; the court tradesmen, seeing that they were in danger of insult from their display of the royal arms, took them down; and this became the signal for pulling down the royal insignia everywhere, and dragging them through the mud. The arsenal, the artillery depôt, and the powder-mills, were all emptied with extraordinary despatch, and every soldier or government servant who carried arms was disarmed, as soon as met. The prefect of the Seine went, at seven in the morning, to inform the minister, that if the Hotel de Ville were not properly guarded, he feared it would be entered, and a provisional council of the people be established therein; but the minister still did not consider the matter serious, thought the people would be scared back to their homes when Paris should be declared in a state of siege, and drove off to attend a council at St. Cloud, where the king and royal family now were. When the magistrate returned from this interview, the Hotel de Ville was in the hands of the people, who had turned out the guard of sixteen men, and were running up to the belfry, where they rang the tocsin, and hung out the tricoloured flag, with crape for mourning; and the eloquent flag streamed to the wind, in the sight of all Paris. Presently there was another, streaming from the steeple of Notre Dame, whose great bell was kept tolling, to call the people to arms. Soon after this was accomplished, bodies of soldiery appeared, to guard the edifices which were already in the possession of the citizens. In the course of the morning, there were various encampments of troops in different parts of the city; but no one seems to have remembered that they would want food, for none was provided. Marshal Marmont now sent a letter and report to St. Cloud, to alarm the king, and assure him that it was necessary to yield immediately; that if measures of pacification were instantly offered, there might yet be time to save the royal dignity; but that to-morrow it would be too late. This letter is declared to have been missent or suppressed.

When the ministers returned from St. Cloud, they assembled and remained at the Tuileries, believing that they should no longer be safe in their own houses, and that they ought to be on the spot, ready to hold council with Marshal Marmont, who was now—Paris being in a state of siege—the head of the government. Almost as soon as they had arrived, a remarkable deputation was shown into the presence of Marshal Marmont. Five deputies came, sent by the liberal members of their body, to propose a truce, for the saving of life, till communication could be had with the king. The marshal appeared disposed for peace, on his own part, but declared that his orders were positive to enforce the decrees of the govern-

ment. He offered to send a message to St. Cloud; and
did so. He inquired if the deputies had any objection to
see Prince Polignac; they expressed themselves willing,
and he went into an adjoining room. Returning almost
immediately, he intimated that, as nothing could be done
till an answer arrived from St. Cloud, there would be no
use in their seeing Prince Polignac. It was afterwards
made known, that orders had been issued for the arrest of
five or six of the leading liberal deputies, some of whom
were of this negotiating party; that the intended victims
passed through the presence of the officers charged to arrest
them; and that, on their departure, Marshal Marmont
countermanded the orders, which could not now be executed without too much hazard.

The marshal sent one of his aides-de-camp, Colonel
Komierowski, to St. Cloud with a letter which related
the mission of the deputies, and referred the king to the
bearer for an account of what was passing in Paris. It
was four o'clock when the messenger left Paris. When he
arrived at St. Cloud, the king was at cards, and some of
the ladies were in the orangery, silently listening to the
distant firing. They had all been informed by an officer
of the royal suite of what was going on; but the king
comforted himself with the thought that everybody always
exaggerates dangers. The messenger did his duty well.
He delivered the letter into the king's own hand, observing that an answer could not be given too speedily;
that it was not the populace, but the whole people that
had risen. 'It is a formidable revolt, is it?' inquired the
king. 'Sire,' replied the soldier, 'it is not a revolt; it is
a revolution.' The king desired him to retire, and return
to his presence to receive his answer, when the letter
should have been read ; and at the end of twenty minutes
of anxious waiting, he was called in. The dauphin and the
Duchess de Berri were present; and it was unchecked by
them that the king gave the message which he chose to
send to Marshal Marmont—a message so cold and cruel,
as well as foolish, as to extinguish any lingering feelings
of compassion for his loss of the sovereignty of France.
His verbal message was that Marshal Marmont must hold
on—' concentrate his forces, and act with the masses '—

that is, he was to put down the people by military force, at all events. It also signified the king's displeasure at the dispersion of the forces over Paris. The method prescribed was already impossible. The greater number of the soldiers had gone over to the people; those that remained were too few for the work, and they were hungry, weary, and distressed. At night, orders were sent in the quietest way possible to such of them as were at the Hotel de Ville, where fighting had been going on, without result, for many hours, to return to the Tuileries in the best way they could. Since the morning of the preceding day, there had been no issue of provisions to the soldiers; and now, when in a famished condition they reached the Tuileries at midnight, after fighting all day in a burning sun, there was neither food nor drink for them. They were promised some at daybreak, but it was not to be got. The officers bought up from the bakers whatever bread they had; but it went a very little way. It was no wonder that it was found next morning that a large proportion of the troops of the line were not to be depended on.

There was little rest for anybody that night. The soldiers were murmuring; and their commander was in great anguish of mind, which caused a miserable irresolution in his purposes. He disapproved the ordinances as much as any man in Paris, and had said so to M. Arago the Monday before; but his professional duty constrained him —or he thought it did—to fire upon the citizens who had his sympathies in their enterprise. He was required to fulfil his professional duty under every kind of disadvantage. His troops were too few, and many of them untrustworthy; food and ammunition fell short; he lay under the displeasure of the king, and was not on good terms with the ministers. Marshal Marmont was a wretched man that night. All night the tocsin rang, banishing sleep from the city. All night the people were cutting down the trees of the Boulevards, and building up new barricades. On the 29th, however, these were no longer wanted. The soldiers no longer came out against the people. They were posted 'in masses,' as the king desired, and the people must come up and attack them.

There was a good deal of fighting, in a desultory kind of way; but regiment after regiment unscrewed their bayonets, and joined the people, or at least withdrew from the struggle. Meantime, from early in the morning, a remarkable scene was going forward in the palace of the Tuileries.

The peers had made no demonstration as a chamber; but some of them had fought as private men on the side of the people. Early in the morning of the 29th, the Marquis de Semonville, who held a high office in the Chamber of Peers, went to the Tuileries, saw Marmont, who carried despair in his countenance, and requested from him an interview with Prince Polignac. The marquis was accompanied by M. d'Argout; and their account of the interview has never been disputed. The marquis peremptorily requested Prince Polignac to withdraw the ordinances, in order to stop the effusion of blood, and preserve Paris; or, at least, to resign. Prince Polignac replied, with cold politeness, that he had no power of his own to take either step, without consultation with the king. The other ministers said the same thing; but their whole manner conveyed to the two peers the impression that they were 'under the influence of a power greater than their own will;' that as they had tempted and urged on the king to this pass, he would not now let them draw back. At length, Prince Polignac, with the same calm politeness, yielded so far as to propose to retire, to deliberate with his colleagues. While he was out of the room, the marquis urged Marmont to arrest the ministers, as the shortest way of putting an end to the slaughter in the streets; the governor of the Tuileries offering to do the deed, and the marquis himself proposing to go to St. Cloud, to work upon the king. Marmont was convulsed with agitation; he shed tears of indignation and passion, in the conflict between the convictions of his judgment and his professional duty; but he had yielded and was about to sign the requisite orders, when Peyronnet came in, and said in a voice of great emotion, as he stood behind the marquis: 'What! not gone yet?' The intention to yield was clear from the tone and manner of these few words. The marshal wrote something different from what he had intended; he wrote a pressing entreaty to the king to give way. The governor put the two peers instantly into a carriage for St. Cloud; Prince Polignac and some of his colleagues entered another, and the two carriages reached St. Cloud at the same time. Their arrival, and the disorder and agitation of their appearance created no little astonishment there; for even yet the royal family insisted upon it that all their informants exaggerated the confusion. The king taunted the marquis with this in the interview which ensued.

During that interview, the king was as obstinate as ever about the ordinances and his 'system' of government. It was only by presenting plainly to him his personal danger from the hands of the populace, and his responsibility for the lives and fortunes of his family, that the marquis could make any impression upon him whatever. It was not a moment for scruples; and the marquis therefore laid upon the king the sole responsibility for anything that might happen to his family through his refusal to yield. This at length brought tears to the old man's eyes; he drooped his head upon his breast, and said in a low and agitated voice: 'I will request my son to write, and assemble the council.'

After a short deliberation, is was resolved that the ordinances should be revoked, and a new ministry appointed; but, either from some difficulty about the new appointments, or from some lingering hope of better news, the decision was kept secret till the evening; and then it was too late.

The ministers fairly gone, Marmont ordered the soldiers to act only on the defensive, and proclaimed a truce at various points; but he was not much attended to, and, in fact, not understood. In some places, the conflict raged more than ever; and elsewhere, more and more soldiers went over to the people. In the afternoon, the citizens had penetrated everywhere; and Marmont found himself suddenly compelled to leave the city, if he wished to preserve his force at all. He could not even give notice of his intention to several scattered companies, which he was obliged to leave to their fate. Most of them, however, made their way out, and joined him on the road to

St. Cloud. His only hope now was to guard the person of the king, and the safety of the royal family. On the road, the soldiers met the dauphin, with two aides-de-camp. They formed in battalions to receive him. They supposed that he would address the troops, and invite them to follow him to Paris; but he only rode rapidly, and in dismal silence, along their front, and turned back towards St. Cloud, whither they followed him with heavy hearts. Their case was a hard one. Their good-will towards the people and their cause was such, that they spared life to the utmost that was consistent with their military duty, while they were pelted with stones, and treated as enemies by the populace; and, at the same time they had no encouragement on the side of their professional duty; their wants were not cared for; they were not supported by an efficient command; nor were their spirits cheered by a single demonstration in favour of the royal cause. Throughout the whole struggle, not one solitary cry of 'Long live the king!' was heard. And now, when all was over, and they were going to the presence of the king, the king's heir had not one word of thanks or sympathy to address to them; but, on the contrary, he seemed to doubt whether they had done their duty. Some of them must have wished themselves with those of their comrades who had fallen—with the old grenadier, one of the heroes of Austerlitz, who fell mortally wounded this day by a ball from the musket of a citizen, exclaiming: 'I was a good Frenchman, however.'

The troops, on their arrival at St. Cloud, were encamped in the avenues of the park; but still, no provision of food or comfort was made for them. Those who had their pay in their pockets bought of the bakers; the others were at last fed by requisitions on the nearest inhabitants. In the evening Marmont delivered a sort of proclamation, in which he declared the revocation of the ordinances, and the change of ministry. The soldiers cried: 'Long live the king!' and set about eating and reposing themselves. The dauphin was indignant with the marshal—called him traitor, ordered his arrest, and took his sword from him with his own hand; but the king checked these proceedings, made some kind of apology for

them, and ordered the troops to be informed that he was
satisfied with their conduct.

The courtiers were the most at a loss what to do. It
was long before they could admit the idea of the popular
victory; but when they did, they took their part with a
primary view to their own security. Up to the night of
the 29th, all had been brilliant, gay, and confident. Next
day, there was an eager looking-out for news; but when,
all day long, nobody entered the park, no deputations, no
messengers, no news-bearers, the silence of consternation
settled down on the palace of St. Cloud. Then, one by
one, the carriages rolled away—attendance slackened—
manners became cold and careless; and, in a few hours,
the great house appeared nearly empty. Only a few
general officers and gentlemen-in-waiting remained—
except, indeed, the disgraced ministers. The king could
not bear this, and he did not know whether he was safe at
St. Cloud; so, at three in the morning of the last day of
July, he set off for Trianon, another country palace, with
his whole family and establishment, except the dauphin
and his attendants, who remained with the troops. The
soldiers were naturally discouraged at this; and some
returned to Paris without asking leave.

The unhappy king could not rest. He went from place
to place, seeing the hated tricolor everywhere along the
road, and forsaken by more and more of his guard of
soldiers, who could not endure being thus dragged about
before the eyes of the victorious people. His displaced
ministers dropped off, except Polignac, who remained
some days in the suite of his sovereign, but concealing
himself from observation. That night—the night of the
1st of August—the king believed that all was lost for
himself; for he heard that the Duke of Orleans had accepted the office of lieutenant-general of the kingdom;
but there might be a hope that the crown might be
preserved for his grandson, the posthumous child of the
Duke de Berri; and in his favour, the king that night
abdicated; and the dauphin resigned his pretensions to
the throne. Again they had to learn that it was too late.
The only notice taken was by sending commissioners from
Paris to advise the departure of the whole royal family

for Cherbourg, whence they were to leave the kingdom; and to require the delivery of the crown jewels. It was impossible to resist. The jewels were delivered up; the last orders to the troops were issued while the chambers met in Paris, according to the king's first appointment, and in defiance of his subsequent decree of dissolution. The last orders to the troops were to repair to Paris, after having seen the royal family depart; and to submit themselves to whatever authority they might find supreme in the capital. On the morning of the 4th, the poor king affected to give the order for departure, though the commissioners remained to accompany him to the coast, and were, in fact, the masters. As he passed between the ranks of his soldiers, and among the flags under which they were to fight no more, tears were in his eyes, and in theirs; and these tears seem to have been the only mark of regret that he met with during the whole process of his dethronement. The royal party moved as slowly as possible towards the coast. They lingered—they courted sympathy—they looked in every face they met for comfort; but there was no comfort for them, for they had not deserved it. They had done nothing to secure either the respect or affection of the nation; and they now met with nothing but indifference or mere compassion. No one injured them; no one insulted them; no one withheld the observances of ordinary civility; but it was impossible for them not to see that no one cared for them. For the children, indeed, some emotion was shown—banished as they were from their birth-right before they were old enough to know what they had lost.

When the train arrived on the heights above Cherbourg, the spectacle that met the eyes of the travellers was very affecting. The vessels in the harbour carried the tricolor, all but two; two ships in the distance, whose sails were hung out, and all evidently ready for immediate departure. These were American vessels engaged to carry the royal family into exile. The travelling-party drove through the town without stopping, and immediately went on board the *Great Britain*, the soldiers on the quay presenting arms, and their officers saluting in grave silence, as the exiles passed. Captain Dumont d'Urville

—who afterwards perished by fire in the dreadful railway
accident near Versailles—waited on the king, to inquire
whither he should have the honour of escorting him.   'To
Spithead,' was the reply.

The pilot who took them out of port related, on his
return, that as the unhappy family saw the shores of
France grow dim and dimmer in the distance, their sobs
and lamentations became more and more irrepressible.
The king alone preserved his calmness.   In twenty-four
hours from their sailing—that is, before three o'clock in
the afternoon of the 17th of August—the vessels anchored at Spithead.   Two of the king's suite were put on
shore, in order to proceed to London, to learn the pleasure
of the king and ministry of England.   As it was reported
to the exiles that the people of Portsmouth, in their joy at
the emancipation of France, meant to hang out the tricolor all over the harbour, the vessels were removed
from their first station, and moored off Cowes, in the Isle
of Wight.

The English ministers had to consult the foreign ambassadors; and it was two days before their answer arrived.
The decision was that Charles X. should be received, but
as a private individual; under which character he thenceforth bore the title of the Count de Ponthieu.   From this
time till October the exiles lived at Lulworth, in Dorsetshire; but there were reasons—some assigned and more
supposed—why they should be recommended to reside
further from the coast, and in a place less immediately
accessible from France.   William IV. offered for their use
the palace of Holyrood, where the ex-king had resided
during his former exile.   There the family lived in retirement, occupied with the education and prospects of the
young king, Henry V., as they called him.   The dethroned
sovereign had nothing to suffer from remorse, or even mis-
giving.   He never ceased to believe and say that the
ordinances were necessary; that the revolution would have
happened exactly as it did if he had never issued them;
and that the French nation had misrepresented his intentions.

What the French nation did next, we shall see hereafter.
The conduct of the people during the three days was

singularly noble. No deed of meanness, and scarcely one of violence, is reported, at a time when public opinion was the only law. The historical education of the French people may not have fitted them for the full understanding and enjoyment of combined liberty and order; but of the strength at once of their patriotism and self-command, in an hour of crisis, no doubt remained in any mind in Europe, after the spectacle of the three days.

As for the late ministers, they were tried by special commission. Prince Polignac was arrested on the night of the 16th of August, when he was on the point of escaping to Jersey. He preserved his calmness throughout, sending in to the government a letter of extraordinary confidence, in which he demanded his freedom, and permission to retire with his family to the tranquillity of the domestic hearth, at home or abroad. If, however, his detention should be decided upon, he requested that his place of imprisonment might be the fortress of Ham, where he had undergone a long captivity in his youth. His life and the lives of his colleagues were spared. They were sentenced to imprisonment for life—Polignac and Peyronnet at Ham—to confiscation of all their goods, and outlawry; to a condition, in short, of civil death.

The loss of life during the three days was much less than could have been expected, and than was believed at the time by those engaged. On the side of the troops, the loss is estimated at about 250 killed, and 500 wounded. On the popular side the numbers are more certainly known. The killed were 788, and the wounded 4500.

While the state of France, viewed in connection with politics at home, was disturbing the mind of the sick King of England, he had to bear a series of vexations on a personal matter, in which he was really ill-used. Among the killed at Waterloo was the Duke of Brunswick, whose young heir was left to the guardianship of the King of Hanover. The boy turned out ill; and there was no end to the trouble he gave to his guardian. He concluded by publishing libels against George IV., which positively asserted charges too serious to be allowed to pass; as, for instance, that he, the duke, had been excluded from his rights for long after he came of age. Though the inces-

sant brawls and disgraces of the young man showed the
world that he was not worth attending to, it was necessary to put some check upon him; and his refusal to recognise certain political acts of his guardian—liberal changes
which were valued by his subjects—rendered some interposition necessary. He must also be rebuked for having
sent a challenge to the Hanoverian minister, Count
Munster. The courts of Vienna and Berlin tried to bring
the young man to reason and penitence, to avoid the
serious disgrace of a virtual trial before the diet; but he
would not yield. An appeal was therefore made to the
diet, by both the subjects and the guardian of the duke.
The affair was gone into, and judgment given against the
duke on every point. He was enjoined to fulfil the
pledges given to his subjects, and to make apology and
reparation to his guardian. But he paid no attention to
the judgment; made no apology—withdrew no libels—
made no advances towards his subjects. Such was the
state of things in 1829. During the revolutions of the
next year, occasion was taken to settle his affairs. He
was deposed, by universal consent, and his younger brother
put in his place. Of course he complained loudly and
long; but his unfitness for power was so evident that no
one aided him, and everybody advised him to be quiet.
The judgment of the diet relieved George IV. from all
apprehension for his reputation as the duke's guardian;
but the affair was one of the annoyances which embittered
the close of his life, and which he had no longer strength
of body or mind to bear cheerfully.

The pope, Leo XII., died in February of this year 1829.
His reign had been short—only five years and a half; and
it had not been distinguished by any remarkable events,
or indications of character or ability in himself. His
tendencies were despotic; but he had not force of mind to
withstand the liberalising influences of the time; so he
indulged his predilections merely by increasing the number
and aggrandising the condition of his clergy. The King
of the Netherlands forbade him to meddle in the management of the Catholic ecclesiastical seminaries of that kingdom; and he yielded. The French nation vexed him
sadly by retrenching the power of the Jesuits in France;

but he yielded.   And now, at the age of sixty-nine, he
laid down his predilections and his vexations together in
the grave.   His successor had as much reason as himself to
feel how times were changed for popes.   The new pope,
Cardinal Castiglione, took the title of Pius VIII.   One of
his first acts was excommunicating the town of Imola,
which lay under his displeasure.   But neither the inhabitants of Imola, nor anybody else, seemed to be at all aware
of the infliction; and the affairs of that town and of the
world went on as before.   Times were indeed changed for
popes ; but it seems as if popes were not changed.   Pius
VIII. excepted from the amnesty usually published on the
accession of a pope, all political offenders, declaring such
to be of the nature of assassins, undeserving of the mercy
of even the compassionate church.   Thus the new pontiff
did not enter upon his reign altogether in the spirit of the
gospel, of which he professed to be the high-priest.

The war between Russia and Turkey was soon over.
The Russian army swept all before it; and when it had
come like a hurricane down the Danube, and was seen descending the southern slopes of the Balkan, there was
nothing more to be done but to obtain the best terms for
the Porte that the conqueror would grant.   On the 20th
of August, the Russian general, Diebitsch, took Adrianople,
the second city of the empire, without firing a shot; so
utterly confounded were the 80,000 inhabitants by the
speed of his approach.   On the Black Sea the Russians
were unopposed; and every post yielded to them.   It now
only remained to take Constantinople.   Up to this time
the Porte had refused all negotiation and offers of mediation.   It was a religious war; and if the Christians were
permitted to mediate, all the infidel subjects of the Porte
would rise in rebellion, and the true faith would succumb.
This was the answer given to, or allowed to be inferred
by the ambassadors of France, England, and Prussia, who
had returned to Constantinople in June.   But when the
Russians were in full march on the capital, and the sacred
flag itself did not raise enough of the faithful to daunt the
foe, the gallant rulers of Turkey yielded to necessity, and
sent two plenipotentiaries to Adrianople, to treat with the
Russian general.   The terms granted appeared at first

sight very liberal; but Russia obtained what she most desired—money in abundance, and a protracted hold upon the country. Besides the indemnity to Russian merchants, amounting to about £800,000, Turkey was to pay the expenses of the war, in ten yearly instalments of half a million sterling each. During these ten years the Turks were not to be rid of the Russian presence. On the payment of the first instalment, the Russians were to evacuate Adrianople; on the second, to retire beyond the Balkan; on the third, to quit the Danube; and so on: but they were not to evacuate the Turkish dominions till the payments were all made, and the ten years expired. As for the question of territory, Russia left to the Porte more than might have been expected, retaining some portions here and there which would be useful auxiliaries to future conquests. It was a galling thing, however, that the whole of the left bank of the Danube was gone, and that no Mohammedan might possess a foot of land, or even reside there; and yet more, that the methods of administration set up by the Russians in the provinces were to remain; and worse still, that no Russian in any part of the Turkish dominions was to be subject to any government but his own. Henceforth the Russians might come and go, and conduct themselves as they pleased, with or without the connivance of the authorities at home, and they could be controlled only by means of their own ambassador and consuls, whose predilections would naturally be on the side of their countrymen. The truth was, all was now over with Turkey; and her political existence was henceforth nothing but a mere show, granted to the solicitations of the three powers which deprecated her open destruction.

Of course, Turkey was in no condition to refuse any terms which might be proposed to her in regard to Greece. The Turks in Greece not being reinforced, had yielded almost everywhere to the arms of the Greeks and their allies; and the three powers might now fix the boundaries of Greece, and arrange its affairs as they would. This had been begun in a protocol prepared by the three powers in March; but the President of Greece, Capo d'Istria, objected to it. The National Assembly, which he convoked at Argos, on the 23rd of July, was composed mainly of his partisans; and they occupied their time till the 18th of August, chiefly in uttering sentiments on peace, and in compliments to the president. By that date, however, the three powers were transacting the business of Greece more effectually at Constantinople, where Russia forced upon the Turkish government the acceptance of the protocol of March. To prevent Russia having too much influence, however, in the disposal of Greek affairs, the conferences on the subject were, by agreement of the three powers, now to be carried on in London, where, from this time, neither the Turkish government, nor the President of Greece, had any part in the deliberations. The three powers, seeing the helplessness of the other parties concerned, took the matter into their own hands, somewhat unceremoniously, offering some compensation to Turkey, by proposing a narrower boundary for Greece than that assigned in the March protocol.

It was presently determined that Greece should be wholly released from Turkish rule; and that the powers which had thus created a new state should appoint its form of government. The monarchical form having been chosen, as of course, the next question was who should be its king. In order to avoid jealousies, all princes connected with the courts of the three powers were excluded. The first to whom the new crown was offered was Prince John of Saxony. He declined it. Prince Leopold of Saxe-Coburg, the widower of our Princess Charlotte, and at this day King of the Belgians, was supposed at the time to be eager for the sovereignty of Greece; and to him it was offered, in January 1830, by the representatives of England, Russia, and France.

The negotiators were rather surprised by the prince's method of proceeding. He had no idea of an unconditional acceptance or rejection; and believing the possession of Candia to be essential to the security of the sovereignty of Greece, he asked for Candia. There were other stipulations, too; and the offerers of the crown found themselves still involved in negotiations, when they had believed that they had only to confer a dignity. There was goodwill on both sides, however; and by the month of April it was understood by all parties that Prince Leopold had

accepted the crown of Greece. The prince himself, however, did not consider his acceptance to be beyond recall;
for on the 21st of May he finally and conclusively declined
the crown of Greece.

Various reasons for this conclusion have been assigned.
One which is most generally agreed upon is, that the
President of Greece had frightened him from his enterprise. Prince Leopold had written to Capo d'Istria on
the 28th of February, to announce his prospects and
intentions, and to address his future subjects through
their present ruler. The reply of the president, and the
report of the proceedings of the senate at Napoli, which
reached the prince in May, and have been made public,
certainly leave no ground of surprise that any rational
man should decline a task so hopeless as that of governing
Greece, while her internal state and foreign dangers were
what they were thus shown to be. For the prince's
reasons for drawing back, there is no need to look beyond
the fact that the senate refused to accept the arrangements
of the three powers, in regard to so important a matter as
the boundaries of the state. But other causes might
easily be, and were, alleged. By that month of May, it
had become clear that George IV. was dying; and Prince
Leopold, the uncle of the young princess who was to
succeed the next aged and feeble heir to the throne, might,
as brother to the regent Duchess of Kent, be a personage
of great political consequence, in case of the princess
coming to the throne before she was of age. Again, there
is no need to go so far as this for the prince's reasons.
There was perhaps scarcely a child in England who,
hearing anything of the matter at all, did not feel an
uneasy sense of the vulgarity of a new crown, manu-
factured by statesmen in a cabinet. Children, and all unsophisticated people, feel the vulgarity of new rank, and of
the lowest dignity, in an assemblage of high ranks.
Every one understands that it may be better to be of high
station among commoners than a new-comer into the
lowest order of the peerage. If it is so with the common
dignities of society, how much stronger must the feeling
be about that highest position whose main dignity is
derived from associations of antiquity! But for historical

associations, a crown has, in our age, absolutely nothing in it at all. If conferred by the united impulse of a nation, the honour of sovereignty is still the highest conceivable ; but such a position is, in the present age of the world, one of leadership—one of personal responsibility —which is only impaired by reference to hereditary associations. There may have been reasons of policy for placing a crown on the apex of the destinies of Greece ; but, whatever might be the tastes of the parties most nearly concerned, it is certain that the tastes of Western Europe were offended by the act of turning a venerable symbol into a politic bauble. And it is very conceivable that though a sensible man might, in the hope of use-fulness and true honour, get over his objection to the insignia of his new office, it is no wonder that, upon the hope of usefulness and true honour being reduced to painful doubt, he should give way to his disgust, and decline the office and its titles and decorations together.

It was not till two years after this time, not till the year 1832 was far advanced, that the three powers could procure the acceptance of the crown of Greece by a European prince ; and then the new sovereign was a mere boy. Otho, a younger son of the King of Bavaria, with nearly three years of his minority yet to run, went to Greece, as king, in December 1833, with little chance of composing its dissensions, and affirming his empire. The only thing that can be said is, that where a boy must fail, the ablest man might have succeeded no better.

CHAPTER X.

Distress in England—State of the King—Duke of Wellington—State of Parties—Mr. Peel—Press Prosecutions—King's Speech—Reductions—Removal of Duties—East India Committee—Removal of a Judge—Welsh and Scotch Judicature—Forgery—Jewish Disabilities—Parliamentary Reform—Duke of Newcastle—Illness of the King—His Death—His Life and Character.

THE year 1830 opened gloomily—not only in England, but throughout Europe, and even in America. In Russia, great efforts were made to raise subscriptions to feed the labouring-classes, who were suffering under the depression of agriculture, from bad seasons and other causes. Throughout the whole of Germany and Switzerland there were stirrings of discontent, which gave warning of revolutionary movements to follow. In the rural districts of the north of France, that strange madness of rick-burning, which afterwards spread fearfully in England, had begun. The educated classes of England spoke of it at first with contemptuous amazement, as showing the desperate ignorance of the rural population of France; not yet dreaming how soon the proof would be brought home to them that our own agricultural labourers were in a similar condition of savagery. In the United States the pressure upon the least opulent class was extreme; and that prosperous country came to the knowledge of real and extensive distress. At home, the distress was so fearful that even the sanguine Duke of Wellington, with all his slowness to see the dark side in politics, and all his unwillingness to depress his valetudinarian sovereign, felt himself obliged to take emphatic notice of it in the royal speech; and the debates on the address, which were keen and protracted in both Houses, turned chiefly on the dispute whether the distress, which all admitted to be intolerable, was pervading or partial. The duke maintained that there were some parts of the kingdom where the distress was not pressing; the opposition maintained that there were none. The duke spoke of the ranges of new houses that were rising in the neighbourhood of most of the large towns, and declared that he had heard of no complaints on the part of the retail traders; while his opponents looked upon these ranges of new houses as monuments of the speculative mania of five years before; declared that they stood empty, or that their inhabitants were pining with hunger within the walls, unable to pay rent, and allowed to remain only because the owners knew that they could get no other tenants, and it was better for new houses to be inhabited than left empty. The interest of money was never known to be lower; and the manufacturers' stocks, with which their shelves were too well loaded, had suffered a depreciation of 40 per cent. The chancellor of the exchequer, we find, spoke this session of topics of 'consolation,' and no longer of 'congratulation;' and one subject of earnest deliberation with the ministers was whether they should propose a property-tax. They resolved against it; but the deliberation indicates the pressure of the time. The restless spirits of the mercantile and political world, who, in seasons of distress, want to be doing something for immediate relief, turned now, as usual, to the ready device of an issue of paper-money. This was urgently demanded, not only by many half-informed people throughout the country, but by some who should at least have known that they had better not speak on this subject unless they understood it. This idea—of an issue of paper-money— seems to have lain under the opposition to the address in both Houses, and to have been the real drift of the amendments proposed. And yet money was abundant throughout this period of distress; and as has been said, the interest of money never was lower.

The national discontent with the government was very great; and the discontent of the government with itself was hardly less. The continuance of the administration would not have been permitted for a day or an hour after the meeting of parliament, but for one consideration—the understood state of the king. And some members of the administration would not have borne the galling yoke of their military chief's authority, if they could, with any

honour or humanity, have left him, or known what to do
with themselves when free.

The state of things was understood to be this. The king,
always selfish and swayed by his passions, had been an
occasion of incessant difficulty to his ministers since the
failure of his prosecution of his queen. The sense of
weakness and loss of self-respect consequent on that failure
had added distrust of his servants to all the evil tempers
which existed in him before. His caprices became
incalculable. Like all jealous and suspicious people, he
was fond of having little plots of his own—sly ways of
putting his ministers to the proof, or disconcerting and
spiting them; so that, between this jealousy and his constitutional infirmity of purpose, matters had now come to
such a pass that his decisions and commands were worth
nothing. He changed his orders between night and
morning; and held contradictory opinions or notions from
day to day. It had become necessary to rule him first, in
order to rule the country. By some means or other, he
must be held to his pledges, and brought back to declared
opinions, and supported in the enforcement of his orders.
The Duke of Wellington could do this better than any
one else. At least, it was certain that if he failed, no one
else could succeed. The times were too grave for any
trifling—for any ungenerous driving on of party objects.
Nothing would have been easier than to turn out the
Wellington ministry any day; and nothing could be
harder than it was to some of the subordinates of the
premier to remain under his humiliating rule; but then
no other government was possible in the existing state of
affairs; and the consequences of leaving the king and
country without a ministry were too fearful to be braved
by the hardiest. All were aware, too, that there must be
a change before long, and every one was disposed to put
off all struggles of parties till the fair opportunity of a
new reign.

Rarely has a minister held a more lonely position than
the Duke of Wellington did at this date. He had no
party, no colleagues, no support of any kind—unless it
were that questionable support of which the country heard
much at the time—of fashion in London drawing-rooms.

There could hardly have been so many reports prevalent, and we could hardly meet with so many allusions to this kind of support in the records of the time, if there had not been some truth in the allegation that the duke was the fashion among the ladies in the higher circles in London, and that these talking ladies did no good to their hero, nor added any security to the chances of the perilous time by their exaltation of the despot of the day. Just as the court ladies of Charles X. were praising the vigour of Prince Polignac, the great ladies in London were praising the Duke of Wellington; and probably the consternation of the English ladies at what they saw before the year was out was nearly as great as that of the French ladies when they beheld their idol consigned to prison and civil death. Happily, however, the cases presented no further parallel. If Paris is France, London is not England; and England possesses a parliament with which no minister dreams of meddling, and a press which, as the Duke of Wellington found by an experience less disastrous than that of his friend Polignac, cannot be assailed with impunity.

First, for the Parliament—that is, the House of Commons —at this time. The opposition consisted of three parties, while the ministerial party was nothing. Mr. Peel was the only minister whom anybody saw or thought of in the Lower House; and his only natural and organised supporters were those who, under the name of adherents of the ministry, have no opinions, or are never asked for any, and therefore afford no particular credit to a government. Mr. Peel was observed with intense interest, and spared or supported by a generous admiration and sympathy, which graced the time, but could not long have put off the struggle of parliamentary conflict. The premier and he had carried the Catholic question in the best possible manner and temper that the circumstances admitted. Mr. Peel's sacrifices were universally respected ; his sincerity universally confided in thus far; and his present difficult position generously considered. He stood, in fact, the supporter and administrator of liberal principles ; and in order to be fraternised with by the leaders of the liberal opposition, it was only necessary that he should also

profess those principles which he was actually working
out. For this he was evidently not yet ready. His heart
could not yet be with those whom he had regarded as
antagonists during his whole political life; his heart was
naturally still with the allies with whom he had lived,
and worked, and fought, till now. This was easily com-
prehended; and it was known that he had suffered much
in his private and public relations on account of his recent
political conduct; and that he must suffer under the stern
rule of his chief; and that he must have his share of
difficulty in the relations of the cabinet with the king;
and therefore was he observed with intense interest—and
time was given him—and he was spared or supported by a
generous admiration and sympathy. Mr. Canning had
specially exempted him from censure for the secession
which he complained of in every other case; the Liberals
exempted him from the mockery and censure with which
they visited his comrades in conversion on the Catholic
question; and now, the liberal section of the opposition
exempted him from the censure with which they visited the
other managers of a perplexed and almost profitless session
—a session marked at the time as that which had exhibited
most talk and least work of any since the Conquest.

The premier's view of the opposition was, without disguise, one which did not secure him any indulgence
from it. The bulk of the opposition was the liberal party,
now strengthened and graced by an abundance of parliamentary talent, while its weakness of administrative
ability was, of course, not yet shown; and animated by
victory, hope, and expectation. Another powerful, though
small party, in opposition, was that of the 'Canningites,'
led by Mr. Huskisson in these his last days. The old
Tories made up the third party—not a very numerous
one, but strong in the energies of grief, disappointment,
and fear. The duke's tactics were well understood. He
expected to hold his position by playing off these parties
against each other. He did not see, as others did, that the
causes of their disunion had mainly disappeared, while,
amidst the heavings of this volcanic time, new ground had
arisen on which they might stand together, and look
abroad upon the agitations of the political sea. The duke

was blind to this, because he was not yet aware of the critical character of the times. He had seen the dangers of Ireland, and shown that he could yield to necessity, and do what was required. But he did not comprehend the state of France, nor entertain the least doubt that his friend Polignac would conquer there; and he was to speak a few words, the next November, which should show the existing generation and a remote posterity that the needs and destinies of England were no clearer to him than, as he should by that time have learned, were now those of France.

As for the union which was possible and probable between these three opposition parties—a union more probable at present than any practical antagonism—it must be remembered that a touchstone of political integrity had been applied universally in the Catholic emancipation measure. It was now clear which men had opinions and could hold to them. No one could be present at the debates of this session, and not see that a new feeling of mutual respect had grown up between the prominent men who had for life advocated, and for life opposed, Catholic emancipation. The dignity of irresistible victory belonged to the one set; and the dignity of adherence to conviction under the new adversity of opposition belonged to the other; and the mutual recognition attracted both to a cordial co-operation on questions on which they happened to agree. Then again, the Huskisson party was strongly united with the Tories on the subject of parliamentary reform, and with the Liberals on that of free-trade. And a clear understanding could not but exist among all the three in regard to the Wellington administration—that it could not, and must not, continue long; and that the utmost care and delicacy were necessary to support it as long as it was necessary, and to displace it in the least perilous time and manner. It is the belief of many that the premier was slow in becoming aware that he held office by the mercy of the opposition which he had expected to manage and control. It is certain that his experience with regard to Irish questions had not yet humbled him enough; and that the coming year was one of most painful discipline to him. He was first to learn, in the spring, however slow he might be in receiving the lesson, that his government was in itself quite powerless; and next, in the summer, how France spurned the government which had not beforehand seemed to him monstrous; and in the autumn—but that lesson shall be revealed in its own time. In the long life of the Duke of Wellington, perhaps no one year has taught him so much political truth, under a regimen of such severe discipline, as the year 1830.

He began the year with a course of action so weak and blind as really helped to justify the popular belief in France, and in some quarters at home, that he and Prince Polignac were, if not in league, at least actuated by strong sympathy. He began the year with a war, on his own account, against the press.

Perhaps no act of the Duke of Wellington's has ever injured him so much as this. It instantly lessened his power, and wholly altered the popular estimate of his character. Much of his power was derived from the impression, till then universal, that his self-reliance was not only indomitable, but so lofty as to be beyond the reach of foolish or malignant censure. Some persons had been rather surprised at his condescending to quarrel with Lord Winchilsea's random assertions; but now, when he directed the attorney-general to prosecute the *Morning Journal* for libels against the king, the government, and himself individually, people looked at one another, and asked whether this could be the man who was supposed to have the world under his feet. The libels complained of were very abusive; but they were, for the most part, extremely vague. One allegation of corruption, supposed to refer to the lord chancellor, was distinct; and it might, perhaps, be necessary to the reputation of a judge to rebut it; but, when the lord chancellor proceeded to prosecute on his own account, the editor of the paper made an affidavit that the charge did not refer to the lord chancellor. Upon this, the government pursued the charge, instituting a new prosecution for the same libel, as affecting some one member of the government, whoever he might be; and this proceeding, taking place after the defendant had disclosed his line of defence, was universally regarded as harsh and vindictive. But it was reasonable in comparison with the other prosecutions, which were for such vague charges as 'treachery, cowardice, and artifice,' and such gossip as that the king had been observed to look coldly on the Duke of Wellington, and giving hints of the reasons why the king did not appear in public. It was no small humiliation to the duke that he had to be reminded by the verdict of the jury, on the second of the three trials, that the time succeeding the passage of the Catholic Relief Bills was one of extreme excitement, when some allowance should be made for vehemence of temper, and intemperance of language. The prime-minister, who best knew the opposition of men's minds, should have been the first to make this allowance; and that he did not, materially damaged his reputation. The private chaplain of the Duke of Cumberland avowed himself the author of some of the libels; yet the printer and publisher were pursued for them. The duke's plea was, that such publications prevented the public excitement from subsiding; but there could be no doubt of the irritation being greatly aggravated by the prosecutions themselves. The Whig attorney-general, who remained in the ministry on the ground of the government being conducted on Whig principles, never recovered the ground he lost in the national esteem by these prosecutions. Mr. Scarlett after this obtained dignities, office, and title; but he was always felt to be a fallen man. Some contemporaries ascribed the whole proceeding to his, as others did, to Prince Polignac's influence over the mind of the Duke of Wellington. The *Examiner* of that date says of the proceeding: 'This may be hypochondria, or it may be Scarlett; for surely it cannot be intended to countenance the measures of Prince Polignac, and to persecute the press with a view to preserving conformity of councils. The coincidence is, at least, curious.' Under any supposition—whether the duke was spontaneously despotic, or whether he was wrought upon by Prince Polignac on the one hand, or Mr. Scarlett on the other—the reputation of the ministry, and especially of the premier, was deeply injured by these conflicts with the press. The editor of the *Morning Journal* and one of the proprietors were punished by fine and imprisonment.

The king's speech delivered by commission on the 4th of February, announced the peace concluded between Russia and Turkey; the continuance of the Portuguese quarrel; the distress among the agricultural and manufacturing classes at home, and the hope of the government that considerable reductions of expenditure might take place, without injury to the public service. The subject of improvements in the administration of the law was also recommended to the consideration of parliament; and measures were announced to answer this object, and prepare for a revision of the practice and proceedings of the superior courts.

Before the ministers could announce their plans of retrenchment, they formally pledged themselves to the principle and practice, to be pursued without hesitation or delay. Only a week after the opening of parliament, Sir James Graham brought forward a motion for a general reduction of the salaries of official persons, on the ground of the restoration of the value of money by Mr. Peel's bill of 1819. This motion was withdrawn in favour of a resolution proposed by Mr. Dawson, secretary to the treasury, urging, in the form of an address to the king, reduction of the persons employed in the departments of civil government, and of their salaries. Mr. Hume's motion for a committee of economical inquiry was also withdrawn, that the ministers might be left free to produce their plan. They did this on the 19th of February.

Such reductions as were now to be proposed almost always disappoint the popular expectation, because they must necessarily bear a very small proportion to the vast expenditure of a country ancient enough in its form of government and society to inherit the consequences of old financial errors, and to lie under heavy obligations of good faith. Not only ignorant demagogues in remote districts of the country, but some members of the House who should understand the history of British finance better than they do, point to the large amount of annual expenditure, and then to the small proposals of reduction, and scoff at the administration of the day—taking no pains to separate the expenditure of the administration of the day from that to which the present generation is bound by the pledges of a

former one. On the present occasion, there was less of this
method of complaint than usual—leading members in each
section of opposition making haste to declare that the
reductions proposed went beyond their expectations. The
reductions amounted altogether to £1,300,000; a large
sum out of the £12,000,000 from which alone they could
be deducted; but not an amount whose remission would
be any effectual relief to the country. All who knew best,
in each party, agreed that nothing further could at present
be done in the departments of the army and navy; a conclusion which was not, however, allowed to pass without
some severe taunting of the ministers about the state of
Ireland, which would not yet admit of any diminution of
the military force stationed there. It had been concluded
too hastily, some months before, that the pacification of
Ireland would follow upon the relief of the Catholics; and
now, Mr. Peel's mention of 'the two great hostile parties
in Ireland' was received with ironical congratulations by
those who did not see that the disturbed state of Ireland
was owing to the long delay of the measure of emancipation, which had exasperated the passions of parties to an
indomitable point.

The duties removed were those on beer, cider, and
leather, by which the direct relief to the people was calculated at £3,400,000; and the indirect at so much more as
would justify an estimate of £5,000,000 for the whole
boon. A prospect was held out of reducing the interest
on some portions of the national debt; and a searching
examination was going forward in every department of
government, into the minutest divisions of the public expenditure. This session gave the most important financial
relief to the nation of any since the peace; and the ac-
knowledgements of this by the liberal members of opposition were full and gracious. Mr. Baring regretted that
the project of annually paying off a portion of the principal of the national debt was surrendered for the sake of
present relief; but most people thought that the fact of a
deficit was hint enough to attend first to the immediate
pressure upon the people. The repeal of the beer-duty
met with great opposition from the landed interest in the
House, who would have preferred a repeal of the malt-

tax ; and from the agitation of the brewers and publicans, who were alarmed at the idea of cheap beer, and of the throwing open of the trade which was proposed to take place at the same time. But the measures suggested by the chancellor of the exchequer were all carried.

The government had promised, at the close of the preceding session, that a committee of parliament should be appointed this year to consider the whole subject of the jurisdiction and charter of the East India Company, as that charter was soon to expire. A committee was accordingly appointed this spring, the vast importance of its duties being emphatically indicated by Mr. Peel. The subjects of the Company had been computed to amount to ninety millions ; and the welfare of millions more was implicated with theirs ; it was therefore impossible to overrate the seriousness of the inquiry whether the territorial and commercial powers of the Company should be continued ; and if continued, on what understanding and what terms. The Company had kept silence as to their own desires and intentions ; the government had no propositions to make, or opinions to express ; and the committee entered upon its work with every possible appearance of impartiality, and security for it. There was some remonstrance, here and there, about the appointment of three or four India directors to serve on the committee ; but the objection gave way before the need that was felt of their information on the affairs of India and of the Company. The result of the investigations of this committee will appear hereafter.

The speech had referred to proposed improvements in the administration of the law. One great improvement which took place this session—an incident so remarkable as to deserve special mention—was the removal of an unjust judge. The crown was addressed by both Houses of parliament, praying for the removal of the judge of the High Court of Admiralty in Ireland—Sir Jonah Barrington—who had been lately discovered to have been guilty of malversation in the years 1805, 1806, and 1810. The facts were clear, and part of the evidence consisted of documents in the handwriting of the accused, which showed that he had appropriated to his own use some of

the proceeds of derelict vessels adjudicated on by himself.
He was, of course, removed. The shock which this proceeding caused throughout the country testified strongly
to the confidence—so unhesitating as to become natural—
which society in England has in the integrity of its
judges.

An important alteration in the administration of the
law was, that Wales was annexed to the English judicature, its own separate system being abolished. Instead of
twelve, there were to be henceforward fifteen English
judges; a new judge being added to each of the three
courts of King's Bench, Common Pleas, and Exchequer.
In Scotland, two courts were abolished—the High Court
of Admiralty and the Commissary Court; and thus the
Court of Session had more to do. It was thought, however, that the Court of Session had still more judges than
were necessary; and their number was reduced from
fifteen to thirteen.

Mr. Peel brought in a bill, on the 1st of April, to cir-
cumscribe the infliction of the punishment of death for
forgery. He proposed to abolish the death penalty in all
cases where the forgery could have been defied by any
degree whatever of care on the part of the person injured,
preserving it only in cases of the forgery of the great seal,
the privy seal, and the sign-manual; in forgeries of wills,
on the public funds, on bank or money notes or orders, or
representatives of money in any shape. This bill, important as it was, did not meet the views of those who
believed that the punishment of death for forgery did not
discourage the crime, and did hinder conviction for it;
and Sir James Mackintosh proposed and carried a clause
repealing the penalty in all cases of forgery but that of
wills. The Lords restored the bill to its original state,
and sent it down so late in the session as to cause a question whether it should be accepted in the Commons, or
thrown out, in the moral certainty that no lives would be
forfeited under portions of a law which it was understood
would be repealed in a few months. On the whole, it was
thought best to take at once what was offered, and seek
the rest hereafter; and Mr. Peel's bill passed.

The cause of the Jews was advocated strongly in the

House this session, as it was likely to be after the admission of the Catholics to parliament. Mr. Robert Grant opened the subject, and was supported at once by many of the ablest men in the House; and afterwards by a considerable body of petitions from the towns. There was a majority of 18 in favour of the introduction of the bill; but it was thrown out on the second reading by a majority of 228 over 165. The arguments against the admission of the Jews to parliament were of the usual untenable and mutually contradictory sort. The Jews were too few to be worth regarding, but they would overthrow the Christianity of the legislature; some Jews once hated the Founder of Christianity, and therefore all Jews would now seek to overthrow his Church. Nobody wished it; and then, again, the desire to favour Jews showed the prevalent disposition to infidelity. All the petitions on the subject were in favour of the Jews; there was not one against them: and this proved how carefully they must be kept out, as a class of infidels powerful through popular sympathy. The most amusing plea was, that it was unreasonable to admit Jews while Quakers were excluded; to which the friends of the Jews replied, by offering to admit the Quakers immediately. To us it is strange to look back now, and see how long ago the Quakers were admitted, while the Jews still stand waiting outside; it is strange to think that that method of management still subsists by which the hypocrite and lax holder of opinion find entrance without difficulty to the national councils, while the conscientious Jew, one of a body of singularly loyal and orderly and useful subjects, is excluded on account of a difference of belief on matters which, as is shown by the fundamental diversities of faith which exist within the walls of parliament, can have nothing to do with the business which goes forward there. The real difficulty probably is, in all such cases, that men suppose a proselyting tendency in all who differ from themselves. In the case of the Catholics, there might be some colour of reason for such an apprehension; but as everybody ought to know, there can be none such in the case of a Jew. A Jew no more desires to make Gentiles Jews, than a peer desires to make all the commonalty peers. In both cases, the privilege must come from the fountain of privilege, and its value lies mainly in its restriction. The Jews consider themselves the peerage of the human race, and accordingly have no tendency to proselytism.

At the beginning of this session it is probable that no one foresaw what a vigorous growth of the political life of the nation was about to take place through the agitation of the question of parliamentary reform. This was beyond human foresight; because as yet the French revolution had not taken place, and its stimulating influence upon the politics of England could not be anticipated. But the subject of parliamentary reform was not neglected. The Marquis of Blandford was still too angry with parliament for passing the Catholic Relief Bill, still too firmly persuaded that the people of England were averse to Catholic emancipation, to give up his attempt to destroy the existing constitution of the House of Commons. The spectacle is curious of the zeal of this violent anti-Catholic gentleman, in the most 'radical and revolutionary' question of the day; a zeal so vehement and rash, that long-avowed advocates of reform of parliament could by no means keep it in check, or prevent its throwing ridicule on their great cause. The Marquis of Blandford moved a very extraordinary amendment to the address on the 5th of February; an amendment which he called a 'wholesome admonition to the throne.' This amendment declared—what would have astonished the king very much if it had been carried—that the House was determined that his majesty should not be the only person in his dominions left ignorant of the astounding fact of the deep and universal distress of the nation, and the consequent impending danger to the throne, and all the venerable institutions of the country. The reason assigned for the distress was the deviation from the true principle of representation, shown in the existence of purchaseable seats in parliament; by means of which the House was filled with men who considered their own interests alone, and heaped a ruinous weight of taxation upon the country; to remedy which, the king was exhorted to revert to the wisdom of our ancestors, and to make the House of Commons once more a representation of the popular will.

On account of the truth mixed up with exaggeration and
error in the long amendment of the marquis, several of
the liberal members voted for it; but all agreed that the
subject was too vast and important to be dealt with as an
amendment on the address; and that a more definite
statement of the object desired must be proposed before
the House could pass a really useful vote on any part of
the subject.

As early as the 18th of the same month, accordingly,
the marquis was ready to put the House in possession of
his plan. Though the French revolution had not yet
happened, the old Tories might be excused for thinking
that the world was coming to an end, when they saw the
Marquis of Blandford making advances to Mr. O'Connell,
in promotion of the most 'revolutionary project' of the
century; and Mr. O'Connell, again, fraternising with
the Polignac ministry and the Bourbons, and expending
all the virulence of his abuse on the liberals of France.
We have on record some of the sayings of the time
which reveal the state of men's minds. First, we have
the old Tory, Lord Eldon, who writes of the Wellington
policy as 'establishing a precedent so dangerous, so
encouraging to the present attempts at revolution under
the name of reform, that he must be, in my judgment, a
very bold fool who does not tremble at what seems to be
fast approaching. Look, too, at France. The ministers
beat in the chambers, on the first day, by a very considerable majority! What the Duke of Wellington will
do, I pretend not to guess. What will be said now about
the fact that all the occasional laws against sedition have
been suffered to expire? Heaven save us now! for in
man there is no sufficient help.' Then we have the Tory
turned Radical, by the consternation which only plunged
Lord Eldon 'in very low spirits.' The Marquis of
Blandford said that 'the honourable and learned member
for Clare had expressed sentiments on this momentous
topic in which he most cordially concurred. He was
happy to see that honourable gentleman devote his talents
to the reprobation of so execrable a system, and he could
assure him that he would gladly join heart and hand with
so efficient a coadjutor in procuring its abolition.' And

next we have this member for Clare, this efficient
coadjutor in the cause of parliamentary reform in London
vituperating the men who were risking their all in vindicating the principle of parliamentary representation in
Paris. 'I a Liberal!' exclaims Mr. O'Connell, at this
juncture. 'No: I despise the French liberals. I consider them the enemies, not only of religion, but of liberty;
and I am thoroughly convinced that religion is the only
secure basis of human freedom.' The assumption that
because the French liberals resisted tyranny, they therefore resisted religion, is worthy of Lord Eldon; but a
stroke of absurdity follows, too gross for even Lord Eldon.
Mr. O'Connell summed up by declaring himself a Ben-
thamite. To the end of his days he cherished his hatred of
all liberalism in France, probably from his leaning towards
the authority of the Jesuits. That he had no faith in the
Orleans family, and no congratulations to offer on their accession, is not to be wondered at; but his loyalty to the old
Bourbons was a trait which, in the self-styled Liberator of
Ireland, was too much for most men's gravity. 'The
Liberals,' he rashly and ignorantly declared, 'do not
desire any liberty save that of crushing religion, and once
again imbruing their hands in the blood of the clergy'—
an assertion which is merely an exaggeration of the terrors
of the 'Protestant' members of the House of Lords about
the Irish Liberals. Such were some of the curious incidents of the time.

The Marquis of Blandford's plan was radical indeed.
He proposed that a committee of parliament should be
chosen by ballot, who should inquire into the condition of
all the cities and boroughs in the kingdom, and should
report to the home secretary all that had forfeited the fair
conditions of representation; as if this last was a point so
clear as to be left to the decision of any 'committee
chosen by ballot!' The home secretary was immediately
to notify the forfeiture to these constituencies and to the
public through the *Gazette;* and the vacancies were to be
filled up by representation of large towns, hitherto excluded. No compensation was to be given to the proprietors of disfranchised boroughs, unless such conciliation
should be absolutely requisite to the passage of the measure.

All members were to be paid; city and borough representatives two pounds, and county members four pounds per day; and all were to have been hitherto residents among the constituencies which they represented. Copyholders and certain leaseholders were to enjoy the franchise; and Scotland was to be placed on the same footing with England. The most obvious objection here is to the vagueness about the true principle of representation by which the committee were to try the existing state of the cities and boroughs of England. If, as the mover declared, abundant information and authority were to be found in the law and history of England, it was clearly necessary to find and arrange them—to fix the test—before proceeding to the trial. That such a proposition should be entertained at all, and debated through a long sitting, showed the earnestness that existed for some measure of parliamentary reform. Lord Althorp moved, as an amendment, at a late hour, the resolution: 'That it is the opinion of this House that a reform in the representation of the people is necessary.' The majority against the amendment was 113; and then the original motion was negatived.

The question about the destiny of East Retford was brought forward again; that question which had cost Mr. Huskisson his seat in the government two years before. He voted as formerly; and there were 99 votes in favour of the transference of the representation to Birmingham; but 126 voted on the other side; and thus, in the opinion of many, cast the die which turned up 'revolution.' There are many who believe, at this day, that if the representation of Birmingham had been permitted at that time, a bit-by-bit reform would have taken place, instead of the sweeping measure which its enemies might be permitted to call 'revolution.' In Mr. Huskisson's speech on this occasion we find the first historical mention of the political unions, which were now to form so prominent a feature of the times. The notice was this: 'He saw in Birmingham, lately, an association which, as far as he could perceive its elements, principles, and operations, seemed exactly formed on the model of the Catholic Association; for it had its subscriptions, its funds, its meetings, its discussions, and its agitator. The pur-

pose of this association was to raise a universal cry for
parliamentary reform—to carry the question by exaggera-
ting the difficulties, abuses, and distresses of the country.
Admiring, as he did, the talent of the gentleman who
took the lead (Mr. Attwood) at the Birmingham meeting, he, for one, would much rather see that gentleman
in the House of Commons—as fortunately he saw the
honourable member for Clare in the House of Commons.
He would rather see the leader of the Birmingham meeting here as the representative of that town, than in conducting such an association, sending forth those statements and appeals to the country, which was, perhaps, too
prone, at the present moment, to act on the apprehensions
generated by them.' Is it possible that Mr. Huskisson
did not see—he who had so clear an eye for some things
less evident—that when the attention of any portion of
the English people is once fairly fixed on the principle of
any one of their institutions, the yielding of a single point
of detail can never satisfy them? If Birmingham had at
that time obtained representation, and had sent Mr.
Attwood to parliament, did he suppose that the Birmingham Union would have dissolved, any more than the
Catholic Association would have dissolved if Mr. O'Connell
had been permitted to take his seat after his first election
for Clare? The Birmingham Political Union was formed
for the promotion of the whole question of parliamentary
reform, and not only for obtaining a representation of its
own town. If this enfranchisement had been granted
now, the success would have stimulated Manchester and
Leeds, and other places, to a similar pursuit of their
object; and then the old Tories would have charged the
government with the consequences of yielding to popular
movements. As it was, the denial answered the same
purpose, of stimulating the popular will. The truth was,
the time was come for the change. It mattered little,
except as to the tempers of the parties concerned, whether
government gave assent or denial. The time was come
for the rending of the garments which the nation's life
had outgrown; and the agreement or refusal to mend the
first slit could make but the difference of a day in the
providing of a new suit. The Duke of Wellington was

soon to show that he saw nothing of this; but if Mr.
Huskisson did not, it is only a fresh proof how little those
who stand in the midst of a crowd of events can see
before them.

Lord John Russell brought forward the subject of the
representation of large towns, by moving for leave to bring
in a bill to enable Birmingham, Manchester, and Leeds to
return members to the House of Commons; and this was the
occasion of Mr. Huskisson's last speech on parliamentary
reform. He supported the motion, but under protest
against any extension of the boon beyond special and very
pressing cases. There is an interest in reading his statement of his views, though his views may not be ours, as
the last words we shall be able to give of one whose
memory will ever be precious to his country. ' To such a
measure of reform,' as the present ' he should give his
cordial support. As to a more extensive parliamentary
reform—a measure founded upon the principle of a
general revision, reconstruction, and remodelling of our
present constitution—to such a general revision, and
change of our constitution, he had been always opposed;
and while he had a seat in that House, he should give it his
most decided opposition. He conceived that if such an
extensive reform were effected, they might go on for two
or three sessions in good and easy times, and such a
reformed parliament might adapt itself to our mode of
government and the ordinary concerns of the country;
but if such an extensive change were effected in the constitution of parliament, sure he was that whenever an
occasion arose of great popular excitement or reaction,
the consequence would be a total subversion of our constitution, followed by complete confusion and anarchy,
terminating first, in the tyranny of a fierce democracy, and
then in that of a military despotism, these two great
calamities maintaining that natural order of succession
which they have always been hitherto seen to observe.
He was therefore opposed to such an extensive change
and revision of our representative system. It might be
easy to raise objections to the boroughs, and by separating
the representative system into its various constituent parts,
to point out evils and abuses in several of them; but it

was a waste of time, and a perversion of common sense, to
look at it in that way. He would take it as a whole, and
regarding our present system as one aggregate, he was
opposed to any material change in it.'

Weak words—to be the last from such a man ! With
the explosive elements of wrong involved, as he allowed,
in this aggregate, was the entireness to be best preserved
by leaving the explosive elements to burst and shatter
everything connected with them, or by taking them out
while they might yet be safely handled? These were
weak words to be the last from such a man; but the wisest
men are weak when they prophesy of the future under the
instigation of fear instead of the inspiration of faith. The
motion was lost by a majority of 48. The subject was
brought up again in May, however, when Lord John
Russell took occasion to propose two resolutions in the
place of a motion of Mr. O'Connell's, which was negatived.
Mr. O'Connell's motion was for leave to bring in a bill to
establish universal suffrage, triennial parliaments, and
vote by ballot. Lord John Russell's resolutions were in
favour of an increase in the number of representatives,
and for the additional ones being given to large towns and
populous counties. This incessant bringing-up of the
subject during the session, by Tory, Whig, and Radical
leaders, testifies to the progress of the question in the
national will. The French revolution might accelerate
the demand and the movement; but these preceding
transactions show that parliamentary reform would have
been required and obtained without the awakening of any
new sympathy with any foreign people.

The man in all England who, at this critical season, did
most to promote the cause of parliamentary reform, was
the Duke of Newcastle. He made an avowal so broad and
clear of his belief that the franchises of the citizens of
Newark were his own, as much as any property whatever
that he held, that many were startled into a contemplation
of the actual system itself, who might otherwise have continued to argue about mere words. The independent voters
of Newark sent up a petition to parliament complaining of
the undue influence of the Duke of Newcastle in the elections, which he exercised without any apparent recollection

of the statute which prohibits the interference of peers in elections. The Duke's influence was mainly derived from his being the lessee of crown-lands, amounting to 960 acres, which formed a sort of belt round three-fourths of the town of Newark. The ministers declared plainly in the House that they had no intention of renewing the lease of these lands to the Duke of Newcastle; and this being the case, and the exposure and disgrace very complete, the committee asked for was considered by the majority not to be needful. The most really useful part of the affair, however, was the innocent amazement of the peer himself at such an interference with his use of his influence; an amazement expressed in words which were never let drop for a day during the continuance of the reform agitation, and which are a proverb to this hour: 'May I not do what I will with mine own?' He had looked upon the electors of Newark as his 'own;' but the 587 who had resisted his dictation, and striven to return an independent member, were very far from answering to the peer's notion of what Newark electors ought to be; and a great blessing the country from this time felt it to be, that there were 587 electors within the duke's belt of land who were not his 'own.'

The general impression that the king was very ill continued in the absence of all reliable information about his state, and notwithstanding the activity of the preparations for his customary birthday fête in April. It became known at length, however, that those preparations were countermanded; and on the 15th of April his majesty's physicians issued a bulletin, announcing that the king was ill of a bilious attack, accompanied with difficulty in breathing. The bulletins during this illness were extraordinarily deceptive; and the nation was kept as nearly as possible in the dark about the king's state to the last—almost every bulletin declaring him better, till, as a contemporary observed: 'Amidst these accumulated betternesses, the nation was wondering why he was not well, when it heard that he was dead.' It is supposed that the king insisted on seeing the bulletins, and that the physicians feared the responsibility of making them true. This is a mockery which should have been prevented by some means or other.

On the 24th of May, however, a message from the king to both Houses of parliament, indicated the truth. The message told that the king was so ill that it was inconvenient and painful to him to sign papers with his own hand, and that he relied on the readiness of parliament to consider without delay how he might be relieved of this labour. There was no doubt in this case about the reality of the bodily illness, nor of the ability of the king to understand and give orders about the business brought before him; but the danger of the precedent was very properly kept in view, and the provision for affixing the sign-manual without trouble to the king was fenced about with all possible precautions, which could prevent the authority from being used by the creatures of an insane sovereign. The stamp was to be affixed in the king's presence, by his immediate order given by word of mouth, to obviate mistake of any sign by head or hand; a memorandum of the circumstances must accompany the stamp; and the document stamped must be previously endorsed by three members of the privy-council. The operation of the bill was limited to the present session, that, if the king's illness should continue, the irregular authority asked for must be renewed at short intervals. The bill was passed on the 28th of May; and the occasion for its use was over within a month. The king died at three o'clock in the morning of the 26th of June. The final struggle was sudden and short. He was sitting up when he felt what appears to be the peculiar and unmistakable sensation of death. He leaned his head on the shoulder of a page, exclaimed: 'O God! this is death!' and was gone. The immediate cause was the rupture of a blood-vessel in the stomach. Ossification of some of the large vessels about the heart had begun many years previously; and, before the end, the complication of diseases had become terrible.

The Kings of England and France were beckoned down from their thrones nearly at the same time. George IV. died just after his brother of France had issued his canvassing proclamation—his last words to his people—and before the result could be known; and both sovereigns were in a state of discontent, anger, and fear at the state of the popular mind, and in view of the future. Two men more unhappy than they were at this time could hardly have been found in the dominions of both.

It would indeed be difficult to point to a more unhappy life, through its whole extent, than that of George IV. Nothing went well with him; and as his troubles came chiefly from within, he had none of the compensations which have waited upon the most unfortunate of kings. Kings defeated, captive, dethroned—or diseased in body, or betrayed in their domestic relations—have usually had solace from noble emotions, strenuous acts, or sweet domestic affections. But our unhappy king had none of these. Through life he achieved nothing. He was neither a warrior, nor a statesman, nor a student, nor a domestic man. If he had been even a mechanic, like Louis XVI. the locksmith, it would have been something. He was nothing but the man of pleasure ; and, even in an ordinary rank, no one leads such a life of pain as the man of pleasure. In his rank, where real companionship is out of the question, even that life of pain is deprived of its chief solace—the fellowship of comrades. The 'first gentleman in Europe' might make himself as vulgar as he would in the pursuits of dissipation ; he was still prince, and therefore excluded from the hilarity which cannot exist where there is not equality.

His youth was unhappy. His parents disliked and restricted him, and thus drove him early into distrust and offence. What his married life was is seen in the story of his queen. If he loved his only child, she did not love him ; and he lost her. He had no friends; and if he chose to give that name to any of his counsellors, he knew that he had often their disapprobation and their compassion. Between himself and his people there was no tie, nor any pretence of one. He never showed the least desire for their happiness, which involved any personal sacrifice. He showed himself capable of petty resentments; he showed himself incapable of magnanimity. He let it be seen that the best government of his reign took place against his will, while he attempted disgraceful acts which did not succeed. He surrounded himself with persons whom the nation could not respect, while his selfish prodigality at their expense checked every growth of that loyalty which springs from personal attachment and esteem. Faulty as was his temper, his principles were no better. We have seen in the course of this history that his word was utterly unreliable; and other proofs stood out from the whole surface of his life. If it is asked whether there was no good to set against this amount of evil, the only answer, probably, that could be given by those most disposed in his favour is, that he was kindly and warm in his feelings towards those whom he took for his companions, whatever their deserts; and that he could be extremely agreeable and winning, and even outwardly dignified, when he chose. Like all princes, he had his flatterers; and while he lived, praises of the sovereign were afloat, as they are in every reign. The glories and blessings which accrued to the nation in his time, naturally appeared to belong more or less to him at the moment. But it is not so after the lapse of twenty years. When we now look back upon the close of the war, the breaking up of the Holy Alliance, the reduction of taxation, the improvement in freedom of speech and the press, the emancipation of the Dissenters and the Catholics, and the establishment of the principle and some of the practice of free-trade, we involuntarily regard these as the acts and experience of a nation without a head. If it is now a conviction very common among us, that besides that irresistible influence which emanates from personal character, the sovereign has, with us, no longer any power but for obstruction, it is certain that no one person has done so much to ripen and extend this conviction as George IV. He declined the noble prerogative of rule over the heart and mind of his people by personal qualities, while using such opportunities as he had of reminding them of his obstructive power; and his death was received by them with an indifference proportioned to such deserts.

He died in the sixty-eighth year of his age, and the eleventh of his reign; previous to which he had held the regency for ten years.

CHAPTER XI.

Character of the Reign—Achievements—Desiderata—State of Opera-
tives—Crimes and Punishments—Accidents—Arts and Edifices—
Hanwell Asylum—Drainage—Railway—Reading for the Blind—
Scott's Novels—Shakspeare Festival—Actors—Irving—Religious
Parties—Conversions of Catholics—Intolerance of Opinion—Dis-
senters' Marriages—Press at Calcutta—Stamp Duty—Protector of
Slaves—Treaty with Brazil—Spring-guns—Society for the Diffusion
of Useful Knowledge—Necrology—Political Deaths—Travellers—
Men of Business—Artists—Men of Letters—Philosophers—Philan-
thropists.

AT the close of the first reign since the peace, it is easy to
see that a great improvement in the national welfare had
taken place, though the period was in itself one of gloom
and agitation. The old Tory rule was broken up, like an
ice-field in spring, and the winds were all abroad to prevent its reuniting. There were obstacles ahead; but so
many were floating away behind, that the expectation of
progress was clear and strong. On every account it was
a good thing that the old Tory rule was broken up; but
chiefly for this—that when the thing was done by the
strong compulsion of fact, of necessity, men were beginning
to look for the principle of the change, and thereby to
obtain some insight into the views of the parties that had
governed, or would or might govern the country. Men
began to have some practical conception that the Tories
thought it their duty to govern the people (for their good)
as a disposable property; that the Whigs thought it their
duty to govern as trustees of the nation, according to their
own discretion; and that there were persons living and
effectually moving in the world of politics, who thought
that the people ought to govern themselves through the
House of Commons. This perception once awakened, a
new time had from that moment begun, of which we are
at this day very far from seeing the end. With the departure of George IV. into the region of the past, we are
taking leave of the old time, and can almost join in even

Lord Eldon's declarations about the passing away of the things that had been, and the incoming of a new and portentous age of the national history, though we do not sympathise in his terrors and regrets, nor agree with him that what had been dropped was that which should have been retained, and that whatever should supervene was to be deprecated because it was new. We have, what the old Tories have not, and cannot conceive of, the deepest satisfaction in every proof that the national soul is alive and awake, that the national mind is up and stirring. There was proof of this, at the close of this reign, in what had been done, and in what was clearly about to be done; and this trumpet-call to advance was heard above loud groans of suffering, and deep sighs of depression; and the nation marshalled itself for the advance accordingly.

As for the facts of what had been done, the old Tory rule by hereditary custom, or an understanding among the 'great families' whom Mr. Canning so mortally offended, was broken up. Exclusion from social right and privilege on account of religious opinion was broken up; that is, the system was, as a whole, though some partial exclusion remained, and remains to this day. In the same manner, the system of commercial restriction was broken up, though in practice monopoly was as yet far more extensive than liberty of commerce. Slavery was brought up for trial at the tribunal of the national conscience; and, whatever might be the issue, impunity at least was at an end. The delusion of the perfection of existing law was at an end; and the national conscience was appealed to, to denounce legal vengeance and cruelty, to substitute justice in their place. Hope had dawned for the most miserable classes of society; for, while some of the first men in the nation were contending for an amelioration of the criminal law in parliament, one of the first women of her time was going through the prisons, to watch over and enlighten the victims of sin and ignorance. The admission of a new order of men into the cabinet; the bending of the old order, even of the iron duke himself, to their policy; the emancipation of Dissenters and Catholics; the adoption of some measures on behalf of slaves; the partial adoption of free-trade; the continued ameliorations of the criminal law through the efforts of Sir S. Romilly, Mr. Peel, and Sir James Mackintosh; and the interest excited in the condition of prisoners by the exertions of Mrs. Fry—are features in the domestic policy of England which must mark for ever as illustrious the first reign succeeding the peace.

Its chief misfortune, perhaps, is that it introduced a method, which some consider a principle of government—which cannot, from its nature, be permanent, and which no one would wish to be so. Now began, with the Catholic relief measure, that practice of granting to clamour and intimidation what would not otherwise have been granted, which has ever since been the most unfavourable feature of our political history. The mischief began with the delay in granting the Catholics their fair claims; and those who caused that delay are answerable for the mischief. They are doubtless right in deprecating the evil, and in calling it a revolutionary symptom or fact; but they are wrong in laying it at any door but their own. It was not till the Whigs came into power that the greatness of the evil was evident to everybody; and then, when the Whigs alone were blamed for it, the censure was unjust. The earlier liberal measures were pushed forward in good time. Mr. Canning's foreign policy, and Mr. Huskisson's free-trade, and all the ameliorations of the criminal law, were the results of the ideas of the men who offered them; offered before the nation was ready to demand them in a way not to be refused. With Catholic emancipation the change came. The leading members of the government avowed their disinclination for the measure, and that it was extorted by necessity. In the story which we shall have next to tell, we shall see the consequences. They did not appear immediately; for, though reform of parliament would have been extorted from an unwilling government, there was happily a willing government ready to grant it. It was as much the result of the ideas of the men who gave it as Mr. Canning's foreign policy, and Mr. Huskisson's free-trade; and all the world knew that the members of the government had advocated this reform for long years past, through evil and through good report; and they could, therefore, now bestow the boon with con-

summate grace. But the history of other transactions will
not prove so gratifying. We shall have occasion to see
how the Whigs were, not only what all rulers of our day
must be—the servants, instead of the masters, of principles
of policy—but the servants, instead of the rulers, of the
loudest shouters of the hour; and with the less dignity from
their being the professors of popular principles. Dangerous
as it might be to see a Wellington and a Peel yielding to
popular demands what they would never have originated,
there might be, and there was, a certain dignity in it—a
touch of heroic mournfulness which is altogether absent
in the other case—when leaders professedly liberal do not
originate measures, but have them extorted against their
own convictions, by the clamour of their own preponderating party. As we shall see, there has been too
much of this in a succeeding time; and some fearful consequences have probably to be met hereafter; but this is
the place in which to fix the reproach where it is due—to
charge upon the anti-Catholic portion of the aristocracy
the consequences, be they what they may, of first compel-
ling concessions to popular intimidation, and turning back
the government from its glorious post of guide and ruler
of the will of the people, to the ignominy of being its
reluctant follower and servant.

As for what remained to be done—obviously in the
view of all the people—the House of Commons must
be reconstituted; municipal government must be purified;
slavery must be abolished; something must be done to
lighten the intolerable burden of the poor-law; the corn-
laws, and as a consequence, the game-laws, must be repealed; religious liberty must be made complete; the
youth of the nation must be educated; and something
remained over and above, and still remains—more important and more pressing, if all men could but see it, than all
these put together: the industrious must have their deserts
of food and comfort. The poor-law, the corn-law, taxation,
and education—these, if properly taken in hand, and
amended to the utmost, might do something; but whatever they might leave over must be done. It cannot, in the
nature of things, happen for ever, or for very long, that
men in rural districts shall toil every day and all day

long, without obtaining food for themselves and their
children; or that men in the towns should sit at the
loom, or stand over the spindles through all the working-
hours of the day, for their whole lives, till age comes upon
them, and then have no resource but the workhouse.   The
greatest work remaining to be done, was to discover where
the fault lies, and to amend it while there was yet time.
We shall hereafter see what has been done to this end;
and must then draw our inferences as to what remains to
be done.

In 1829, the weavers of Lancashire and Cheshire were
earning, at best, from 4s. 4½d. to 6s. per week when at
work. The most favoured had to wait a week or two
between one piece of work and the next; and about a
fourth of the whole number were out of employ altogether.
The parishes made allowances in the proportion necessary
to enable these people to procure food and shelter; and
the burden became so heavy, that a continually increasing
number of rate-payers sank down into the condition of
paupers.   At this time, a cotton-mill was burned down at
Chorley, in Lancashire; and there was reason to suspect
that the fire was not accidental—disputes having taken
place between the proprietors and their men about wages.
The factory was rebuilt; and persons were employed at
the rate of wages formerly given. An advance was soon
demanded and refused. The spinners turned out; and
they used every effort to prevent others from taking their
places; but, where so many were in need, hands were
sure to be found. Four of the new workers lodged in the
house of one of the overseers. At one o'clock in the
morning (June 17, 1830), a tremendous explosion shook
the house to its foundation, destroyed the furniture, and
blew out all the doors and windows—without, however,
materially injuring any of the inmates. A common break-
fast-can, containing gunpowder, had been let down the
chimney, and ignited by a slow match. Here was one
symptom of the state of society which could not long exist.
Amidst fearful records of the destruction of property in
the manufacturing districts by men wild with hunger, we
meet with the yet more sickening stories of the Hibners
and Philps, who hardly escaped from the hands of the

mob for their treatment of parish apprentices. The name of Esther Hibner is familiarised to all ears by its infamy. The sum of her history is, that she treated her apprentices as the most barbarous and depraved of slaveholders treats his slaves, whom he would rather torture than make a profit of. She starved them; she beat them; she pulled out their hair; she had them ducked; till, happily, one died of the ill-usage, and the others were in consequence rescued. Esther Hibner was hanged. In this case, protection came when only one life had been sacrificed; but the succession of cases that was revealed at this time, and the general impression conveyed by the evidence, caused a conviction that the pauper apprentices were too many and too helpless to be properly cared for; and that there must be something intolerably wrong in the state of society which permitted them to swarm as they did. During the same period, a case here and there appeared at the police-offices, or came to the knowledge of inquiring men, which showed that if the amount of pauperism was becoming unmanageable, so were the abuses of pauper funds. The corruption of morals caused by the parish allowance for infants was more like the agency of demons than the consequence of a legislative mistake. In many rural districts, it was scarcely possible to meet with a young woman who was respectable; so tempting was the parish allowance for infants in a time of great pressure. And then again, there were the pauper marriages; old drunkards marrying the worst subjects they could find in the neighbouring workhouses, for the sake of the fee of two or three pounds given to get rid of the woman. The poverty of the industrious, the violence of the exasperated, the cruelty of the oppressor, the corruption of the tempted, the swindling of the corrupt, and the waste of the means of life all round, to a point which threatened the stability of the whole of society; these were things which could not long endure, and which made the thoughtful look anxiously for a change. The amount of poor-rate expenditure for relief at this time was between six and seven millions annually; and incessantly on the increase.

First among the changes needed was the introduction of an abundance of food. While, however, men, women, and

children, were actually wan and shrunken with hunger,
they saw a sight which turned their patient sighs into
angry curses. When the poor Irish lay hands on grain
about to be exported, we do not wonder at the act, though
we would fain make them understand that by the sale of
that grain comes the fund which is their only resource for
the payment of their labour, and their consequent means
of bread, and hope of next year's crop. But when the
hungering peasant sees whole breadths of wheat devoured
or laid waste before his eyes by the hares and pheasants
of his rich neighbour, what can be said that shall deter
him from putting in for his share? During this period
the jails were half filled with offenders against the game-
laws; and besides the melancholy stories so frequent as to
weary the newspaper reader of poaching affrays, in which
men of the one party were killed by violence in the night,
and men of the other party were afterwards killed by law,
we find a new order of offences rising up under the vicious
system. We find that men prowled about in the fields
near the great game covers, strewing and sowing poisoned
grain. Country gentlemen were not then so well aware
as later events have made some of them of the danger of
suggesting to the ignorant peasant the use of poison, in
any kind of self-defence against his neighbour. But if the
evil had never spread beyond the poisoning of pheasants
and hares, there was enough in it to induce any thoughtful and humane man to inquire whether he was not pursuing his sports at too great a cost. If he did not know,
and would not learn, the amount of social injury that he
was causing in the useless consumption or destruction of
food, it was clear to all eyes that he was causing his
brother to offend by his persistence in the pursuit of a
mere amusement. Some transactions of this time between
the country gentlemen and their peasant neighbours
remind us but too strongly of the days before the first
French Revolution, when the great man of the chateau
kept the neighbouring cottagers up all night, whipping
the ponds, to silence the frogs. Subsequent events showed
that these cottagers were of opinion that, as they were to
toil for the great man in the day, he should have protected,
instead of forbidding, their sleep at night; and events

were now at hand which indicated something of the feeling of the ignorant and suffering peasantry against the landed interests of England.

It is during this period that we come upon the traces of the practice which is, beyond all others, the opprobrium of our time—the practice of poisoning for the gratification of selfish passion. The perpetrators are of a different order from those of whom we read in the history of past centuries—of whom we read with a shudder at the thought of living in such times; but the crime is as desperate in our day, and, it is to be feared, more extensive. Then, it was the holders of science and their intimates that did it—those who ought best to have known the value of human life and the irredeemable guilt of cruel treachery. In our day, it is the lowest of the low who do it; people whose ignorance and folly, offered in evidence on their trial, make us aghast to think how, when, and where we are living, with beings like these for fellow-citizens. We look upon these fellow-citizens of ours as upon ill-conditioned children, killing flies for their amusement, and breaking windows in their passion. They know nothing of the sacredness of human life, of virtue, decency, good fame, or of doing as they would be done by. They want something—money, or a lover, or a house, or to be free of the trouble of an infant; and they put out the life which stands in the way of what they want. Time and experience appear to show that this is but the beginning. Their sluggish faculties seem to be pleasurably animated by the excitement of the act; and they repeat it, till, at the present time, we find cases of men and women who have been poisoning relations and neighbours by the score, during a period of ten or fifteen years. The guilt and the shame lie with the whole of society, which has permitted its members—hundreds of thousands of them—to grow up as if they were not human beings at all, but a cross between the brute and the devil. We can see the horror of the existence of such a class in another country, and shudder at the atrocious mental and moral condition of the *canaille* at the time of the first French Revolution; but it may be questioned whether France had at that time anything to reveal more sickening than our wholesale child-murder for the sake of the profits from burial-clubs, and the poisonings which sweep off whole families in the hamlets of our rural districts. In the year 1828, the idea seems to have been so new and appalling as to make us feel, in the reading, ashamed of the familiarity which has grown up in ten years. In 1828, Jane Scott was found guilty, at the Lancaster assizes, of having murdered her mother by poison. She had been previously tried for the murder of her father; but had escaped through the death of a witness. Before she was hanged, she confessed both murders, and also that she had poisoned an illegitimate child of her own, and one of her sister's. The object of her parricide was to obtain property, which might tempt an acquaintance to marry her. Her age was twenty-one. She seems to have acted under the superficial excitability of a child, rather than from any fury of passion. This first case of a long series is here given expressly as such. Henceforward a general mention must suffice; for the crime becomes more and more frequent. Next to the pain of the fact is that of hearing what is proposed as a remedy. Far and wide now, men are proposing to restrict and impede the sale of poisons, as if any mechanical check could avail against a moral mischief so awful! It is not in barring out any knowledge once obtained that safety can be found, but in letting in more without restriction or delay. We have had warning of this for many years now; yet no system of national education is in practice, or likely to be so. Sectarian quarrels have come in the way. To this hour men are disputing about the order of religious education that shall be given, and insisting upon the right to communicate exclusively each his own views, while one generation after another passes off into the outer darkness, and beings, called human, are, after leading the life of devils, dying the death of brutes. Let this case of Jane Scott be preserved and perpetuated till we have done our duty by the living of her class, and then forgotten as soon as may be; for, in holding up to view her dangling corpse, we are gibbeting ourselves.

At the close of our last period, mention was made of the affrays caused by the practice of body-snatching. In the present period, we have a long array of such narratives,

and something worse.   It had been for some time suspected
that various ingenious methods were constantly in use to
meet the demand of the hospitals for subjects for dissection.
Among others, the detection of a single case of fraud in
obtaining the body of a person unknown, dying in a
workhouse, caused a suspicion that such frauds were
frequent.   A man and woman presented themselves to
claim the body of a man who had dropped down dead on
Walworth Common, declaring that the woman was the
sister of the deceased.   From their appearance of anxiety
and grief, and the circumstantial story they told, no
doubt of the relationship was entertained, till it was
accidentally discovered that these people had sold the
body to St. Bartholomew's Hospital for eleven guineas.
The only way in which the culprits could then be reached
was by prosecution for stealing the clothes of the deceased.
It had become pretty evident now that the requirements
of science must be met by some arrangement which should
facilitate the procuring of bodies for dissection; and
already individuals here and there were doing what they
could by making known that they had by will left their
own bodies for dissection.   Some few had even sold their
own bodies for that purpose, receiving at once a portion of
the sixteen guineas, which was then the average price of
such an article.   But in the year 1828, a disclosure was
made, which, while it startled everybody, warned such
negotiators as we have mentioned to be careful as to the
parties with whom they made their bargain.   By an accidental discovery of a dead body, recognised as that of a
woman in good health a few hours before, in the house
of a man named Burke, at Edinburgh, it was revealed that
a system of murder had been going on for some time, in
order to supply 'subjects' to the dissecting-rooms.   Burke
himself confessed fifteen murders which he and his accom-
plice Hare had perpetrated together.   Their practice was
to note any helpless half-wit and unfriended person in the
streets, invite them home, make them first merry and then
stupidly drunk, and then suffocate them by covering the
mouth and nose, and pressing upon the body.   The medical
men do not appear to have noticed any suspicious appearances about the corpses brought to them, or to have made

any troublesome objections to the stories told in each case
to account for the possession of the body. The only
observation on record is that Dr. Knox, in one case,
'approved of it as being so fresh.' The horror of the
medical men must have been extreme when the truth was
revealed. The consternation of the public was excessive.
Probably it was not known to any one, or ever will be,
how far the practice of burking—as the offence was henceforth called—extended at that time ; how much was true
of the dreadful stories of murder current in every town
and village in the kingdom. Most people believed at that
time that it was the custom of not a few gangs of murderers
to clap plasters on the mouths of children and unsuspicious
or helpless persons, to strangle them, and sell them to
the doctors; and it is probable that the crime was suggested by the fear, and by the notoriety of the case of
Burke and Hare ; while the practical jokes instigated by
the general apprehension were, no doubt, numerous. The
crime was superseded by improved care on the part of
surgeons, and by legislation, which supplied them with
what they wanted. But the memory of the occasion is
kept alive by the new term which it supplied. Since that
date, we have had the verb 'to burke;' which meanst o
stifle or extinguish any subject or practice, from motives
of self-interest. The execution of the murderer took place
at Edinburgh in January 1829, when the spectacle of
popular rage and vindictive exultation was fearful. Shouts
arose from a multitude vast beyond precedent—shouts to
the executioner of : 'Burke him ; give him no rope ; burke
him !' And at every convulsive throe, a huzza was set
up, as if every one present was near of kin to his victims.
When the body was cut down, there was a cry for 'one
cheer more !' and a general and tremendous huzza closed
the diabolical celebration.

   This was not the only crime of this period which
stimulated legislation. A shock was given to the general
feeling by the execution of a man known and habited,
though disowned, as a Quaker, for forgery. The case was
so clear and so common—a case of rash embezzlement,
covered by the forgery of bills, in the hope of retrieval
before the time came round—that there could be no doubt

about his punishment while others were so doomed; but the peculiarities of the case quickened the efforts of those who disapproved of capital punishment for forgery. Hunton was executed on the 8th of December; and on the 27th of the same month, a case of embezzlement occurred, which eclipsed all prior adventures of the kind. A member of parliament, treasurer of St. Bartholomew's Hospital, and a partner in the banking-house of Remington, Stephenson, & Co., absconded, in company with a clerk of the bank. Some suspicion was excited in the minds of the gentlemen who were his securities at the hospital, by the culprit, Mr. Rowland Stephenson, leaving home at four o'clock in a December morning; and they obtained from the president a cheque for £5000 on the bank, whereby the balance at the bank might be lessened. The cheque was presented and paid at eleven o'clock; and at half-past one the bank stopped. The delinquents got off from the Welsh coast for Savannah.

A crime more remarkable than these, and unspeakably odious to public feeling, was that of the abduction of a young lady, an only child, by the conspiracy of a rapacious family. The Wakefields were the conspirators, and one of them was the principal in the case—the husband as he hoped to be, and as he was, in the eye of the law, till a divorce could be obtained; a process which was quickly completed in a case where the universal sympathy was with the wronged parents, and their deceived and affectionate child. This young lady, aged only fifteen, was fetched away from school at Liverpool, on false pretences; and then made the victim of her attachment to her parents, by means of stories of their illness, pecuniary embarrassment, and so forth; so that she was carried to Gretna Green, and married there, and then conveyed abroad, where she was soon overtaken and rescued by her uncle. She went through the suffering of the prosecution of her enemy, and of the divorce process; married not long afterwards, and died early. The brothers Wakefield were imprisoned for three years—Edward Gibbon Wakefield in Newgate, and his brother William in Lancaster Castle.

A delinquent who has ever since been a standing satire

on the gullibility of English men and women, made his first appearance in public in May 1830. Joseph Ady then wrote his first recorded letter, offering mysterious advantages on payment of a sovereign; and, the promised advantages not being apparent, he was brought before a magistrate on a charge of swindling. And he has never since left off swindling, in precisely the same manner, making, it is believed, a good living for many years, by the credulity of his correspondents. He baffled the ingenuity of every one who wished to stop his career, till the assistance of the Post-office authorities was called in. By making him responsible for the postage of his unaccepted letters, he has been checked at last, and laid up as a debtor to the postmaster-general. But in the intervening eighteen years, it may be safely alleged that no one person in the kingdom has consumed so much time and patience of the magistrates in London, or, in his character of swindler, so tickled the fancy of the wide public—a multitude of whom, all the while fully aware of his dealings with others, hesitated to forego the chance of some great advantage which might be purchased for one sovereign. Many are the young and old ladies; many the shopkeepers, with entries of bad debts, possibly recoverable in their books; many the professional men, experienced in the odd turns of human life and fortunes, who have held a letter of Joseph Ady's between the finger and thumb, waiting for some suggestion which would save them from shame and ridicule in the act of sending a sovereign to the noted Joseph. He is an old man now; but who will say that he is too old to find more dupes, if ever he escapes from the grasp of the postmaster-general?

At four o'clock in the morning of Monday, the 2nd of February, 1829, a man passed through the minster-yard at York, and saw a light in the building. Supposing that somebody was at work about a vault, he took no notice; and, indeed, the last thing likely to occur to any one was that York Minster could be on fire. Between six and seven, a boy, one of the choristers, passing the same way, set his foot on a piece of ice and fell on his back, when, dusk as it was, he saw that smoke was coming out at various parts of the roof. He ran to the man who had the keys. On entering, it was found that the fine carved wood-work of the choir was all on fire. That carving, done in the fourteenth century, with its curious devices, long become monumental, was evidently doomed. The preservation of any part now seemed to depend on the roof not catching fire; but the wood of the roof was extremely dry, and it presently kindled as a tongue of flame touched it here and there; and at half-past eight it fell in. The mourning multitude who looked on now told each other that their beautiful minster was gone. But such exertions were used that the flames were checked, less by the efforts of the people—though everything possible was done—than by the failure of any combustible substance when the tower was reached. The great east window, the glory of the fabric, suffered but little; and the stone-screen which separated the communion-table from the Ladye Chapel was capable of repair. The clustered pillars of the choir were ruined, being of magnesian limestone, and splitting into fragments under the action of the fire.

On inquiry, it was immediately ascertained that the mischief was done by an insane man, named Jonathan Martin, who believed himself directed by a divine voice to destroy the minster. He told his wife of his supposed commission; and she nearly diverted him from his purpose by asking what was to become of their child. The voice, however, urged him again; he travelled to York, secreted himself in the minster on the Sunday evening, struck a light at night with a razor, flint, and tinder, shouted 'Glory to God!' till he was weary, and at three in the morning collected the cushions, set fire to them with a bundle of matches, broke a window, and let himself down to the ground outside by the knotted rope of the prayer-bell. Such was his own account; and several persons testified to having heard noises in the cathedral in the course of the night. How it was that no one of them took steps to ascertain the cause has never been explained. At the end of a month, the estimates for the restoration were prepared, and a meeting was held, the tone of which was so earnest and spirited as to leave no doubt that the work would be well and completely done. Happily, some drawings of the stalls and screen of the choir remained in the hands of the dean and chapter, which facilitated the imitation of the work destroyed; and it was resolved that the imitation should be as complete as possible. The poor lunatic was of course so confined as to be kept out of the way of further mischief. He had done enough for one lifetime.

On the 27th April, there was a yet more serious alarm; for Westminster Abbey was on fire. A little after ten at night, flames were seen issuing from the north transept. As the news spread, it caused a pang in many hearts—so strong seemed the probability that the fashion of burning cathedrals would spread, as the fashion of desperate crimes is wont to spread, among infirm brains. The anxiety of the moment was about the difficulty of getting at the place that was burning. The dean was out of town; but his function was well filled, and the mischief soon stopped. A cast-off screen, used in the Westminster plays, and put away here, with other lumber, in a corner, was on fire, and falling, had kindled the boards. When an entrance was obtained, the flames were climbing rapidly to the roof; and it was considered certain that the delay of half an hour would have caused the destruction of the building. There was for some time a good deal of mystery about the origin of the fire. The only thing clear at first was that it must have been done by somebody secreted among the lumber; but the finding of a mass of lead in a strange place, and traces of hob-nailed shoes, were thought to show that thieves had come to steal lead from the roof, and that the fire was caused by them.

A fearful accident occurred during this period, which occasioned a useful amount of discussion—the coroner's jury sitting for six weeks. A new theatre—the Brunswick Theatre—had been recently erected in Wells Street, for the eastern part of London. The walls, twenty-two inches thick, supported a cast-iron roof. The architect thought this roof enough, though not too much, for the walls to support; and when he saw the proprietors adding one weight after another—suspending the carpenters' shops, heavy scenes, &c., from the roof—he gave repeated warnings of the danger of the experiment. The theatre was opened on Monday, the 25th of February, the audience little dreaming, as they left it, what a danger they had

escaped. On the Friday following, the 29th, at the time
of rehearsal, when many people were in the theatre, the
walls gave way, and the iron roof came crashing down.
Ten houses on the opposite side of the street were destroyed, and some passengers and a dray and horses crushed.
Eleven persons within the theatre were immediately
killed, and twenty were seriously hurt. The jury returned
a verdict of strong censure against the proprietors, in
which the architect was not implicated.

The most interesting class of casualties which happened
during this period was that of Thames Tunnel accidents.
Every man, woman, and child, who read newspapers had
some ideas and feelings about this great work. They
knew that though many persons had thought of tunnels
under rivers, none had been able to make them ; and that,
in this case, the credit of doing the thing was infinitely
greater than that of conceiving of it. They had some idea
of the great commercial importance of this work ; but the
predominant interest was from sympathy with the gallant
engineer, Mr. Brunel. The tunnel itself was begun with
the year 1826 ; and the first nine feet were easy—the soil
being stiff clay. Through this substance, the celebrated
shield of Mr. Brunel pushed its way, inch by inch, as the
worm, from whose boring process he took the idea of his
enterprise, works in its cylindrical shell, by hair-breadths,
through the hardest wood. Before the middle of February,
the workmen came to a dangerous part, a tract of loose,
watery sand, and for thirty-two days there was momentary danger of the river breaking in. On the 14th of
March, they came to clay again ; and they went on very
happily, boring through it till they had built 260 feet of
their great cylinder. On the 14th of September occurred
the first breach, when the river poured down upon the top
of the shield. The engineer had foreseen the danger, and
provided against it. A month after, the same thing
happened again ; and again his foresight had been equal
to the occasion. With a few alarms, the work went on
well till the following April ; when the soil became so
moist, that men were sent down from a boat in a diving-
bell, to see what was the matter. The men left behind
them a shovel and hammer at the bottom of the river, and

these tools were presently washed into the tunnel on the
removal of a board—showing how loose was the soil
throughout the eighteen feet which lay between the top
of the tunnel and the bottom of the river. In the middle
of May, some vessels moored just above the tunnel-works;
and this occasioned an unusual washing of the waters
overhead. On the 18th occurred the first great irruption
of the river. In it came, sweeping men and casks before
it, glittering for a moment in the light of the gas-lamps,
and then putting them out, and blowing up the lower
staircase of the shaft. The workmen barely escaped; and
one who was in the water was rescued by Mr. Brunel.
The roll was instantly called, and not one was absent.
The cavity above was closed with bags of clay; and before
August was out, the traces of the disaster were cleared
away, and all were at work again as if nothing had happened. By the beginning of 1828, the middle of the river
was reached; and, whatever had been the wear and tear
of anxiety, vigilance, and apprehension, for two years, the
engineer had thus far succeeded without the loss of a
single life. On the 12th of the next August, a rush of
water occurred which caused the death of six men. Mr.
Brunel himself was hurt; and his life was saved only by
the rush of water carrying him up the shaft. When the
river-bottom was explored, by means of the diving-bell,
the cavity was found to be so large that scarcely any one
but Mr. Brunel would have thought of filling it up; but
he undertook and achieved it—four thousand tons of clay
being required for the purpose. But the directors were
discouraged, the funds were exhausted, the tunnel was
shut up for seven years; and Mr. Brunel had to bear the
long mortification of this suspense. He knew the substantial character of the work, as far as it had gone; and
he never lost the hope of being permitted to finish it;
and, meantime, he had the sympathy of a multitude of the
English people in his toils, his sufferings, and his indomitable courage and perseverance. It was no uncommon
thing in those days, to overhear little boys telling their
sisters the story of the enterprise, or arguing with each
other as to whether it would ever be completed; and in
the factories, and farmsteads, and public-houses of the

land, the romance of the tunnel engaged a large share of
true English pride and hopefulness.

Some other public works prospered better; and one
great event in the commercial history of this period was
the opening of St. Katharine's Dock. The privileges of
the older docks were to die out between the years 1822
and 1827; and some of the principal merchants of London
considered it desirable at once to obviate a renewal of dock
monopolies, and to provide for present and future expansion
of commerce, by building a new dock. They procured
their bill in 1825; and proceeded to take down eight
hundred houses, and St. Katharine's Hospital, founded in
1148, by Maude, spouse of King Stephen—re-establishing
this hospital and appurtenances in Regent's Park. The
first stone of the new dock was laid in May, 1825; and it
was actually finished and opened in October, 1828, though
the mere circuit-wall, lofty and secure, comprehends an
area of twenty-three acres, and there is accommodation
within for 120 ships, besides smaller craft, and for 110,000
tons of goods. The most noticeable circumstance in connection with St. Katharine's Dock is perhaps the new
economy of time and convenience in loading and unloading
vessels, from the use of scientific principles and methods
discovered since the last erections of the kind. The
capital employed exceeded £2,000,000.

The markets of London were much improved during this
period—the Duke of Bedford building the handsome edifice
in Covent Garden, which occupies the place of the dirty,
inconvenient, and unsightly buildings which formerly
stood in the centre of the market area; Fleet Market being
opened in November 1829; and Hungerford Market begun
in 1830. Besides the convenience and advantage to health
conferred by the markets themselves, they occasioned the
opening of new streets, and the removal of many nuisances.
The old Fleet Market became the present Farringdon
Street; and Hungerford Street was rebuilt, on a new site,
and with an increased width of ten feet. Elsewhere, the
street improvements were very great; much space being
cleared round St. Martin's Church, by which a close neighbourhood was ventilated; and yet greater advantages
gained by the removal of Exeter Change and the adjacent

houses. Men's minds were by this time turned to the
subject of street-improvement—which means primarily
health-improvement—in London; and that course of action
was beginning which, with the help of railway facilities,
will end only, we may hope, with the laying open every
court and alley where men live, to the passage of the air
of heaven.

The health and pleasure of the Londoners were beginning to be considered in regard to the parks, as well as
the streets. In 1827, St. James's Park, which was before
as little beautiful as any piece of ground in such a place
could well be made, was laid out anew, with such exquisite taste as makes it one of the finest walks in the
world. In the same year, Hyde Park was much improved
by drainage and planting. The Regent's Park was continually improving by the growth of its plantations, and
becoming as much a favourite of promenaders as any park
in London. On its outskirts, too, there was now a great
and increasing attraction. The Zoological Gardens, begun
in 1825, were opened to visitors in the spring of 1828;
and those who came to enjoy the wise and profitable pleasures of the place soon amounted to hundreds of thousands,
so as to guarantee the self-support of the institution. The
opening of the first Zoological Gardens in England deserves
to be noted in any history of popular interests—so great
is the privilege of an airy walk among a vast variety of
the creatures, winged and four-footed, which we may read
of as peopling all the lands of the globe, but can here alone
ever hope to see.

The king was during this period pleasing himself, but
nobody else, with the erection of Buckingham Palace.
Whatever may be thought of his gentlemanly qualities in
other ways, his subjects agreed, when they looked at the
Brighton Pavilion, and at his Pimlico palace, that he had
not good taste in building and architecture; for his edifices
were neither healthful, convenient, nor beautiful. The
cost of Buckingham Palace was enormous; partly from
frequent changes of plan in the sovereign and his architect, which went to impair the beauty of the structure, as
well as to increase the expense. The one alteration of
raising the wings cost £50,000; and the whole affair little,

if at all, less than £500,000. Parliament did not permit this extravagance to pass unreproved, a committee of the House of Commons issuing a strong censure upon it in 1829. A nearly similar sum was voted by parliament for the preservation and improvement of Windsor Castle; and no one was heard to object to this item of the national expenditure. The preservation of this old royal castle is truly a national duty; and the manner in which it was done was satisfactory and gratifying to the best judges.

The new Post-office bears inscribed on the frieze above the columns of the façade the date of the reign of George IV., 1829. Yet it was set about in 1815, after the old situation in Lombard Street had been found unfit for the enlarged and increasing business of the establishment. It is amusing to read now, in the papers of the time, the accounts of the vastness of the new establishment, as transcending even the needs of the expanding postal communication of the day. If any one could have foreseen what was to happen to the postal communication of Great Britain within a few years, a somewhat different tone would have been used. But it is well that men should enjoy the spectacle of their own achievements for a while, before they become abashed by a knowledge of the greater things yet to be done. The new Post-office will always be considered fine in aspect; and, in 1829 it might fairly be called vast in its dimensions and arrangements, however much these may need enlargement to meet the wants of a later time.

During the same year, London University was advancing; the ground was clearing for the erection of King's College; and the Athenæum Club-house was preparing for the reception of its members at the opening of the next year. The club had been in existence six years; and it was now so flourishing as to be able to build for itself the beautiful house which overlooks the area where the regent's palace of Carlton House stood at the time of its origin. These modern clubs are a feature of the age worthy of note; for they differ essentially from the clubs so famous in the last two centuries. The two have no condition in common, except that of admission by ballot, or by consent of the rest, however expressed. Dr. John-

son's account of a club is, that it is 'an assembly of good
fellows, meeting under certain conditions;' but there is
implied in this a degree of mutual acquaintanceship and
fellowship which do not exist in the large modern clubs,
where the object is not political or literary, or even social,
but merely the personal convenience and enjoyment of
the members, who use for this object the principle of the
economy of association. The modern club is a mixture of
the hotel, the home, and the reading-room. The member
calls for what he pleases, and is waited on as at a hotel;
he goes in and out, and lives in splendid apartments
without daily charge, as at home, his subscription covering his expenses; and he sees newspapers and books, and
meets acquaintances, as at the reading-room. Of the convenience of the arrangement, of the soundness of the principle of the economy of association, there can be no doubt;
and it is on this account—because it may be hoped that
the principle will be extended from these clubbists to
classes which need the aid more pressingly—that the
London clubs of this century form so important a feature
of the time. There is some complaint that these luxurious
abodes draw men from home, make them fond of a bachelor-
life, and tend to discourage marriage—already growing too
infrequent among the upper classes of society—and to
lessen the intercourse between men and women of education; objections which will never be practically available
against the clear daily convenience of such institutions.
The remedy will be found, if it is found, not in unmaking
these associations, but in extending them to a point which
will obviate the objections. Already, the less opulent
classes are stirring to prove the principle of the economy
of association in clubs, where the object is, not bachelor
luxury and ease, but comfort and intellectual advantage,
in which wife and sister may share the general table,
library, and lecture-room; where those whose daily business lies far from home may enjoy mid-day comfort and
evening improvement at a moderate expense, through the
association of numbers. The city-clerk, the shopman,
the music and drawing-master and mistress, the daily
governess, married persons, and brothers and sisters, can
now live out of town, can dine here and see the newspapers,

and stay for the evening lecture, while enjoying the benefit
of an abode in the country, instead of a lodging in a close
street in the city. When the experiment has been tried
somewhat further, and found to succeed, it may be hoped
that women will have courage to adopt the principle, and
to obtain more comfort and advantage out of a slender
income than a multitude of widows and single women do
now. In a state of society like our own at present—a
transition state as regards the position of women—the lot
of the educated woman with narrow means is a particularly
hard one. Formerly, every woman above the labouring-
class was supported by father, husband, or brother; and
marriage was almost universal. In the future, possibly
marriage may again become general; and if not, women
will assuredly have an independent position of self-main-
tenance, and more and more employments will be open to
them, as their abilities and their needs may demand. At
present, there is an intervening state, in which the condition of a multitude of women of the middle class is hard.
Marriage is not now general, except among the poor. Of
the great middle class it is computed that only half, or
little more, marry before middle age. It is no longer
true that every woman is supported by husband, father,
or brother; a multitude of women have to support themselves; and only too many of them, their fathers and
brothers too; but few departments of industry are yet
opened to them, and those few are most inadequately paid.
While this state of things endures—which, however, cannot be for long—there is a multitude of educated women
in London, and the country-towns of England, living in
isolation on means so small as to command scarcely the
bare necessaries of life. They are dispersed as boarders in
schools and lodging-houses, able to obtain nothing more
than mere food, shelter, and clothes; without society,
without books, without the pleasures of art or science,
while the gentlemen of the London clubs are living in
luxury on the same expenditure, by means of the principle
of economy of association. When such women have looked
a little longer on the handsome exterior of these club-houses,
and heard a little more of the luxury enjoyed within, it
may be hoped that they will have courage to try an

experiment of their own ; clubbing together their small means
—their incomes, their books and music—and make a home
where, without increased expenditure, they may command
a good table, good apartments, a library, and the advantages
and pleasures of society. It seems scarcely possible that
the new-club principle of our time, already extending,
should stop short of this, while so many are looking forward to a much wider application still. Those who think
this a reasonable expectation will consider the opening of
the Athenæum Club-house, with its 1000 members, and
that of the United Service and other neighbouring joint-
stock mansions, a sign of the times worth noting.

Two large public buildings were rising at this time
within a few miles of London, which have nothing in
common but their date. There was a grand stand on
Epsom race-course, of which nothing more need be said
than that was said at the time; that it was 'on a more
magnificent scale than the stand at Doncaster.' What
does the subject admit of more? The other edifice was
the Metropolitan Lunatic Asylum at Hanwell; of whose
destination so much might be said as to need a volume.
We can merely note here what a history of the time requires
—that the mode of life within those walls was almost as
new as the edifice itself ; and there were things to be seen
there far nobler and more interesting than any architec-
tural spectacle ever offered to the eyes of men. The
building up that was to go on within was far grander
than any that could be seen without—the building up of
the overthrown faculties — the restoration of shattered
affections. The Middlesex magistrates secured the services
of Dr. and Mrs. (afterwards Sir William and Lady) Ellis
as superintendents ; and their method of management
stands in noble contrast with that of former times, when
the insane were subjected to no medicinal or moral treatment, but only to coercion. Instead of being chained, and
left in idleness and misery, the patients here were immediately employed, and permitted all the liberty which their
employment required. Not only might they be seen
gardening with the necessary tools; but the men dug
a canal, by which stores were brought up to the building
at a great saving of expense. A score of insane men

might be seen there, working with spade, pickaxe, and shovel; they built the wall; they kept the place in repair; they worked and lived much as other men would have done; and from first to last, no accident happened. They attended chapel; and no interruption to the service ever occurred. The women earned in their work-rooms the means of buying an organ for the chapel-service. No sign of the times can be more worthy of notice than this—that the insane had begun to be treated like other diseased persons, by medicine and regimen, and with the sympathy and care that their suffering state requires. As for the results, the recoveries were found to be out of all proportion more numerous than before, and continually increasing; the pecuniary saving of a household of working-people over that of a crowd of helpless beings raving in a state of coercion was very great; and of the difference in the comfort of each and all under the two systems, there can, of course, be no doubt. The Hanwell Asylum was not, even at first, the only one in which the humane and efficacious new method of treating insanity was practised; but, as the metropolitan asylum, built at this date, it was the most conspicuous, as were the merits of Dr. and Mrs. Ellis, from their having been many years engaged and successful in the noble task of their lives.

We find during this period much improvement going on in drainage and enclosure of land, and extension of waterworks. The Ewbank drainage, by which 9000 acres of land in Cardiganshire were reclaimed for cultivation, was completed in 1828, with its embankments, cuts, three miles of road, and stone bridge. In a small insular territory, the addition of 9000 acres to its area of cultivation is not an insignificant circumstance.—At the same date we find an achievement of somewhat the same kind notified in the records of the year, in those capital letters which indicate the last degree of astonishment. Chat Moss, lying in the line of the Manchester and Liverpool Railway, was under treatment for the formation of the line; and we are told, that 'horses with loaded waggons, each weighing five tons, are constantly moving over those parts of the moss which originally would scarcely bear a person walking over it.'—The marvels of this first great English railway were open-

ing upon the world by degrees. This solidifying of Chat
Moss was enough at first. Next, we find that two locomotives were put to use on the works, to draw the marl and
rock from the excavations, at a saving of nearly £50 a
month in one case, and more in the other. But the
highest astonishment of all was experienced on occasion
of the race of locomotives on the line, for a prize of £500,
when 'the Rocket actually accomplished one mile in one
minute and twenty seconds; being at the rate of forty-five
miles an hour.' If men had been told at even that late
date at what speed our Queen would be travelling twenty
years later, they would have been as truly amazed as our
great-grandfathers could have been at the notion of travelling from London to Edinburgh in a day. It is very
interesting to observe how strong was the exultation,
twenty years ago, when any improvement in road-making
turned up; how anxious men were to publish new facts
about the best methods of skirting hills, managing differences of level, and connecting the substructure and super-
structure of the mail-roads, so as to facilitate to the utmost
the passage of the mails. We find earnest declarations of
the increase of postal correspondence, of the evils of delay,
and of the benefits of rapid communication between distant
places. These notices seem to us now clear indications of
the approach of the railway age; but no one then knew it.
What these complaints, and declarations, and desultory
toils indicated, we can now recognise, but our fathers—
except a philosopher here and there—could not then
foresee. Nor shall we perhaps learn philosophy from the
lesson, nor perceive that every urgent want, every object
of restless popular search, foreshows a change by which
the want will be met, and the search rewarded. As men
were anxiously and restlessly mending their old roads up
to the very time of the opening of the great first English
railway, so may we be complaining and toiling about some
inadequate arrangement which needs superseding, while
on the verge of the disclosure of the supersession. It
would save us much anxiety and some wrath, and render
us reasonable in our discontents, if we could bear this in
mind as often as we come into collision with social difficulties, whether they be mechanical or political; for social

difficulties of both orders come under the same law of remedy.

In 1828, a committee of the professors of the University of Edinburgh were employed on a very interesting service —witnessing how, by means of a special method of printing, the blind ' were able to read with their fingers as quickly, or nearly so, as we could suppose them to do with their sight in ordinary circumstances. Since that time, the method of printing for the blind by raised letters, to be traced with the fingers, has been much extended; and embossed maps are largely brought into use, to teach them geography. The question of the existence of a faculty by which space could be apprehended and reasoned about, without any aid from the sense of sight, was proved by the case of Dr. Saunderson; and it is very interesting to watch its working in children who have never seen light, when they learn geography by means of these embossed maps. And the printing of books for their use has been facilitated from year to year, till now the number of books to which they have access is greatly increased, and their cost much diminished. The honour of the invention, in the form under notice, was assigned to Mr. Gall, by the committee of Edinburgh professors ; and it is an honour greater than it is in the power of princes to bestow.

Before this time, the public had become aware of Sir W. Scott's claim to the undivided authorship of the Waverley Novels. In 1827, the copyrights of the novels, from *Waverley* to *Quentin Durward*, with those of some of the poems, were sold by auction, and bid for as if the successive editions of these wondrous works had not already overspread the civilised world. After the unparalleled issue which had amazed the book-trade for so many years, the competition for the property was yet keen ; the whole were purchased by Mr. Cadell for £8500 ; and he made them produce upwards of £200,000. What would the novelists of a century before—what will the novelists of a century hence, if such an order of writers then exists—think of this fact? Genius of a high quality finds or makes its own time and place ; but still the unbounded popularity of Scott as a novelist seems to indicate

some peculiar fitness in the public mind for the pleasure
of narrative fiction in his day. And it might be so ; for
his day lay between the period of excitement belonging to
the war, and that later one of the vast expansion of the
taste for physical science, under which the general middle-
class public purchases five copies of an expensive work on
geology for one of the most popular novels of the time.
Certain evidences, scattered through later years, seem to
show that while the study of physical science has spread
widely and rapidly among both the middle and lower
classes of our society, the taste for fiction has, in a great
degree, gone down to the lower. Perhaps the novel-
reading achieved by the middle classes during Scott's
career was enough for a whole century ; and in sixty years
hence the passion may revive. To those, however, who
regard the changes occurring in the office and value of
literature, this appears hardly probable. However that
may be, the world will scarcely see again, in our time, a
payment of above £8000 for any amount of copyright of
narrative fiction.

A great festival was held at Stratford-upon-Avon in April
1827, on Shakspeare's birthday, and the two following
days—from the 23rd to the 25th inclusive. There was a
procession of Shakspeare characters, music, a chanting of
his epitaph at the church, banquets, rustic sports, and
a masquerade, chiefly of Shakspeare characters. Such
festivals—commemorating neither political nor warlike
achievement, but something better than either—are good
for a nation, and themselves worthy of commemoration in
its history.

Some old favourites of the drama, or rather of the stage,
went out during this period ; and some new ones came in.
Fawcett retired, after having amused and interested the
crowd of his admirers for thirty-nine years ; and Grimaldi,
the unequalled clown, took his farewell in a prodigious
last pantomime. There was something unusually pathetic
in his retirement, however, sad as are always the farewells
of favourite actors. He was prematurely worn out. As
he said that night, he was like vaulting ambition—he had
overleaped himself. He was not yet eight-and-forty ; but
he was sinking fast. ' I now,' he said, ' stand worse on

my legs than I used to do on my head.' This was a melancholy close of the merriment of Grimaldi's night and of his career. But there is seldom or never an absence of favourites in the playgoing world. While, according to Lord Eldon, the sun of England was about to set for ever —while a Catholic demagogue was trying to force his way into parliament, to the utter destruction of Church and State, and everything else—Lord Eldon thus writes : ' Amidst all our political difficulties and miseries, the generality of folks here direct their attention to nothing but meditations and controversies about the face, and figure, and voice, of the new lady who is come over here to excite raptures and encores at the Opera-house—namely, Mademoiselle Sontag. Hardly any other subject is touched upon in conversation, and all the attention due to Church and State is withdrawn from both, and bestowed on this same Mademoiselle Sontag. Her face is somewhat too square for a beauty, and this sad circumstance distresses the body of fashionables extremely.'

Mademoiselle Sontag did not stay very long ; and her birdlike warblings were forgotten in the higher interest of the appearance of another Kemble the next year. The young Fanny Kemble, then only eighteen, came forward in October 1829, under circumstances which secured to her beforehand the sympathy of the public, as her name insured for her a due appreciation of her great talents. She came forward to retrieve her father's affairs and those of Covent Garden Theatre ; and her success was splendid. For two or three seasons, she was the rage. There were always those who, true to art, and loyal to Mrs. Siddons, saw that her niece's extraordinary popularity could not last, unsustained as it was by the long study, experience, and discipline—to say nothing of the unrivalled genius— of Mrs. Siddons ; but the appearance of the young actress was a high treat, though a temporary one, to the London public. She went to America, and married there ; and subsequent appearances in England have not revived the enthusiasm which her first efforts excited.

The dramatic world is not more sure of a constant succession of enthusiasms than the religious. It is at this time, in 1828, that we first hear of that extraordinary man

who was soon to turn so many heads; the greater number
by a passing excitement, and not a few by actually crazing
them. The way in which we first hear of the Rev.
Edward Irving is characteristic. It was by the fall of a
church in Kirkcaldy, from the overcrowding of the people
to hear him. The gallery fell, and brought down much
ruin with it. Twenty-eight persons were killed on the
spot, and one hundred and fifty more or less injured.
Among the killed were three young daughters of a
widowed mother, who never more lifted up her head, and
was laid by their side in a few weeks. What Irving was
as a sign of the times we shall have occasion to see hereafter; for, for seven years from this date, and especially
during the first half of that period, he was conspicuous in
the public eye, and doing what he could, under a notion of
duty, to intoxicate the national mind. What he had been,
up to the first burst of his fame, we know through the testimony of one who understood him well: 'What the
Scottish uncelebrated Irving was, they that have only
seen the London celebrated—and distorted—one can never
know. His was the freest, brotherliest, bravest human
soul mine ever came in contact with. I call him, on the
whole, the best man I have ever, after trial enough, found
in the world, or now hope to find. The first time I saw
Irving was six-and-twenty years ago, in his native town,
Annan. He was fresh from Edinburgh with college
prizes, high character, and promise. He had come to see
our schoolmaster, who had also been his. We heard of
famed professors, of high matters classical, mathematical,
a whole wonderland of knowledge; nothing but joy, health,
hopefulness without end, looked out from the blooming
young man.' It was in 1809 that he was this 'blooming
young man.' The rest of the picture—what he was just
before his death at the age of forty-two—we shall see but
too soon.

These were times when some such man as Edward
Irving was pretty sure to rise up; times certain to excite
and to betray any such man who might exist within our
borders. The religious world was in an extraordinary
state of confusion, with regard both to opinion and conscience. The High-Church party was becoming more and
more disgusted with the appeals of the day to the vulgar

' Protestantism' ; of the mob, while it was no less alarmed at the concessions made to the popular will on both civil and ecclesiastical matters. The most earnest members of this party were already looking towards each other, and establishing that sort of union which was immediately to cast discredit on the hitherto honoured name of Protestantism, and very soon to originate the *Tracts for the Times*. This party had lost its trust in the crown; it had no sympathy with parliament, and saw that it must soon be in antagonism with it; and its only hope now was in making a vigorous effort to revive, purify, and appropriate to itself the Church. This exclusive reliance upon the Church appears to have been, as yet, the only new point of sympathy between this party and Rome; but it was enough to set men whispering imputations of Romanism against its members. While such imputations were arising and spreading, the Low-Church party were zealous among the Romanists to convert them; and the registers of the time show their great success. Conversions from popery figure largely among the incidents of the few years following Catholic emancipation; and nothing could be more natural. There were in the Catholic body, as there would be in any religious body so circumstanced, many men who did not know or care very much about matters of faith, or any precise definitions of them, who were of too high and honourable a spirit to desert their Church while it was in adversity, who had fought its battles while it was depressed, but were indifferent about being called by its name after it came into possession of its rights. Again, amidst the new intercourse now beginning between Catholics and Churchmen, it was natural that both parties, and especially the Catholics, should find more common ground existing than they had previously been aware of; and their sympathy might easily become a real fraternisation. Again, there might naturally have been many Catholics constitutionally disposed to a more inward and ' spiritual' religion than they received from a priest who might add to the formalism of his Church an ignorance or hardness which would disqualify him for meeting the needs of such persons. Under these influences we cannot wonder that conversions from popery were numerous at that time; but

we may rather wonder what Lord Eldon, and other pious
Protestants thought of a fact so directly in opposition to
all their anticipations. Protestantism had its day then,
when its self-called champions least expected it; and
popery has had its day since, when the guardians of the
church, or those who considered themselves so, were least
prepared for it. An extraordinary incident which occurred
in the midst of these conversions was the defence set up
by the counsel for the defendants in an action for libel,
brought by the Archbishop of Tuam against the printer
and publisher of a newspaper. The libel complained of
was an assertion that the archbishop had offered a Catholic
priest £1000 in cash, and a living of £800 a year, to
become a Protestant. Serjeant Taddy declared the allegation to be purely honourable to the archbishop, instead of
libellous, as, by a whole series of laws, he was authorised
to bestow rewards on Catholics who should submit to conversion; and under this head of his argument he brought
forward the atrocious old laws of Queen Anne and the first
Georges, by which bribes to Protestantism, on the one
hand, were set against penalties for Catholicism on the
other. The defence was purely ironical; but the judge
had to be serious. He pronounced these old laws irrele-
vant, being Irish; and, not stopping there, declared their
intention to be, not to bribe, but to grant a provision afterwards to those 'who, from an honest conviction of the
errors of the Romish Church, had voluntarily embraced
the purer doctrines of Protestantism.'

The moderate Churchmen, meanwhile, were dissatisfied
with the prospect opened by the conflicts of the High and
Low Church parties; and some of them began to desire a
revision and reconstitution of the whole establishment.
Dr. Arnold writes: ' What might not —— do, if he would
set himself to work in the House of Lords, not to patch up
this hole or that, but to recast the whole corrupt system,
which in many points stands just as it did in the worst
times of popery, only reading " king," or " aristocracy" in
the place of " pope." ' Again, when disturbed by the
moral signs of the times : 'I think that the clergy as a
body might do much, if they were steadily to observe the
evils of the times, and preach fearlessly against them. I

cannot understand what is the good of a national Church, if it be not to Christianise the nation, and introduce the principles of Christianity into men's social and civil relations, and expose the wickedness of that spirit which maintains the game-laws, and in agriculture and trade seems to think that there is no such sin as covetousness, and that if a man is not dishonest, he has nothing to do but to make all the profit of his capital that he can.' Men were too busy looking after the faith of everybody else to attend to the moral evils of the times; and yet, no party was satisfied with the Church, or any body of Churchmen of its own. This was exactly the juncture to excite and betray Edward Irving.

Amidst these diversities of faith, there never was a time when diversity of opinion was less tolerated. Amidst the vehement assertion of Protestantism, its famous right of private judgment was practically as much denied, with impunity and applause, as it could have been under popish ascendency. The fact of the illegality of bequests for the encouragement of popery was brought prominently before the public in 1828, by a claim of the crown against the Bishop of Blois. The Bishop of Blois had put out a book, when resident in England at the beginning of the century, which he believed might serve the cause of religion permanently; and he invested a large sum of money, appointing trustees, who were to pay him the dividends during his life, and apply them after his death to the propagation of his work. It seems as if the bishop had discovered that his bequest was likely to be set aside as illegal, at the present time of eager controversy; for he petitioned in the Rolls Court that his bequest might be declared illegal and void, and that the stock might be retransferred to himself. But here the crown interposed, demanding the stock in question, on the ground that the money, having been applied to a superstitious use, was forfeited to the crown—any proviso of the testator in prevention of such forfeiture being an evasion of the law. The master of the rolls, however, decreed justice to the bishop, giving him back his money, while deciding that he must not put it, in the way of bequest, to such 'a superstitious use' as spreading a book in advocacy of the faith that he held. The whole transaction looks like one not belonging to our own century. The laws were ancient; but the use made of them by the crown, on the plea of the contrariety of the book to the policy of the country, is disheartening to look back upon as an incident of our own time.

One small advance in religious liberty was, however, made in 1828, when the question was raised whether baptised Jews should be permitted to purchase the freedom of the city of London. In 1785, the Court of Aldermen had made a standing order that this privilege should not be granted to baptised Jews; and an application now, nearly half a century afterwards, by the brothers Saul, who had been always brought up in the Christian faith, though children of Jewish parents, was thought a good opportunity for one more struggle for religious liberty, after the failure of many in the intervening time. Much discussion having been gone through, the old-fashioned order was rescinded, and the petitioners were directed to be sworn in.

Some extraordinary and painful scenes which took place during this period at the marriages of Protestant Dissenters, foreshowed the near approach of that relief to conscience which was given by the Dissenters' Marriage Bill. One wedding-party after another delivered protests to the officiating clergymen, and declared to persons present their dissent from the language of the service, and that it was under compulsion only that they uttered and received it. One clergyman after another was perplexed what to do; and there was no agreement among them what they should do. One refused to proceed, but was compelled to give way; and another took no notice. One rejected, and another received, a written protest. Some shortened the service as much as possible; and others inflicted every word with unusual emphasis. Such scandals could not be permitted to endure; and more and more persons saw that the Dissenters must be relieved and silenced by being made free to marry according to their consciences.

Two or three awkward questions arose at this time in our dependencies on questions of liberty, which were in each case decided in favour of the subject against the

government.   The East India Company were so rash as
to attempt at the same time to coerce the press at Calcutta,
and to impose a stamp-duty of doubtful legality, when the
period of the expiration of their charter was drawing on.
The council at Calcutta prohibited the publication of any
newspaper or other periodical work by any person not
licensed by the governor and council; and the licenses
given were revocable at pleasure.   Englishmen were not
likely to submit to such restrictions on the liberty of
printing, at any distance from home; and the men of
Calcutta, after the regulation had been registered there,
looked anxiously to see what would be done at Bombay.
Two of the three judges of the Supreme Court of Bombay
refused to register the regulation, as contrary to law; and
the Calcutta authorities were therefore ignominiously defeated.   And so they were, by the ordinary magistrates,
about the same time, on another occasion of equal importance.   The government wished to pay the expenses of the
Burmese war by a new stamp-duty, which was pronounced
by the whole population of Calcutta unjust and oppressive,
and even illegal.   All argument of counsel, all petition
and remonstrance being found unavailing, the inhabitants
resolved to petition parliament.   They obtained permission
from the sheriff, as usual, to meet for the purpose; but
the sheriff was visited with a severe reprimand from the
council, and the meeting forbidden.   The next step was
to hold a meeting as an aggregate of individuals, instead
of in any corporate capacity; and public notice of this
intention was given.   The council, while professing to
have 'no objection' to the inhabitants petitioning parliament—a thing to which they had no more right to
object than to the inhabitants getting their dinners—sent
an order to the stipendiary magistrates to prevent the
meeting, and if necessary, to disperse the assemblage by
force.   The magistrates consulted counsel, and finding
that each of them would be liable to an action for trespass
for disturbing a lawful meeting, they declined acting, and
the meeting took place.   Here was foreshown some of the
future under the new charter.

In 1827, we first hear of the new functionary, the protector of slaves, and of proceedings instituted by him.

An order in council was promulgated in Demerara, in
January 1826, which had, after vehement disputes, been
previously promulgated in Trinidad, by which, among
other provisions, a protector of slaves was ordained to be
appointed, who was to be cognizant of all proceedings
against slaves, and against persons declared to have injured
slaves; and to see that justice was done to the negroes.
He was to assert and maintain the right of the slaves to
marriage and to property; and to look to their claim to
emancipation. In 1827, the first claim of a slave to purchase liberty was made in Berbice; and the protector
carried the cause. The opposition set up by the owner of
the woman whose case was in question, exhibited the
vicious assurance which was an understood characteristic
of West India slaveholders. The plea—there, in that spot
where marriage among slaves had been a thing unheard
of, and where purity of morals was, naturally, equally
unknown—was, that the money with which the slave
desired to purchase her freedom had been obtained by
immoral courses—the woman having had a mulatto child.
The plea, odious from its hypocrisy, was rejected on a
ground of law. The protector claimed for himself, as the
legal officer concerned, the power of determining whether
the money had been honestly earned. He had ascertained
that it had been honestly earned. The result was, that
the woman and her child were declared free on payment
of a sum fixed by appraisers. Thus, not only was a great
inroad made on the despotism of slavery, but a prophecy
was given forth to the whole world, that greater changes
were impending. The wedge was in, and the split must
widen. In the same year, a treaty for the abolition of
the slave-trade was made with Brazil, the emperor
engaging that the traffic should cease in three years from
the ratification of the treaty; after which the act of trading
in slaves was to be considered as piracy.

A proceeding, big with prophecy of the fate of all
remnants of feudality, is noticeable in the Scotch High
Court of Justiciary in 1827. A gamekeeper of Lord Home
being indicted for murder for having set and charged a
spring-gun, by which a man was shot dead, the counsel of
the accused began his defence, by asserting the legality of

the act of setting and charging a spring-gun. Certain
English judges—Abbott, Bailey, and Best—had delivered
an opinion, a few years before, that the act was lawful,
and morally defensible. As the practice was abolished in
this same year, 1827, we may spare ourselves the pain and
shame of citing the arguments—the prejudices under the
name of opinions—which English judges could bring
themselves to deliver at so late a date as the nineteenth
century. The men and their judgments are gibbeted in
the pages of the *Edinburgh Review.* The Scotch judges
now, after hearing full and fair argument, decided against
the legality, as well as the morality, of the act; and
declared the accused liable to prosecution for wilful murder.
' The general doctrine of the law, even in England,' their
lordships agreed, ' was, that it will not suffer, with
impunity, any crime to be prevented by death; unless the
same, if committed, could be punished with death.
Poaching would not be so punished. Spring-guns were
secret, deadly, and, at the same time, dastardly engines
. . . . It was an aggravation that they did in a secret,
clandestine, and dastardly manner, what durst not be
openly attempted.' To ordinary persons, the case always
seemed clear enough. The man who set a spring-gun
either meant to shoot somebody, or he did not. If he did,
he was guilty of murderous intent. If not, why set the
gun at all? Much was said, in the days of spring-guns,
and very properly, of the number of persons, not poachers,
who were shot; of the constant danger to children, old
people gathering sticks, or, as Sydney Smith has it, ' some
unhappy botanist or lover.' But the one point of murderous intent, if any intent at all, is enough—enough to
stamp our age with barbarism to the end of time. 'If a
man is not mad,' says Sydney Smith, 'he must be pre-
sumed to foresee common consequences; if he puts a
bullet into a spring-gun, he must be supposed to foresee
that it will kill any poacher who touches the wire; and
to that consequence he must stand. We do not suppose
all preservers of game to be so bloodily inclined, that they
would prefer the death of a poacher to his staying away.
Their object is to preserve game; they have no objection
to preserve the lives of their fellow-creatures also, if both

can exist at the same time; if not, the least worthy of
God's creatures must fall—the rustic without a soul; not
the Christian partridge—not the immortal pheasant—not
the rational woodcock, or the accountable hare.' If it
appears an idle task to be presenting matters so plain,
even after it had long been decided that it was unlawful
to kill a dog which is pursuing game in a manor—Lord
Ellenborough declaring that 'to decide the contrary would
outrage reason and sense'—we can only say that we are
presenting a picture of the times under our hand; times
when such a remonstrance as this was needed in England.
'There is a sort of horror in thinking of a whole land
filled with lurking engines of death—machinations against
human life under every green tree—traps and guns in
every dusky dell and bosky bourn; the *feræ naturâ*—the
lords of manors, eyeing their peasantry as so many butts
and marks, and panting to hear the click of the trap, and
to see the flash of the gun. How any human being,
educated in liberal knowledge and Christian feeling, can
doom to certain destruction a poor wretch tempted by the
sight of animals that naturally appear to him to belong to
one person as well as another, we are at a loss to conceive.
We cannot imagine how he could live in the same village,
and see the widow and orphans of the man whose blood
he had shed for such a trifle. We consider a person who
could do this to be deficient in the very elements of morals
—to want that sacred regard to human life which is one of
the corner-stones of civil society. If he sacrifices the life
of man for his mere pleasures, he would do so, if he dared,
for the lowest and least of his passions. He may be de-
fended, perhaps, by the abominable injustice of the game-
laws, though we think and hope he is not. But there
rests upon his head, and there is marked in his account,
the deep and indelible sin of *blood-guiltiness.*' This is the
deep and indelible sin which is marked in the account of the
nation, under the head of its game-defences, till, as before
recorded, Lord Suffield obtained a parliamentary prohibition of man-traps and spring-guns, in the session of 1827.

As a winding-up of the improvements of this period,
and in rank the very first, we must mention the systematic
introduction of cheap literature, for the benefit of the

working-classes. A series or two of cheap works had been issued before, chiefly of entertaining books meant for the middle classes; and there was never any deficiency of infamous half-penny trash, hawked about the streets, and sold in low shops. The time had now arrived for something very different from either of these kinds of literature to appear.

Immediately upon the establishment of mechanics' institutes, it was found that the deficiency of attainable books in science and literature was a serious misfortune. Men can learn little from lectures, unless they can follow up their subjects by reading; and hearty efforts were made to collect libraries, and form reading societies. These efforts convinced all concerned in them of two facts—that books were dreadfully expensive, and that many that were eminently wanted did not exist; elementary treatises on scientific subjects, by which students might be introduced into the comprehension of a new subject by a more rational method than through a wilderness of technical terms. The friends of popular enlightenment began, upon this, to consider whether the want could not be supplied; whether works truly elementary could not be issued so cheaply as to meet the needs of the members of mechanics' institutes; and in April 1825, Mr. Brougham, Lord John Russell, Dr. Lushington, Mr. Crawford, William Allen, and others, formed themselves into a society, under the name of the 'Society for Promoting the Diffusion of Useful Knowledge.' Large subscriptions were offered, and all looked promising, when the commercial convulsions of the time stopped the progress of the work; and little more was done than in the way of preparation, till November 1826, when Mr. Brougham assembled the friends of the enterprise, and the organisation of the society was completed. The issue of works began on the 1st of March 1827, in the form of pamphlets of unexampled cheapness; and the publication was continued fortnightly for a long period. The subscriptions declined when the society was once fairly in operation; and after the first year, it was mainly supported by the sale of its works. The society was incorporated by a charter, in 1832, and before the virtual expiration of its efforts and

powers, it had done great service to the existing generation; though not precisely—as happens with almost all
social enterprises—to the extent, or in the mode, contemplated.   The profession—and, no doubt, the intention—
was to teach the elements of all the sciences, moral as
well as natural; politics, jurisprudence, and universal
history as well as physical science.   As Mr. Brougham
said, in his *Treatise on Popular Education:* 'Why should
not political, as well as all other works, be published in
a cheap form, and in numbers?' and he proceeded to
assign good reasons why they should; but it was not done.
In the laudatory and exulting notice of the operations of
the society, some months after its works were spread over
the kingdom, the *Edinburgh Review* slides in a hint: 'We
trust, however, that the appearance of the ethical and
political treatises will not be unnecessarily delayed.'
They never came; and the consequences to the society
and to the public were very serious—too serious to be
passed over without grave mention.   Some of the leading
promoters of this society became the rulers of the country
a short time afterwards.   Those whom they had invited
to be their readers were aware of their own lack of
political and historical knowledge; and that this knowledge
was at that period of our history, of the highest importance to them.   They desired it and asked for it; it was
promised to them, but not given.   It was promised by men
about to enter into office; and when they were in office, it
was not given.   While a vast change was taking place in
the constitution, and a multitude of men were eager to
learn the history and bearings of this change, they were
put off with treatises on dynamics and the polarisation of
light.   Explanations of the fact might, perhaps, be easily
given; but the fact was injurious to the spread of the
knowledge which the society was willing to afford.   The
calm observers of the time presently saw that the position
of the Whig ministry after the passage of the Reform Bill
was seriously affected by the popular persuasion, whether
right or wrong, that the Whigs desired to preclude them
from political knowledge.   So much for what this important association failed to effect.   It is very animating
to observe and note what it achieved.

The actual distribution of tens of thousands of copies of works of a high quality, is by no means the leading fact of this case—great as it is. A more important one is the raising of the popular standard of requirement in literature and science. It is no small matter to have issued the *Penny Magazine* at the rate of nearly 200,000 copies per week; but it is a greater to have driven out of the market the vast amount of trash to which the *Penny Magazine* was preferred. The society's *Almanac* is a great boon; but a part of the good is, that it excluded the absurd old-world almanacs, and immediately caused an improvement in those issued by the Stationers' Company. Other cyclopædias and family libraries followed upon the different series issued by the society; and the Christian Knowledge Committee set up their *Saturday Magazine*, after the model of the *Penny Magazine*. There being, as provided by the charter, no division of profits in the society, the gains from their more popular works went to set up works of great value which could not possibly pay; such as their *Statistics of the British Empire*. A reduction in the cost of maps generally followed the appearance of the society's Atlas. When to these great benefits we add the consideration of the value of the works published—the *Penny Cyclopædia*, the *Library of Entertaining Knowledge*, the *Journal of Education*, the *Gallery of Portraits*, the geographical and astronomical maps, with many a series besides—we shall see that the institution of this society was an important feature of its times, and one of the honours belonging to the reign of George IV. It did not succeed in all its professed objects; it did not give to the operative classes of Great Britain a library of the elements of all sciences; it omitted some of the most important of the sciences, and with regard to some others presented anything rather than the elements. It did not fully penetrate the masses that most needed aid. But it established the principle and precedent of cheap publication—cheapness including goodness—stimulated the demand for sound information, and the power and inclination to supply that demand, and marked a great era in the history of popular enlightenment. Bodies of men are never so wise and so good as their aggregate of individual wisdom and goodness pledges

them to be; and this society disappointed the expectations
of the public, and of their own friends, in many ways;
but this was because the conception and its earliest aspira-
tions were so noble as they were; and it is with the conception and original aspiration, that, in reviewing the
spirit of the period, we have to do. Any work suggested
is sure to find doers—one set, if not another; it is the
suggestion that is all-important in the history of the
time.

Within two years after the death of the Duke of York,
happened that of his sister, the Queen of Würtemberg,
the eldest daughter of George III. After she became the
second wife of the King of Würtemberg, she had little
connection with England; and the tidings of her death
were chiefly interesting as reminding men that one generation was passing away, and another coming. She died on
the 6th of October 1828, in her sixty-third year.

In January 1830, a death happened in the political
world, which occasioned extraordinary relief to all dull, or
indolent, or in any way incapable or unworthy members
of the House of Commons. Mr. Tierney, the castigator—
the unremitting satirist of incapacity and unworthiness
in any sort of functionary—died suddenly on the 25th of
that month. He had long been known to be suffering
under an organic disease of the heart; and he was found,
dead and cold, sitting in his chair in the attitude of sleep.
The most notorious single event in the political life of Mr.
Tierney, was his duel with Mr. Pitt in 1798, the fault of
which appears to have lain wholly with Mr. Pitt, who
charged Mr. Tierney with 'a wish to impede the service
of the country,' and refused to retract, when time and
opportunity were afforded. Both parties left the ground
unharmed. Mr. Tierney was generally regarded as a sort
of concentrated parliamentary opposition; but he was in
office for short periods at different times of his life; first,
as treasurer of the navy under Mr. Addington, in 1803;
and last, as master of the Mint under Mr. Canning, in 1827.
He represented many places in parliament during his
political life of forty-two years; and died member for
Knaresborough.

It was in May of the same year that Sir Robert Peel,

the father of the minister, died at the age of eighty. He
was originally a cotton manufacturer; and in that business he early obtained great wealth, which enabled him to
become an extensive landed proprietor, a benefactor to the
borough of Tamworth, where his influence soon tran-
scended that of the Townshends, and a member of parliament who discharged his function well. He was an able
and conscientious public man, and blessed in his domestic
relations, dying in the midst of a family of above fifty
descendants. His politics were high Tory. He considered
the national debt a national blessing, believed everything
to be right that was done by Mr. Pitt, and was unable so
to perceive that the times were changing as to take any
pleasure in the political acts of his son during the last
two or three years of his life. His life was interesting as
an indication of the greatness of the career laid open to
ability and industry, under favouring circumstances, in
our country; and his death was interesting, not only as
conferring title and increased wealth on his illustrious son,
but as giving him that freedom of speculation and action
which had necessarily been more or less restrained of late
by virtuous filial regards.

Two great Indian officers, both Scotch by birth, died in
1828 and the following year—Sir David Baird and Sir
Thomas Munro. Sir David Baird had been one of Tippoo
Saib's prisoners, chained by the leg in a dungeon; after
which he lived to receive the thanks of parliament four
times—for his services in India in 1799; in Egypt in
1803; in the Danish expedition in 1807; and in the Penin-
sula in 1809, after the battle of Corunna, at which time he
was made a baronet. He had been governor of Fort-
George two years when he died, on the 18th of August
1829.—Sir Thomas Munro was governor of Madras at the
time of his death, which happened by a sudden attack of
cholera in July 1828. Having spent his life in Indian
service, he was anxious to return to England in 1823, but
was entreated by the directors to remain. He received his
baronetcy in 1825. Capable in every way, as he had
shown himself to be as a soldier, his most eminent services
were wrought in a nobler field, in settling, governing and
fostering one conquered province after another that was

put under his charge. His just and humane government was his highest title to honour.

Two African explorers died within this period—Mr. Salt, on the 30th of October 1828 ; and Major Laing, at some time not perfectly known, but supposed to be during the autumn of 1826. Major, then Lieutenant Laing, having been sent with his regiment to Sierra Leone, experienced the passion for African exploration, which has proved fatal to so many brave adventurers in all times ; and, after various expeditions on political business to tribes residing not far from the western coasts, he was made happy by an appointment to proceed, *via* Tripoli, to Timbuctoo, in order to ascertain the course of the Niger. By that time the discoveries of Denham and Clapperton had roused much expectation and ambition, which it was Major Laing's hope to gratify. On the 14th of July 1825, he married the daughter of the British consul at Tripoli, and two days after set forth on the expedition from which he never returned. There is a good deal of mystery about his fate. On the 21st of September he wrote from Timbuctoo the last letter ever received from him ; and in this letter, which conveys an impression of discomfort and danger, he declares his intention of leaving the great town the next morning. He was well satisfied with his own views about the course of the Niger, and declared himself laden with information, from 'records' which were 'abundant' at Timbuctoo. Of all this he promised to write from Sego, in two or three weeks ; but nothing more was heard of him but from some Arabs, whose testimony could not be relied on. All agreed that he was killed, and that his property was stolen ; but where, in that fearful desert, his bones are whitening, and what was done with his effects, no real knowledge has ever been obtained.—Mr. Salt was the companion of Lord Valentia in his eastern travels ; and he published his drawings, by which Lord Valentia's work is illustrated in a valuable manner. His familiarity with Oriental customs and languages caused him to be selected by the government for a mission to Abyssinia, to carry presents to the emperor, and afterwards to be our consul-general in Egypt. He died at a village between Cairo and Alexandria, after having added much to our knowledge of Eastern countries. He was a native of Lichfield, and received his education at the grammar-school of that city.

Among the promoters of the useful arts who died during this period, we find one strange humorist—Dr. Kitchener, whose name was supposed to be an assumed one by a multitude who had read his cookery-books, without being aware that he had written upon optics and music before he committed himself to gastronomic science. We say, ' read his cookery-books,' because it is impossible not to read them, if one looks at them at all, so full are they of sense and appropriate learning, and of sly fun. Dr. Kitchener was educated at Eton and Glasgow, was nominally a physician, but did not trouble himself about practice, as he had an independent fortune and bad health. He suffered under complicated disease for many years before his death, which happened when he was fifty years of age, suddenly, from a spasmodic affection of the heart. It was his state of disease, and not epicurism, which made him so refined a teacher of the laws of luxury. The laws of luxury were, in his opinion, involved in those of health ; and he taught both together, to the great advantage of a multitude of readers, numerous beyond computation. He amused himself with experiments in cookery, and was to the last degree exact about the preparation of his food ; but with him this was an intellectual pursuit, followed up with an aim—his own habits being regular, and even abstemious, except on occasion when an attack of peculiar disease caused a craving for an enormous quantity, according to his own account, of animal food. His chief delight was in music, and he was a student of natural philosophy. As he is probably the only man who will ever give us the overflowings of a scientific and gentlemanly mind in the form of witty cookery-books, he should find a place in the records of his time. He died in February 1827.

In the next year died the man to whom chiefly our country owes the introduction of the muslin manufacture —Mr. Samuel Oldknow, who reached his seventy-second year. When quite a young man, he tried the experiment of manufacturing muslin handkerchiefs, at Anderton, near Bolton, in Lancashire. In a few years, he established a great manufactory at Stockport, and afterwards at Mellor, in Derbyshire. The results were that, as regarded himself, he grew rich, and became a great landed proprietor and agriculturist—being president of the Derby Agricultural Society at the time of his death; and, as regards the public, that the manufacture is now brought to such a point of perfection that we can bring cotton from India, make it into muslins rivalling those of India themselves, and sell them in India at a lower price than the native fabric can be sold for on the spot. Mr. Oldknow had the energy and perseverance which invariably distinguish public benefactors of his order. He seldom saw a muslin dress in any drawing-room, of a pattern that was new to him, but he had the pattern, with improvements, in the loom the next day. It was a great benefit and blessing to his mind that he could interest himself in agricultural pursuits. The penalty which improvers in the useful arts usually have to pay for their privilege is that they cannot rid themselves of their object; as an eminent ribbon-designer was heard to say that it was the plague of his life that he saw ribbons everywhere—ribbons in the winter fire, ribbons in the summer evening clouds, and wherever there was form and colour. Mr. Oldknow must have dropped his muslins when in his farmyard, and among his crops.

The great printer, Luke Hansard, died in 1828, at the age of seventy-six. His father, a Norwich manufacturer, had died early in embarrassed circumstances. At the end of his apprenticeship to the printing business, Luke Hansard went to London, with one guinea in his pocket. The very next time that he had a guinea in his pocket, he sent it to Norwich to pay a debt of his father's—his father having then been dead some years. Mr. Hughs of Great Turnstile, was then, in 1774, printer to the House of Commons; and Luke Hansard became a compositor in his office. In two years he was made a partner; and from that time his career, as sketched in the report of a committee of the House of Commons on parliamentary printing (1828), was nothing short of illustrious. He improved the extent and quality of the parliamentary printing beyond what had been dreamed of. Employed by Mr. Orme in

printing his *History of India*, he informed himself so
thoroughly on Indian subjects, that he was Burke's right
hand in selecting evidence from India documents for the
trial of Warren Hastings.   It was he who supplied without delay, and without the commission of an error, the
unequalled demand for Burke's *Essay on the French Revolution*. Dr. Johnson secured him for his printer; and Porson
pronounced him the most accurate of Greek printers.
When Mr. Pitt was perplexed how to get the report of the
secret committee on the French Revolution printed, under
such impossible conditions as his own illegible handwriting, extreme haste, and absolute secrecy, Luke Hansard
promised that the thing should be done ; and the minister
was amazed by the sight of the proof-sheets early the next
morning. After the union with Ireland, the parliamentary
printing increased so much that Mr. Hansard declined all
private business except during the parliamentary recess,
when he liked to have it, to keep his great corps together
and in practice. His great corps once thought they had
him and his affairs in their own hands. In no business
could a strike of workmen be more fatal than in this ; and
in 1805, when strikes were the fashion, Hansard's men
thought themselves sure of any wages they chose to ask.
But they did not yet know their employer. The greater
the danger, the better prepared was such a man to meet
it. He had foreseen the event, and had devised plans, and
taught them to his sons, by which the art of printing
might, by extreme subdivision of employment, be practised
by untrained hands. He let his workmen go; picked up
great numbers of unemployed men from the streets and
stable-yards, put on a working-jacket, and, with his sons,
went from one to another, showing how the business was
to be done, and aiding in it. He was an early riser ; and
his plans—so original, so various, and so singularly successful—were made in the clearness and coolness of the
morning, before those were awake who were to execute his
schemes. He was little seen out of the range of his business; and that business was of so wide a range as to afford
constant exercise to all the faculties of his mind. It united
the interests of the scholar, the literary man, and the politician, with those of the vast mechanism of his business.

He had the excellent health which is the natural privilege
of men who work the whole of the brain equably and
diligently—the faculties which relate to the body, the
intellect, and the affections. Up to the age of seventy-
five, he felt no change in his powers; nor was any failure
apparent to his friends. At that time he experienced
paralysis of the left eye. It disappeared; but when the
business of the session began, he declared his conviction
that this would be his last season of regular work; but
that he would work on while parliament sat. And so he
did; and he had the gratification of printing the report on
printing in which his labours are immortalised. When
this was done, and parliament rose, he felt himself sinking,
and summoned to his presence the principal persons in his
establishment, taking a solemn leave of them, and declaring his belief that he should see them no more. We
cannot but hope that some of them knew how he came to
London, and what he did with his first spare guinea. He
died a few weeks after this leave-taking, saying farewell
to each member of his family individually, explaining
what provision he had made for them, and offering to each
his blessing and a parting gift. Such was the life of Luke
Hansard, which speaks for itself. The particulars given
will not be too many for those who, hearing the name of
Hansard incessantly, may not be aware how it came to be
connected with the printed debates of the Lords and
Commons of England.

Just at the time when George III. came to the throne, a
youth belonging to Bath was apprenticed to a jeweller
there—a youth of high spirit, little industry, a strong love
of pleasure, good talents, and especially a remarkably
refined taste, which contrived to show itself before he
knew anything of art. When this gay lad heard of the
accession of the young king, and of the splendours of the
coronation, he little dreamed how much he should hereafter have to do with this king and all his family; nor
how it would be his own industry that would make a way
for him into the royal presence and employment. This
somewhat harum-scarum youth, apt to go into a violent
passion, apt to sing and dance rather than to work, was
Philip Rundell, who was to die one of the richest and

best-known men in England. A new apprentice came into
the business at Bath, a few months before he left it, to be
trained to take his place ; and the new apprentice's name
was Bridge. Here we have the Rundell and Bridge whose
firm is known all over Europe. Never were two men
more unlike than Mr. Rundell and Mr. Bridge ; yet the
partnership turned out admirably, by their undertaking
different departments. Mr. Rundell studied art, *con amore*,
became an unequalled judge of diamonds, and worked indefatigably—absolutely revelling in the gratification afforded
by his business to his intellect and taste, when once it had
expanded to a point which satisfied his desires. He was
very irascible ; but his people knew him, and revered his
generosity, through his bursts of temper. No one ever left
his employment on account of his temper. But he was
not the man to go about for orders among the great—
always excepting the royal family. Mr. Bridge, amiable,
gentlemanly, and as able in his way as his partner, undertook this part of his business. And he sacrificed no independence by it. On matters of taste in their department,
Messrs. Rundell and Bridge were called on to advise, and
not to be dictated to. If it is asked how they reached
this point of eminence, the only answer is, that they won
it. Mr. Rundell was placed by his relations as a partner
in the ancient jewellery establishment of the Golden
Salmon on Ludgate Hill; and there, if he had been an
ordinary man, he might merely have made a competence, as
an ordinary jeweller, in a respectable house. When the
senior partner retired, leaving his money in the concern,
Mr. Rundell invited Mr. Bridge to be his partner. In
liberality of views the partners were one. They studied,
and they largely bought, pictures, statues, gems—every
species of antique beauty that they could obtain access to ;
and that they obtained access to so many as they did, in
those days of continental warfare, is a proof of their zeal
in the pursuit of peaceful art. It was for the sake of art
that they executed their celebrated 'Shield of Achilles.'
It was not ordered ; it was not likely ever to be bought.
But they communicated their idea to Mr. Flaxman, and
paid him £620 for his model and drawing of the shield.
George IV. and the Duke of York, and two noblemen, had

each a cast of this shield, in silver-gilt; and the jewellers
now stood before the world as artists; and they gathered
into their establishment all the talent, foreign as well as
native, which promised to advance their art. It was about
1797 that they became diamond-jewellers to the royal
family, on the retirement of their predecessor; and Mr.
Rundell retired from business in 1823; so that his intercourse with royalty extended over twenty-six years; and
a long time that was to be handling and taking care of
many of the finest jewels in the world. He was in the
habit of giving away money freely. To persons out of the
line of relationship, he gave sums not exceeding £200;
and he is supposed to have given away about £10,000 in
this manner. To his relations he presented gifts varying
from £500 to £20,000; and in this way he distributed
about £145,000 during his life. Besides this, he settled
annuities on a considerable number of persons, that he
might not keep them waiting till his death; and at last
he left property far exceeding a million. It was not the
money that it brought, nor yet the fame, which made his
success in life precious to him. It was the high gratification of his faculties and taste. And he enjoyed this long;
for he had worked well during the last two-thirds of his
life. His mind remained clear to the last; and he was
eighty when he died, on the 17th of February 1827.

His life carries us over from the department of the useful
arts to that of art, properly so called. But first we must
note the melancholy case of the engineer to whom we owe
the design for Waterloo Bridge, and the institution of
steam-passage from London to Margate and to Richmond.
Mr. George Dodd was the son of Mr. Ralph Dodd, who
effected some excellent engineering in his day. His unhappy son, in his best years, revived the idea of the
Strand Bridge; and on its being seriously undertaken,
was appointed resident engineer, with a salary of £1000 a
year. This situation he hastily resigned; but he received
£5000 in all from the company. His habits, however, put
prosperity out of the question, great as were his talents.
Those whom he had served could not save him from himself; and he lived to be brought up to the Mansion House
as a drunken pauper. He asked for a week in prison, after

which he would begin life afresh. He was taken care of
in the infirmary of the prison ; but he rejected medicine
and advice, and sank at the end of the week, killed by intemperance, at the age of only forty-four. He died in
September 1827.

In the preceding March died a patient artist who had
devoted thirty years of incessant labour to engraving the
cartoons of Raffaelle. Thomas Holloway was scarcely
heard of as an engraver till a book came out which
presently became the rage—Dr. Hunter's translation of
Lavater, for which Holloway had engraved seven hundred
plates. He was made historical engraver to the king ;
and when he was about fifty, applied himself to the great
work of the cartoons, six of which were nearly completed,
and the seventh begun, when he died in the eightieth year
of his age. What a succession is here of men engaged in
virtuous and intellectual toil, who lived in health, and
died in a clear and serene old age !

Many people have seen the bust of Nelson which is
placed in the Common Council-room at Guildhall; and
the bust of Sir Joseph Banks at the British Museum ; and
the colossal heads of Thames and Isis on Henley Bridge ;
and some know the statue of George III. at the Register
Office at Edinburgh. These are all works of the Hon.
Mrs. Damer, whose father was the General Conway
(afterwards Field-marshal) to whom the largest share of
Horace Walpole's correspondence was addressed. To this
lady Horace Walpole left Strawberry Hill, with £2000 to
keep it in repair, on condition that she lived there, and
did not dispose of it to any one but his great niece, Lady
Waldegrave. Mrs. Damer's marriage was unhappy ; and
her husband destroyed himself nine years after their
union. She had no children ; and from the time of her
husband's death, she applied herself to the study and
practice of art. She went to Rome for improvement, and
returned to be the acknowledged head of amateur sculpture
in Europe. She was always at work ; and her work is in
many great houses, valued as her gift, as well as for real
merit. One of her last achievements was a bust of
Nelson, which she sculptured for the King of Tanjore, at
the request of her relative, Sir Alexander Johnston, then

governor of Ceylon. Great was the sensation excited when the bust reached its destination ; and its reception by the gazing multitude was such as to encourage further attempts to foster the artistic faculties of the natives of our dependencies. Mrs. Damer directed that her apron and tools should be buried with her. Let us hope that her example does not lie buried with them. She was in her eightieth year, and died on the 28th of May 1828.

Another amateur-artist, better known as a patron of art, who died during this period, was Sir George Howland Beaumont, the friend of Sir Joshua Reynolds, to whom Sir Joshua left his picture, by Sebastian Bourdon, of the 'Return of the Ark.' This picture Sir George Beaumont presented, with fifteen others, to the National Gallery, a short time before his death. He was in parliament for one session; but his heart was in private life—in his home, his painting, and his friends. He was a liberal and judicious patron of art and artists ; and the idea we form of him from Wordsworth's Works, the Life of Wilkie, and other pictures of the time, is genial and endearing. He was one of those whose pursuits and tenor of life promise and deserve old age. He was seventy-three when he died, and then his death was from an attack of erysipelas. The event happened on the 7th of February 1827.

George Dawe, the painter, died in 1829. The latter part of his life was spent on the continent, and most of his works were done there, as he was first painter to the Emperor of Russia. He was a Royal Academician ; and a picture of his, 'The Demoniac,' hangs in the council-room of the academy. He realised a very large fortune at St. Petersburg, but died in England, and was buried at St. Paul's. The Russian ambassador and Sir Thomas Lawrence led the pall-bearers.

Only three months afterwards, Sir Thomas Lawrence was himself carried to burial in St. Paul's, with as much pomp as rank and wealth can contribute to the honour of genius. Great as Sir Thomas Lawrence was, the abiding impression of him is and will be, that he was not all that nature intended him to be. His early promise was most marvellous. At six years old he took crayon likenesses ; those of Lord and Lady Kenyon still existing to show the

wonderful spirit the child could put into his drawings,
which were also strong likenesses. At the age of eight
he saw a Rubens—the first good picture he had ever seen.
He could not leave it; and when he was fetched away he
sighed : 'Ah! I shall never be able to paint like that!'
At ten he painted historical pictures; and one especially
—'Christ reproving Peter'—manifested such promise as
makes it a matter of infinite regret that he spent his life in
painting portraits, even though that life establishes a new
era in portrait-painting in England. At thirteen he
received from the Society of Arts, for his copy of the
'Transfiguration,' the great silver-gilt palette, and a
premium of five guineas; and yet at sixteen he was very
near going upon the stage. There was something to be
said for this fancy. He was full of personal beauty,
grace, activity, and accomplishments; a hearty lover of
Shakspeare, and a wonderfully fine dramatic reader. He
was also very intimate with the Kembles. Indeed, he
was early engaged to a daughter of Mrs. Siddons; but the
father doubted the prudence of the connection, and the
young lady afterwards died. Thus far Lawrence had
studied under Mr. Hoare at Bath—an artist of exquisite
taste, who fostered the boy's powers. At seventeen,
Lawrence's father took him to London, and petitioned for
an interview with Sir Joshua Reynolds. Sir Joshua was
manifestly struck on the instant with the extraordinary
beauty and manners of the youth, and gave close attention, during a long silence, to the young artist's first
attempt in oils—a picture of 'Christ bearing the Cross.'
It was an anxious pause for both father and son; and the
son at least thought that all was over, and that he should
never be a painter, when Sir Joshua found fault with his
colouring in many particulars. It was Sir Joshua's way,
however, to get all the fault-finding done first, and then to
praise; and this was what he was doing now. When he
had raised the lad's spirits again, he said, impressively, but
mildly : 'It is very clear you have been copying the old
masters; but my advice to you is to study *nature*. Apply
your talents to nature, and don't *copy* paintings.' Then
followed an invitation to call whenever he liked; and the
great man's kindness never failed during the four years

that he continued to live. Lawrence succeeded him in his office of principal painter in ordinary to the king. Honours were showered upon him from this time, and wealth flowed in, to be immediately dispersed in acts of generosity, or by habits of carelessness. He never married; he made money at an unequalled rate; yet he was never rich. Of course, it was said that he gamed; but this was so far from being true, that he conscientiously abstained from billiards—at which he had never played for money—because his fine play occasioned immoderate betting; and he thought it as wrong to occasion gambling in others as to game himself. At Christmas 1829, he consulted a friend about insuring his life for £5000, and resolved to effect the insurance on the 8th of January; but on the 7th he was dead. Between 1792 and 1818 he was painting the portraits of half the aristocracy of England; and then he was called to paint the royalty of Europe. The regent sent him to the congress at Aix-la-Chapelle, to paint the potentates there assembled; and he proceeded afterwards to various courts to complete his commission. He had never been abroad before—had never seen Rome, nor even the pictures that Paris had to show. Before his return he was elected, on the death of West, president of the Royal Academy. After his return he went on portrait-painting to the time of his death. His service to art was in idealising portraits. He had that *bonhommie* of genius which showed to him at once not only the best side of whatever human phenomenon met his eye, but all that a face and figure were capable of being under the best influences; and that ideal he had power to present. His portraits of children are beautiful beyond parallel. His own face and manner were most attractive to children. They would hang upon his neck, and sit on his knee to be fed; and their antics in his painting-room were as free as in the fields; and not a trait of frolic or grace ever escaped him. We have a myriad such traits, caught at a glance, and fixed down for ever. At Christmas 1829, as we have seen, Sir Thomas Lawrence believed himself, as he then said, likely to attain a good old age. He declared his health to be perfect, except that at night his head and eyes were heated, so that he was glad to

bathe them. On Saturday, January 2nd, he dined, with
Wilkie and others, at Mr. Peel's. On Tuesday, though not
feeling very well, he was busy at the new Athenæum
Club-house, about whose interior decoration he was much
interested. On Wednesday, the 6th, he wrote a note to
his sister, to say that he could not dine with her on
Thursday, but would come on Friday—the day he meant
to insure his life. On Thursday evening, being better
than for some days before, he received two friends, with
whom he conversed very cheerfully. Before they had left
the house they heard a cry from his servant, which made
them return to the room, where they found him dead in
his chair. He had told his servant that he was very ill
—that he must be dying. His disease was ascertained to
be extensive ossification of the heart. He was sixty years
of age.

One of Lawrence's famous portraits was of Miss Farren,
the bewitching actress, of whom our grandfathers could
not speak without enthusiasm. This lady, become Countess
of Derby, died in April 1829. Among her captives she
reckoned Charles James Fox, who spent evening after
evening behind the scenes at Drury Lane; but there was
no coquetry on the lady's part. She became the second
wife of the Earl of Derby in 1797; was received at court;
and, to the end of her days, was considered the most
accomplished lady in the peerage. It may be a question
whether, under the happiest domestic circumstances, it is
wise to exchange the excitement of artistic life for the
level dulness of aristocratic existence; but Miss Farren's
case is a proof that it may be done without scandal, or
open bad consequences; and all will agree that, supposing
an opening to aristocratic life to be a good thing, artistic
genius is a nobler avenue than the commoner one of
wealth.

Before this time, and for some years afterwards, there
was a good deal of disputation going forward as to the
best method of learning a foreign language; whether in
the old plodding way by grammar and dictionary, or by
the new method of Mr. Hamilton—by interlinear trans-
lations, in which each foreign word was placed above or
below the equivalent English one. The dispute at times

ran high, the advocates of each method not seeing that both may be good in their way. If people found that they could, by Mr. Hamilton's means, learn to read a foreign language more speedily and easily than by beginning with the grammar, they would certainly become Hamiltonians, whatever their opponents had to say to the contrary; and if parents wished to give their children a thorough grammatical knowledge of a foreign language, they would put the grammar and dictionary before them, as of old. A great number, too, would use both methods at once— the ancient, for a knowledge of the construction; the modern, for a knowledge of the idiom, and of its affinity with their mother-tongue. In the midst of the controversy, and of great success, Mr. James Hamilton, author of the Hamiltonian system, died at the age of fifty-nine, in September 1829.

Of men of letters there died, during this period, William Gifford; Professor Jardine; Mitford, the historian; and Professor Dugald Stewart.—Gifford's career was a remarkable one. He worked his way upwards from the lowest condition of fortune and education; his spirit and his love of knowledge being indomitable. He became known, when cabin-boy of a ship, to a surgeon of Ashburton, Mr. Cookesley, who so exerted his interest and his own generosity as to send the aspiring boy to Oxford. Earl Grosvenor afterwards took him into his house, to be tutor to his son. He was intimate with Canning, and became the editor of the *Anti-Jacobin*; and afterwards, for a long course of years, of the *Quarterly Review*, which he edited from its origin in 1809 till within two years of his death. His learning, his industry, his literary taste, his unscrupulousness as a partisan, and his intense bigotry, all favoured him in making the *Quarterly Review* what it was; worthy of immortality for its literary articles, and sure of an undesirable immortality as a monument of the extreme Toryism of its day—with all its insolence, all its selfishness, unscrupulousness, and destitution of philosophy. Cold and cruel as Gifford was in his political and satirical writings, he had a warm heart for gratitude and for friendship. He was generous in his transactions, and courteous in his manners; and he thus won a cordial

affection from his friends, while he provoked a feeling of
an adverse kind from the public at large. He left a
considerable portion of his property to a member of Mr.
Cookesley's family; and died on the last day of the year
1826, at the age of seventy.—Professor Jardine, who
taught logic at Glasgow College, and won to himself the
respect and affection of a wide circle of eminent men, once
his pupils, died, at the age of eighty-four, on the 28th of
January 1827.—Mitford, the historian of Greece, reached
the age of eighty-three, and died in February of the same
year. His history was universally read, and celebrated
accordingly, in its early days ; but this was mainly because
it was uncontroverted and left unrivalled. Since the
great recent expansion of the philosophy of history,
Mitford's work has fallen into discredit, from which it is
not likely to recover.—Professor Dugald Stewart is never
spoken of by those who knew him without affection and
admiration, on account of the amiability and charm of his
character and manners. He early devoted himself to
metaphysical speculation, and became the most popular
lecturer on mental philosophy ever known in this country.
For a long course of years, his lecture-room was crowded ;
and his circle of pupils was enlarged indefinitely by his
frequent publication of his lectures, under one form or
another. The service that he rendered to philosophy was,
however, confined to that of interesting a wide public in
the subjects which occupied his mind. He added nothing
to the science which he undertook to teach; but rather
drew away from the track of real science many minds
which might have followed it, if they had not been enticed by the graces of his desultory learning into a
wilderness where he indicated no path at all. No comprehensive principle is to be found amidst the whole mass
of his works ; no firm ground under his speculations ; no
substance beneath his illustrations. Nothing that he
wrote under the name of philosophy could cohere for a
moment under the test of science. And the science was
already abroad—the strong breeze which was to drive
before it the mists of mere speculation. Prince Metternich
—who, whatever had been his political sins, understood
and appreciated as well as any man the nature and

benefits of true science—had before this time, when
Austrian ambassador at the French court, guaranteed to
Dr. Gall the expenses of the publication of his work on
the functions of the brain; a work which has already
begun to change the aspect of both medical science and
mental philosophy throughout the civilised world. Dr.
Gall's work had been prohibited—as first-rate scientific
achievements are apt to be everywhere—by the government
at Vienna in 1802. In 1810, Prince Metternich himself
had secured its presentation to the world. Before the
close of the war, it had begun to modify the views of
physicians and philosophers abroad; and soon after the
war, when continental ideas began to reach Great Britain,
the scientific discoveries of Dr. Gall were heard of in
England; and they received in Scotland, before the death
of Dugald Stewart, that primary homage of outrageous
abuse from partisans of old systems, which invariably
precedes an ultimate general reception. The noise reached
the placid man; but it did not disturb him. He had lived
a long and tranquil life—amused with speculation, un-
disturbed by difficulties which were not apparent to him,
unspoiled by adulation, unabashed by the excess of his
popularity, cherished by family and friends, and undoubting
about the permanence of his works. Those works it is
impossible to characterise in any philosophical sense; for
no basis is assigned for them; and no proof of any part of
them is anywhere offered. The most positive part of them
is a protest, sometimes expressed, sometimes implied,
against the philosophy of Locke. They contain some
recognition of facts of the mind which there is no attempt
to account for; and much desultory information and
disquisition which are entertaining to read; and would be
more so if the reader could forget his constant unsatisfied
craving for that analysis and reasoning which are always
professed in the mere undertaking of such subjects, but
are in the writings of Dugald Stewart nowhere to be
found. He reached the age of seventy-four, and died in
June 1828—two months before the great German physician and philosopher who was to extinguish the Will-o'-
the-wisps which, in the name of the Scotch philosophy, had
beguiled multitudes while the continent and its science

was closed to us.   Dr. Gall died in the neighbourhood of
Paris, aged seventy-one, on the 22nd of August 1828.

A young man died during this period, whose name
should perhaps be mentioned on account of the popularity
of a poem which he published; such popularity, won by
such a poem, being a curious sign of the times.   The Rev.
Robert Pollok, who had been educated at Glasgow, issued
a long poem called *The Course of Time*, which immediately
went through many editions, in spite of faults so offensive,
and such an extraordinary absence of merits, as completely
perplexed all the authoritative literary critics of the day.
The truth seems to be that Mr. Pollok's readers and admirers were the whole of that great and opulent body
called, in common conversation, the religious world—the
great body which has a conscientious objection to the
cultivation of taste by familiarity with the best models
in art and literature; with whom music is objectionable,
as 'exciting the passions,' painting as 'frivolous,' and
Shakspeare and our other classics as 'profane.'   When a
novel—Hannah More's *Cœlebs*—came in the way of this
portion of the public, a novel which they might read, they
carried it through a succession of editions presently; and
now that a poem had come in their way, a poem that they
might read, they devoured it so ravenously as to set the
world and the reviews of the day wondering how it might
be.   The young author left the world before his brief fame
reached its height.   He was on his way to Italy, con-
sumptive, when he died, in September 1827.

In the days of the first French Revolution, when the
excitement of the occasion brought out all existing
enthusiasms in one form or another, many women found a
voice, and listeners to their voice, who would have been
little attended to at other times.   Among these was Helen
Maria Williams, a lady who had previously published
some poems of small account, but whose political writings,
animated by a sincere enthusiasm, were eagerly received
both in England and in France.   She was an ardent re-
publican; and she was feared and hated accordingly by one
party, and extolled by another.   She was a woman of good
intentions, warm benevolence, and considerable powers;
but, that there was a want of balance or sagacity in her

mind, seems to be shown by the fact, that she died a
champion of the Bourbons and their rule. Her most celebrated works were her *Farewell to England, Sketch of the
Politics of France*, and *State of Manners and Opinions in the
French Republic.* She died at Paris, before the breaking
out of the second revolution, which would have perplexed
and alarmed her extremely. Her death took place in
December 1827.

There is something interesting, and perhaps profitable,
in noting cases of individuality of character, which make
themselves felt and heard of amidst the organic movement
of a highly civilised society ; and we may therefore note
the death of a lady whose story is still told by many firesides, where a grey-headed elder sits in the seat of honour.
There were two high-born young ladies, of the families of
the Marquis of Ormond and Lord Besborough, who, before
the breaking out of the first French Revolution, distressed
their relations by an early disgust with the world, and
longing for absolute seclusion. They left their homes
together in 1779, and settled in retirement ; but their
families brought them back, and endeavoured to separate
them, that they might not encourage one another's 'romance.' The consequence was that they eloped ; and it
was some time before they could be traced. They settled
near Llangollen, in Wales, where, for some years, the
country-people knew them only by the name of ' the ladies
of the vale.' Their friends hoped and believed that they
would grow tired of their scheme ; but they did not.
They had refused marriage ; and friendship, and the tranquillity of a country-life, appeared to satisfy them to the
end. It is true, those who visited them during the latter
years of their lives were struck by their inquisitiveness
about the affairs of the world, and especially about the
gossip of high life in London. A singular sight it was,
we are told, the reception of a visitor by these ancient
ladies, in their riding-habits, with their rolled and pow-
dered hair, their beaver hats, and their notions and
manners of the last century, perfectly unchanged. Amidst
the storms of revolutions, when the world was gathered
into masses to contend for great questions, this quiet side-
scene of romance and individuality is worth glancing at

for a moment. Lady Eleanor Butler died in her Llangollen cottage on the 2nd of June 1829. She must have
been about seventy years of age. Her companion followed
in a few months.

It seems as if the world were destined to be stripped of
its most eminent men of science during the period under
review. Laplace and Volta died on the same day, March
5, 1827—the one in France, and the other in Italy; and
soon afterwards, three deaths took place in England within
six months, which made scientific foreigners inquire of
travellers : ' Whom have you left ?'—On the 22nd of December 1828, died Dr. Wollaston, the most illustrious
member of a family distinguished for science through three
generations. The father and two uncles of William Hyde
Wollaston were all Fellows of the Royal Society. He, in
whose fame the distinction of his family is now concentrated, was born on the 6th of August 1766. His profession was that of a physician; but he left it early in a fit of
wrath at not being elected to a desired office in St. George's
Hospital. He never repented of his hasty determination;
and from his devotion to science he reaped all kinds of
rewards. He was eminently useful to his race; he was
happily occupied; he was highly honoured; and he was
very rich. One of his discoveries—that of a method by
which platinum can be made ductile and malleable—
brought him in £30,000; £10,000 of which he gave away
at a stroke, to a relation who was in embarrassed circumstances. Dr. Wollaston's organisation was in favour of
his accomplishing with certainty and completeness whatever
he undertook. His bodily senses were particularly acute
and delicate; his understanding clear and patient; and
his habits of thought and language eminently correct.
From his singular accuracy of observation and reflection,
he was able to pursue a method of research which would
nave been impossible to another kind of man. He was
able to diminish and simplify the material and apparatus
of his experiments in chemistry and natural philosophy to
a degree which appeared incredible to those who first
heard of his methods. He could carry on a process in a
thimble which the world would wonder at; and he would
draw out from that little galvanic battery, a wire too

slender to be seen but in a full light. With an apparatus which would stand on a tea-tray he would effect what another man would require a roomful of utensils to do. A grain of any substance would serve his purposes of analysis as well as another man's pound. This peculiarity, though chiefly interesting as characteristic of the man, is useful also, as suggesting to other labourers the practicability and benefit of simplifying the processes of chemical research. To a certain extent, his example may be imitable, though no one else is likely to arise gifted with his delicacy of sense, acuteness of sagacity, and precision of understanding, which made small amounts of evidence as good as large, if only they were indisputable. As for the immediate practical results of his labours, we have mentioned one whose profit to himself showed its immediate utility. He discovered two new metals, rhodium and palladium. Then we owe to him the camera-lucida; and that boon to practical chemists, the sliding scale of chemical equivalents; and that great help to crystallographers, the goniometer, or angle-measurer, by which the angle contained between two faces of a crystal can be measured with a degree of accuracy never before attainable. But it is an injury to great chemical discoverers to specify as the result of their labours those discoveries which take the form of inventions. We are thankful to have them; but they are a small benefit in comparison with the other services of such men. Their true service is in their general furtherance of science; their pioneering in new regions, or opening out new methods of procedure, whose importance cannot be at once communicated to, or appreciated by, the multitude of men. It is a good thing to invent a useful instrument, for the service or safety of society and men; but it is a much greater thing to evolve a new element, to discover a new substance, to exhibit a new combination of matter, and add confirmation to a general law. Wollaston did much in both ways to serve the world. He died of a disease of the brain which, however, left his mind clear to the last. He employed his latter days in dictating to an amanuensis an account of the results of his labours. When he was speechless and dying, one of his friends observed aloud that he was in a state of unconsciousness; whereupon, he made signs for paper and pencil, wrote down figures, cast them up, and returned the paper, and the sum was right.   He was in the sixty-third year of his age.

Dr. Thomas Young went next. He was the son of Quaker parents, whom he astonished not a little by his ability to read at two years old. He appears to have been able to learn and to do whatever he chose ; and that, with such versatility, he had any soundness of science at all seems surprising. His first passion was for languages, even for the Oriental; and to this we owe the vast benefit of an introduction to the interpretation of the hieroglyphics of Egypt. It was Dr. Young who was the first to read the proper names in the hieroglyphic and enchorial inscriptions on the Rosetta stone, by a comparison of them with the third—the Greek inscription; and it was on this hint that Champollion proceeded in his elaborate researches. It is by this service, and his re-invention or revival of the theory of the undulatory character of light, that Young is chiefly known ; though there is hardly a department of natural science on which he did not cast some wondrous illumination. It is a common mistake of superficial readers to suppose that there must have been three or four Dr. Youngs at work in different regions of the world of science. He was the last secretary of the Board of Longitude ; and then sole conductor of the *Nautical Almanac*. His writings are too numerous for citation. He was a physician by profession ; but the greatest service he rendered in that province was by his testimony to the empirical character of medical treatment, and the absence of all real science in that department of pursuit. He was himself too scientific to be a good practical physician, or to make his patients think him one. Where he saw no guiding principle, he could not pretend to a decision that he did not feel; and he was open in his complaints of the darkness which involves the laws of the human frame. When he said this in his lectures at St. George's Hospital, and avowed that his idea of the advantage of skill in medical practice was the advantage of holding a larger number of tickets in a lottery over a smaller, the students were offended, as this was, as Arago observes, a doctrine which students of medicine do not like

to hear. From this cause of unpopularity, and from his
instructions being too high and deep for the comprehension
of his class, his lectures were not well attended, nor was
his practice large; as the least scientific and therefore most
confident practitioners must have, with the anxious and
trusting sick, the advantage over those who are more
aware of consequences while more doubtful about causes,
till the laws of the human frame are less obscure than they
as yet are. From these disappointments, and other causes
of irritation, Dr. Young was not a happy man; and the
controversies in which he was engaged are painful records
of the aberrations from the serenity of science induced by
those self-regards which the love of science should cast
out. He was hardly and insultingly treated; but he
might not have been so, if his temper had been worthy of
his vocation. He and his enemies are gone down to that
common resting-place where there is no more strife; and
the testimony remains, of which Arago was the utterer,
that among philosophers he must always be held to be one
of the greatest whom England has produced in modern
times.

The man who, of this group, presented the most strongly
to the popular observation the attributes of genius, was
Davy. In his case, there was no occasion to offer, upon
trust, assertions of his greatness, or assurances that a future
generation would become aware that he was a transcendent
man in his way. People all knew it during his life,
whether they understood anything of his services to science
or not. His ardour, his eloquence, his poetical faculty,
the nature of his intense egotism, his countenance, his
manners—before he was spoiled—and his pleasures, all
spoke the man of genius, from moment to moment. He
brought the poet's mind into philosophical research, and
the results were as brilliant as might be expected from
such a concentration of such faculties as his. The world
will for ever be the better for them. Those who know
nothing else about him have heard of the Davy-lamp, and
know what a service he rendered by tracking death
through the foul caverns of the earth, to bind and disarm
him. This was only one of many immediate practical
services which he rendered to society before the eyes of

all men—the wise and ignorant together; but the wise
know that there is a host more behind, which the multitude must as yet take upon trust. The genius of the
Cornish boy made itself felt by society before he had
reached mature years ; and when he lectured in London at
the beginning of the century, he was probably the most
popular man of his time—so clear were his expositions, so
beautiful his experiments, and so bewitching his ardent
eloquence. When we call him perhaps the most popular
man of his time, we mean with the listening public ; for
he was not popular in private life. Besides the degree of
wildness which appears in all the evidence of his life and
writings, there was an excessive egotism, a lack of magnanimity, an insufferable pride and vanity united, which
destroyed all pleasure on both sides in his intercourses with
others than his flatterers. His visit to Paris ended badly,
hearty as was the welcome accorded to himself and his
discoveries by the French philosophers. The serenity of
a life of scientific research was not his. He had manifold
and intense enjoyments ; but not the peace which occupies
the unsophisticated mind when employed in its noble
researches into the secrets of nature. His ambition did
not take the direction of wealth. About money, he was
simple-minded and generous. As for the rest, such men
are so rare that they may well be permitted the isolation
of egotism when they must have so much isolation of
other kinds. It is happy for themselves, and for those
about them, if they can preserve the childlike nature,
innocent, humble, and loving, which bears the truest
affinity to genius ; but if the world comes in to strip
genius of its natural graces, we must not reckon too
hardly with a being so singularly circumstanced, but
honour and glory in the gifts that remain, and let the
losses go. Davy was born at Penzance, in December 1778.
He arrived in London in 1801 ; was knighted in 1812 ;
and was afterwards, in 1818, made a baronet; but, his
marriage being childless, his title died with him. He
became president of the Royal Society in 1820; went
abroad in ill health in 1825, and again, and finally, in the
early part of 1828, dying at Geneva on the 29th of May,
1829. The authorities of Geneva decreed a public funeral;

and there was wide-spread mourning in England when the
news arrived that her great philosopher had sunk into the
grave at the age of fifty-one. Davy and Wollaston never
crossed each other's path, the character of their minds and
their methods of pursuing science being essentially unlike.
Wollaston was the elder by twelve years; and on some
occasions he was called the Mentor of the younger and
more brilliant genius; but they generally worked apart,
and certainly without mutual hindrance, if without co-
operation. Whilst Wollaston was busy with his thimble,
and a shaving of metal, and a pinch of earth, using the
most delicate manipulation and refined observation, Davy
was rushing about in his laboratory, among heaps of apparatus and masses of material, holding to his work for days
and nights together, or half-killing himself by respiring
fatal gases. Wollaston never declared a fact or a doctrine,
even to his own mind, till the verification of every step of
the evidence was complete; while Davy intrepidly published the proofs of the error of his own former published
opinions. Wollaston was seldom or never wrong; Davy
was often miraculously right. Both had sagacity not to
be surpassed; but the sagacity of the one was clear insight, and of the other excited prevision. Both men were
too great to be confined within the limits of their own
science. Wollaston was a man of various reading and
open intellect; and he was capable of genuine intercourse
with minds of various character. Davy had not that
liberality; but his own pursuits were diversified. He
loved sport—fishing and fowling—with all the intensity
of his nature. He was fond of what he thought to be
mental and moral philosophy, and attached an unaccountable value to his writings on such subjects. That estimate, however, must be regarded as one of his wildnesses,
and as another instance of that opposition which is so
common between great men and everybody else as to what
they can do best and worst. The inspiration of Davy's
genius could not but leave some traces in his miscellaneous
writings, and we find accordingly a passage of beauty here
and there; but if there is philosophy in them, it is such as
may be dropped through the dreams of the night. Amidst
his mass of achievements, we may well throw out without

slight what there was of mistake and transient; but
Wollaston left as little as it is possible for fallible and
tentative man to leave for rejection, and much, very much,
for which the world will ever be the better. They were
two wonderful and truly great men; and at the date
under our notice, and for long after, the scientific world
felt blank and dreary without them.

Major Rennell is considered the first Englishman who
ever attained a high and permanent reputation as a geographer. He began life in the navy, and early showed what
he was capable of in surveying. After being in India, he
was induced to leave the navy for the army; and he went
out to Bengal as an officer of engineers. His Bengal atlas,
and some charts of great value, appeared before long. His
greatest work is *The Geographical System of Herodotus;* a
work of the highest interest and importance to untravelled
scholars, and a marvel in its way, from the fact that
Major Rennell could not read Greek, had no better translation of Herodotus than Beloe's, and was actually able to
detect the errors of the translation, by his sagacity and his
geographical knowledge together. He assisted Dr. Vincent
in making out the track of Nearchus for his Commentary
on Arrian's account of that voyage; he assisted Sir
William Jones in his Oriental collections; and it was he
who made out Mungo Park's track, from his journals
and descriptions; and by comparing Park's account with
prior discoveries, formed the map which accompanies the
Travels, with an approach to correctness since proved to
be truly surprising. One of his most remarkable and
interesting works is his *Observations on the Topography of
the Plain of Troy,* which the lovers of Homer rushed to
read, and have studied ever since. As a practical boon,
none of his labours are more important than his account of
the currents in the oceans navigated by European ships.
This excellent man and eminent public benefactor lived to
the age of eighty-eight, being born near Chudleigh, in
Devonshire, in 1742, and dying on the 29th of March 1830.
Though he never reached a higher rank than that of
major in the army, and surveyor-general of Bengal, he
had abundance of honours in the scientific world, being a
member of the chief learned societies in Europe. His

must have been an eminently happy life—full of diversity and interest, full of innocence and uprightness, and of achievements of the most unquestionable value to the whole society of the civilised world.

Among the philanthropists whose lives and labours closed during this period, the name of Pestalozzi ought not to be omitted; for, though a foreigner, he was a benefactor to our country and people. One of the most remarkable results of the peace was the improvement in methods of education in countries which had for many years been shut up within themselves, but could now freely communicate with each other. Pestalozzi was the principal medium of this benefit to England. He was a Swiss, born at Zurich, in 1746; and his benevolence led him to surrender all the ordinary views of young men entering upon the profession of the law, and to devote himself to the service of the ignorant and poor. As director of an orphan institution at Stanz, he obtained experience, and the opportunity of testing the value of some of his ideas on the training of the human mind. Here he was seen at work by various English travellers, or his pupils were encountered here and there; and his popular works were made known among us, and the rage for the Pestalozzian method of education which ensued can never be forgotten by those who witnessed it. This Pestalozzian method was in fact the Socratic, but applied to little children, with whom Socrates himself would probably not have used it. Hitherto, common-place and unreflecting parents and teachers had gone on in the old method—putting everything into a child, and not thinking of bringing anything out; while reflecting and able teachers had of course done both. Now, everything was to be done by the interrogative method, and nothing was to be received by the memory which could in any way be made otherwise accessible. The suffering of a multitude of children was at first very great, as under every new fashion in education; and there are many who rue the prevalence of that fashion to this day. But this was no fault of Pestalozzi's. It was not his way to tease a little child with questions that it could not see the drift of, till every fibre in its frame was quivering with irritation. It

was not his way to work a child's reasoning faculties
before they ought to have been appealed to at all; or to
forbid the natural and pleasant exercise of the flourishing
memory of childhood, till a little creature might be seen
clutching a vocabulary or chronological table, as most
children lay hands on a fairy tale. He interrogated his
pupils only on subjects which they were able and ready to
understand, and on which they had ideas which they
could produce on easy solicitation. But the truth was,
his procedure was more a peculiar talent than a system,
and it was impossible that it could be extensively imitated
without serious abuse, for which he was, all the while, in
noway responsible. Serious as were the abuses at first in
England, as no doubt elsewhere, the benefits given us by
Pestalozzi unquestionably and immeasurably surpassed
them. The mischief was one which was certain to work
its own cure; while all that was noble and true must live
and grow. Pestalozzi's respect for the human mind, wherever he found it—his sense of its equal and infinite rights,
under all circumstances—his recognition of the diversity of
its faculties—his skill in enlarging its scope—and sub-
stantiating its knowledge; all this was like a new idea to
a nation of parents, who had been too long shut up alone
with old methods, and debarred from intercourse with
thinkers abroad. Since that time, English children have
had a better chance in education—those of them who are
educated at all; a better chance of a natural and timely
development of their various faculties, physical, intellectual, and moral. Therefore it is that we may fairly
class Pestalozzi among our national benefactors, and record
his death among the national losses. He died at the age
of eighty-two, on the 17th of February 1827.

Another educator died during this period, whose name
should not be ungratefully passed over—Dr. Watson, of
the Deaf and Dumb Institution in the Kent Road, London.
Without going into any general account of the education
of the deaf and dumb, we may note, in explanation of Dr.
Watson's services, that the most fatal oversight in that
branch of education has been that of supposing that a full
communication of mind and reception of ideas can be
obtained by written language and gesture. Written

words and gesture are but the signs of language, after
all; and without oral communication, the mind cannot
possibly be fully exercised and cultivated. This difficulty
is, to all appearance, insuperable; but men have risen up,
from time to time, who saw that though the deaf and dumb
can never be brought to an equality of cultivation with
those who have the full use of speech, much is gained by
giving them spoken as well as written language; and Dr.
Watson was the man who gave the deaf and dumb more
power in this direction than any preceding teacher.
Bulwer, the chirosophist, opened up the track in England
in the seventeenth century; and his work, dated 1648,
plainly shows that he taught articulate speech, as well
as the written and hand language. Wallis followed,
being a contemporary of Bulwer, and anxious to engross
the merit which belonged truly to him. Dr. Wallis had
great merit; but he is proved not to have been a dis-
coverer. Articulate speech had been found attainable for
the born deaf previously in Spain, and subsequently in
Holland, where Dr. Amman published his method in full;
and during the eighteenth century, Germany and France
followed. Henry Baker taught various deaf and dumb
persons to speak; but he bound them over not to reveal
his method; and, though he half promised Dr. Johnson
to make it known, he never did so. Thomas Braidwood
began his career in 1760, at Edinburgh, and carried to some
extent the practice of articulate speech among his pupils.
When he removed to London, in 1783, Dr. Watson studied
and worked at his institution, and made up his mind to
devote himself to the education of that unfortunate class, of
whom there are not fewer than 13,000 in our islands; and
in his eyes the practice of articulate speech was indispensable to the attainment of such cultivation as could be
afforded. For five-and-forty years he laboured at his
benevolent task, and he carried the capability of speech
much higher than any predecessor. In regard to the
general run of his pupils, an authority declares: 'Some of
the pupils articulate not unpleasantly; their reading is
monotonous, but their animation in ordinary conversations,
especially on subjects of interest to them, gives a species
of natural tone and emphasis to what they say.' This,

great as it is, is not all. A few days before Dr. Watson's
death one of his private pupils was called to the bar by
the Honourable Society of the Middle Temple. Here
were tidings for a good man to receive on his death-bed !
The days of miracles will never be over while human
benevolence is unexhausted ; and here we have, for a sign
of our own times, a good man soothed to his rest by the
blessings of the dumb. Dr. Watson died on the 23rd of
November 1829, in the sixty-fifth year of his age.

It is not a purely melancholy task to make up this
account of our national losses. In the presence of great
deeds, the doers fade into shadows even during their life,
except to the few to whom they are dear for other reasons
than their deeds. The shadowy form is dissolved by
death, and we strain our eyes to catch the last trace, and
sigh when it is gone ; but the substance remains in the
deeds done, and yet more in the immortal ideal of the
man.

BOOK IV.

——◆◆——

CHAPTER I.

William IV.—King's Message—Regency Question—**Manners of the** Commons—Prorogation—Dissolution—Sympathy with France—**Mr.** Brougham—Yorkshire Election—New House—Death of Mr. Huskisson—O'Connell and the Viceroy—Repeal of the Union—Rickburning—Anxieties of Parties—Opening of the Session—The Duke's Declaration—Alderman Key's Panic—Change of Ministry.

THE valetudinarian king was gone, with his moods and caprices; and with him went all the considerations of expediency which had determined the political conduct of the year, on every side. It was not now necessary to have the most peremptory man in the empire to hold its first office, for the purpose of keeping its sovereign in order. There was no longer an incessant appeal to the generosity of the three bodies in opposition to abstain from joining to throw out the ministry. There need no longer be a mere show of transacting business, while in reality nothing was done—through the mechanical character of the administration on the one hand, and the desultory forbearance of the opposition on the other. It was no longer necessary that the country should be without a government in fact, while the nation was kindling and stirring under the news from France, which became more interesting every day. There was now a king who did not shut himself up with his discontents and his flatterers, but who walked in London streets with his umbrella under his arm, and gave a frank and sailor-like greeting to all old acquaintances, whoever they might be. There was no longer a king who regarded every contravention of his prejudices as a personal injury; but one who sincerely and kindly desired the welfare of his people, without any regard to his personal feelings. He gave an immediate

and strong proof of this by continuing the Duke of
Wellington and his colleagues in power, notwithstanding
a well-understood personal disinclination, and from the
pure desire not to unsettle public affairs till the national
will should have shown itself in the elections. He had
not been many days on the throne, when he took the
opportunity, at some public collation, of proposing the
Duke of·Wellington's health, and declaring, in a manner
more well-meant than dignified, that it was a mistake to
suppose that he had any ill-feeling—any feeling but of entire confidence in his good friend, the Duke of Wellington.
A steady man, of determined will, he certainly did
require as head of his government, as every British
sovereign must, in days when sovereigns have little power,
and scanty means of knowledge of the national mind and
needs ; and in this case, the sovereign was at no time a
man of ability, and often liable to attacks of incapacitating illness ; and he was sixty-five years of age ; but he
was honest, unselfish, and earnestly desirous to do his
duty well ; so that the steadiness of his prime-minister
was required, not to control him, but to inform, and
guide, and aid him in the fulfilment of his function.
There was in no direction any necessity for the Wellington
ministry to remain in power, unless by the wish of the
nation ; and what the desire of the nation was, the
elections would soon show.

The late king had died on the 26th of June. On the
29th, William IV. sent down his first message to parliament—just after the unhappy King of France had addressed his last words to his people, and while the elections
were proving that he had lost all. King William's
message, after adverting to the loss sustained by himself
and the nation, declared his opinion that the sooner the
necessary new elections took place the better, and recommended the Commons to make provision, without delay,
for the maintenance of the public service during the interval between the close of the present session and the
meeting of the new parliament.

This was very well, as far as it went ; but it struck
everybody on the instant that there was an enormous
omission. The king was childless ; and the Princess

Victoria, who was to succeed him, if he died without heirs, was only eleven years old. Without express provision, there is no recognition by the law of the minority of a sovereign; and if the king should die before the new parliament met, this child would be sovereign without control, unless some provision were made for a regency. Something must be done about this, many members of both Houses and of all parties said; but they took a day to consider how they should proceed. On this first day, they spoke merely on that part of the message which related to the death of the late king—the Duke of Wellington's motion in reply being seconded by Lord Grey, and Sir Robert Peel's by Mr. Brougham. All was thus far civility and harmony; a civility and harmony which endured for that day only.

On the 30th, Lord Grey in the one House, and Lord Althorp in the other, moved for the delay of a day in replying to the message in the understood hope that the king would send down a request to parliament to consider the subject of a regency. The grounds on which the ministers resisted this proposition were such as now excite astonishment. They talked of the excellence of the king's health, of 'not indulging in such gloomy forebodings,' of this not being a matter of pressing necessity, and of its being so important in its nature that it should be left for the deliberation of a new parliament, instead of being brought forward when the minds of members were occupied with their approaching election conflicts; the fact remaining clear to all men's minds, that by an overturn of the king's carriage, or a fall of his horse, or the slipping of his foot, or an attack of illness, the country might be plunged into inextricable difficulty, from which the legislation of a day or two now might save it. The Dukes of Newcastle and Richmond, Lords Wellesley and Londonderry, and even Lord Eldon, voted with Lord Grey, though the duke had said that he should regard a defeat as the signal for the dissolution of the ministry. The ministry, however, obtained a majority of forty-four in the House of Peers, and of forty-six in the Commons. The general conviction resulting from this affair was that all compromise was now over; that the duke was laying aside his method of balancing the sections of opposition against each other, and intending to try his strength, while the opposition no longer thought it necessary to spare him. Mr. Brougham lost no time in taking out in full the licence which he had of late, on the whole, denied himself, and on this night used language, and excited uproar, which deprived the opponents of parliamentary reform of their plea of the dignity and decorum of the House as then constituted. Some one having complained of a 'peculiar cry'—whether a baa, a bray, or a grunt, Hansard does not say—a 'peculiar cry which was heard amidst the cheers of the House,' Mr. Brougham observed that 'by a wonderful disposition of nature, every animal had its peculiar mode of expressing itself; and he was too much of a philosopher to quarrel with any of those modes.' And presently after, he called up Sir Robert Peel to a personal altercation, by saying, after a reference to the Duke of Wellington : 'Him I accuse not. It is you I accuse—his flatterers—his mean, fawning parasites.' Such quarrels are always got rid of with more or less quibbling and ill grace ; but it should be noted that they did occur before the great opening of the representation which was now near at hand. Much was said by the enemies of parliamentary reform of the vulgarity of manners which would certainly show itself in the House when the manufacturing towns were represented ; but at this time it was the complaint of strangers who attended the debates, that not only violence of language was occasionally very great, but that offensive noises—the braying, baaing, crowing, mewing of animals—were ventured upon and tolerated in the House to an extent which would not be thought of in any other association assembled for grave purposes.

The king's answer to the address contained no allusion to the subject of a regency ; nor did he make any reference to it in any form. The omission was daring ; but nobody doubted that the ministers pressed upon him, as upon parliament, the consideration of 'a great present inconvenience' being of more consequence than 'a remote future risk ;' and the king did not die during the recess, so as to put the fallacy to the proof. How much he thought of dying during those weeks, and whether he felt like a

family man who is prevented by vexatious accidents from
making his will, and who grows nervous about his personal safety till the thing is done, there is no knowing;
but the matter was discussed with deep interest in the
homes of the land—children and adults wondering whether
the little princess was aware of her position—whether, if
the king were now to die, she would have the sense to
desire a regency for some years, or whether she would
choose to rule according to her own pleasure; and if so,
what kind of persons she would select for her ministers.
There was another consideration uppermost in all minds,
and largely concerned in the question, though it could not
be openly spoken of in parliament. After the king's
death, the Duke of Cumberland would be her eldest uncle.
He must succeed to the crown of Hanover, which descends
only to male heirs. Would he go to Hanover and stay
there, and let England alone? To say that the Duke of
Cumberland was unpopular throughout the empire, would
be to use language too feeble for the fact. He was hated;
and hated with that mixture of fear which belongs to total
disesteem. It was widely felt that the princess would not
be safe, if unprotected by a regency on ascending the
throne in childhood; and it was generally believed that
the nation would not submit to any kind or degree of rule,
governance, or influence from the Duke of Cumberland.
This being the state of the royal family, and the warning
condition of France being before all eyes, it was an act of
extraordinary rashness in the ministry to insist on the dissolution of parliament before any provision had been made
for a regency.

It was carefully pointed out, when the king came down
to prorogue parliament, that he appeared to be in excellent
health. There was something exhilarating in the sight of
a king in excellent health, coming down with an open
face and frank demeanour, to meet his parliament. He
wore his admiral's uniform under the royal robes. There
was not much in his speech; for the session did not supply
much matter. The most important point was that with
which the speech concluded; an expression of his desire
that, as parliament had declared its will that civil distinctions on account of religious opinion should cease, his

subjects universally should join with him in promoting peace, and burying all such differences in oblivion.

The next day, July 24, parliament was dissolved by proclamation; and in a few hours the bustle of the new elections began. In a few days, some of them were actually decided; for the writs were made returnable on the 14th of September.

The people of England, Scotland, and Ireland, met together in crowds for other purposes than electing their representatives. By this time, the three days in Paris were over; the French people had thrown off the Polignac tyranny, and the English were not slow to congratulate them. Public meetings were held in counties and towns to prepare addresses for this purpose; and a long file of deputations crossed the Channel to present these addresses in Paris. At these meetings men spoke to each other, in high exhilaration, of the bearing of these French events upon their own political affairs. They pointed out to each other how the representation was the central ground of struggle; and how victory there was total victory. They agreed upon the powerlessness of kings, cabinets, and armies, when in opposition to the popular will; and all who were in any degree on the Liberal side in politics saw that now was the time to secure that reform of parliament which was a necessary condition of all other political reforms. That was a stirring time in England. Again, the men of the towns went out early in the summer mornings, or late at night, to meet the mails; and brought news to the breakfast table, or to the eager listeners round the lamp, that Paris was in a state of siege; that the Parisians had taken Paris; that the French king was coming to England; that the chambers had met at the appointed time, as if no impediment had arisen; that the tricolor had been seen in the Thames, and that the Duke of Wellington, riding along the wharves, had turned away his head from the sight with unconcealed anger and mortification; that, though the king had called the duke his friend, it was clear that we could not have an intimate of Prince Polignac for our prime-minister; that almost the whole newspaper press of England was hostile to the present administration; and, finally, that the men of Yorkshire

had sent such a requisition to Harry Brougham to become
their representative as left scarcely a doubt of his triumphant return; a portentous sign of the times, if such
should be the issue.

There is something very affecting to those who were of
mature years at that time in looking back upon these
glories of the Harry Brougham who was the hope and
admiration of so large a portion of the Liberal body in the
nation. As he himself said, he had now arrived at the
pinnacle of his fame; he had attained an honour which
could never be paralleled. When he said this, he did not
contemplate decline; nor did those who listened to him;
nor did the Liberal party generally. Those who did were
some close observers who had never had confidence in
him, and who knew that sobriety of thought, and temperance of feeling, were essential to success in a commanding
position, though they might not be much missed in one
of struggle and antagonism. These observers, who had
seen that with all his zeal, his strong spirit of pugnacity,
his large views of popular right and interests, Henry
Brougham gave no evidences of magnanimity, patience,
moderation, and self-forgetfulness, felt now, as throughout
his course, that power would be too much for him, and that
his splendid talents were likely to become conspicuous disgraces. This was what was soon to be tried; and in the
interval he stood, in these times of popular excitement,
the first man in England; called by the popular voice to
represent the first constituency in England, in a season
when constituencies and their chosen representatives were
the most prominent objects in the nation's eye. Mr.
Brougham had been twenty-one years in public life; his
endowments were the most splendid conceivable, short of
the inspiration of genius; and they had been, thus far,
employed on behalf of popular interests. Men thought of
his knowledge and sagacity on colonial affairs, shown
early in his career; they thought of his brave and faithful
advocacy of the queen's cause; they thought of his labours
for popular enlightenment—of his furtherance of Mechanics' Institutes, of the London University, and of the
Society for the Diffusion of Useful Knowledge; they
thought of his plans for the reform of the law, and his

labours in making justice accessible to the poor; they thought of his mighty advocacy of the claims of the slave, and of his thundering denunciations of oppression in that and every other relation; and they reasonably regarded him as a great man, and the hope of his country.   It was so reasonable to regard him thus, that those who had misgivings were ashamed of them, and concealed them so anxiously, that it is certain that Mr. Brougham had as fair a field as any man ever had for showing what he could do. But, though those who knew him best concealed their doubts, the doubts were there; doubts whether his celebrated oratory was not mainly factitious—vehement and passionate, but not simple and heartfelt; doubts whether a temper of jealousy and irritability would not poison any work into which it could find entrance; doubts whether a vanity so restless and insatiable must not speedily starve out the richest abilities; doubts whether a habit of speech so exaggerated, of statements so inaccurate, would not soon be fatal to respect and confidence; doubts about the perfect genuineness of his popular sympathies—not charging him with hypocrisy, but suspecting that the people were an object in his imagination, rather than an interest in his heart—a temporary idol to him, as he was to them.   These doubts made the spectacle of Henry Brougham at the head of the representation of Great Britain an interesting and anxious one to those who knew him well, whether from personal intercourse or from a close study of his career. With all the other Liberals of England, it was an occasion of unbounded triumph.   He has since publicly and repeatedly referred to this period as that of his highest glory; and there are now none, probably, who do not agree with him.   At this Yorkshire election, when four representatives were required, five candidates came forward, and Mr. Brougham stood next to Lord Morpeth, who headed the poll.

A very few days were enough to show the ministers what they had to expect from the new House.   The Tory magnates whom they had offended by their liberal measures, took this opportunity of revenging themselves, and returned members opposed to them, who, though not Liberals, served the purposes of the Liberals nearly as well as if they had been comrades. Two brothers and a brother-in-law of Sir Robert Peel were thrown out. Mr. Hume came in for the county of Middlesex, while the Duke of Newcastle was causing the return of members hostile to the ministry. Their faithful friend the Duke of Rutland could not carry the county of Cambridge; and Lord Ebrington was returned for Devonshire. No cabinet minister obtained a seat by anything like open and popular election. Of the eighty-two county members, only twenty-eight were avowedly on the ministerial side, while forty-seven were avowedly on the other side. Of the twenty-eight members representing the greatest cities, three were ministerialists, and twenty-four Liberals. Such being the state of things where the elections were open and popular, and the proprietors of close boroughs being still steady anti-Catholics, the fate of the ministry was sealed, and known to be so, before the summer was over. Even the revolutions on the continent, now following one another with a rapidity which, at a different time, would have pressed all the Conservatives in England into close union, had not at present that effect. The great soldier, the peremptory commander, the iron duke, must be got rid of; and then, all good Conservatives would join at once, and see what must be done to save the Church and the State. The ministry, on their part, hoped to effect some good understanding in the interval betwixt August and November. In September, an event occurred which seemed to open some prospect of this; though the ministers themselves were too much touched and grieved at heart to think of such a result so soon as some of their less interested adherents.

The first great English railway was completed, and the line from Liverpool to Manchester was opened on Wednesday, the 15th of September. The Duke of Wellington, Sir Robert Peel, and other great men, arrived to take part in the ceremony, which was to have been succeeded by a banquet at Manchester. Mr. Huskisson was already on the spot, having arrived, as soon as the state of his feeble health permitted it, to visit the constituency of Liverpool, who had elected him in his absence. Before the trains left Liverpool, a particular request was made that none of the

company would leave the carriages, and the printed bills
exhibited a caution to the same effect; but when the trains
stopped at Parkside, several of the party alighted, and a
mutual friend of the Duke of Wellington and Mr. Huskisson thought that this would be a good opportunity for
bringing them together, and putting an end to the coolness
which had existed between them since Mr. Huskisson's
dismissal from the cabinet. Both parties were willing
and cordial. When the duke saw Mr. Huskisson approaching, he advanced and held out his hand, and almost before
the friendly grasp was loosened, some one took alarm at
the approach of a locomotive, and there was a general cry
to those who were standing in the road: 'Get in, get in!'
If Mr. Huskisson had stood still beside the car, he would
have been safe. Whether, feeble and nervous from illness,
he was attempting to get round the open door of the car,
in order to enter it, or whether he was merely holding by
it, appears not to be known. The event was that the open
door by which he held was struck by the locomotive, and
threw down Mr. Huskisson, who fell, with his leg doubled
across the rail, so that the limb was instantly crushed. He
was at once aware that the accident was fatal; and he died
that night, at the parsonage at Eccles, where he was conveyed with all skill and tenderness. The ministers were in
no spirits for further public exhibition that day, and they
would fain have withdrawn; but it was represented to
them how serious would be the public alarm, in such a
place as Manchester; how report would exaggerate the
mischief if they were not seen; and how fatal might even be
the effect on future railway travelling of a false panic that
day; and they consented to proceed. All was now gloom,
and the chief guests refused to leave the car at Manchester,
or do more than the public safety required.

It was not they who immediately began to consider
what effect this mournful death would have on their
political position; but, as was natural, there were many
who did. The 'Canningites' would now merge into
another party. For some time there had been no sufficient
peculiarity of doctrine or principle to necessitate their
forming a separate party; and that they did stand aloof,
was owing to the state of feeling between the duke and

Mr. Huskisson. That was all over now. There was no quarrel which survivors ought to keep alive; and it was hoped that the Grants and Lord Palmerston would strengthen the ministry in the Lower House. It was too late for this, however. The ministry had done their utmost, and in vain, to exclude Mr. Charles Grant from Inverness; and Mr. Robert Grant had thrown out a brother of Sir Robert Peel's at Norwich. The few remaining ʻCanningites' advanced towards liberalism from this day. The only hope now was that the bringing forward of the parliamentary reform question in revolutionary times would alarm all but the extreme Liberals into union at the last moment.

Up to the last moment, indeed, matters looked gloomy enough. In October the viceroy of Ireland, through his secretary, Sir Henry Hardinge, issued a proclamation intended to prevent the meeting of an association for promoting the repeal of the union. The prohibition was positive and comprehensive; but British governments, and British officials, did not yet know Daniel O'Connell; how impossible it was to restrain him by law in the prosecution of his enterprises, or to have dealings with him, as between man and man. Daniel O'Connell issued his proclamations forthwith, in which he arraigned ʻthat paltry, contemptible, little English soldier, that had the audacity to put his pitiful and contemptible name to an atrocious Polignac proclamation;' and laid down the law about obtaining the repeal of the union. He declared, as he continued to declare to the end of his life, that the repeal of the union was just at hand, and that ʻno power on earth could prevent it, except the folly or the crimes of some of the Irish themselves.' He proposed ʻthat a society should be formed to meet in Dublin, to be called the Association of Irish Volunteers;' the motto of the society to be ʻ1782,' over the word ʻ*Resurgam.*' The members were to be unarmed, open in all their proceedings, and to be active, in the first place, in procuring petitions from every parish in Ireland in behalf of repeal of the union. In the course of his speeches and proclamations on this matter, Mr. O'Connell used language with regard to Sir H. Hardinge, for which he was called to account by that gentleman. A recurrence to this fact seems to take us back to a distant time indeed; all modern recollections of O'Connell being such as to attach an idea of ridicule to any person resenting his foulness of language. On this occasion he behaved as disgracefully as possible, shuffling about what expressions he did or did not use, and refusing to accept a challenge. There cannot be a finer spectacle in our time than an honourable man refusing to fight a duel, from a conviction of the sin and folly of that kind of ordeal in a Christian nation and a modern age. But then it is essential that he be an honourable man, observing the Christian rule of doing as he would be done by, and peaceable and inoffensive, as truly brave and considerate men always are. It was far otherwise with O'Connell; he was the bully all over; the most foul-mouthed railer of his time; and, till men left off calling him to account, he always fell back upon his conscientious objection to duelling. He indulged in offence, and then made a merit of declining the penalty. As his sons grew up, he permitted them, two or three times, to fight his duels for him; but the public cry of disgust and indignation was so strong, that he at length forbade his sons to fight in his quarrels, and made a merit out of that. The correspondence on occasion of this offence to Sir H. Hardinge settles the matter for ever about O'Connell's honour, and the possibility of having dealings with him, as between man and man; and it is referred to here as an evidence that all parties who afterwards courted him, or allied themselves with him, more or less, for whatever political purposes, were not entitled to complain when he betrayed, insulted, and reviled them. That any terms should have been held with O'Connell, by governments, English public, or gentlemen, in or out of parliament, after his present agitation for repeal, and his published correspondence with Sir H. Hardinge's aide, in October 1830, is one of the moral disgraces of our time. It shows that a man's abilities and political influence can secure to him an impunity for bullying, cowardice, and falsehood, which would drive a man of meaner talents and power from any society in the land. It is at this time that we find first recorded that expression of O'Connell's which he used, with the utmost freedom of application, for the rest of his life. The administration was 'base, bloody, and brutal;' and henceforward, every law, every cabinet, every person, and every party, that he objected to, was 'base, bloody, and brutal;' and it really appears as if every successive party to whom the epithets were applied, winced under them as if they had never been used before, or as if they carried any weight.

Our country and our time have, since this date, rung with the Irish cry of 'Repeal of the Union!' and this seems the occasion on which to look and see what it means. There are many in France and Germany, and a multitude in America, who would be surprised that any question could be made as to the meaning of that cry. They suppose the case to be plain enough; that England conquered Ireland, and has ever since oppressed her; draining her of her produce, insulting her religion, being indifferent to her discontents, and careless of her woes. They suppose that the entire Irish people wish to be wholly separated from England, and insist that a nation which desires to live by itself, and to govern itself, should be allowed to do so. Of course, they believe that the reason why England does not let Ireland go, is that the territorial possession and its produce are of consequence to England. Such was the story told by O'Connell to the world; though it is utterly impossible that he could have believed it himself. He had too much warrant in history for some of his complaints. It was true that Ireland had once been fiercely conquered and cruelly oppressed; that, till now, her Catholic population had been bitterly insulted by exclusion from political rights on account of their faith; that the Church of seven-eighths of her people was still insulted by the presence of an established Episcopal Church, and endowed Protestant meeting-houses; and that a large proportion of her people were in a condition of political discontent, and intolerable social misery. Thus much was true; but O'Connell, in his addresses to the ignorant among his countrymen, and to the world abroad, never failed to cast the blame of ancient tyranny on the existing generation; never failed to impute the purely social miseries of Ireland to political causes; never failed to suppress the

fact that Ireland had any imperial rights at all, or to
throw contempt and ridicule on benefits which he could
not ignore ; never held forth to his countrymen the means
of welfare which they had in their power, if they would
but use them, and, above all, never made the slightest
rational attempt to show how the repeal of the union
would cure their woes and give them peace and comfort.
Any one who studies his speeches, as a series, may see that
he knew the truth, from the directions in which he levels
his vituperation and his sarcasm.   He certainly knew that
the miserable tenure of land, and multiplication of a destitute population, were the chief causes of the miseries of
Ireland, and that, as a natural consequence, the people
would not work, and were prone to outrage.   He certainly
knew that these evils could not be cured by a parliament
sitting in Dublin.   He certainly knew that nearly all
persons of education and property in Ireland were averse
to a repeal of the union, and did not choose that it should
take place.   He certainly knew that such a complexity of
interests had grown up between England and Ireland
during their imperial connection as made separation impossible, and that the interests of Great Britain would no
more permit her to have for an independent neighbour an
insular nation in a state of desperate and reckless misery
—as Ireland would be, if left to her own turbulence and
poverty—than her conscience would permit her to cast off
from her protection a people whom she had formerly helped
to make miserable.   From O'Connell's speeches, during a
course of years, it is clear that he well knew all these
things; yet it was his custom to speak, when on Irish
ground, as if all the Irish desired repeal—as if the Dublin
parliament would truly represent the Irish people—as if
Irish industry would thrive when commerce with England
should be stopped—as if repeal would give to every man
for his own, the land he lived on—as if Irish turbulence
were merely the result of English provocation—and as if
all had been well in Ireland till the British connection
began, and would be immediately well again if that connection could be dissolved.   As for the reasons why any
man should plead such a cause in such a way, they seem
clear enough in this case.   Among the ignorant of his

own countrymen and uninformed foreigners, he obtained
credence enough to give him great power; and this power
sustained him in his chosen career as an agitator in Ireland. Moreover, he believed, and truly, that it gave him
great importance in England—great power of annoyance
to the government—great power of obstruction in parliament—a power of intimidation which he could take up
at any time when he had an object to gain for himself
or his country. He raised the repeal cry whenever any
benefit to Ireland was moved for, to hasten it, as he
thought; and again, whenever it was granted, to save the
awkwardness of acknowledgment; and he raised it in the
autumn of every year—unless some other cry was abroad
which would spare this for once—when the O'Connell rent
was to be collected. As for the question of repeal itself,
let us see how it stands, apart from the prejudice which
O'Connell connected with it.

People had different opinions about what the effect
would be in Ireland of granting measures which had been
too long delayed. When the Duke of Wellington was
proposing Catholic emancipation, he said, at his own table,
at a ministerial dinner: 'It is a bad business; but we are
aground.' Lord Sidmouth asked: 'Does your grace think,
then, that this concession will tranquillise Ireland?' 'I
can't tell. I hope it will,' the duke replied. He shortly
discovered and owned his mistake. The duke was no
philosopher, to be sure; but, if he had been, he would
have seen that the union itself, though working well on
the whole, worked very slowly, because it had been too
long delayed. And this other great measure, being much
too long delayed, could not be expected to 'tranquillise
Ireland,' so as to gratify the eyes of existing statesmen
with the spectacle of tranquillity.

The slightest observation of Ireland, and the most
superficial knowledge of her history, must convince every
one, that if she had been an independent kingdom from
1782, or earlier, she would have been from that time in
a state of misery and ruin which could not have been
allowed in any civilised quarter of the world, either
for her own sake or that of her neighbours. The civil
wars of her factions, and the hunger of her swarming

multitudes, must presently have destroyed her as a nation. If she had been up to this time an ally, or self-governing province of Great Britain, instead of being incorporated with her, her ruin could hardly have been less complete. In such a case, it is impossible to prevent the weaker going to the wall.   It is impossible to prevent more or less abuse of power by the stronger party, and to obviate the jealousy or sycophancy of the leading men of the weaker, who make their own people their prey.   We have a picture of Scotland, before and after the union, which may enlighten us much in regard to the case of Ireland, though Scotland never was subject to the worst economical evils of Ireland ; economical evils which are the true cause of her miseries, and which can be remedied only by her intimate connection with a country of superior industrial condition and habits.

' If any one doubts,' says an eminent Scotchman, ' of the wretchedness of an unequal and unincorporating alliance, of the degradation of being subject to a provincial parliament and a distant king, and of the efficacy of a substantial union in curing all these evils, he is invited to look to the obvious example of Scotland.   When the crowns only were united, and the governments continued separate, the weaker country was the scene of the most atrocious cruelties, the most violent injustice, and the most degrading oppressions.   The prevailing religion of the people was proscribed and persecuted, with a ferocity greater than has ever been systematically exercised, even in Ireland ; her industry was crippled and depressed by unjust and intolerable restrictions ; her parliaments corrupted and overawed into the degraded instruments of a distant court ; and her nobility and gentry, cut off from all hope of distinction by vindicating the rights, or promoting the interests, of their country at home, were led to look up to the favour of her oppressors as the only remaining avenue to power, and degenerated, for the most part, into a band of mercenary adventurers, the more considerable aspiring to the wretched honour of executing the orders which were dictated from the south, and the rest acquiring gradually those habits of subserviency and selfish submission, the traces of which are by some

supposed to be yet discernible in their descendants. The
Revolution, which rested almost entirely on the prevailing
antipathy to popery, required, of course, the co-operation
of all classes of Protestants; and, by its success, the
Scottish Presbyterians were relieved, for a time, from
their Episcopalian persecution. But it was not till after
the union that the nation was truly emancipated, or
lifted up from the abject condition of a dependent, at once
suspected and despised. The effects of that happy consolidation were not, indeed, *immediately* apparent; for the
vices which had been generated by a century of provincial
misgovernment, the meannesses that had become habitual,
the animosities that had so long been fostered, could not
be cured at once by the mere removal of their cause. The
generation they had degraded must first be allowed to
die out, and more perhaps than one generation; but the
poison tree was cut down, the fountain of bitter waters
was sealed up, and symptoms of returning vigour and
happiness were perceived. Vestiges may still be traced,
perhaps, of our long degradation; but for forty years
back, the provinces of Scotland have been, on the whole,
but the northern provinces of Great Britain. There are
no local oppressions, no national animosities. Life, and
liberty, and property, are as secure in Caithness as they
are in Middlesex, industry as much encouraged, and wealth
still more rapidly progressive; while, not only different
religious opinions, but different religious establishments,
subsist in the two ends of the same island, in unbroken
harmony, and only excite each other by a friendly
emulation to greater purity of life, and greater zeal for
Christianity. If this happy union, however, had been
delayed for another century; if Scotland had been doomed
to submit for a hundred years more to the provincial
tyranny of the Lauderdales, Rotheses, and Middletons,
and to meet the cruel persecutions which gratified the
ferocity of her Dalzells and Drummonds, and tarnished the
glories of such men as Montrose and Dundee, with her
armed conventicles and covenanted saints militant; to
see her patriots exiled, or bleeding on the scaffold; her
teachers silenced in her churches and schools, and her
courts of justice degraded or over-awed into the in-

struments of a cowardly oppression—can any man doubt, not only that she would have presented, at this day, a scene of even greater misery and discord than Ireland did in 1800; but that the corruptions and animosities by which she had been desolated would have been found to have struck so deep root as still to encumber the land, long after their seed had ceased to be scattered abroad on its surface, and only to hold out the hope of their eradication after many years of patient and painful exertion?'

In the Irish case, England had indeed much, very much, to answer for in not having immediately and strenuously given the fullest possible effect to the union; in having continued the disabilities of the Catholics, and in still maintaining a church establishment useless and hateful to seven-eighths of the Irish people. But, by means of the union, agriculture was improving in Ireland, and manufactures were advancing every year. Throughout the north, life, liberty, and property were secure to a degree never known before. The whole island had begun to be governed by the wisdom and impartial rule of the British government, instead of by turbulent native factions; and now a way was, however late, freely opened into the imperial legislature. What a benefactor would O'Connell have been to his country, if he had now used patriotically the rights so hardly gained! If he, and the Irish members he had brought into the legislature with him, had used their imperial rights for the thorough realisation of the union, their country might by this time have been, not prosperous and peaceful and satisfied—for her troubles could not be annihilated so speedily—but advancing towards such a condition. He, and he alone, could control the impatient Irish temper; he set himself diligently to exasperate it. He could have won the peasantry to industry and conscientious thrift; he drew them off studiously from their labours to roam the country in attendance on his political agitation. He could have united their wills and voices in a calm and effectual remonstrance against their remaining wrongs, and demand for rights yet due; but he bade them spurn the benefits granted, and taught them to put a foul construction on every act of the government and people of which they were now a part, and trained them to a passionate contempt and hatred of the law, which was all they had to look to for security and social existence. To all this he added that worst and ultimate act of promising to those who would believe him, the repeal, and the speedy repeal, of the union; well knowing that that repeal was rendered impossible by the united will and judgment of England, Scotland, and the most enlightened and influential part of Ireland. He promised a federal allegiance to the British sovereign, who would not receive such a partial and pernicious allegiance. He promised a parliament in Dublin, where parliaments had never been anything but assemblages of jobbers and faction leaders. He promised Irish-laws, while corrupting the people out of any capacity for obedience to law at all. He promised the exclusion of British commerce, while without British commerce the Irish could not live. He promised everything he could not perform, and that no sane and shrewd man—and O'Connell was sane and shrewd—would have performed if he could; and everything which could most effectually draw off the vast multitudes of the Catholic peasantry of Ireland from the remedy of their social hardships, from the duty to their own households, and their welfare in the state. Whether he gained any objects by threatening and annoying the governments of his day, we may see hereafter. Whether he and his companions in the legislature might not have gained more by honest political endeavours —gained more even in definite achievements, as well as in personal and national character, and in British sympathy for Ireland—there can be no question. Thus early, however, in the summer and autumn of 1830, O'Connell exhibited the programme of his political course. One of the troubles of the Wellington ministry during this October was the state of Ireland, where the magistrates of Tipperary were obliged to apply for military force, to put down outrage; where one repeal association after another was prohibited by the viceroy, the people believing their liberties assailed in each case; and where O'Connell—on all other occasions the partisan of the Bourbons—bade the people look to the revolutions of France and Belgium for examples what to do, and counselled a run on the banks throughout Ireland, in order to show government the danger of resisting their demands.

Nearer home, too, a strange new trouble was arising, which it was extremely difficult to cope with. A year or two before this time, English gentry had been holding up hands and eyes at the atrocious barbarism of the peasantry in the north of France, who burned corn-ricks in the night. People observed to one another on the awful state of stupidity and malice in which any society must be sunk where such a crime could spread; a crime so foolish, so suicidal, as well as malicious! What could induce a peasantry to destroy their own food? What a set of idiots they must be! But, as soon as the dark long nights of October and November came on, the same thing was happening in our agricultural counties, and particularly in Kent. The mystery appears never to have been completely explained. Here and there, perhaps, was seen some skulker—some shabby stranger, wandering about in copses, and behind enclosures, or hiding in sheds, or dropping into the public-house, all ear and no tongue, or patting farm boys and girls on the back, and having confidences with them. Such people were seen here and there; and there were several instances in which young persons on trial for incendiarism accused the principal witness of having enticed them to do the act, and then got the reward by informing against them. But, if these things were true, they do not account for the origin of the practice. There was considerable distress; but not nearly so pressing or threatening as during two or three preceding years. There was, as there always is among an ignorant population, some discontent with machinery; but it did not appear that the farmers who used machinery were more pursued by the incendiary than others. It was probably from all these causes, in turn, from some imported knowledge of what had been done in France, and from that never-failing propensity in human nature, by which extraordinary crimes—crimes which produce vast effect by a rapid and easy act, gratifying the relish for power in an untrained mind—spread like a fashion of a season; but, however it was, that autumn was a memorable time to all who lived in the southern agricultural

counties of England. The farmers and their families had
no comfort in their lives. All day they looked with unavoidable suspicion upon the most ill-conditioned of their
neighbours, and on every stranger who came into the
parish. All night, they were wakeful; either acting as
patrols, or looking out towards the stackyards, or listening
for the rumble of the fire-engine. Those who were fully
insured did not like the idea of fire close to the dwelling-
house; and there were some serious doubts about the
stability of some of the insurance offices, under a pressure
for which no prudence could have provided. The farmers
who were not insured need not think of it; for no offices
would do new business, on any terms that farmers could
offer, during the rick-burning period. If a man, weary
with patrolling for three or four nights, hoped for a night's
sleep, and went the last thing to his rickyard, and explored
every corner, and visited every shed on his premises, he
might find his chamber illuminated by his burning ricks,
by the time he could get upstairs. If the patrol, after a
similar search, looked round as they shut the gate, some
one of them asked what that blue speck in the air was; and
before he could be answered, a blue flame would run,
rocket-like, along the ridge of a stack, and down its sides,
and in one minute the farmhouse windows would be
glittering, and the sheds would seem to come out into the
yellow light, and the pond would be burnished, and all
darkness would be suddenly annihilated, except in the
shadows cast by the mounting and spreading flames. How
it was done was never learned. Some believed that a particular stack in a yard was previously wetted with some
liquid that would blaze up with a spark; and so few
persons were apprehended in the very act, or under very
strong suspicion, that it was a widely spread belief that
some kindling substance was directed upon the prepared
stack from a distance. Several persons declared, and were
more or less believed, that they saw the blue spark traverse
the air and descend; and now and then, a long slender
wire was said to be found among the ashes. A considerable number of persons saw the fire begin before their very
eyes, without being able to discover traces of trespassers.
This was naturally a time for malicious or encroaching

persons to send threatening letters; and for foolish jesters
to play off practical jokes; and for timid persons to take
needless alarms; and for all the discontented to make the
most of their grievances; and a dreary season of apprehension indeed it was. It is memorable even to those who
lived in towns, and conducted no business and had no
enemies, and feared no evil for themselves. It was a great
shock to such to find themselves living in a state of society
where such things could be. In Kent, there were gibbets
erected on Penenden Heath, and bodies swung there in the
December winds—bodies of 'boys about eighteen or nine-
teen years old, but looking much younger;' brothers, who
had said to each other, on arriving at the spot, and seeing
the gallows: 'That looks an awful thing.' And from
Kent, the deadly fashion spread into Hampshire, Wiltshire,
Buckinghamshire, Sussex, and Surrey. The military were
harassed with fruitless marches, their nightly path lighted
by fires from behind, whichever way they turned. Large
rewards were offered—£500 for a single conviction; and
these rewards were believed to have been now and then
obtained by the instigators, while poor tools were given
over to destruction. A special commission was ordered
to proceed into the shires where this kind of outrage
abounded; and the subject was one of several unwelcome
topics in the king's speech in November.

The opening of this parliament was awaited throughout
the country with anxious expectation. In September,
when tidings of new continental revolutions were arriving,
almost day by day, the funds fell; and what Lord Eldon
and the ministers called 'London'—that is, the aristocracy
with whom they had intercourse, and who remained
clustered together in the metropolis in a very unusual
manner—was in gloomy apprehension of the fall of the
monarchy; not because there were any threatenings of the
monarchy, public or private, but because other monarchies
were falling. The aristocracy shook their heads over the
free-and-easy sayings and doings of the new sailor-king.
'I hear,' wrote Lord Eldon, 'that the condescensions of
the king are beginning to make him unpopular. In that
station, such familiarity must produce the destruction of
respect. If the people don't continue to think a king

somewhat more than a man, they will soon find out that
he is not an object of that high respect which is absolutely
necessary to the utility of his character.' It may be
doubted whether anybody in England was at that time
saying anything more injurious to monarchy than this.
Lord Eldon, however, did what he could towards preserving the monarchy, by rebuking the king for improper
condescension. The anecdote is an interesting one, as
presenting both these old men—so perfectly unlike each
other—in a favourable light. Lord Eldon went up with
the Bishop of Bristol to present an address. As Lord
Eldon was retiring, the king stopped him, and said: ' My
lord, political parties and feelings have run very high, and
I am afraid I have made observations upon your lordship
which now '——. Here Lord Eldon interrupted him, and
said: ' I entreat your majesty's pardon—a subject must
not hear the language of apology from the lips of his
sovereign ;' and then the dutiful subject passed out from
the presence of his rebuked king. If the Tories were
right in supposing the existence of the monarchy to depend
in any considerable degree on the personal reserve and
dignity of the sovereign, it was assuredly very unsafe
under the open-hearted sailor-king.

This same ' London ' believed in October that, in consequence of the removal of Mr. Huskisson, negotiations
were going on between the ministry and ' Palmerston and
Co.,' the survivors of the ' Canningites,' but on a footing
which yielded far too much to the requisitions of this
remnant of a party; on the footing of pledges for some
kind of parliamentary reform—which could hardly have
been true—some measure about tithes, and some close
dealing with the civil list. Whether these reports had any
foundation or not, they are of importance to us now, as
showing that the great Tory world of London was prepared for some assertion of the necessity of these measures,
and would not have been surprised if they had been
brought forward by the duke himself. When night closed
in on the 1st of November, nobody knew, except those
who were seated round the tables of the ministers, what
the disclosures of the speech were to be next day. For
five days the swearing in of members of parliament had

been going on; but the session was not opened till the
2nd of November.

When the speech was promulgated, it was found to be
the most offensive that had been uttered by any British
monarch since the Revolution. Now, indeed, unless it
could presently be shown that the king had been made a
tool of by his ministers, there might soon be some ground
for the Tory apprehensions about the unpopularity of the
sovereign. Except a surrender of the civil list to the consideration of parliament, and a recommendation to provide
a regency in case of his death, there was no topic which
gratified the expectation of the people. There was much
regret at the disturbed state of Europe; determination to
uphold the treaties by which the political system of
Europe had been established; indignation, contempt, and
horror, about disturbances in England and Ireland; a
pledge to use all the powers of law and constitution to put
down and punish such disturbance; and a lecture on the
supreme happiness of those who live under British institutions. While men were gathering together in streets
and public buildings to discuss this speech, the turbulent
in exasperation at its insolence, and the thoughtful in
regret at its hardness, the prime-minister settled everything—the fate of his government, and the course of public
affairs for years to come—by a few sentences in the opening debate, which made some people ask whether he had
lost his senses, while they revived the Tory party with
hopes that some hidden resources of power existed to
justify the apparent rashness. In the debate on the
address, the Duke of Wellington uttered that celebrated
declaration against reform in parliament, which immediately overthrew his power at home, and his reputation as
a statesman throughout the world. His personal friends
have since accounted for the apparent madness of uttering
those words at that moment, by saying that it was a mistake owing to his deafness; and this is quoted as his own
plea. A deafness had been long growing upon him which
had now become considerable; and it was declared on his
behalf that if he had heard what had been said by men
of his own party, and what was passing on the benches
behind him, he would not have made such a declaration in

that place and at that time, and without consultation with
his colleagues. But the plea goes for nothing in his defence.
It does not disprove his ignorance—an ignorance extraordinary and culpable in a member of administration—of
the popular opinion and will; and it proves a most repre-
hensible carelessness, want of concert with his colleagues,
and want of deference for their judgment, on a matter of
supreme importance. The memorable sentences were these,
uttered with the coolness and confidence with which he
would have delivered a lecture on the British constitution
in a mechanics' institute:

'The noble earl [Grey] had alluded to the propriety of
effecting parliamentary reform. . . . . He had never
heard or read of any measure, up to the present moment,
which could in any degree satisfy his mind that the state
of the representation could be improved, or be rendered
more satisfactory to the country at large than at the
present moment. He would not, however, at such an
unseasonable time enter upon the subject, or excite discussion, but he should not hesitate to declare unequivocally
what were his sentiments upon it. He was fully convinced
that the country possessed at the present moment a
legislature which answered all the good purposes of
legislation, and this to a greater degree than any legislature ever had answered in any country whatever. He
would go further and say, that the legislature and the
system of representation possessed the full and entire
confidence of the country—deservedly possessed that confidence; and the discussions in the legislature had a very
great influence over the opinions of the country. He
would go still further and say, that if at the present
moment he had imposed upon him the duty of forming a
legislature for any country, and particularly for a country
like this, in possession of great property of various
descriptions, he did not mean to assert that he could form
such a legislature as they possessed now, for the nature of
man was incapable of reaching such excellence at once;
but his great endeavour would be to form some description
of legislature which would produce the same results. The
representation of the people at present contained a large
body of the property of the country, and in which the

landed interests had a preponderating influence. Under these circumstances, he was not prepared to bring forward any measure of the description alluded to by the noble lord. He was not only not prepared to bring forward any measure of this nature, but he would at once declare, that, as far as he was concerned, as long as he held any station in the government of the country, he should always feel it his duty to resist such measures when proposed by others.'

On that same night, Mr. Brougham gave notice in the Commons of his intention to bring forward, in a fortnight, the question of parliamentary reform. The next day, the unrepresented men of Birmingham were telling each other in the streets that the prime-minister of the country had declared that the representation could not be improved; and perhaps some traveller, on his way from Marlborough to Salisbury, gazing as he passed on the little mounds of Old Sarum, enclosing its few bare acres, where no living creature dwelt, would think of the two members sitting in the Commons, to represent this patch of ground, and would say to himself, with some amusement, that the prime-minister of the country had declared that the representation could not be improved. There were thousands of inhabitants of Leeds and Manchester, sustaining hundreds of thousands of labourers—five to one of rural labourers—who conferred ominously on the minister's satisfaction at the preponderance of the landed interests in the legislature. While the ferment was spreading and rising in the country, the liberal party in both Houses of Parliament were looking in a spirit of calm and confident expectation upon the struggles and difficulties of the rash and helpless administration. Some members of the cabinet took pains to intimate, the next night after the duke's declaration, that he spoke for himself alone; Sir George Murray owned himself in favour of some moderate reform; Sir Robert Peel would not declare any opinion on a subject as yet wholly indefinite. In the Commons, Mr. Tennyson conjured the country to await in quiet the downfall of the duke, which was now sure to happen, and by no means to let the duke's opinion on reform go for more than any one man's opinion was worth;

and in the Lords, the Earl of Winchilsea proposed to lay
before the king the opinion of parliament in regard to the
incapacity of his ministers. It was as yet only the 4th of
November; but this was a season when hours told for
days. In forty-eight hours the duke was in the embarrassment of another scrape, in which there was so
much of the ludicrous mixed up with what might have
been very serious, that the subject was ever a most
exasperating one to the great soldier.

In justice to him, it must be remembered how his mind
had been wrought upon for some months past, in sympathy
with his friend Polignac, in apprehension for that distribution of power in Europe which he had been concerned
in establishing; and by the daily increasing disturbances
in our rural districts, which exactly resembled those that
preceded the revolution in France. It must be remembered how little he really knew the people of England;
and how, to a mind like his, the mere name of revolution
suggests images of regicide, and of everything horrible;
images which were, no doubt, in his mind when he turned
away, as he was seen to do, from the spectacle of the tricolor floating in the Thames. These things mark him as
unfit to be the prime-minister of England in 1830; but
they soften the shame of the thought that the high
courage of the great soldier sank under a senseless alarm
given by an alderman of London. This Alderman Key
had been elected to serve the office of lord mayor for the
coming year; and the king and queen and the ministers
were to dine with him at Guildhall on the 9th of
November. On the 6th, the alderman addressed a letter
to the prime-minister, the tone and wording of which
should have shown to any man of sense that it was not a
communication to be acted upon, without large confirmation of its statements. This letter warned the duke
that a certain number of desperate characters intended to
make an attack upon him near the hall; and it plainly
desired that, as the civil force would not be enough for
the duke's protection, he would not come without a strong
military guard. The next night, Saturday, Sir Robert
Peel sent a letter to the lord mayor, to state that their
majesties declined visiting the city on the 9th. The

ministers pleaded that they had received other letters, besides that from Alderman Key; and, but for this, the case would have been much simplified; for the poor man expressed, again and again, the deepest contrition for his folly in writing as he had done, when he saw how serious were the consequences of the act. In the course of Sunday, a deputation from the committee of the feast waited three times on the ministers; and the duke's declaration was that either the banquet must be postponed, or a large military force must be put in possession of the city. The banquet was postponed.

In the morning, the consternation in the city was extreme. No one knew what was the matter; but that there must be something terrible, there could be no doubt. Some said that there was to be a 5th of November on the 9th; some, that while their majesties were dining, the gas-pipes were to be cut, Temple Bar blockaded, the royal personages made prisoners, and London sacked. There was no nonsense that could not find belief on that fearful Monday, though everybody agreed that no sovereign had ever been more popular than William IV., who had not done an ungracious thing, nor spoken an ungracious word, except that speech a few days before, which everybody knew to be solely the work of his ministers. On that Monday morning, consols fell three per cent. in an hour and a half; careful citizens renewed the bolts and bars of their doors, lined their shutters with iron plates and laid in arms and ammunition, in expectation of the sacking of London. Before the end of the week, the most alarmed were laughing at the panic; but not only was the mysterious panic a fearful thing at the moment, but the natural effects were very vexatious. There was a good deal of desultory and unmeaning rioting, by such disorderly citizens as thought that if they had the discredit, they might as well have the fun. And, worse than this, an unfounded impression went abroad through all the world, that it was not safe for the King of England to pass through the streets of his own capital, to dine with its chief-magistrate.

Day by day now, it became only a question of weeks about when the administration would go out; whether before the Christmas recess or after. Before a single week from the panic, they were out. On the 15th, Sir Henry Parnell made his promised motion for a select committee to examine the accounts connected with the civil list. The debate was not long, the ministers declaring that simplification and retrenchment had been carried as far as was possible ; and the opposition desiring to have it proved whether the matter was so. On the division, the government were left in a minority of twenty-nine, in a House of 437 members. Mr. Hobhouse asked Sir Robert Peel whether the ministers would retain their seats after such a division ; but he received no answer. He was about to press the question, when Mr. Brougham proposed to wait till the next day for the answer and the appointment of the committee just decided upon. The committee, however, was appointed at once ; the reply was waited for. The ministers afterwards declared that they might not have considered this division on the civil list reason enough for their resignation, by itself ; but that they considered with it the probable result of Mr. Brougham's motion for parliamentary reform, which was to be debated on the night after the civil list question.

On that evening, the 16th, the Duke of Wellington came down to announce to the Lords that his resignation of office had been presented and accepted, and that he continued in his position only till his successor should have been appointed. In the other House, Sir Robert Peel made the same declaration on behalf of himself and all the other members of the administration.

Lord Althorp immediately requested Mr. Brougham to defer his motion on parliamentary reform, which was too important to be debated while the government of the country was in an unsettled state. Mr. Brougham expressed great reluctance, and threw the responsibility upon the House of delaying the matter till the 25th ; declaring that he would then bring it forward, whatever might be the condition of circumstances, and whoever might be his majesty's ministers. No one had any doubt about who, in the main, would be his majesty's ministers. It was well understood that the great day was at hand when the British polity was to renew its youth and replenish its

life.   Some who walked homewards from their parliamentary halls to their own firesides, through the darkness
of that November night, told each other that a brighter
sun than that of midsummer was to arise to-morrow, en-
cumbered and dimmed at first, probably, by clouds and
vapours, but destined to send down its vital warmth and
light through long vistas of remote generations.

CHAPTER II.

The Grey Ministry—Regency Bill—Official Salaries—State of Ireland
—The Cholera.

THERE was no doubt in any quarter as to who would be
the new premier, or what would be the general composition
of the ministry.   The anti-Catholic party was broken up
and humbled.   The demand of the people for a liberal
government was strong; and there was no one to say that
it should not be obeyed.   The king requested Lord Grey
to form a government; and he agreed to do so, on condition that reform of parliament should be made a cabinet
question; a condition immediately granted.   As the news
spread through the land, it excited a stronger sensation
than men of a future time could perhaps be easily made to
understand.   The interest felt for Lord Grey was strong.
Men remembered his advocacy of reform of parliament in
the last century; his patient and dignified assertion of the
principle and ultimate necessity of the case during a long
course of years, obscure and unprosperous for him; and the
deep melancholy of his unhappy speech against Canning,
three years before, when he spoke of his own political career
as over, and his political loneliness as complete.   Now, with
more years upon his honoured head, he stood at the summit
of affairs, empowered to achieve with his own hand the great
object of his life and time, and surrounded by comrades of
his own choice and appointment.   This trait of the time
interested the hearts of hundreds of thousands; but to the
millions there was something far more exciting still.

The year which was closing was called the year One of the people's cause.

It was now fifteen years since the peace. Of these fifteen years, the first seven had been dark and troubled under a discouraging and exasperating Tory rule, during which, however, by virtue of the peace, good things were preparing for a coming time. During the last eight years, there had been vicissitudes of fortune—some exultation and prosperity—more depression and distress, as regarded the material condition of the people; but the country had been incomparably better governed. It was under this better government that the people had learned striking and virtuous lessons about their own power—lessons which had prepared them to require wisely, and conduct magnanimously, the greatest revolution in the history of their country.

It was in the leisure of the new peace that a multitude of minds had received the idea, and made it their own, that the shortest and only safe way of procuring all reforms and all good government was by making the representation as true as it could be made. This became the vital principle of the political life of Great Britain, as soon as the excitements of the war died away; and it must long continue to be so. Among the many reasons which make us now and for ever deprecate war, the chief is, and should ever be, that we would not have the national mind and will called off from this great truth and aim—that the first duty, and most unremitting obligation of a people living under a representative system, is to make the representation true and perfect. In this year One of the people's cause, the people were ready; and they were blessed with rulers who were willing to make a beginning so large and decided as to secure the permanence of the work, as far as they carried it, and its certain prosecution through future generations. It is nothing that they did not foresee this further prosecution, nor believe it when it was foretold to them. Great deeds naturally so fill the conceptions and sympathies of the doers, that they are—except a great philosopher here and there—finality-men; but those who are not so immediately engaged see further, and remember that sound political institutions are made perfect very slowly, and by a succession of improvements. There were many, therefore, who in that day of exultation saw more cause for rejoicing than did those who were proudest of the immediate triumph. They saw in the parliamentary reform of Lord Grey a noble beginning of a great work which it might take centuries to perfect, and in every stage of which the national mind would renew its strength and gain fresh virtue and wisdom. They appreciated the greatness of the first effort, by which the impediments to true representation were to be removed, and some steps taken towards a recognition of the vast commercial interests which had risen up in modern times; but they saw that the due equalisation of the landed and commercial interests, and the true proportion of the representation of property and numbers, could not be attained at a stroke, and that much of the noble work of parliamentary reform must remain to occupy and exalt future generations. The wisest and the most eager, however, the oldest and the youngest, desired nothing more than what they now saw; their nation, as a whole, demanding and achieving its own self-improvement, instead of ringing bells and firing cannon about bloody victories obtained in the cause of foreign governments.

It was news enough for one day that this great era was opening, and that Lord Grey stood on the threshold. By the next day, the people were eager to know who were to be his helpers. The newspapers could not give the list of the ministry fast enough. In reading-rooms, and at the corners of streets, merchants, bankers, and tradesmen took down the names, and carried them to their families, reading them to every one they met by the way; while poor men who could not write, carried them well enough in their heads; for most of the leading names were of men known to such of the labouring class as understood their own interest in the great cause just coming on.

Next on the list to Lord Grey was Lord Althorp, as chancellor of the exchequer. He was known as an advocate of the ballot; as having been forward in questions of retrenchment and reform; and as being a man, if of no eminent vigour, of great benevolence, and an enthusiastic love of justice. His abilities as a statesman were now to be tried. Mr. Brougham's name came next. He was to be lord chancellor. It was amusing to see how that announcement was everywhere received with a laugh; in most cases, with a laugh which he would not have objected to—a laugh of mingled surprise, exultation, and amusement. The anti-reformers laughed scornfully—dwelling upon certain declarations of his against taking office, and upon his incompetency as an equity lawyer; facts which he would not himself have disputed, but which his party thought should be put aside by the pressure of the time. To his worshippers there was something comic in the thought of his vitality fixed down upon the woolsack, under the compression of the chancellor's wig. Some expected a world of amusement in seeing how he got on in a position so new; how the wild and mercurial Harry Brougham would comport himself among the peers, and as the head of the law. Some expected from him the realisation of all that he had declared ought to be done by men in power; and as the first and most certain boon, a scheme of national education which he would carry with all the power of his office and his pledged political character. Others sighed while they smiled; sighed to give up the popular member for Yorkshire, and feared that his country had had the best of him. Lord Lansdowne, the president of the council, was held in a quiet, general respect. Lord Durham, the John George Lambton who had ever fought the people's battle well, was hailed with great warmth. He was lord privy seal. There were some 'Canningites,' who were received with good-will, without much expectation. Charles Grant, president of the Board of Control; Lord Palmerston, foreign secretary; Lord Melbourne, home secretary; and Lord Goderich, as colonial secretary. The only anti-Catholic and anti-reform member of the cabinet was the Duke of Richmond, who was postmaster-general. How he found himself there was a subject of speculation on all hands. The other members of the cabinet were Sir James Graham, at the Admiralty; Lord Auckland, at the Mint and Board of Trade;·and Lords Holland and Carlisle. Out of the cabinet, there were the names, among others, of Lord John Russell, pledged to parliamentary reform; Mr. Charles Poulett Thomson, pledged to repeal of the corn-laws; and Sir Thomas Denman and Sir William

Horne, as attorney and solicitor general. Lord Anglesey was again viceroy of Ireland, and Lord Plunket the Irish lord chancellor. The chief-secretary for Ireland was Mr. Stanley. Such was the government about to conduct the great organic change in the British constitution which the anti-reformers were still resolved should never take place.

There was a suspension of business in parliament while the re-election of some of the ministers went on. One defeat was ludicrous enough. Mr. Stanley, the heir of the house of Derby, was thrown out at Preston by Henry Hunt, who was not yet, it thus appears, seen through by all his followers as by Bamford.

The first business to be proceeded with was the Regency Bill, which had already been delayed too long. By this bill it was provided, that in the case of the birth of a posthumous child of the king's, the queen should be regent during the minority. In the other case, the Duchess of Kent was to be regent, if the Princess Victoria should come to the throne during her minority; unless, indeed, the Duchess should marry a foreigner.

Lord Wynford proposed a grant of additional powers to the magistracy in the disturbed districts, where matters were going on from bad to worse; but the ministers declared that the existing powers of the law were sufficient, if duly put in force: but they did not conceal their opinion that a more active and sensible set of men might be brought into the commission of the peace. How serious was the aspect of the times we find by the gazetting of an order in council, that the Archbishop of Canterbury should prepare a prayer for relief from social disturbance; which prayer was to be read in all the Episcopal churches and chapels of England and Scotland.

In the Commons a select committee was appointed, on the motion of the chancellor of the exchequer, to inquire what reductions could be made in the salaries and emoluments of offices held by members of either House of parliament, during the pleasure of the crown. This was a graceful beginning of the business of retrenchment by the ministers—this offer to reduce, in the first place, their own salaries. As the new administration had much to do in preparing, during the recess, the great measures to which they were pledged, they moved for a long interval, and parliament was adjourned to the 3rd of February 1831.

At the close of this year One of the people's cause, there was as much disturbance in Ireland as if the government in London had been composed of the rankest anti-Catholics. O'Connell set himself up against Lord Anglesey; organised insults to him on his arrival; encouraged tumultuous processions and meetings, by which he was himself to be thanked for his advocacy of repeal of the union; and put out addresses, in defiance and reply to the proclamations of the viceroy, the whole tenor of which was to rouse the strong passions of the Irish artisans and peasants against the government, the law, and the imperial connection, from which, at this juncture, so many benefits might be expected. His interspersed exhortations were to observe the law; his influence went to excite that fever of the mind which is sure to throw off law, sooner or later: and thus inauspiciously began the new reign of the popular viceroy, Lord Anglesey.

By this time the dread of something more awful than Irish disturbance and Kentish rick-burning was stealing into the heart of the nation. All reports of the Asiatic cholera which Englishmen had listened to, had been to their ears and imaginations like the accounts which have come down to us of the desolating plagues of the middle ages—something horrible to conceive of, but nothing to be afraid of, as if it could ever reach us. But now it was known—known by orders of the privy-council—that the plague had spread from Asia into Europe, and was travelling north-westwards, exactly in the direction of our islands. All that was at present proposed was an attention to the quarantine laws; but the imagination of the people naturally went further than the letters of the privy-council. If George IV. and the Wellington ministry had lived through the year, its close would have been a season of almost unequalled gloom. But the nation now had an honest-hearted and unselfish king, a popular ministry, and a prospect of immeasurable political benefits. So that it was in a mood, on the whole, of hope and joy that they saw the expiration of the year One of the people's cause.

CHAPTER III.

Popular Discontents—Prospect of Conflict—Ministerial Declaration—
Reform Bill brought forward—Reception of the Bill—Debate—First
Reading—Second Reading—Defeat of Ministers—True Crisis—The
Palace—The Lords—The Commons—Prorogation—Dissolution.

THE year 1831 opened gloomily. Those who believed that
revolution was at hand, feared to wish one another a happy
new year; and the anxiety about revolution was by no
means confined to anti-reformers. Society was already in
a discontented and tumultuous state; its most ignorant
portion being acted upon at once by hardship at home and
example from abroad; and there was every reason to expect
a deadly struggle before parliamentary reform could be
carried. The ignorant and misled among the peasantry
and artisans looked upon the French and other revolutions
as showing that men had only to take affairs into their
own hands, in order to obtain whatever they wanted; and,
in their small way, they took matters into their own
hands. Machine-breaking went on to such an extent, that
men were tried for the offence in groups of twelve or
twenty at a time; and the January nights were lighted
up by burning barns and ricks, as the preceding months
had been. On the 3rd of January, a Manchester manufacturer was murdered in a manner which gave a shock to
the whole kingdom. He left his father's house to go to
the mill, in the evening, when it was dark; he was
brought home dead within ten minutes, shot through the
heart, in the lane, by one of three men who were lying in
wait for him. The significance of the case lay in the circumstance that it was a murder from revenge, occasioned
by a quarrel about the trade union. There was fear lest
the practice should spread; lest every manufacturer who
refused to employ men belonging to a trade union—and
there were many such—should be liable to be picked off

by an assassin, appointed by lot to be the instrument of the vengeance of his union. A reward of £1000 for the detection of the murderer was offered by the secretary of state, and another £1000 by the father and family of the victim; but no clue was obtained at the time nor for some years afterwards.

As for the dangers which might follow upon the action of government on the great question, the coolest heads had the strongest sense of them. The apprehensions of the anti-reformers were all about the consequences of the Reform Bill, if carried. The apprehensions of the most thoughtful reformers were of the perils attending its passage. On a superficial view it might appear that the result was so certain, that the way could not be much embarrassed; but there was not only the anti-reforming aristocracy to be encountered on the one hand, but large masses of malcontents on the other. In the estimate of the anti-reform forces might be included—possibly, under certain circumstances — the sovereign; certainly, the House of Peers—almost a whole House of Peers, made desperate, not only by fear of loss of political power, but by spoliation of what they considered their lawful, and a wholly inestimable property; next, the aristocracy, in the House of Commons and out of it, who had influence and property of the same kind at stake; and, lastly, the whole body of Toryism in England—a party never small, and at this time made particularly active and desperate by a sincere belief that the constitution was likely to be overthrown, and that the English nation would presently be living under mob-rule. Large numbers of this party, who had not the remotest interest in borough property, were as fierce against the reform measure as the peers themselves, from this tremendous fear. There was quite as much folly among the lowest classes on the other side. The hungry and the desperately ignorant, who are always eager for change, because they may gain and cannot lose, believed that parliamentary reform would feed and clothe them, and bring work and good wages, and a removal of all the taxes. It was too probable that a protracted opposition would raise these poor people in riot, and turn the necessary revolution, from being a peaceable one, into an over-

throw of law and order.   It is necessary to take note of this
state of things, in order to understand and appreciate the
action of the middle classes during the two following
years.

While the ministers were hard at work, preparing their
mighty measure, the middle classes were preparing for
their support.   The action of the non-electors during this
month of January was as powerful a satire on the then
existing system of representation as could have been displayed.   The vast populations of Leeds, Birmingham, and
Manchester, and countless hosts of intelligent and enlightened tradesmen and artisans elsewhere, sent shoals of
petitions to parliament for a reform of the House of Commons ; and they did something more effectual by forming
political unions, or preparing for their immediate formation, in case of need.   This was the force which kept the
peace, and preserved us from disastrous revolution.   These
people knew what they were about, and they went calmly
to their work.   Of course, the anti-reformers complained
of compulsion, of extorted consent, of unconstitutional
forces being put in action.   This was true, since they themselves compelled the compulsion, and called out the unconstitutional forces.   There was no question about the fact,
but only about the justification of it.   No one denies that
occasions may and do occur when the assertion of a nation's
will against either a corrupt government or a tyrannical
party is virtuous, and absolutely required by patriotic
duty.   The fearful and trying question is, when this ought
to be done, and how men are to recognise the true occasion
when it comes.   There probably never was an occasion
when the duty was more clear than now.   The sovereign
and his ministers were on the side of the people ; and if
the opposing party should prove disloyal to sovereign and
people for the sake of their own political power and mercenary interests ; if they held out till the one party or the
other must yield, it was for the interest of peace, law,
order, loyalty, and the permanence of the constitution,
that the class most concerned—the orderly middle class,
who had the strongest conceivable stake in the preservation of law and peace—should overstep the bounds of
custom, and occupy a debatable land of legality, in support

of the majority of the government and the nation. They felt
that they occupied the strong central position whereby they
upheld the patriotic government above them, and repressed
the eager, untaught, and impoverished multitude below
them; and they saw that whatever might best secure the
completion of the act which must now be carried through,
they must do. They therefore prepared themselves for all
consequences of their determination that parliamentary
reform should take place. Some formed themselves into
political unions; some held themselves ready to do so, if
need should arise; all made a more rapid progress in
political knowledge and thought than they could perhaps
have antecedently supposed possible in the time: when
the period of struggle arrived they did their duty magnifi-
cently; and their conduct stands for ever before the world,
a model of critical political action, and a ground of confidence in the political welfare of England in all future
times.

When the Houses reassembled, on the 3rd of February,
Lord Grey made the expected declaration that a measure
of parliamentary reform was in readiness to be brought
forward in the other House. He intimated that the work
had been laborious, and in its first stages, difficult; but
that it had been the desire of the ministers to prepare a
scheme, 'which should be effective, without exceeding
the bounds of a just and well-advised moderation;' and
that they had succeeded to their wish—the whole government being unanimous in their adoption of the measure as
an exponent of their principle and aim. When Lord John
Russell afterwards brought the measure forward, he declared the whole scheme to be Lord Grey's; and there
was assuredly no mind in England which had more
earnestly, or for more years, meditated the subject. The
execution was universally understood to have been confided in chief to Lord Durham; and there was assuredly
no heart more in the work, or more true to the principles
of popular freedom. The profoundest secrecy was observed
as to the scope and details of the measure, to the very last
moment. It was of great consequence that it should be so,
in order that the eager friends and foes of the measure
should not rush into conflict on any misunderstanding or

fragmentary knowledge. The very few persons who were necessarily admitted to the confidence of the government felt this confidence to be a heavy burden. One, deeply engaged and hard-worked, said afterwards that he was almost afraid to sleep, lest he should dream and speak of what his mind was full of. The great day of disclosure was the 1st of March, when Lord John Russell had the honour—though not a cabinet minister, but on account of his long advocacy of the cause—of bringing forward the measure in the Commons. On that day, the friends of the ministry had dinner-parties, where the guests sat watching the clock, and waiting for tidings. The lord chancellor had promised the hostess of one of these parties that no one should be earlier served with the news than she; and anxiously she sat, at the head of her table, till the packet was brought in which the lord chancellor had despatched, the moment he found that Lord John Russell had begun his speech. As she read aloud, exclamations of surprise at the scope of the scheme burst forth. And so it was, all over the kingdom. During the recess, some of the liberal papers had conjured the people to receive thankfully whatever measure the ministers might offer, and be assured that, however inadequate, they could not have more. Other papers had been more true to their duty, exhorting the people to take nothing less than the whole of what they demanded. If they understood their principle, and were earnest in their demand, they ought not to yield an inch of their ground. It now appeared that there was no faltering on the part of the ministers; no desire that the people should surrender an inch of their ground. They knew that there could be no half-and-half dealing with boroughmongery. It was a vice which must be extinguished, and not an indulgence which might be gradually weakened. By this bill, the practice of boroughmongery was cut up by the roots. This was the essential feature of the measure. Whether the further reforms advocated were complete or inadequate, this opened the way to all else. 'Like Sinbad,' as was said at the time, 'we have first to dash from our shoulders the " Old Man of the Sea," and afterwards to complete our deliverance.' It will afterwards appear how partial was the representation proposed to be given, and how inadequate and faulty were the constructive arrangements. But there were not two opinions at the time as to the ministers having gone further than anybody expected, and proposed a measure which could never be withdrawn without a deadly struggle, nor stand without becoming a dividing-line between the old history of England and the new.

It was a great night—that night of the 1st of March 1831—when for the first time a response was heard from within the vitiated House to the voice of intelligence without. This House had long been the property or the tool of powers and parties adverse to the general weal. While the world without had been growing wiser and more enlightened in political principle, this assembly had made no progress or had deteriorated, till the voice of general intelligence had given it unmistakable warning that it must either reform itself or succumb. The last and effectual warning was the demand of an administration which should invite the House of Commons to reform itself; and here, at least, on this memorable night, was the response— the answering hail—for which the stretched ear of the vigilant nation was listening, to the furthest boundary of the empire. While the occasion appeared thus serious to those who brought it about, there were listeners, and not a few, in the House that night, who could not receive Lord John Russell's exposition otherwise than as an audacious jest. Others came away at the end, and said they could give no clear account of it; and that there was no need, as ministers could have no other intention than to render office untenable for those who must presently succeed them. Thus blind were the anti-reformers, after all the long and threatening warnings they had received. But a few hours opened their eyes. The morning newspapers exhibited the scheme, with all its royal and ministerial sanctions; and that which appeared a jest the night before was now pronounced a revolution.

The proper occasion for giving a specific account of the Reform Act will be when its provisions were finally settled. It may suffice now to say, that, in the words of Lord Grey, 'representation, not nomination, is the principle of the Reform Bill;' that, in pursuance of this principle, sixty 'rotten boroughs' were deprived of the franchise; and 168 borough seats were abolished.   A few small boroughs were retained—to the dissatisfaction of reformers generally—for the purpose of admitting an order of members not likely to be returned for large towns or counties, and providing for some little representation of the small-borough class of citizens.   The reformers were also sorry that fifty-four members were given to counties which had hitherto been opposed to popular interests; and the stopping short at the representation of the middle classes was disapproved by a multitude in the middle and upper classes, as much as by the excluded artisans themselves.   Wise statesmen and observers know well that the strongest conservative power of a country like ours resides in the holders of the smallest properties.   However much the nobleman may be attached to his broad lands, and his mansions and parks, and the middle-class manufacturer or professional man to the station and provision he has secured for his family, this attachment is weak, this stake is small, in comparison with those of the artisan who tastes the first sweets of property in their full relish.   He is the man to contend to the last gasp for the institutions of his country, and for the law and order which secure to him what he values so dearly.   The commonest complaint of all, made by the restless and discontented spirits of any time, is that their former comrades become 'spoiled' from the moment they rise into the possession of any ease, property, or social advantage; and they do truly thus become 'spoiled' for any revolutionary or disorderly purpose.   By all to whom this fact was clear it was thought a mistake to have stopped at the proposed point in the communication of the franchise; but they knew that it was an error which might and would be corrected in a future time, and were content to wait.   They saw how the clumsy ancient methods of conducting political affairs, in the rough, as it were, at the bidding of a few individual wills, were giving way to the more comprehensive, refined, and precise methods of government by representation; and that, when this new philosophical practice had gone somewhat further, the value of the artisan class, as the nicest of political barometers, would be practically acknowledged.   To them, to

their union of popular intelligence and strong love of property, would rulers and all propertied classes hereafter
look for the first warnings of approaching disturbance, the
earliest breathings of conservative caution; and to representatives of this class will a welcome assuredly be given
in the councils of the nation, as our political procedure
improves in elevation and refinement. The reduction of
the number of members of the Commons was not at first
objected to on any hand. As Lord John Russell observed:
'It is to be considered that when this parliament is reformed, there will not be so many members who enter parliament merely for the sake of the name, and as a matter of
style and fashion;' not so many, he went on to say, who
were travelling abroad during the whole session, or who
regarded the House as a pleasant lounge, and not an
arduous field of duty. The 168 displaced members were
not therefore to be succeeded by an equal number. There
was to be a decrease of 62, making the total number of
representatives 596. The parishes and suburbs of London
were to send eight new members, and the large towns in
the provinces 34; all these together not equalling the new
county representation.

On the whole, it was concluded by the reform party that
the measure should be received as most meritorious and
sufficiently satisfactory, on account of its bold dealing
with corruption—of its making a complete clearance for
further action; but that it was not a measure of radical
reform. As a contemporary observed: 'The ground,
limited as it is, which it is proposed to clear and open to
the popular influence, will suffice as the spot desired by
Archimedes for the plant of the power that must ultimately govern the whole system.'

It was thus that the authors of the measure expected it
to be received by the reform party. In the course of the
debates on the bill in the House of Peers, Lord Sidmouth,
who supposed Lord Grey to have been carried by circumstances far beyond his original intentions, said to him: 'I
hope God will forgive you on account of this bill—I don't
think I can.' To which Lord Grey replied: 'Mark my
words; within two years you will find that we have
become unpopular, for having brought forward the most

aristocratic measure that ever was proposed in parliament.'
Lord Althorp did not conceal his opinion—he avowed it
—that the Reform Bill was the most aristocratic act ever
offered to the nation ; and the wonder is who could doubt
it, while the new county representation preponderated
over the addition to the towns. The inestimable virtue
of the bill—that which made it the horror of the ' borough-
market' men, as the Marquis of Blandford called them—
was the destruction of borough property by the substitution of election for nomination.

As for the reception of the measure by its enemies—
we have seen that when Lord John Russell opened the
business, it was supposed to be a jest, or a factious
manœuvre. The staid Hansard, usually so strictly ad-
hering to bare reporting, here gives us a passing glimpse
of the aspect of the House when Lord John Russell read
the list of boroughs proposed for disfranchisement. In
the course of his reading ' he was frequently interrupted
by shouts of laughter, cries of "Hear, hear!" from
members for these boroughs, and various interlocutions
across the table.' And what was it that they were about
to lose? There was a man living, speaking, and preaching in those days, who could convey more wisdom in a
jest, more pathos in a burlesque sketch, than other men
could impress through more ordinary forms ; and he has
left a picture of the ' borough-market' which, as the last
and unsurpassed, ought to be put on permanent record :
' So far from its being a merely theoretical improvement,
I put it to any man, who is himself embarked in a profession, or has sons in the same situation, if the unfair influence of boroughmongers has not perpetually thwarted
him in his lawful career of ambition and professional emolument? "I have been in three general engagements at
sea," said an old sailor—" I have been twice wounded ; I
commanded the boats when the French frigate, the
Astrolabe, was cut out so gallantly." " Then you are made
a post-captain?" "No; I was very near it; but Lieutenant Thompson cut me out, as I cut out the French
frigate; his father is town-clerk of the borough for which
Lord F—— is member; and there my chance was
finished." In the same manner, all over England, you

HISTORY OF THE PEACE. [BOOK IV.

will find great scholars rotting on curacies—brave captains
starving in garrets—profound lawyers decayed and moul-
dering in the Inns of Court, because the parsons, warriors,
and advocates of boroughmongers must be crammed to
saturation, before there is a morsel of bread for the man
who does not sell his votes, and put his country up to
auction; and though this is of everyday occurrence, the
borough-system, we are told, is no practical evil. . . .
But the thing I cannot, and will not bear, is this: what
right has this lord, or that marquis, to buy ten seats in
parliament, in the shape of boroughs, and then to make
laws to govern me? And how are these masses of power
redistributed? The eldest son of my lord has just come
from Eton—he knows a good deal about Æneas and Dido,
Apollo and Daphne, and that is all; and to this boy his
father gives a six-hundredth part of the power of making
laws, as he would give him a horse, or a double-barrelled
gun. Then Vellum, the steward, is put in—an admirable
man; he has raised the estates—watched the progress of
the family Road and Canal Bills—and Vellum shall help
to rule over the people of Israel. A neighbouring country
gentleman, Mr. Plumpkin, hunts with my lord—opens
him a gate or two, while the hounds are running—dines
with my lord—agrees with my lord—wishes he could
rival the Southdown sheep of my lord—and upon
Plumpkin is conferred a portion of the government.
Then there is a distant relation of the same name, in the
county militia, with white teeth, who calls up the carriage
at the opera, and is always wishing O'Connell was hanged,
drawn, and quartered; then a barrister, who has written
an article in the *Quarterly*, and is very likely to speak, and
refute M'Culloch: and these five people, in whose nomination I have no more agency than I have in the nomination
of the toll-keepers of the Bosphorus, are to make laws for
me and my family—to put their hands in my purse, and
to sway the future destinies of this country; and when
the neighbours step in, and beg permission to say a few
words before these persons are chosen, there is a universal
cry of ruin, confusion, and destruction; we have become
a great people under Vellum and Plumpkin—under
Vellum and Plumpkin our ships have covered the ocean—

under Vellum and Plumpkin our armies have secured the strength of the Hills—to turn out Vellum and Plumpkin is not reform, but revolution.'

In recognising the truth of this picture, and declaring that such a state of things could not have endured much longer, we must remember the cost of the breaking up to those who nobly volunteered to do it. The framers of the Reform Bill were noblemen and gentlemen of high family, who were laying down hereditary possessions of their own, while requiring the same sacrifice from others. The borough-wealth of the Russell family was known to be enormous; yet the Duke of Bedford cheered on Lord John Russell in his task. If we read with tender admiration of loyal noblemen and gentry who brought their wealth to the feet of an unprosperous sovereign, and made themselves landless for the sake of their king, what must we feel at this great new spectacle of the privileged classes divesting themselves of privilege for the sake of the people—for the honour and integrity of the country? It was a great deed; and posterity will ever declare it so. It is objected by some that these peers and gentlemen were well aware, and indeed openly avowed, that they could not retain this kind of wealth, nor, perhaps, any other, if reform of parliament were not granted; they apprehended a convulsion, and said so; declaring also that this was the reason why their reforms were made so prompt and sweeping. This is quite true; but it is precisely this which shows how superior these men were to the selfish greed which blinded the eyes of their opponents. They had open minds, clear eyes, calm consciences, and hands at the service of their country; and they therefore saw things in their true light, and turned the pressure of an irresistible necessity into a noble occasion of self-sacrifice, and disinterested care for the public weal; while the opposite order of borough-holders saw nothing, believed nothing, knew nothing, and declared nothing, but that they would not part with their hereditary property and influence. When they protested that to take away their borough property was 'to destroy the aristocracy,' they passed a severer satire upon their order than could have been invented by any enemy. If the aristocracy of

England could not subsist but upon a rotten-borough foundation, it was indeed a different order from that which the world had, for many centuries, supposed; but no one could look upon the dignified head of the prime-minister, or the countenances of his self-sacrificing comrades in the House of Peers, without feeling that the world was right, and that those who said anything so derogatory to the aristocratic tenure in England were basely and sordidly wrong. Lord Eldon was one of these; and in his speech at the Pitt Club, supposing that point granted, he went on to his view of the consequences; in the course of which we find him, who ought to have known better, falling into the vulgar error of the aristocracy, of supposing only one class of society to exist below that wealthy one with which they are compelled by their affairs to have business. Lord Eldon, like others who must know better, included under one head ('the lower classes') everybody below the wealthiest bankers—manufacturers, tradesmen, artisans, labourers, and paupers; as we now and then hear fine people confusing the claims of great capitalists and humble cottagers, announcements in town-hall meetings and gossip in servants' halls. Lord Eldon must have known, but he seems to have forgotten, that there is a large proportion of society composed of the ignorant and hopeless classes, lying below the rank from which he rose; yet this is the representation he gives of the happy state of the English people which was to be broken up by the Reform Bill, through its destruction of the aristocracy. 'The aristocracy once destroyed,' he declared to his brother Pittites, 'the best supporters of the lower classes would be swept away. In using the term "lower classes" he meant nothing offensive. How could he do so? He himself had been one of the lower classes. He gloried in the fact; and it was noble and delightful to know that the humblest in the realm might, by a life of industry, propriety, and good moral and religious conduct, rise to eminence. All could not become eminent in public life—that was impossible; but every man might arrive at honour, independence, and competence.'

What?—every man?—he whose early years are spent in opening and shutting a door in a coal-pit, who does not know his own name, and never heard of God?—or any one of thousands of hand-loom weavers, who swallow opium on Saturday nights, to deaden the pains of hunger on Sundays?—or the Dorsetshire labourer, whose only prospect is that his eight shillings a week may be reduced to seven, and the seven to six, but never that his wages may rise? May 'every man' of these arrive at honour, independence, and competence? Truly, Lord Eldon did his best to prove how sorely these 'lower classes' needed some kind of representation in parliament, or at least the admission of some who might make known their existence and their claims.

The debate which followed the introduction of the Reform Bill extended over seven nights, between seventy and eighty members delivering their views in the course of that time. The adversaries of the measure argued on grounds more contradictory than are often exhibited, even on great occasions like the present. Some cried out that democracy was henceforth in the ascendant, while others were full of indignation that the qualification was raised, and so many poor freemen disfranchised. Some complained of the qualification as too low, and others as too high. Some insinuated pity for the sovereign, as overborne by factious ministers; others were disgusted at the parade of the king's sanction, and intimated that it was nothing to them what the king thought. Of all the objections uttered, none rose higher in matter or tone than a deprecation of change in a country which had been so great under the old laws; and a remonstrance against lessening the proportionate power of the House of Lords.

On the side of the measure, there was a brief statement of objections on the score of deficiency; but an agreement to work cordially for the bill as it was offered, in the hope of supplying its deficiencies afterwards. Many would have desired an extension of the franchise downwards, as well as upwards and laterally, as was now provided by the removal of many restrictions. Yet more had hoped for the ballot, to purify the elections, and for a shortening of the duration of parliaments. But all agreed to relinquish their minor objects for the time, to secure the overthrow of borough corruption; and the great cry was agreed upon which from that hour rang through the land for above a year: ' The bill, the whole bill, and nothing but the bill.'

There was to be no division on the first reading. Neither party seemed disposed to bring the matter to any test so soon; the ministers apprehending being left in a minority, and their opponents not being yet combined for an organised resistance. The bill was read a first time on the 14th of March.

And now began the great stir among the middle classes which kept the country for nearly two years in a state which was called revolutionary, and with justice; but which showed with how little disturbance of the public peace that prodigious growth of political sentiment can take place which is the resulting benefit of a principled revolution. At each stage of the business there was some disorder, and much noble manifestation of intelligence and will. Illuminations were called for foolishly at times, and windows broken—especially at Edinburgh in the course of this spring. Lists of placemen and pensioners, containing incorrect items and invidious statements, were handed about at a season when it was dangerous to inflame the popular mind against an aristocracy already too much vituperated. Many of the newspapers were not only violent on their own side, but overbore all rights of opinion on the other, as insufferably as the rankest of the Tory journals; and, naturally enough, a multitude of the ignorant believed that all the taxes would be taken off, and that every man would have the independence and competence that Lord Eldon talked about, if the Reform Bill passed, and regarded accordingly those who stood between them and the bill. These were the sins and follies of the time; and it is marvellous that they were no worse.

Some will ask even now, and many would have asked at the time, whether the determination of the political unions to march on London in case of need, was not the chief sin and folly of the time. We think not, while feeling strong sympathy with those who come to an opposite conclusion. In judging of the right and wrong of a case so critical, everything depends on the evidence that exists as to what the principles and powers of the opposing parties really were. This evidence we shall find disclosed in the history of the next year. Meantime, in the March and April of 1831, the great middle class, by whose intelligence and determination the bill must be carried, believed that occasion might arise for their refusing to pay taxes, and for their marching upon London, to support the king, the administration, and the bulk of the nation, against a small class of unyielding and interested persons. The political unions made known the numbers they could muster; the chairman of the Birmingham Union declaring that they could send forth two armies, each fully worth that which had won Waterloo. On the coast of Sussex, ten thousand men declared themselves ready to march at any moment; Northumberland was prepared in like manner; Yorkshire was up and awake; and, in short, it might be said that the nation was ready to go up to London, if wanted. When the mighty processions of the unions marched to their meeting-grounds, the anti-reformers observed with a shudder that the towns were at the mercy of these mobs. The towns were at their mercy; but they were not mobs; and never were the good citizens more safe. The cry was vehement that the measure was to be carried by intimidation; and this was true. The question was whether, in this singular case, the intimidation was wrong. The ministers were vehemently accused of resorting to popular aid, and making use of all possible supports for the carrying their measure, in violation of all established etiquette. Lord Eldon thought them extremely vulgar, it is evident. The truth was that the popular aid resorted to them; and that they did consider the times too grave for etiquette, and the matter in hand far too serious to be let drop, when a momentary vacillation on their part would bring on immediate popular convulsion. So, they did declare in public, at the lord mayor's Easter dinner—what Lord Eldon thought 'perfectly unconstitutional'—that they had the king's confidence and good wishes: they did wait in silence to see whether it would become necessary for the political unions to act; and they did not retire from office when left with a majority of only one, but bore with all taunts and sneers, and preferred a neglect of propriety and precedent to a desertion of the cause to which they had pledged their fidelity. We cannot reckon any of these things, though irregular and portentous, among the sins and follies of the time, but rather among its noblest features. Among these we should reckon also a public declaration against the bill, put forth by several hundreds of merchants, bankers, and eminent citizens of London; a declaration which, though proved mistaken in its view, was in its diction and manner, calm, loyal, and courageous. If the opposition of the anti-reformers generally had been more of this character, there would have been less marshalling of political unions.

Some of the experienced old Conservatives thought it one of the sins and follies of the time, that their own party made no preparation for combined action against the bill. It was on the second reading that the ministers had been left with a majority of one, in the fullest House ever known to have divided—the numbers being, besides the speaker and the four tellers, 302 to 301, making a House of 608. The ministers did not resign on this; and the people illuminated because they did not. The Easter holidays were at hand; and immediately after, the bill was to be considered in committee. These Easter holidays were the time when, as the experienced old Conservatives thought, their party should have been organising for opposition; but the party were very confident that it was quite unnecessary to take such trouble. The late vote had shown that the Whigs could not carry their measure. They were, their opponents declared, a factious set, who vulgarly stayed in office as long as possible, and were preparing all possible trouble for their successors; but they were now proved too weak in the Commons to be formidable to the Lords. 'All will be lost,' Lord Eldon wrote in this interval, 'by the confidence with which people act, and with which they persuade themselves that all will be safe. Lord Sidmouth, on the day in which the second reading of the bill was carried, spoke to me of the majority by which it would undoubtedly be lost and negatived. And now the few, very few individuals here whom I see, speak of the rejection of the bill, as if it was certainly to be rejected, though no two persons agree as to what shall be the course of the measures by which its rejection can be accomplished.'

On the 18th of April, the Commons went into committee on the Reform Bill; and on the 19th, ministers were defeated on the point of reducing the number of members in the House. General Gascoyne moved that the numbers should not be reduced; and he obtained a majority of eight over ministers.

On the 21st, or rather on the morning of the 22nd, there was another defeat, which brought matters to a crisis. The opposition, after losing much time in talking about anything but the question before the House, refused to go into the consideration of a question of supply. They moved and carried an adjournment against the chancellor of the exchequer, leaving ministers in a minority of 22. This act of the opposition was looked upon, by some stretch of construction, as a refusal of the supplies. In the morning, the ministers offered their resignations to the king; but he would not accept them. He desired that they should go on with the Reform Bill, and get it carried as well as they could; but, unfortunately, though very naturally, he objected to the first measure which they considered essential —the dissolution of the new parliament, now in the midst of its first session.

Though other parts of that mighty struggle might appear more imposing, more dangerous, more awful, in the eyes of common observers, the real crisis lay within the compass of this day—the 22nd of April. The ministers themselves said so afterwards. When, in a subsequent season, the very ground shook with the tread of multitudes, and the broad heaven echoed with their shouts, and the Peers quaked in their House, and the world seemed to the timid to be turned upside down, the ministers were calm and secure; they knew the event to be determined, and could calculate its very date; whereas now, on this 22nd of April, they found themselves standing on a fearful Mohammedan bridge—on the sharp edge of chance, with abysses of revolution on either hand. The people were not aware of the exigency; and the ministers were not, for the moment, aided by pressure from without. The doubt—the critical doubt—was whether the king could be persuaded to dissolve the parliament.

The probable necessity of this course, and the king's repugnance to it, had been discussed throughout London for some days, and especially on the preceding day. The administration and the cause were injured by the understood difficulty with the sovereign ; and it was in a manner perfectly unprecedented that Lord Wharncliffe, on the night of the 21st, had asked Lord Grey in the House whether ministers had advised the king to dissolve parliament. On Lord Grey declining to answer the question, Lord Wharncliffe gave notice that he should move to-morrow an address to the king, remonstrating against such a proposed exertion of the royal prerogative. After what happened in the other House at a later hour, there was nothing to be done but to enforce upon the king the alternative of losing his ministers or dissolving parliament; and the next morning Lord Grey went to the palace for the purpose of procuring a decision of the matter. He and a colleague or two walked quietly and separately across the Park, to avoid exciting notice. For some hours there appeared little chance of a decision; but at length the perplexed sovereign began to see his way. He was yielding—had yielded—but with strong expressions of reluctance, when that reluctance was suddenly changed into alacrity by the news which was brought him of the tone used in the House of Lords about the impossibility that he would actually dissolve parliament, undoubted as was his constitutional power to do so. What! did they dare to meddle with his prerogative? the king exclaimed; he would presently show them what he could and would do. He had given his promise, and now he would lose no time; he would go instantly—that very moment—and dissolve parliament by his own voice. ' As soon as the royal carriages could be got ready,' his ministers agreed. ' Never mind the carriages; send for a hackney-coach,' replied the king— a saying which spread over the kingdom, and much enhanced his popularity for the moment.

Lord Durham ran down to the gate, and found but one carriage waiting—the lord chancellor's. He gave orders to drive fast to Lord Albemarle's, the master of the horse.

Lord Albemarle was at his late breakfast, but started up on the entrance of Lord Durham, asking what was the matter. 'You must have the king's carriages ready instantly.' 'The king's carriages! Very well : I will just finish my breakfast.' 'Finish your breakfast! Not you! You must not lose a moment. The king ought to be at the House.' 'Lord bless me! is there a revolution?' 'Not at this moment; but there will be if you stay to finish your breakfast.' So the tea and roll were left, and the royal carriages drove up to the palace in an incredibly short time. The king was ready. and impatient, and walked with an unusually brisk step. And so did the royal horses, in their passage through the streets, as was observed by the curious and anxious gazers.

Meantime, the scenes which were taking place in the two Houses were such as could never be forgotten by those who witnessed, or who afterwards heard any authentic account of them.

The peers assembled in unusual numbers at two o'clock to hear Lord Wharncliffe's motion for an address to his majesty, praying that his majesty would be graciously pleased not to exercise his undoubted prerogative of dissolving parliament; every one of them being in more or less expectation that his lordship's speech might be rendered unavailing by some notification from the throne, though few or none probably anticipated such a scene as took place.

Almost immediately, the lord chancellor left the woolsack. Could he be gone to meet the king? Lord Shaftesbury was called to the chair, and Lord Wharncliffe rose. As soon as he had opened his lips, the Duke of Richmond, a member of the administration, called some of their lordships to order, requesting that, as bound by the rules, they would be seated in their proper places. This looked as if the king was coming. Their lordships were angry; several rose to order at the same time, and said some sharp things as to who or what was most disorderly; so that the Duke of Richmond moved for the standing order to be read, that no offensive language should be used in that House. In the midst of this lordly wrangling, and of a confusion of voices rising into cries, boom! came the sound of cannon

which announced that the king was on the way! Some of
the peeresses had by this time entered, to witness the
spectacle of the prorogation. For a few minutes, something
like order was restored, and Lord Wharncliffe read his
proposed address, which was as strong a remonstrance, as
near an approach to interference with the royal prerogative, as might be expected from the occasion. The lord
chancellor re-entered the House, and, without waiting for
a pause, said, with strong emphasis : 'I never yet heard
that the crown ought not to dissolve parliament whenever
it thought fit, particularly at a moment when the House
of Commons had thought fit to take the extreme and unprecedented step of refusing the supplies.' Before he could
be further heard for the cries of 'Hear, hear!' shouts were
intermingled of 'The king! the king!' and the lord
chancellor again rushed out of the House, rendering it
necessary for Lord Shaftesbury to resume the chair. Every
moment now added to the confusion. The hubbub, heard
beyond the House, reached the ear of the king—reached
his heart, and roused in him the strong spirit of regality.
The peers grew violent, and the peeresses alarmed. Several
of these high-born ladies, who had probably never seen
exhibitions of vulgar wrath before, rose together, and looked
about them, when they beheld their lordships below pushing
and hustling, and shaking their hands in each others' faces.

Lord Mansfield at length made himself heard ; and he
spoke strongly of the 'most awful predicament' of the
king and the country, and on the conduct of ministers in
'conspiring together against the safety of the state, and of
making the sovereign the instrument of his own destruction ;' words which naturally caused great confusion. He
was proceeding when the shout again arose : 'The king!
the king!' and a commanding voice was heard over all,
solemnly uttering : 'God save the king!' Lord Mansfield
proceeded, however. The great doors on the right side of
the throne flew open : still his lordship proceeded. Lord
Durham, the first in the procession, appeared on the threshold, carrying the crown on its cushion : still his lordship
proceeded. The king appeared on the threshold ; and his
lordship was still proceeding, when the peers on either
side and behind laid hands on him, and compelled him

to silence, while his countenance was convulsed with agitation.

The king had a flush on his cheek, and an unusual brightness in his eye. He walked rapidly and firmly, and ascended the steps of the throne with a kind of eagerness. He bowed right and left, and desired their lordships to be seated while the Commons were summoned. For a little time it appeared doubtful whether even the oil of anointing would calm the tossing waves of strife; but, after all, the Peers were quiet sooner than the Commons.

That House, too, was crowded, expectant, eager, and passionate. Sir Richard Vyvyan was the spokesman of the opposition; and a very strong one. A question of order arose, as to whether Sir Richard Vyvyan was or was not keeping within the fair bounds of his subject—which was a reform petition; whereas he was speaking on ' dissolution or no dissolution.' The speaker appears to have been agitated from the beginning; and there were several members who were not collected enough to receive his decisions with the usual deference. Honourable members turned upon each other, growing contradictious, sharp, angry—even abusive. Lord John Russell attempted to make himself heard, but in vain: his was no voice to pierce through such a tumult. The speaker was in a state of visible emotion. Sir Richard Vyvyan, however, regained a hearing; but, as soon as he was once more in full flow, boom! came the cannon which told that the king was on his way; and the roar drowned the conclusion of the sentence. Not a word more was heard for the cheers, the cries—and even shouts of laughter; all put down together, at regular intervals, by the discharges of artillery. At one moment, Sir Robert Peel, Lord Althorp, and Sir Francis Burdett, were all using the most vehement action of command and supplication in dumb show, and their friends were labouring in vain to procure a hearing for them. The speaker himself stood silenced by the tumult, till the cries took more and more the sound of ' Shame! shame!' and more eyes were fixed upon him till he could have made himself heard, if he had not been too much moved to speak. When he recovered voice, he decided that Sir Robert Peel was entitled to address the

House. With occasional uproar, this was permitted ; and
Sir Robert Peel was still speaking when the usher of the
black rod appeared at the bar, to summon the Commons to
his majesty's presence. Sir Robert Peel continued to
speak, loudly and vehemently, after the appearance of the
usher of the black rod ; and it was only by main force, by
pulling him down by the skirts of his coat, that those near
him could compel him to take his seat.

The hundred members who accompanied the speaker to
the presence of the king rushed in 'very tumultuously.
There is an interest in the mutual addresses of sovereign
and people in a crisis like this which is not felt in ordinary
times; and the words of the speaker first, and then of the
king, were listened to with extreme eagerness.

The speaker said: 'May it please your majesty, we your
majesty's most faithful Commons approach your majesty
with profound respect; and, sire, in no period of our
history, have the Commons House of parliament more
faithfully responded to the real feelings and interests of
your majesty's loyal, dutiful, and affectionate people;
while it has been their earnest desire to support the
dignity and honour of the crown, upon which depend
the greatness, the happiness, and the prosperity of this
country.'

The king spoke in a firm, cheerful, and dignified tone
and manner. The speech, which besides referred only
to money-matters and economy, and to our state of peace
with foreign powers, began and ended thus : 'I have come
to meet you for the purpose of proroguing this parliament,
with a view to its immediate dissolution. I have been
induced to resort to this measure, for the purpose of ascer-
taining the sense of my people, in the way in which it can
be most constitutionally and most authentically expressed,
on the expediency of making such changes in the representation as circumstances may appear to require, and
which, founded upon the acknowledged principles of the
constitution, may tend at once to uphold the just rights
and prerogatives of the crown, and to give security to the
liberties of the people. . . . In resolving to recur to the
sense of my people, in the present circumstances of the
country, I have been influenced only by a paternal anxiety

for the contentment and happiness of my subjects, to promote which, I rely with confidence on your continued and
zealous assistance.'

' It is over !' said those to each other who understood the
crisis better than it was apprehended by the nation at
large.   ' All is over !' whispered the anti-reformers to each
other.   The members of both Houses went home that
April afternoon, hoarse, heated, exhausted—conscious that
such a scene had never been witnessed within the walls of
parliament since Cromwell's days.   The ministers went
home, to take some rest, knowing that all was safe ; that
is, that to the people was now fairly committed the people's
cause.

A proclamation, declaring the dissolution of the parliament, appeared next day ; and the new writs were made
returnable on the 14th of June.

CHAPTER IV.

General Election — Popular Action — Riots — New House — Second
Reform Bill—Committee—Bill passes the Commons—First Reading
in the Lords—Debate—Lord Grey—The Bishops—The Bill lost—
Prorogation—Vote of Confidence—Riots at Derby and Nottingham
—At Bristol—Prevalence of Order.

THE people thoroughly understood that their cause was
now consigned to their own hands.   In all preceding ' revolutions '—to adopt the term used by the anti-reformers
—they had acted, when they acted at all, under the direction of a small upper class who thought and understood
for them, and used them as instruments.   Now, the
thinkers and leaders were of every class, and the multitude acted, not only under orders, but in concert.   If
for every nobleman and legislator who desired parliamentary reform for distinct political reasons there were
hundreds of middle-class men, for every hundred middle-
class men there were tens of thousands of the working-
classes who had an interest, an opinion and a will in the
matter, which made them, instead of mere instruments,

political agents. The whole countless multitude of reformers had laid hold of the principle that the most secure
and the shortest way of obtaining what they wanted was
to obtain representation. This was a broad, clear truth
which every man could understand, and on which every
earnest man was disposed to act as men are wont to act
on clear and broad truths; and the non-electors felt themselves called upon to put forth such power as they had,
as a means to obtaining the power which they claimed.
The elections were, to a wonderful extent, carried by the
non-electors, by means of their irresistible power over
those who had the suffrage. Times were indeed changed
since the century when Leeds and Manchester had, for a
short time, been allowed to send members to parliament in
Cromwell's days, and had then again been quietly disfranchised, almost without a murmur on any hand. In
those old days, these populous towns had been admitted
to the representation, because legislators, looking abroad
from their point of survey, saw that in reason they ought
to be. They were to be represented now because the
inhabitants themselves demanded it, for reasons which
it was their turn to propound. For some time they had
been preparing to enforce their demand; and the first
obvious occasion for action was now, when a House of
Commons was to be returned whose special business it
was to reform itself.

The great unrepresented towns were co-operated with
all over the country—even in rural hamlets, and scattered
farmsteads. In such places, half-a-dozen labourers would
club their earnings to buy a weekly newspaper—these
costing sevenpence, at first price—on the second day; and
the one who could read best read aloud the whole of the
debates after the memorable 1st of March, to his companions, as they crowded round him in a shed, by the
light of a single tallow candle. Rural artisans walked
miles after working-hours to the nearest towns, to learn
what was posted up on the walls, and said in public-
houses. By the time the elections were to take place,
tens of thousands of working-men knew something more
than the mere names of Russell, Grey, and Brougham,
and their leading opponents: they knew their ways of

thinking and speaking, their aims and their plans; and
this was an inestimable help in showing such political
students what to do. It is true, few of these novices were
very wise on their great subject, and a multitude were
ignorant and prejudiced : some wished for foreign war,
and some for civil war, as a vent for their own pugnacity;
some were for persecuting their neighbours who differed
from them ; and others drew glorious pictures of the
wealth they should all enjoy when every man had a vote,
and had voted away all the taxes; but even the most
ignorant and unreasonable were in a better condition than
before—more able to understand reason—more fit to be
influenced by their wiser neighbours—better qualified to
trust the authors and influential promoters of the great
measure. As for the higher orders of non-electors, the
intelligent men of the towns—by combining their lights,
they easily saw what to do. They combined their will,
their knowledge, and their manifest force, in political
unions, whence they sent forth will, knowledge, and
influence, over wide districts of the land. And the
electors, seeing the importance of the crisis—the unspeakable importance that it should be well conducted—joined
these unions, and by their weight of character, intelligence,
and station, preserved them from much folly and aimless
effort, kept up the self-respect and sobriety of the best of
the non-electors, and curbed the violence of the worst.
Wealthy capitalists, eminent bankers, members of the late
parliament, and country gentlemen, agreed over their wine
that they ought to join the political union of the district,
and went the next morning to enrol themselves. When
face to face in their meetings with their neighbours of
lower degree, they taught and learned much : new open-
ings for action appeared; daily opportunities offered for
spreading knowledge, proposing sound views, and discoun-
tenancing violence. They were startled by sudden appa-
ritions of men of minds superior to their own—men of
genius and heroism—rising up from the most depressed
ranks of non-electors ; and they, in their turn, were found
to be imbued with that respect for men as men which is
the result of superior education, but which the poor and
depressed too often conceive not to exist among the idle

independent, whom they are apt to call the proud. Such
was the preparation going forward throughout the country
while the ministers were at their work in London; the
rapid social education of all ranks, which may be regarded
as another of the ever-springing blessings of the peace,
and by which the great transition from the old to the new
parliamentary system was rendered safe. That the amount
of violence was no greater that it was, remained, and still
remains, a matter of astonishment to the anti-reform party,
and was a blessing scarcely hoped for on the other side.
After the three days in Paris, in the preceding July,
thoughtful Englishmen asked each other with anxiety,
whether it was conceivable that their own countrymen
would behave, in a similar crisis, with such chivalrous
honour and such enlightened moderation as the French
populace. The question was not now precisely answered,
because the crisis was not similar—the British king and
his ministers being on the side of the people, and the
conflict being only with a portion of the aristocracy of
birth and wealth; but there was enough of intelligence
and moral nobleness in the march of the English movement, to inspire Englishmen with a stronger mutual
respect and a brighter political hope than they had ever
entertained before.

Such evidence as there was at present, was window-
breaking on illumination nights, and hustlings and
threatenings in the streets, at the election time, which
compelled some anti-reform candidates and their agents
to hide themselves. A few scattered instances of this kind
of disturbance occurred in England; and in Scotland the
riots were really formidable. The anti-reformers there
carried all before them, from their possessing almost a
monopoly of political power. These election days and
illumination nights are the occasions when brawlers and
thieves come forth to indulge their passions and reap their
harvest; and in Edinburgh and London they made use of
their opportunity, to the discredit of the popular cause.
On the dissolution of parliament, the lord mayor sanctioned the illumination of London; and the windows of
the Duke of Wellington, Mr. Baring, and other leading
anti-reformers, were broken. After the Edinburgh elec-

tion, the lord provost was attacked on the North Bridge, and with difficulty rescued by the military. We happen to know what was thought on the occasion by a reformer noted for his Radicalism: ' As dash went the stones,' he says, ' smash fell the glass, and crash came the window-frames, from nine o'clock to near midnight, reflection arose and asked seriously and severely what this meant: was it reform? was it popular liberty? Many thousands of others who were there must have asked themselves the same questions. . . . . The reform newspapers were content to say that the riots reflected no discredit on reformers; the rioters were only " the *blackguards* of the town.". . . . I believe that there is now one problem solved by experience, which was hidden in futurity then— namely, that the greater the number of men enfranchised, the smaller is the number of blackguards." '

The election cry was: ' The bill, the whole bill, and nothing but the bill;' and the result was that such an assemblage of reformers was returned that their opponents styled them a company of pledged delegates, and no true House of Commons. And it was certain that such a thing as they called a true House of Commons they would never more see. Out of eighty-two county members only six were opposed to the bill. Yorkshire sent four reformers; and so did London. General Gascoyne was driven from Liverpool, Sir Richard Vyvyan from Cornwall, Sir Edward Knatchbull from Kent, and Mr. Bankes from Dorsetshire. The Duke of Newcastle could, this time, do nothing with his ' own.' The most remarkable defeat of the ministerial party, but one which was sure to happen, was at Cambridge University, where Lord Palmerston. and Mr. Cavendish were driven out by Mr. Goulburn and Mr. W. Peel.

After re-electing the speaker, and hearing from the king's own lips a recommendation to undertake the reform of their House, the Commons went to work again. The bill was introduced on the 24th of June; but the second reading stood over till the 4th of July, that the Scotch and Irish Reform Bills might be brought in. The debate lasted three nights, when a division was taken on the second reading, which gave the ministers a majority of 136 in a House of 598 members.

It was clear that the ministers were so strong that they were sure of their own way in this House; but the strain upon the temper and patience of the large majority was greater than they would have supported in a meaner cause. When we remember that the minority sincerely believed that they were now witnessing the last days of the constitution, we cannot wonder at their determination to avail themselves of all the forms of the House, and of every passing incident, to delay the destruction of the country. They avowed their purpose, and they adhered to it with unflinching obstinacy. The House went into committee on the 12th of July; and it was at once evident that every borough was to be contended for, every population return questioned, every point debated on which an argument could be hung; and this, not on account of the merits of the case, but merely to protract the time, and leave room for 'fate, or Providence, or something,' to interfere. If at midnight, in the hot glare of the lamps, any member dropped asleep, a piqued orator would make that a cause of delay, that he might be properly attended to to-morrow; and another time, the House would sit till the summer sunshine was glittering on the breakfast-tables of the citizens, the opposition hoping to wear out the vigilance of the proposers of the bill. The people grew angry, and the newspapers spoke their wrath. It was all very well, they said, to insist on the fullest discussion of every principle; but to wrangle for every item, after the principle had been settled—to do this with the avowed object of awaiting accidents, and in defiance of the declared will of the nation at large, was an insolence and obstruction not to be borne. When, towards the end of the month, people began to ask when and how this was to end, the ministers moved that the reform business should take precedence of all other; and it was arranged that the discussion should proceed from five o'clock every day. Before August came in, however, signs appeared of an unappeased discontent on the part of the non-electors, who dreaded lest the heats of August in town, and the attractions of that month in the Scotch moors, should draw off their champions from their duty; and it became known in the House that a conference had taken place between the political unions of Birmingham, Manchester, and Glasgow, in order to agree how long they would wait. The majority in the House thought it right to intimate such facts, to prove the danger of the times. The minority called it stifling discussion by threats, and considered whether they could not be a little slower still, in assertion of their constitutional right of debate. Weeks passed on; the summer heats rose to their height, and declined; the days shortened; honourable members, haggard and nervous, worn with eight hours per night of skirmishing and wrangling, pined for fresh air and country quietness; and still every borough and every population statement was contested. It was the 7th of September before the committee reported. On the 13th and two following days the report was considered, when only a few verbal amendments were proposed. The final debate occupied the evenings of the 19th, 20th, and 21st of September; and at its close, the bill passed the Commons by a majority of 109; the numbers for and against being 345 to 236. Both London and the country had grown tired of waiting, and had somewhat relaxed their attention when they found that the members might be relied on for remaining at their posts; but on this occasion, all were as eager as ever. The House was surrounded by crowds, who caught up the cheers within on the announcement of the majority; cheers which were renewed so perseveringly that it seemed as if the members had no thoughts of going home. There was little sleep in London that night. The cheering ran along the streets, and was caught up again and again till morning. Such of the peers as were in town, awaiting their share of the business, which was now immediately to begin, must have heard the shouting the whole night through. It is certain that it was the deliberate intention of the greater number of them to throw out the bill very speedily. If the acclamations of that night did not raise a doubt as to the duty and safety of their course, they must have been in a mood unlike that of ordinary men, meditating in the watches of the night.

Before daylight, the news was on its way into the country; and wherever it spread, it floated the flags, and woke up the bells, and filled the air with shouts and music. In the midst of this, however, the older and graver men turned to each other with the question: ' What will the Lords do?' Lord Grey's speech, in opening the debate in the House of Peers, shows to those who read it now that he had a precise foresight of what the Lords would do, and particularly the bishops. Lord Althorp, attended by a hundred of the Commons, carried up the bill to the Peers, the day after it had passed the Lower House; but the debate took place on the question of the second reading; extending over five nights, from the 3rd to the 7th of October. It was an exceedingly fine debate, as might have been expected from its nature. Not only did the accomplishments of the noble speakers come into play, but they had never before spoken on a subject which concerned them so nearly, which they at once so thoroughly understood and so deeply felt; and their minds were roused and exercised accordingly. No position could be more dignified than that of Lord Grey. He was safe from the taunt under which the Duke of Wellington had winced, and under which many a minister has since winced—that he was the slave of popular clamour; for he could point back to the year 1786, when he voted with Mr. Pitt for shortening the duration of parliaments; and to a time before the old French Revolution, when he voted for Mr. Flood's measure of parliamentary reform. Standing on this high ground of principled consistency, the venerable statesman was at liberty from all self-regards to be as great in his bearing as his measure was in its import. And truly great he was. From this day, for many months he was subject to a series of provocations which must often have worn his frame and sickened his spirit; but he never stooped to anger or impatience. His conscience calm and clear, his judgment settled, his knowledge and his powers concentrated in his measure, he could maintain his stand above the passions which were agitating other men. And he did maintain it, through all the personal fatigue and mental weariness of months. Through the vacillations of the king above him, and the raging and malice of the peers around him, and the surging of the mob far below him, for which he was made responsible, he preserved an

unbroken yet genial calmness, which made observers feel
and say that, among the various causes of emotion of that
time, they knew nothing so moving as the greatness of
Lord Grey. On this opening night of the debate—the
3rd of October—he stood, by virtue of his experience and
the meditation of half a century, like a seer, showing the
issues of such procedure, on the one hand or the other, as
their lordships might adopt. Among his other warnings,
that to the bishops stands out conspicuously and propheti-
cally. ' Let me respectfully entreat those right reverend
prelates,' he said, after an acknowledgment of their deserts
and dignities, ' to consider, that if this bill should be rejected by a narrow majority of the lay peers—which I
have reason to hope will not be the case; but if it should,
and that its fate should thus, within a few votes, be decided by the votes of the heads of the Church, what will
then be their situation with the country. Those right
reverend prelates have shown that they were not indifferent or inattentive to the signs of the times. . . . . They
appear to have felt that the eyes of the country are upon
them; that it is necessary for them to set their house in
order, and prepare to meet the coming storm. . . . . They
are the ministers of peace; earnestly do I hope that the
result of their votes will be such as may tend to the tranquillity, to the peace, and happiness of the country.' If
the bishops were aware that the eyes of the people were
upon them, they seem to have been ignorant or thoughtless of one of the reasons why. The people, down to the
very lowest of the populace, were willing to bear more on
this question from the most aristocratic of the lay peers
than from any of the spiritual peers. There was no man
anywhere so ignorant as not to see that much allowance
was to be made for noblemen of ancient lineage, called on
to part with hereditary borough property, and with political influence which became more valuable from one session
of parliament to another. The bishops had no plea for
such allowance—commoners by birth as they were, having
no interest in borough property, and no hereditary associations making war against present exigencies. If they
really approved of our representative system, they should
naturally desire its purification; and the whole people

looked to see whether they did or not. If they did, they
would show themselves indeed shepherds of the flock;
if not, they must be regarded as the humble servants
of the hereditary aristocracy; and their Church would
be distrusted in proportion to the worldliness of her
prelates. They did their utmost to ruin themselves and
their Church. One bishop alone—the Bishop of Norwich
—voted in favour of the bill. Twenty-one—exactly enough
to turn the scale—voted against the bill; the majority
by which it was thrown out being forty-one. It was
proclaimed over the whole kingdom, and it will never
be forgotten, that it was the bishops who threw out the
Reform Bill. Newspapers in mourning edges told this,
in the course of a day or two, to every listener in the
land. Every school-boy knew it; every beggar could cast
it in the teeth of footmen in purple liveries on the steps of
great houses. For many months—till some time after the
Reform Bill became the law of the land—it was not safe
for a bishop to appear in public in any article of sacerdotal
dress. Insults followed if apron or hat showed itself in
the streets. And the bench gained nothing by yielding at
last, because everybody knew they could not help it.
While they imputed their yielding to a love of peace, they
could not complain if the people assigned it to a lack of
courage. Whether the deficiency was of sagacity, or
knowledge, or independence, or principle, it did more to
injure the Church throughout the empire than all hostility
of Catholics and Dissenters together. Among the twenty-
two anti-reform voters in the Lords, on the final reading,
a few months after this, there is no bishop's name. Not
the less for this was it everywhere still repeated that it
was the bishops that threw out the Reform Bill, till no
child old enough to understand the words could ever
forget them.

The peers were not tempting fate in blindness. They
knew what was said and thought of them, and what was
threatened in case of their refusal to surrender their
borough interests. They were aware, if they read the
newspapers, that there was a change in the form of the
popular question which every man had been asking his
neighbour. Instead of the question, 'What will the Lords

do?' men were now asking, 'What must be done with the Lords?' and the journals, having taken for granted that four hundred peers were not to stand in the way of an essential improvement desired by king and people, were beginning to discuss whether the king or the people should take the peers in hand; whether, as this was understood to mean, the king should create so many new peers as to obtain a majority for the bill, or the people should refuse to pay taxes till they had obtained a better representation. If the Lords did not read the newspapers—and Lord Grey gave great and general offence, in the midst of his popularity, by declaring that he did not—they had other means of information. On the day of the loss of the bill, Lord Eldon wrote, before going to the work of mischief: 'Making new peers to pass it has been much talked of; but, unless our calculation of numbers is erroneous, and most grossly so, audacity itself could not venture to attempt a sufficient supply of new peers.' Again, on the 5th of October, a remarkable scene had taken place in the House of Lords, before entering on the topic of the night. During the debate, more and more peeresses attended every evening, bringing their daughters and relations, for whom seats were placed below the bar. Instead of two or three ladies, quietly listening behind a curtain, there was now an assemblage on rows of chairs, smiling, frowning, fidgeting—indicating their agitation in every way short of clapping and groaning. The space about the throne was thronged with listening foreigners and members of the other House; and on this evening, the conspicuous figure of the intelligent Hindoo, Rammohun-Roy, was in the midst of the group, his spreading turban attracting many eyes, and his mobile countenance varying with every turn of the discussion. All these, and a very full House of Peers, were present when evidence was brought forward of what the people were thinking of doing with the peers, in case of too obstinate a stand for the rotten boroughs. On occasion of the presentation of petitions, information was given of something ominous which had taken place at a meeting of 100,000 people at Birmingham. After one orator there had, quite unconstitutionally, asked repeatedly and significantly the question, whether the Lords would 'dare' to reject the bill, another had declared his intention to pay no taxes till the bill should have passed; and his declaration had been received with loud cheers. On his desiring those who agreed with him to hold up their hands, a countless multitude of hands was held up; and on his asking for a sign of dissent, not a single hand was held up. While all the peers who spoke upon this news, from Lord Chancellor Brougham to his predecessor, Lord Eldon, denounced such proceedings as unconstitutional, no peer could, from that hour, be supposed ignorant of what he was doing in driving the people and the sovereign to one or the other of these methods of procuring a law which all but a small fraction of society desired and chose to obtain. Yet, on the 7th, they threw out the bill, by a majority in which they gloried, as being much larger than the ministers had anticipated. Their expectation was that all would now go well. Lord Grey had declared, that by this measure the administration would stand or fall. The measure having been lost, the administration must fall. After relating how the final debate lasted till between six and seven in the morning, Lord Eldon wrote: 'The fate of the bill, therefore, is decided. . . . . The night was made interesting by the anxieties of all present. Perhaps fortunately the mob would not on the outside wait so long as it was before Lords left the inside of the House.' Their lordships got home unmolested that autumn morning, and awaited joyfully the tidings of the fall of the administration. But they had far other news to hear. The king meant to prorogue parliament immediately, in order to a speedy re-assembling, and going over of the whole matter again.

This was a prospect full of weariness and anxiety to everybody. As for the king, he came down to the House on the 20th of October, in temper and spirits as yet apparently unchanged; and his speech manifested the unrelaxed resolution of his ministers. It earnestly recommended the careful preservation of tranquillity throughout the country, during the suspense in which the great question was held. As for the peers, some believed, and with too much excuse, that the hour of revolution was really come. 'Our day here yesterday was tremendously alarming,' Lord Eldon had written a week before this time. Many windows had been broken, several peers in-sulted in the streets, and Lord Londonderry struck insensible from his horse, by the blow of a stone. Lord Eldon, while writing of 'the immense mob of reformers,' admits that there was 'hardly a decent-looking man among them ;' and it was indeed the case that the excitement of the time had called out all the disorderly part of society into view and action. Not only the ignorant and violent desirers of parliamentary reform, but thieves and vaga-bonds, made use of the opportunity to stir up the passions under whose cover they might pursue their aims of plunder. This was made clear by the presence of well-know London faces, not only at the window-breaking at the west end, but in the mobs at Derby and Bristol, where the most serious damage was done to the reform cause. 'Everywhere,' Lord Eldon said, 'the mischief is occasioned by strangers from other parts coming to do mischief.' The fact was clear ; only—Lord Eldon called these strangers 'reformers,' while the police called them 'the swell-mob.' Disastrous, indeed, was the injury they did.

The great body of reformers stood firm and calm, because the government did so. The House of Commons had im-mediately followed up the rejection of the bill by a vote of confidence in ministers, which removed all fear of their resigning; and calm patience was certain to carry the great objects of the time. But then came these incendiaries, stirring up riots in Derby and Nottingham first, and after-wards at Bristol—not only discrediting the reform cause, but doing a yet more terrible mischief by perplexing and alarming the king. The king remained to all appearance firm till after the prorogation of parliament, the Derby and Nottingham riots having meantime occurred ; but the more fearful affair at Bristol shook his decision and his courage ; and it is understood that, from that date, the work of his ministers was more arduous than before.

At Derby, some rioters were consigned to jail for window-breaking ; and the jail was carried by the mob, the prisoners released, and several lives lost after the arrival of the military. At Nottingham, the castle was burnt—avowedly because it was the property of the Duke of Newcastle. To all to whom the name and fame of the devoted Lucy Hutchinson and her spouse are dear, this event was a mournful one; but the walls remain, and the beauty of the site cannot be impaired while any part of the building meets the eye. The duke recovered £21,000 from the county, as damages, and certainly appeared to suffer much less under the event than his respectable neighbours of the reform party. He evidently enjoyed his martyrdom.

The Bristol mobs have always been noted for their brutality; and the outbreak now was such as to amaze and confound the whole kingdom. It will ever remain a national disgrace that such materials existed in such quantity for London rogues to operate upon. Nothing like these Bristol riots had happened since the Birmingham riots in 1791.

London rogues could have had no such power as in this case if the political and moral state of Bristol had not been bad. Its political state was disgraceful. The venality of its elections was notorious. It had a close corporation, between whom and the citizens there was no community of feeling on municipal subjects. The lower parts of the city were the harbourage of probably a worse seaport populace than any other place in England, while the police was ineffective and demoralised. There was no city in which a greater amount of savagery lay beneath a society proud, exclusive, and mutually repellent, rather than enlightened and accustomed to social co-operation. These are circumstances which go far to account for the Bristol riots being so fearfully bad as they were. Of this city, Sir Charles Wetherell—then at the height of his unpopularity as a vigorous opponent of the Reform Bill—was recorder; and there he had to go, in the last days of October, in his judicial capacity. Strenuous efforts had been made to exhibit before the eyes of the Bristol people the difference between the political and judicial functions of their recorder, and to show them that to receive the judge with respect was not to countenance his political course; yet the symptoms of discontent were such as to induce the mayor, Mr. Pinney, to apply to the home-office for military aid. Lord Melbourne sent down some troops of horse, which were quartered within reach, in the neigh-

bourhood of the city. It was an unfortunate circumstance that, owing to the want of a common interest
between the citizens and the corporation, scarcely any
gentlemen offered their services as special constables but
such as were accustomed to consider the lower classes with
contempt as a troublesome rabble, and rather relished an
occasion for defying and humbling them. Such was the
preparation made in the face of the fact that Sir Charles
Wetherell could not be induced to relinquish his public
entry, though warned of danger by the magistrates themselves; and of the other important fact that the London
rogues, driven from the metropolis by the new police, were
known to be infesting every place where there was hope
of confusion and spoil.

On Saturday, October 29, Sir Charles Wetherell entered
Bristol in pomp; and before he reached the Mansion
House at noon, he must have been pretty well convinced, by the hootings and throwing of stones, that
he had better have foregone the procession. For some
hours the special constables and the noisy mob in front
of the Mansion House exchanged discourtesies of an emphatic character, but there was no actual violence till
night. At night, the Mansion House was attacked, and
the Riot Act was read; but the military were not brought
down, as they ought to have been, to clear the streets.
The mayor had 'religious scruples,' and was 'humane;'
and his indecision was not overborne by any aid from his
brother-magistrates. When the military were brought in,
it was after violence had been committed, and when the
passions of the mob were much excited. Sir Charles
Wetherell escaped from the city that night. During the
dark hours, sounds were heard provocative of further riot;
shouts in the streets, and the hammering of workmen who
were boarding up the lower windows of the Mansion House
and the neighbouring dwellings. On the Sunday morning,
the rioters broke into the Mansion House without opposition; and from the time they got into the cellars, all went
wrong. Hungry wretches and boys broke the necks of the
bottles, and Queen Square was strewed with the bodies of
the dead-drunk. The soldiers were left without orders,
and their officers without that sanction of the magistracy

in the absence of which they could not act, but only parade; and in this parading, some of the soldiers naturally lost their tempers, and spoke and made gestures on their own account, which did not tend to the soothing of the mob. This mob never consisted of more than five or six hundred; and twenty thousand orderly persons attended the churches and chapels that day, to whom no appeal on behalf of peace and the law was made. At a word through the pastors from the magistrates, indicating how they should act, the heads of these families could easily have co-operated to secure the protection of the city. The mob declared openly what they were going to do; and they went to work unchecked—armed with staves and bludgeons from the quays, and with iron palisades from the Mansion House—to break open and burn the bridewell, the jail, the bishop's palace, the custom-house, and Queen Square. They gave half an hour's notice to the inhabitants of each house in the square, which they then set fire to in regular succession, till two sides, each measuring 550 feet, lay in smoking ruins. The bodies of the drunken were seen roasting in the fire. The greater number of the rioters were believed to be under twenty years of age, and some were mere children; some Sunday scholars, hitherto well conducted, and it may be questioned whether one in ten knew anything of the Reform Bill, or the offences of Sir Charles Wetherell. On the Monday morning, after all actual riot seemed to be over, the soldiery at last made two slaughterous charges. More horse arrived, and a considerable body of foot soldiers; and the constabulary became active; and from that time the city was in a more orderly state than the residents were accustomed to see it.

The inhabitants at large were not disposed to acquiesce quietly in the disgrace of their city. Public meetings were held to petition the government to make inquiry into the causes and circumstances of the disturbances, the petitioners emphatically declaring their opinion, 'that Bristol owed all the calamities they deplored to the system under the predominance of which they had taken place.' The magistrates were brought to trial, and so was Colonel Brereton, who was understood to be in command of the

whole of the military.   The result of that court-martial
caused more emotion throughout the kingdom than all
the slaughtering and burning, and the subsequent executions which marked that fearful season.

It was a year before the trial of the magistrates was
entered upon. The result was the acquittal of the mayor,
and the consequent relinquishment of the prosecution of
his brother-magistrates. While every one saw that great
blame rested somewhere, no one was disposed to make a
victim of a citizen who found himself, at a time of extreme
emergency, in the midst of a system which rendered a
proper discharge of his duty impossible. All agreed that
Bristol must no longer be misgoverned; but no one desired
to punish the one man, or the three or five men, in whose
term of office the existing corruption and inefficiency were
made manifest by a sort of accident. Instead of complaining that Mr. Pinney and the other aldermen escaped, men
mourned that Colonel Brereton had not lain under the
same conditions of impunity.

The magistrates believed that they had done their part
in desiring that the commanders of the military would act
according to their discretion. Colonel Brereton believed
that, before he could act, he must have a more express
sanction from the magistracy than he could obtain.
Between them, nothing was done. The mayor was not
the only 'humane' man. Colonel Brereton also was
'humane.' He saw a crowd of boys and women, with
a smaller proportion of men, collected without apparent
aim, and in a mood to be diverted, as he thought, from
serious mischief. While inwardly chafing at being left
without authority—not empowered to do anything but
ride about—he rode in among them, made use of his popularity, spoke to them, and let them shake hands with him.
This would have been well, if all had ended well. But
the event decided the case against him. He knew how
unfavourably these acts would tell on his trial. Full of
keen sensibilities, nothing in him was more keen than his
sense of professional honour. He sank under the conflict
between his civil and professional conscience. He was
crushed in the collision between the natural and the
conventional systems of social and military duty in which

he found himself entangled. He had been too much of the man to make war, without overruling authorisation, on the misguided and defenceless; and he found himself too much of the soldier to endure conventional dishonour. His trial began on the 9th of the next January. For four days, he struggled on in increasing agony of mind. On the night of the 12th, he, for the first time, omitted his visit at bedtime to the chamber of his children—his two young motherless daughters: he was heard walking for hours about his room; and when the court assembled in the morning, it was to hear that the prisoner had shot himself through the heart. The whole series of events at Bristol became more and more disconnected in the general mind with the subject of the Reform Bill, as facts came out which showed that other proximate causes of disturbance would have, no doubt, wrought the same effects, sooner or later, as well as the one which chanced to occur. The question which did, from that time, lie deep down in thoughtful minds was, how long our Christian profession and our heathen practice—our social and military combinations—were to be supposed compatible, after a man who united in himself the virtues of both had been driven to suicide by their contrariety.

It is necessary to note the social disturbances which followed upon the rejection of the second Reform Bill; but it is no less necessary to point out that the turbulence of this, as of all seasons, is easy to observe, while no account can be given which can represent to the imagination the prevailing calmness and order of the time. Calmness and order present no salient point for narrative and description; but their existence must not therefore be overlooked. A truly heroic state of self-discipline and obedience to law prevailed over the land, while in particular spots the turbulent were able to excite the giddy and the ignorant to riot. The nation was steadily rising to its most heroic mood; that mood in which, the next year, it carried through the sublime enterprise which no man, in the darkest moment, had any thought of surrendering.

CHAPTER V.

THE preparations for the renewal of the struggle for parliamentary reform began immediately after the prorogation, and were of a very serious character on every hand. As might be expected from the protraction of the quarrel, each party went further in its own direction; and the king, whose station was in the middle, became occasionally irresolute, through anxiety; an anxiety which plainly affected his health.

On the 31st of October, the London Political Union held an important meeting, which was so fully attended that the multitude adjourned to Lincoln's Inn Fields. The object of the day was to decree and organise a National Union, the provincial associations to be connected with it as branches, sending delegates to the central board. Thus far, all had gone well, as regarded these unions. The administration had not been obliged to recognise their existence, while undoubtedly very glad of the fact. Whether their existence was constitutional, was one of the two great questions of the day. Hitherto, the government were not obliged to discuss it, in public or private, or to give any opinion; for, till now, the unions had done nothing objectionable. Now, however, the difficulty

began. The less informed and more violent members of
the London Union insisted upon demanding universal
suffrage, and other matters not included in the bill, while
the wiser majority chose to adhere to their watchword :
' The bill, the whole bill, and nothing but the bill.' The
minority seceded, and constituted a metropolitan union of
their own, whose avowed object was to defeat the ministerial
measure, in order to obtain a more thorough opening of the
representation. In their advertisements, they declared all
hereditary privileges and all distinction of ranks to be
unnatural and vicious; and invited the working-men
throughout the country to come up to their grand meeting
at White Conduit House, on the 7th of November, declaring that such a display of strength must carry all
before it. The government brought soldiery round the
metropolis, had an army of special constables sworn in—
all in a quiet way—and as quietly communicated with
the union leaders. On the 5th, the Hatton Garden
magistrates informed these leaders that their proposed proceedings were illegal. A deputation begged admission to
the presence of the home secretary. Lord Melbourne saw
them, and quietly pointed out to them which passages of
their address were seditious, if not treasonable, involving
in the guilt of treason all persons who attended their
meeting for the purpose of promoting the objects proposed.
The leaders at once abandoned their design. The ministers were blamed for letting them go, and taking no notice
of the seditious advertisement; but no one who, at this
distance of time, compares the Melbourne and the Sidmouth days, can doubt that the forbearance was as wise as
it was kind. What the offenders needed was better knowledge, not penal restraint, as their conduct in disbanding
plainly showed. The peace of society lost nothing, and
the influence of the government gained much, by the
ministers showing themselves willing to enlighten rather
than to punish ignorance, and to reserve their penalties,
where circumstances allowed it, for wilful and obstinate
violations of the law. The affair, however, alarmed the
sovereign and the more timid of the aristocracy who had
hitherto supported the reform measure.

At the same time, Lord Grey was beset by deputations

from all ranks and classes, urging the shortening of the recess to the utmost, and the expediting the measure by all possible means; and especially by inducing the king to create peers in sufficient numbers to secure the immediate passage of the bill through the House of Lords. All the interests of the kingdom were suffering under suspense and disappointment, and the popular indignation against the obstructive peers was growing dangerous. This proposition of a creation of peers was the other great question of the day.

And seldom or never has there been a question more serious. Men saw now that the word 'revolution,' so often in the mouths of the anti-reformers, might prove to be not so inapplicable as had been supposed; that, if the peers should not come immediately and voluntarily, and by the light of their own convictions, into harmony with the other two powers of the government, it would prove true that, as they were themselves saying, ' the balance of the constitution was destroyed.' Was it not already so? it was asked. Unless a miraculous enlightenment was to be looked for between October and December, was there any alternative but civil war, and, in some way or another, overbearing the Lords? Civil war was out of the question for such a handful of obstructives. The king, commons, and people could not be kept waiting much longer for the few who showed no sign of yielding; and it would be the best kindness to all parties to get the obstructives out-voted, by an exertion of that kingly power whose existence nobody disputed, however undesirable might be its frequent exercise. From day to day was this consideration urged upon the premier, who never made any reply to it. It was not a time when men saw the full import of what they asked; nor was this a subject on which the prime-minister could open his lips to deputations. He must have felt, like every responsible and every thoughtful man, that no more serious and mournful enterprise could be proposed to any minister than to destroy the essential character of any one of the three component parts of the government; and that, if such a destruction should prove to be a necessary condition of the requisite purification of another, it was the very hardest and most fearful of condi-

tions. Men were talking lightly, all over the kingdom, of
the necessity of swamping the opposition of the peers;
they were angry, and with reason, with the living men
who made the difficulty; and nobody contradicted them
when they said that the extinction of the wisdom of these
particular men in the national counsels would be no great
loss; but they did not consider that the existing Roden
and Newcastle, and Eldon and Rolle, were not the great
institution of the British House of Lords, whose function
shone back through the history of a thousand years, and
might shine onwards through a thousand years more, if
the ignorance and selfishness of its existing majority could
be overcome on the present occasion by a long patience
and a large forbearance. Lord Grey was the last man to
degrade his ' order,' if the necessity could by any means
be avoided. It was his first object to carry the reform of
the Commons; but it would well-nigh have broken his
heart to be compelled to do it through the degradation of
the Lords.   At this time, while, from his silence, multitudes
believed what they wished, and confidently expected a
large creation of peers, it is now known that he had not
yet proposed any such measure to the king.

One consequence of the prevalence of an expectation of a
batch of new peers, was the parting off from the obstructive Lords of a large number who were called the
Waverers.   There is always such a set of people in such
times; and greatly do they always embarrass the calculations of the best informed.   These kept the issue in
uncertainty up to the last moment.   On the one part were
the honest and enlightened peers who saw that the end of
borough corruption was come.   On the other part were
the honest and unenlightened, or the selfish, who would
not have our institutions touched on any pretence whatever; and between them now stood the Waverers, hoping
to keep things as they were, but disposed to yield
voluntarily, if they could not conquer, rather than be put
down by an incursion of numbers.

There was something unusually solemn in the meeting
of parliament on the 6th of December.   It may surprise
men now, and it will surprise men more hereafter, to
remark the tone of awe-struck expectation in which men

of sober mind, of cheerful temper, and even of historical learning—that powerful antidote to temporary alarms—spoke and wrote of the winter of 1831-2. A government proclamation, issued on the 22nd of November, with the aim of putting down political unions, was found to be as ineffectual as such proclamations always are against associations which can change their rules and forms at pleasure. It appeared strange that the ministers should now begin to make war upon the unions, when their policy hitherto had been to let them alone; a policy befitting men able to learn by the experience of their predecessors in the case of the Catholic Association. There was a general feeling of disappointment, as at an inconsistency, when the proclamation appeared. It has since become known that the administration acted under another will than their own in this matter. In December, Lord Eldon had an interview with the Duke of Wellington, of which he wrote: ' I sat with him near an hour, in deep conversation and most interesting. Letters *that he wrote to a great personage* produced the proclamation against the unions. But if parliament will not interfere further, the proclamation will be of little use—I think, of no use.' It was certainly, at present, of no use. The National Union immediately put out its assertion that the proclamation did not apply to it, nor to the great majority of unions then in existence. So there sat the monstrous offspring of this strange time, vigilant, far-spreading, intelligent, and of incalculable force—a power believed in its season to be greater than that of King, Lords, and Commons; there it sat, watching them all, and ready to take up any duty which any one of them let drop, and force it back into the most reluctant hands. A dark demon was, at the same time, brooding over the land. It chills one's heart now to read the cholera proclamations and orders of that year, and the suggestions of boards of health, to which men looked for comfort, but from which they received much alarm. Men were not then able to conceive of a mild plague; and what they had heard of the cholera, carried back their imaginations to the plagues of the middle ages. Among many dismal recommendations from authority, therefore, we find one which it almost made the public ill to read of—that,

when the sick could not be carried to cholera hospitals,
their abodes should be watched and guarded, to prevent
communication; that the word 'SICK' should be conspicuously painted on the front of the dwelling, while there
were patients there, and the word 'CAUTION' for some
weeks afterwards. Men began to think of the nightly
bell and dead-cart, and of grass growing in the streets,
and received with panic the news of the actual appearance
of the disease in various parts of the island at the same
time. In the truthful spirit of history, it must be told
that a large and thoughtful class of society were deeply
moved and impressed at this time by what was taking
place in Edward Irving's chapel and sect. Men and
women were declared to have the gift of unknown tongues;
and the manifestations of the power—whatever in the vast
range of the nervous powers of man it might be—were
truly awe-striking. Some laughed then, as many laugh
now; but it may be doubted whether any thoughtful
person could laugh in face of the facts. We have the
testimony of a man who could never be listened to without
respect—of a man whose heart and mind were not only
naturally cheerful but anchored on a cheerful faith—as to
what was the aspect of that season to such men as himself.
In reply to some question about the Irvingite gift, Dr.
Arnold writes: 'If the thing be real, I should take it merely
as a sign of the coming of the day of the Lord—the only use,
as far as I can make out, that ever was derived from the
gift of tongues. I do not see that it was ever made a
vehicle of instruction, or ever superseded the study of
tongues, but that it was merely a sign of the power of God;
a man being for the time transformed into a mere instrument to utter sounds which he himself understood not
. . . . . However, whether this be a real sign or no, I
believe that "the day of the Lord" is coming—that is,
the termination of one of the great αἰῶνες [ages] of the
human race, whether the final one of all or not: that, I
believe, no created being knows or can know. The termination of the Jewish αἰὼν in the first century, and of
the Roman αἰὼν in the fifth and sixth, were each marked
by the same concurrence of calamities, wars, tumults,
pestilences, earthquakes, &c., all marking the time of one

of God's peculiar seasons of visitation.. . . . . My sense of
the evil of the times, and to what prospects I am bringing
up my children, is overwhelmingly bitter. All the moral
and physical world appears so exactly to announce the
coming of the "great day of the Lord"—that is, a period
of fearful visitation, to terminate the existing state of
things—whether to terminate the whole existence of the
human race, neither man nor angel knows—that no entireness of private happiness can possibly close my mind
against the sense of it.' Thus could the thoughtful—
active in the duties of life—feel at this time; and when
men of business proposed to each other any of the ordinary
enterprises of their calling, they were sure to encounter
looks of surprise, and be asked how anything could be
done while the cholera and the Reform Bill engrossed
men's minds. At the same time, London was overhung
with heavy fogs; and that sense of indisposition was
prevalent—that vague restlessness and depression—which
are observable in the seasons when cholera manifests
itself. When the king went down to the House, to open
the session on the 6th of December, it was observed that
he did not look well; and the topics of the speech—the
disputed bill, the pestilence, the distress, the riots—were
not the most cheerful. It was under such influences as these
that parties came together in parliament, for what all knew
to be the final struggle on the controversy of the time.

On the 12th of December, Lord John Russell moved for
leave to bring in a new Reform Bill. It was to be not
less efficient than the last, and the few alterations made
tended to render it more so. There was now also a new
census—that of the year then closing; so that the census
of 1821, with all the difficulties which hung about it,
might be dismissed. The bill was read a first time. The
debate on the second reading began on Friday the 16th,
and was continued the next evening, concluding early in
the morning of Sunday the 18th, when the majority was
162 in a House of 486. The majority was a very large
one; and ministers might rest on that during the Christmas recess; but the spirit of opposition to reform in
general, and to this bill in particular, was growing more
fierce from day to day.

The House met again on the 17th of January, and on the 20th went into committee on the bill. It is amusing to read the complaints of the anti-reformers about being hurried in committee—as if the provisions of the bill were perfectly new to them. Some changes had been introduced since the long summer nights, of which so many had been spent in the discussion of the measure, and these—due mainly to the use of the new census— were considered with all possible dilatoriness. By no arts of delay, however, could the minority of the committee protract its sittings beyond the 9th of March. The report was considered on the 14th. When, on the 19th, the third reading was moved for, Lord Mahon, seconded by Sir John Malcolm, made the last effort employed in the House of Commons against the bill. He moved that it should be read that day six months; and a debate of three nights ensued—worn out as all now felt the subject to be. Worn out as all felt the subject to be, there was a freshness given to it by the thought that must have been in every considerate mind, that here the people's representatives were ending their preparations for a great new period; that they had done their share, and must now await the doubtful event—the one party expecting revolution if the bill did become law, and the other if it did not. All felt assured that they should not have to discuss a fourth bill, and that the issue now rested finally with the Lords. At such a moment, the words of the leaders are weighed with a strong interest. 'At this, the last stage of the Reform Bill,' said Lord Mahon, ' on the brink of the most momentous decision to which, not only this House, but, I believe, any legislative assembly in any country, ever came—when the real alternative at issue is no longer between reform or no reform, but between a moderate reform on the one hand, and a revolutionary reform on the other—at such a moment, it is with feelings of no ordinary difficulty that I venture to address you.' Lord John Russell's closing declaration, when the last division had yielded a majority of 116, in a House of 594, was this: ' With respect to the expectations of the government, he would say that in proposing this measure they had not acted lightly, but after much consideration, which had induced them to think, a year ago, that a measure of this kind was necessary, if they meant to stand between the abuses which they wished to correct, and the convulsions which they desired to avoid. He was convinced that if parliament should refuse to entertain a measure of this nature, they would place in collision that party which, on the one hand, opposed all reform in the Commons House of parliament, and that which, on the other, desired a reform extending to universal suffrage. The consequence of this would be, that much blood would be shed in the struggle between the contending parties, and he was perfectly persuaded that the British constitution would perish in the conflict. I move, sir, that this bill do pass.' It passed; and then 'the next question, "That this be the title of the bill—A Bill to amend the Representation of the People of England and Wales," was carried by acclamation. Lord John Russell and Lord Althorp were ordered to carry the bill to the Lords, and to request the concurrence of their lordships to the same.'

When they discharged their errand, three days afterwards—on Monday, March 26—they were attended by a large number of members of their own House. The first reading in the Lords took place immediately; and the second, which was to be a period of critical debate, was fixed for the 5th of April, but, for reasons of convenience, did not begin till the 9th. Already, on this first night, there was a defection of waverers from the late majority— several peers intimating their intention of voting the bill into committee; some in hopes that it might be improved there into something good, and others because there was now less danger in passing the bill than in refusing it. This conduct, after the anti-reformers had strained every nerve to bring up before the king's face all the opposition that could be aroused throughout the British islands—Lord Roden having presented at the levée on the 28th of February a petition against reform, signed by 230,000 Irish Protestants — discouraged some members of their lordships' House, and exasperated others; so that the conflict of passions within the House was almost as fierce as between their House and the unions. The Duke of Buckingham did what he could to accommodate matters all round, by promising that, if their lordships would throw out the bill on the second reading, he would himself immediately bring in a Reform Bill, by which representatives should be given to all the large towns, and some consolidation of boroughs be effected. Absurd as was the supposition that the country would give up its own bill for one from the Duke of Buckingham, the incident is worth noting as a proof that the high Conservatives were giving way—were surrendering their main arguments of antiquarian analogy, and becoming eager to avow themselves reformers.

The deepest anxiety that had yet been felt was about the division on the question of the second reading in the Lords. The stanch Tories saw that it was ' too clear,' as Lord Eldon said, that their own party would split on this question, and that then it was to be feared the bill would pass. The reform lords saw that another triumph of their opponents would be the doom of their House; while they were by no means sure that the bill would pass even in case of victory now; for the event would be determined by the waverers, who could not be depended on at the last moment. The debate extended over the nights from the 9th to the 13th of April. It was bright morning on the 14th when the votes were taken. The lights had grown yellower and dimmer in the fresh daylight, the faces of the wearied legislators had appeared more and more haggard and heated; and at last, the slanting rays of the morning sun shone full in upon the woolsack, as the keen eyes of the chancellor shot their glances, as wakeful as ever, from under the great wig. The attendance of strangers was as full as it had been twelve hours before; for it was not a scene which men would miss for the sake of food and sleep. It was a quarter past seven on Friday morning, when the House adjourned, after yielding a majority of nine to the administration.

In a few hours, lists were handed about which showed how the minority of forty-one of six months before had been changed into a majority of nine. Seventeen peers had turned round. Twelve who had been absent before, now voted for the bill; and ten who had voted against it before, now absented themselves. Among the twelve were the Archbishop of York, and the Bishops of London, St. David's, Worcester, and Chester. Among the ten was the Bishop of Peterborough. It was the bishops who saved the bill this time; but their deed did not restore the credit their order had lost in October.

The Easter recess, which postponed the meeting of the Houses till the 7th of May, now afforded time for the people to apply that 'pressure from without' which might be necessary to prevent the waverers from spoiling the bill in committee. This 'pressure from without' was spoken of by the peers with an abhorrence and contempt in which it is impossible for any one who appreciates their function not to sympathise. But they had brought it upon themselves; and now they must bear it. The Birmingham Political Union met on the 27th of April, and invited all the unions of the counties of Warwick, Worcester, and Stafford, to congregate at Newhall Hill in Birmingham, on the day of the re-assembling of parliament. Monster meetings were held in all the large towns, and monster petitions sent to the king to yield to the necessity for creating more peers. The Edinburgh meeting, 60,000 strong, was held before the windows of Charles X. at Holyrood; and there he saw the spectacle of an orderly assemblage met to express their concord with their sovereign, and their determination to aid him in obtaining for them the rights to which he was able to see that time had given birth. The cheering of that multitude for 'King William, the father of his country,' must have gone to the exile's heart. The petitions to the king and the Lords from Liverpool, Manchester, Sheffield, Edinburgh, Glasgow, Paisley, Dundee, and indeed from every populous place in the land, were in exactly the same strain, and nearly in the same words. That from Birmingham implored the peers 'not to drive to despair a high-minded, generous, and fearless people, or to urge them on, by a rejection of their claims, to demands of a much more extensive nature, but rather to pass the Reform Bill into a law, unimpaired in any of its great parts and provisions.' The National Union, on the 3rd of May, spoke out plainly enough. Its petition informed the Lords, that if they denied or impaired the bill, 'there was reason to expect that the payment of taxes would cease, that other obligations of society would be disregarded, and that the ultimate consequence might be the utter extinction of the privileged orders.'   Among the serious and solemn petitions which it is a duty to place upon record, there was a fable put forth which should stand beside them, as having done as much for the great cause as any or all of them.   It has passed into a proverb; but its original delivery should be registered, for the benefit of a far future.   At a meeting at Taunton, a clergyman, who felt himself equally at home and free to speak the truth among peers and cottagers, after declaring in regard to the bishops that he 'could not but blush to have seen so many dignitaries of the Church arrayed against the wishes and happiness of the people,' went on to say: 'As for the possibility of the House of Lords preventing ere long a reform of parliament, I hold it to be the most absurd notion that ever entered into human imagination.   I do not mean to be disrespectful, but the attempt of the Lords to stop the progress of reform reminds me very forcibly of the great storm of Sidmouth, and of the conduct of the excellent Mrs. Partington on that occasion.   In the winter of 1824, there set in a great flood upon that town; the tide rose to an incredible height; the waves rushed in upon the houses, and everything was threatened with destruction.   In the midst of this sublime and terrible storm, Dame Partington, who lived upon the beach, was seen at the door of her house with mop and pattens, trundling her mop, squeezing out the sea-water, and vigorously pushing away the Atlantic Ocean.   The Atlantic was roused.   Mrs. Partington's spirit was up; but I need not tell you that the contest was unequal.   The Atlantic Ocean beat Mrs. Partington.   She was excellent at a slop or a puddle, but she should not have meddled with a tempest.   Gentlemen, be at your ease; be quiet and steady.   You will beat Mrs. Partington.'

The congregation of the unions at Birmingham on the 7th of May composed the largest meeting believed to have been ever held in Great Britain.   The numbers did not fall short of 150,000.   The hustings were erected at the bottom of the slope of Newhall Hill, in a position so favourable that the voices of most of the speakers reached

to the outskirts of the great assemblage, and to the throngs
on the roofs of the surrounding houses. The unions poured
in upon the ground in one wide unbroken stream, till the
gazers were almost ready to ask one another whether this
was not a convention of the nation itself. At the sound of
the bugle from the hustings, silence was instantly produced; and Mr. Attwood, the chairman, announced to
the assemblage the object of the meeting—to avow the
unabated interest and resolute will of the people in the
cause of reform, and their determination to support their
excellent king and his patriotic ministers in carrying forward their great measure into law. While the chairman
was speaking, the Bromsgrove Union, which arrived late,
was seen approaching from afar. Their assembled brethren
greeted them with the union hymn—deserving of record
from being then familiar to every child in the land. It
never was so sung before, nor after; for now, a hundred
thousand voices pealed it forth in music which has never
died away in the hearts of those who heard it. Seventy-
four members of the Society of Friends—men of education,
who had just joined the union on principle—might now
know something of the power of music. A different order
of men, who could not be on the ground—some soldiers of
the Scots Greys who had quietly joined the union—must
have listened from within their barracks with a longing to
be on the hill. The Duke of Wellington was reckoning
on their services to finish the business, after all; but the
hymn seems to tell that the warlike intentions were
wholly on one side.

UNION HYMN.

' Lo ! we answer ! see, we come,
   Quick at Freedom's holy call.
We come ! we come ! we come ! we come !
   To do the glorious work of all ;
And hark ! we raise from sea to sea
The sacred watchword, Liberty !

God is our guide ! from field, from wave,
   From plough, from anvil, and from loom,
We come, our country's rights to save,
   And speak a tyrant faction's doom.
And hark ! we raise from sea to sea
The sacred watchword, Liberty !

God is our guide! no swords we draw,
    We kindle not war's battle fires;
By union, justice, reason, law,
    We claim the birthright of our sires.
We raise the watchword, Liberty!
We will, we will, we will be free!'

Spirit-stirring as this was, a more solemn manifestation followed: the plighting of their faith by these hundred thousand earnest men. 'Here,' said one of the speakers, Mr. Salt, 'I call upon you to repeat, with head uncovered, and in the face of heaven and the God of justice and mercy, the following words after me.' Every man bared his head, and, with the true Anglo-Saxon spirit swelling at his heart, uttered slowly, one by one, as they were given forth, these words: ' With unbroken faith, through every peril and privation, we here devote ourselves and our children to our country's cause.'

On this same 7th of May, the Duke of Wellington was beginning to see how the hope of such multitudes as this was likely to be foiled, and relying confidently on the Scots Greys in their barracks for putting down this particular multitude, if it should prove troublesome. Mrs. Partington was going to her cupboard, to bring out her mop. On this same 7th of May, the Lords, on reassembling after Easter, went immediately into committee on the bill; and, as their first act, overthrew the administration. Before the echoes of the hymn had well died away at Birmingham, before the tears were well dried which the plighting of the faith had brought upon many cheeks, the Lords in London had decided, by a majority of thirty-five against ministers, and on the motion of Lord Lyndhurst, to postpone the disfranchising clauses, going first to the consideration of the new franchises. When Lord Grey moved to have the business stand over till the 10th, he was taunted with a desire to delay the bill. Lord Ellenborough 'could assure the noble earl and their lordships that, from the side of the House on which he sat, there was no wish whatever to interpose any delay to the adjustment of the measure.' He went on to intimate that he was ready to proceed with a very large measure of reform. As, however, he had given no notice of any reforming intentions, and as the ministers found themselves in a minority of thirty-five on the very first clause, Lord Grey persisted in asking for and obtaining an interval of three days.

Within those three days it became know that the division on the Monday night, the 7th, was the result of an intrigue which had been going on for many months. The king's personal intercourses had been throughout with some of the highest Conservatives in the country, rather than with his ministers and their connections. He was old, and very dependent on the ladies of his family; he was no statesman; and he had no knowledge of the mind and condition of the people, except through those who surrounded him. His wife, some of his daughters (the children of Mrs. Jordan), and his sisters, were opposed to the new measure, and were kept in constant alarm by their Conservative friends; and they fed the king's mind with apprehensions which unfitted him for the discharge of his duty towards his ministers and his people. Lord Wharncliffe, as representative of the anti-reforming lords, had engaged to Lord Grey, at the beginning of the winter, that the bill should be carried through the second reading if no new peers were made; and accordingly the king was not asked to create peers. That the whole business was to be overthrown in committee, and when, was certainly known in Edinburgh beforehand, when the ministers themselves were in the dark as to what was likely to happen. Orders had also been issued from the Horse Guards for all the officers on furlough to join their regiments before this critical week; and every preparation that could be made by the Duke of Wellington for putting down risings of the people was made. During this week, orders were sent down to the barracks at Birmingham that the Scots Greys should be daily and nightly booted and saddled, with ball-cartridge ready for use at a moment's notice. The Conservatives were determined that there should be a revolution rather than that the Reform Bill should pass.

The people were, however, too strong and too determined to render a revolution necessary. They were indignant on behalf of the ill-used ministers; indignant at the weakness of the king; indignant at the meddling of the royal ladies; and in the last degree indignant at the intrigues of the Tory leaders: but they knew their strength to be so great that they had only to put it forth peaceably to subdue the adverse faction by a manifestation of will, instead of by force of arms. A nobler scene was never enacted by any nation than that of the nine days' waiting while the country was without a government.

On the morning of Tuesday, the 8th, a cabinet council was held, when it was determined to request from the king a creation of peers sufficient to carry the bill. The two highest officers of the realm, the prime-minister and the lord chancellor, went to Windsor, to make this request. As none of the three persons present were likely to report what passed in this interview, it cannot be spoken of with any certainty; but a morning paper which professed to have information, declared that the king wept, and lamented that he must sacrifice his ministers to his wife, his sisters, and his children. The ministers tendered their resignations. On Wednesday morning, a special messenger brought a letter from the king, accepting the resignations of the cabinet. The king came to town the same morning, to hold a levée; and he then formally received the resignations of the whole administration, with those of their friends in the royal household. The Whigs made a complete clearance, leaving not a single official, of any rank, about the king. They had done with the business; and they left a clear field for the anti-reformers. The Duke of Wellington afterwards spoke of his fruitless enterprise of the next nine days as an act of gallant devotedness, in which he was willing to sacrifice himself rather than desert his sovereign in an hour of perplexity and distress. It might be so; and the duke might easily be too much feared, and too much respected, by the intriguers, to be invited to their counsels; but the blame of the royal perplexity and distress should rest where it is due. It was not the king who was deceived and deserted, but his ministers. The honour and fidelity were all on their side; and if the Duke of Wellington went in to the rescue, it was on the appeal of a sovereign who had weakly deserted his faithful advisers and servants, and given himself into the hands of persons no less weak, who had brought him

into a difficulty from which they could not rescue him. If
he had refused to aid his sovereign, the duke said he
'should have been ashamed to show his face in the streets.'
He endeavoured rather 'to assist the king in the distressing circumstances in which he was placed;' meaning,
however, by these 'distressing circumstances,' the advice
of Lord Grey to create peers, and not the position of
humiliation, in regard to Lord Grey, in which a clique of
helpless advisers had placed the sovereign.   On the Wednesday evening, the ministers announced to the two
Houses their relinquishment of the government of the
country; and on the Thursday, the Commons, on the
motion of Lord Ebrington, addressed the king, deploring
the retirement of the late administration, and imploring his
majesty to take none for his advisers who would not carry
the reform measure unimpaired, and without delay.   It
was on this occasion that Mr. Baring declared himself
'entirely ignorant of the cause which had led to the extraordinary resignation;' a statement which first occasioned
loud laughter, and then called up Lord Althorp to make
an explanation, which was listened to in breathless silence,
as he spoke with the calmest deliberation and the strongest
emphasis.   The moment he had uttered the words, there
was 'a burst of cheering, by far the most enthusiastic,
universal, and long continued, ever witnessed within the
walls of parliament.'   Lord Althorp's words were, 'I have
no objection to state—that the advice which we thought
it our duty to offer to his majesty was, that he should
create a number of peers sufficient to enable us to carry
the Reform Bill through the other House of parliament in
an efficient form.'   The same advice was now tendered to
the king by the Commons in the address passed this
night; and he did not feel himself at liberty to neglect it,
even while placing himself in the hands of anti-reformers.
'His majesty insisted,' declared the Duke of Wellington,
a week later, 'that some extensive measure of reform—I
use his majesty's own words—should be carried.'   But the
duke was opposed to all parliamentary reform.   What was
to be done?   The duke proposed a compromise.   He proposed to set aside the question of an 'unconstitutional'
creation of peers by granting a measure of reform 'mode-

rate' enough to be passed by the Lords. He could not himself take office in any administration which would undertake even this; but he would rescue the sovereign from his difficulties by making up a cabinet for him— taking measures meantime for the safety of the country. Such was the extraordinary task which the great soldier undertook with the idea of serving his king and country; and very hard he worked to fulfil his duty. For five days he went about from door to door among his Tory friends; but from first to last, in vain. He had Lord Lyndhurst, the active spirit of the whole transaction, to help him; but there was no anti-reformer except Lord Lyndhurst who could be found to undertake to carry 'a large measure of reform;' and on the 15th, the duke was compelled to announce to the king that all his attempted negotiations had failed.

During this interval, the nation was as busy as the duke. As the news of the division on the night of the 7th spread through the country, men found themselves unable to give their minds to their affairs till the suspense should be relieved. The mail roads were sprinkled over for miles with people who were on the watch for news from London; and the passengers on the tops of the coaches shouted the tidings, or threw down handbills to tell that the ministry had resigned. Then was there such mourning throughout England as had not been known for many years. Men forsook their business to meet and consult what they should do. In some places, the bells tolled; in others, they were muffled. In many towns, black crape was hung over the signs of the king's head; and there was talk of busts of Queen Adelaide being seen with a halter round the neck. These vain shows, however, did not suit the temper of earnest and efficient reformers, who did something better than mourn and threaten. While they went to their serious work, there was much for the mere observer to note and remember: the full streets—for everybody was abroad, from a desire for news, and because it was difficult to sit still at home; the wistful faces of little children, who saw that something fearful was going on, but could not understand what; and, above all, the close watching of the soldiery, wherever there were barracks; for the prevalent expectation now was, from the intimacy between the Duke of Wellington and the king, that a military control was to be attempted. It has since become certain that there were just grounds for this apprehension.

The political unions met early and continually. The National Union declared itself in permanent session; 1500 new members—all men of substance—entered it in one day. Its watchword was: 'Peace, Order, Obedience to the Law.' It passed a resolution 'That whoever advises a dissolution of parliament is a public enemy.' As soon as the news reached Manchester, a petition to the House of Commons was prepared, praying the House to grant no supply till the bill was passed unimpaired: and this petition had received in four hours the signatures of 25,000 persons, and was despatched to London in the hands of three eminent citizens. This petition was the first of a large number which, within a few days, urged the same demand upon the House. The Bolton petition was signed by 20,300 within two or three hours. After reading the Manchester petition to the House, Mr. John Wood, who presented it, declared: 'The whole of the north of England, the deputation from Manchester informed him, was in a state which it was impossible to describe. Dismay, and, above all, indignation, prevailed everywhere. He believed, however, if the House did its duty, that the country might yet be saved; if it would not, he believed the people knew their duty; and if the House would not stop the supplies, the chancellor of the exchequer, whoever he might be, would very soon find that his coffers were unreplenished. Whether such a line of conduct might be right or wrong it was not for him to argue then; but it was his duty as a reformer to state his firm conviction, that if a borough-mongering faction should prevail, the people would take the most effectual mode of stopping the supplies, by telling the tax-collector to call upon them when the Reform Bill had passed into a law.' So much of this kind of statement was offered in the House, the petitions against votes of supply were presented and received with such hearty concurrence, that it became a question everywhere what the Duke of Wellington and Lord Lyndhurst could possibly propose to do with the House of Commons. The present House would certainly never yield up the reform measure; and if, as was reported and believed, the present parliament was to be immediately dissolved, there could be no doubt that the people would return an overwhelming majority of reform members in the new elections.

The Common Council of the city of London were among the petitioners to parliament to refuse the supplies: they declared that all concerned in stopping the passage of the Reform Bill were enemies to their country; and they appointed a permanent committee, to sit from day to day, till the measure should be secured. The Livery of London, assembled in Common Hall, adopted exactly the same course. There can be no doubt that both bodies held themselves ready to communicate and co-operate with the political unions which were expected to march up to London, in case of a prolongation of the struggle. Some of the smaller unions discussed plans of marching peaceably to the metropolis, and bivouacking in the squares—there to wait till the Reform Bill should become law. The great Birmingham Union, now 200,000 strong, was to encamp on Hampstead Heath, or perhaps Penenden Heath, in order to incorporate with it bodies coming from the south. On the movements of this Birmingham Union, which had so lately uttered its sublime vow under the open sky, all eyes were now turned; and there is reason to believe that, what passed at Birmingham immediately determined the issue of this mighty contention.

Declarations began to appear in the Tory newspapers that all reports of the disaffection of the Scots Greys at Birmingham were mere fabrications of the reformers; and that it was a gross and scandalous falsehood that the Duke of Wellington could not rely upon the soldiery. These declarations immediately showed men that such things had been said, and that the reports were considered of importance; and most people believed that they were true. Revelations have since been made which show that there was much truth in them. There had been talk of 'cold iron' on the Tory side, for some days; and the Duke of Wellington had been understood to stand pledged, since the 9th, 'to quiet the country in ten days;' and an

attempt at military government for the time was almost
universally looked for. What the duke's intentions were
precisely is not known, and perhaps it will never be
known ; but circumstances have been revealed which
show that his reliance at first was more or less on the
soldiery ; and that he was informed of the vain nature of
his reliance immediately before he gave up his enterprise.
The earliest hours of his negotiation were employed in
sending out feelers of the disposition of the new police ;
and Colonel Rowan's report was unsatisfactory. From
two of the divisions the answer was, that if it was intended
for the police to act against the people, they could not be
relied on. There were some among the soldiery who reported of themselves to the same effect with the least
possible delay, not even waiting to be questioned ; and
from a passage in a speech of a relative of the Duke of
Wellington's on the 16th, it appears that the disinclination
to oppose the people was concluded to be prevalent in the
army. In the last preceding struggle, in October, the
Duke of Wellington had said to Mr. Potter of Manchester,
who represented the determination of the working-classes
to have reform : ' The people of England are very quiet if
they are left alone ; and if they won't, there is a way to
make them.' In the opinion of his relative, Mr. Wellesley,
member for Essex, he was now, on the 16th of May, finding
himself mistaken. Mr. Wellesley ' was sorry he had shown
so much ignorance of the character of the British people,
in supposing that they were not fit to be trusted with those
liberties to which we, as reformers, say they are worthily
entitled. He had told him so often ; and he was astonished
that a man of such intelligent mind—a man who had led
them on through blood and battle, through danger to
victory—should have so mistaken the character of the
British people, as to suppose that the red coat could change
the character of the man, or to imagine that the soldier
was not a citizen.' Some of the yeomanry corps resigned
during the critical interval ; that of Ware being in such
haste to declare themselves on the side of the people, that
they assembled immediately on hearing of the retirement
of the Whig ministry, and informed the Marquis of Salis-
bury of their resignations by sending them at midnight

to Hatfield House. Of all the forces in the kingdom, the soldiery at Birmingham fixed the most attention, because Birmingham was the foremost place in public observation; because the duke must be able to rely on the soldiery stationed there at such a time, if on any; and because of the reports afloat that the Scots Greys would refuse to act against the people, if called upon.

The officers of the Birmingham Union knew that certain of the Scots Greys were on the union books. Letters were found in the streets of the town, which declared in temperate language that the Greys would do their duty if called on to repress riot, or any kind of outrage, but that they would not act if called on to put down a peaceable public meeting, or to hinder the conveyance to London of any petition, by any number of peaceable persons. Some of these letters contained the strongest entreaties to the people of Birmingham to keep the peace, that they might not compel their sympathising friends among the Greys to act against them. Letters containing similar avowals were sent to the king, to the Duke of Wellington, and to Lord Hill at the war-office. We know this on the testimony of a private of the regiment, who avows himself a party in these proceedings, and who gives us the following clear and impressive account of his own view of the position in which he and his comrades stood; a view which he knew to be shared by many of his comrades, and which he took care should be well understood by the Duke of Wellington: 'The duty of soldiers to protect property and suppress riots expressed then were the opinions which I have since expressed. To write, or say, or think, that in any case we were not to do what we were ordered was a grave offence, nothing short of mutiny. I was aware of that grave fact. I remonstrated with the soldiers who had joined the political union, and succeeded in persuading them to recall their adhesion to it. With the same regard to my own safety, I never went near the political union. Had the time and the circumstances come for us to act according to our design and judgment, and not according to orders, it would have been an occasion great enough to risk all that we were risking. It would have been a national necessity. We would have either

been shot dead, or triumphant with a nation's thanks upon
our heads. For either alternative we were prepared.'
This state of preparation being made known at headquarters on the one hand, and by the whole people of
Birmingham and the midland counties through the newspapers on the other, all plans of military coercion in that
neighbourhood were clearly frustrated.

The first probation of these soldiers was on the Sunday
after the Newhall Hill meeting. At all times hitherto,
the barrack-yard had been the resort of people who liked
' to see the Greys;' and on the preceding Sunday, 'there
were upwards of 5000 people within the gates, most of
them well-dressed artisans, all wearing ribbons of light
blue knotted in their breasts, indicating that they were
members of the political union.' On the next Sunday, the
scene was different indeed. The gates were closed; the
soldiers were marched to prayers in the forenoon, and their
occupation for the rest of the day was rough-sharpening
their swords on the grindstone. This was at the time
that they were kept supplied with ball-cartridge, and
booted and saddled day and night. They were kept so
close within their walls at present, that they did not
know with any precision what was going forward; but
their impression was—and the impression soon became a
rumour—that the Birmingham Union was to march for
London that night, and that the Greys were to bar its
progress. The doubt and dread were not lessened by the
nature of their work. The purpose of rough-sharpening
the swords ' was to make them inflict a ragged wound.
Not since before the battle of Waterloo had the swords of
the Greys undergone the same process. Old soldiers
spoke of it and told the young ones. Few words were
spoken. We had made more noise, and probably looked
less solemn, at prayers in the morning, than we did now
grinding our swords. It was the Lord's day, and we
were *working*.'

The union did not start for London that night. It had
to hold a meeting the next day. There were then 200,000
persons present. They resolved to pay no taxes till the
bill was passed; and they carried a declaration of un-
appeasable opposition to the faction which had misled the

king, and of reasons why the nation should demand the
removal of the Duke of Wellington from the royal counsels.
This declaration was to have been signed, after legal
revision, by all the unionists in the kingdom; but it was
not wanted, any more than the jagged swords of the
Greys. The Birmingham Union met again on the Wednesday for purposes of thanksgiving.

The debating of the newspapers, and of all assemblages
of people, in public and private, as to whether it was or was
not true that the army was not to be relied on, was fatal to
all reliance on the army, and would have been, if every
soldier in the kingdom had been precisely of the duke's
way of thinking. It must have been an extreme surprise
to the great Captain to find already that if the people
would not be quiet, there was *not* a way to make them so
against their will. So it proved, however; and the end of
it was that if the duke would not be quiet, the people had
found a way to make him so. On the second day after
the grinding of swords—on Tuesday, the 15th—Lords
Grey and Althorp intimated to the two Houses the joyful
news that communications were renewed between the
sovereign and themselves which rendered it expedient to
adjourn till Thursday. The words were scarcely uttered,
before there was a rush from the Houses, to spread the
tidings. There was no electric telegraph then; but the
news flew as by electric agency. By breakfast-time the
next morning, placards were up in the streets of Birmingham; and presently the people thronged to Newhall
Hill, after bringing Mr. Attwood into the town. As by
an impulse of the moment, a minister present was asked
to offer thanksgiving; and that prayer, that devout expression of gratitude for their bloodless victory, and their
privileges as exulting freemen, was felt by the throng to
be a fitting sequel to their last week's solemn vow.

It must be some days before the facts could become
perfectly known, or the future certainly anticipated; but
men felt secure enough of the result to begin to return to
their business. There had been a run on the Bank of
England to the extent of above £1,000,000 in small sums.
Now, this began to flow back again; the weaver stepped
into his loom; the blacksmith blew up the fire of his

forge; the husbandmen parted off into the fields; and the merchants of London ceased to crowd the footways of Lombard Street all day long.

In forty-eight hours more there was a rumour in London that by some means unknown the peers had been induced to yield. What the conjuration was which brought about such a marvel was not understood at present; except that some unusual exertion of his personal influence had been made by the king. That the good-behaviour of the peers was not absolutely assured, seemed to be shown by the care with which Lord Grey and his colleagues evaded the question whether they had received any pledge about a creation of peers. By acute observers it was supposed that some method of warning or persuasion had been used by the king; and that he held himself ready, in case of its failure, to create peers to the extent necessary for carrying the bill. This proved to be the truth. The first expedient was successful; and it is entertaining now to see, on looking back to that date, how credit is taken by the Lords who now yielded to this final appeal, for having 'saved the peerage, with what else was left of the constitution.' The final appeal to the Lords—the last practical acknowledgment of their free-will—was in the form of the following circular-letter, dated from St. James's Palace, May 17, 1832:

'MY DEAR LORD—I am honoured with his majesty's commands to acquaint your lordship that all difficulties to the arrangements in progress will be obviated by a declaration in the House to-night, from a sufficient number of peers, that, in consequence of the present state of affairs, they have come to the resolution of dropping their further opposition to the Reform Bill; so that it may pass without delay, and as nearly as possible in its present shape. I have the honour, &c.

HERBERT TAYLOR.'

This, which was called the king's letter to the waverers, removed all difficulties. It was dated on the Thursday; and on that night the Duke of Wellington made his explanation of the transactions of the preceding week, retiring from the House when he had finished, and absenting himself during all the remaining discussions of the Reform Bill. About 100 peers went out with him, and absented themselves in like manner. On the next Monday, the 21st, the peers resumed the discussion of the bill in committee, the Duke of Newcastle protesting against their assuming such an appearance of free-will as this, and desiring that they would read through the whole bill at once, and pass it as quickly as possible—as men acting under open compulsion. The first division took place the next night, on the question of the separate representation of the Tower Hamlets, when the anti-reformers exhibited their largest minority—36 to 91. But this disheartened them; and on the next night only 15 were present. On Thursday, the 24th, 23 were present. On Wednesday, the 30th, the disfranchising sections of the bill were gone through—the tenderest points where all was painful. These sections were read through with little discussion, and no real opposition; and on the same night the committee finished its business. On the 1st of June the report was received, eighteen peers recording their dissent in a protest. On the 4th, Lord Grey was ill; but he went down to the House to move the third reading of his bill. Unfit for exertion as he was, he was called up by an attack on the administration from Lord Harrowby. When he sat down, it was suddenly, from inability to stand and speak; but his last words on parliamentary reform, though not designed to be the last, were a fitting close to the testimony of his whole political life: 'He trusted that those who augured unfavourably of the bill would live to see all their ominous forebodings falsified, and that, after the angry feelings of the day had passed away, the measure would be found to be, in the best sense of the word, conservative of the constitution.' The majority were 106, the minority 22. The question, 'That the bill do pass,' was put and carried; and then a great number of congratulating peers gathered about the venerable minister, who had so majestically conducted to fruition a measure which he had advocated before many of the existing generation of legislators were born, and through long years of discouragement, which ordinary men would have taken for hopelessness. The Commons next day agreed to the few amendments proposed by the Lords, which left untouched the disfranchising and enfranchising clauses; and on Thursday, June 7, the Reform Bill became law, the royal assent being given by a commission, consisting of the lord chancellor, the Marquises of Lansdowne and Wellesley, and Lords Grey, Holland, and Durham.

It is not be supposed that when Lord Grey received the congratulations of his friends, there was no melancholy mingled with his satisfaction, or that he had no sympathy with the stoutest of his opponents. The provocation caused by the long resistance of the peers to a necessary change, might naturally blind the people at large to a portion of their case, and might urge the most lordly of the ministers themselves into a state of popular feeling at which they might afterwards stand surprised. But Lord Grey was too much of a man, too much of a scholar, too much of a peer, not to feel and remember, that by the passage of this act, the ancient glory of the House of his order was declared to have departed. The change could not be prevented. It was rendered so imperative by time, that the course of wisdom was clear—to acquiesce in the change, and to obtain the utmost possible good out of the attendant circumstances. But, however anxious to put an end to the abuses of borough corruption, and the interference of peers with popular representation, such a man as Lord Grey could not but remember the ancient days when the lords of the realm were the parliament of the realm—when there was no middle class, and the peers were the protectors of such popular interests as existed then: he could not but remember the majesty of his House during the centuries when the popular element was advancing and expanding; and though that House had of late fallen from its dignity—become adulterated in its quality, and disgraced by too much of ignorance and sordidness in its self-will and its claims—it still was the British House of Peers which was now overborne and humbled, and made conscious that it existed no longer as a vital part of the English constitution, but for the sake of decorum and expediency. It was natural for the people—

the large majority of whom contemplate the present and the future in all their interests—to enjoy the signal proof now given of the continuous rise and expansion of the popular element in the nation; but the most that could be expected from Lord Grey was to perceive and provide for the fact in the noblest and the amplest manner. His associations were too much concerned with the past to admit of his rejoicing with an unmingled joy. Many of us who rejoiced without drawback at the time, and held the strongest opinions of the folly and selfishness of the Tory peers, can now see that they really were much to be pitied; that it was true that 'the balance of the constitution was destroyed;' and that the change was something audacious and unheard of. In as far as these things were true, the Conservative peers had a claim to the sympathy of all thoughtful persons in their regrets. Their fault and folly lay—that fault and folly which deprived them of popular sympathy—in supposing that the operations of time could be resisted, and their own position maintained, by a mere refusal to give way. They lost more than they need have done by a foolish and ungracious resistance, which served but to complete and to proclaim their humiliation. It is a fact not to be denied, that, as the kingly power had before descended to a seat lower than that of parliament, the House of Peers now took rank in the government below the Commons. It will ever stand in history that the House of Commons became the true governing power in Great Britain in 1832, and that from that date the other powers existed, not by their own strength, but by a general agreement founded on considerations as well of broad utility, as of decorum and ancient affection. In as far as the House of Peers was now proved to be destined henceforward—as the royal function had for some time been—to exist only by consent of the people at large, it might be truly said that the constitution was destroyed; and the prime-minister who had conducted the process could not be insensible, even in the moment of his triumph, to the seriousness and antiquarian melancholy of the fact, however convinced he might be of the historical glories which were to arise out of it.

By the Reform Bill, as passed, the representative system of the British Islands became this ·

In England, the county constituencies, which had before been fifty-two, returning ninety-four members, were now increased by the division of counties to eighty-two constituencies, returning 159 members. In Ireland there was no change. In Scotland, the number of constituencies and members remained as before, but some shifting took place to secure a more equitable representation. The great increase in the county representation is the chief of those features which would soon cause the measure to be called—as Lords Grey and Althorp predicted—'the most aristocratic measure that ever passed the House of Commons.'

All boroughs whose population was, according to the census of 1831, under 2000, were disfranchised. Fifty-six English boroughs, which before returned 111 members, were thus extinguished as constituencies. Such boroughs as had a population under 4000, and had hitherto returned two representatives, were now to have one. These being thirty in number, thirty members were thus reduced. The united boroughs of Weymouth and Melcombe Regis were now to send two members instead of four; and thus was the total reduction of 143 old borough members provided for.

As the total number of representatives was not to be altered, as decided by the House of Commons, the 143 were to be distributed over new or newly arranged constituencies. New and large constituencies in England and Wales received 63. The metropolitan districts and other boroughs with a population of 25,000 and upwards, were now to return two members each; and these took up 22 more. The remaining 21 were to be returned by 21 boroughs whose population amounted to 12,000 and upwards. In Ireland, the increase of the representation was only from 35 to 39 members; with an additional member given to Dublin University. In Scotland, there was much redistribution of the franchise, and change in the formation of constituencies; and the number of town representatives was raised from 15 to 23.

There was much changing of boundaries where a population had grown up outside the old limits, and fixing of limits to the boroughs which had a large new population.

Improvements were made in the practice of issuing writs for new elections, and in the conduct of elections, by the ordaining of convenient polling districts, and the shortening of the time of polling in contested elections. The term of fifteen polling days in county elections was shortened to two in England, Wales, and Scotland, and five in Ireland; and instead of the old process of scrutiny, which occasioned endless delays and vexations, there was to be henceforward only a comparison of the voter's statement as to name and qualification with his description in the register.

In the great matter of the qualification of voters, it was thought impossible to avoid compromise; and some provisions therefore exist which everybody understands must be got rid of sooner or later. The old 'freemen' were permitted to remain among the qualified, the condition of residence being imposed, and all being excluded who had been made freemen since March 1831; the fact being notorious that a multitude of such voters had been created by the corporations, for the sake of defeating the reform measure. The new borough franchise rested on the basis of inhabitancy. Inhabitants of abodes—whose various kinds are specified—of the yearly value of £10, become electors, provided they comply with all conditions of registration, payment of rates and taxes, and length of residence. The privileges of out-voters were abolished entirely, the elector being able to vote only in the place where he resides, or where he has property in land or houses of the required amount. In Ireland, great changes were occasioned by this fixing of the franchise, as the corporations there had been excessively corrupt in the use of the large powers, of which they were now deprived. In Scotland, the franchise was at once, and for the first time, put into the hands of the true constituency, while the town-councils were deprived of the powers which they had grossly abused.

As for the county franchise, it was extended by admitting copyholders and leaseholders, and even, under some circumstances, occupiers, to the franchise which was before confined to freeholders, to the value of 40s.; while freeholders were prevented from voting in both county and borough elections. The most unfortunate part of the bill was that clause proposed by the Marquis of Chandos, by which tenants-at-will in the counties, occupying at a yearly value of £50, have the franchise. By this provision, the power of the great landed proprietors over their tenantry is perpetuated; and hence arises a greater frustration of the purposes of the act than from all other errors and faults together. The county franchise in Ireland was so resettled in 1829 as to be little affected by the present act, such alteration as there was being the admission of certain copyholders, leaseholders, and occupiers. By the new arrangements, the county constituency in Scotland was much enlarged.

As for the qualification of the representative, disabilities on account of profession—as the clerical—and the holding of modern offices under the crown, and of situations of government emolument, remained much as before. Disabilities on account of religious opinion had been already almost entirely abrogated. The qualification for an English, Welsh, and Irish member remained as before in regard to property—namely, a clear estate of £600 a year for a county seat, and of £300 a year for a city or borough seat. The property qualifications were not extended to Scotland at the time of the union; nor were they by the new act. A qualification was formerly required for a Scottish elector which is not necessary for a Scottish representative now.

Such was the Reform Act of 1832, by which the landed interests were brought down some little way from a supremacy which had once been natural and just, but which had now become insufferably tyrannical and corrupt. As the manufacturing and commercial classes had long been rising in numbers, property, and enlightenment, it was time for them to be obtaining a proportionate influence in the government. By this act they did not obtain their due influence; but they gained much, and the way was cleared for more. Great as was the gain thus far, there was a yet mightier benefit in the proof that the will of the people, when sufficiently intelligent and united, could avail to modify the government through the forces of reason and resolution, without violence. This point ascertained, and the benefit secured, all subsided into quiet. Trade and manufactures began immediately to prosper; credit was firm, and the majority of the nation were in high hope of what might be expected from a government which had begun its reforms so nobly, and promised many more. There were some, and not a very few, who declared that the sun of England had set for ever; but yet nobody could see that it was growing dark. Men in general thought that if they had ever walked in broad daylight, it was now.

The king was presently pitied and pardoned as an old man, called late to the throne—more amiable than enlightened, and entangled between public duty and private affections which had been brought by the fault of others into contrariety; but, as was fitting, he never recovered his original popularity. When the Reform Bill was once secure, men no more carried a black flag, with the inscription, 'Put not your trust in princes;' nor a crown stuffed with straw, with the inscription, 'Ichabod;' but neither did they rend the clouds again with cheers for their 'King William, the father of his country.' There was no longer anything to fear from him; but men saw that neither was there anything to hope from him; and he was henceforth treated with a mere decorum, which had in it full as much of compassion as of respect.

As for his ministers, they were idols, aloft in a shrine.

CHAPTER VI.

The Cholera—The Poor-law—Swan River Settlement—Slavery—Canada—India—Irish Church—Tithes—Law Reform—Education—Bank—Municipal Reform—Strength of the Government—Weakness of the Government.

WHILE the Reform Bill was in progress and in jeopardy, little else was thought of; except, indeed, the new plague which had come to overcloud all hearts, and to attract to itself some of the terror which would otherwise have been given entire to the apprehension of coming revolution.

There were many in those days who would have been intensely grateful to know, first, that the cholera would have departed by a certain day, leaving them and their families in safety; and next, that revolution—by which they understood the overthrow of the whole social fabric —would not happen in their lifetime. If they could have been assured of these two immunities, they would have been quite happy, would have believed their way was clear for life, and that affairs would remain in their existing state as long as their own generation had any concern with them. Very different from this view was that taken by braver spirits, with that truer vision given by courage and enlightenment. 'The truth is,' wrote Dr. Arnold in April 1831, 'that we are arrived at one of those periods in the progress of society when the constitution naturally undergoes a change, just as it did two centuries ago. It was impossible then for the king to keep down the higher part of the middle classes; it is impossible now to keep down the middle and lower parts of them. . . . . One would think that people who talk against change were literally as well as metaphorically blind, and really did not see that everything in themselves and around them is changing every hour by the necessary laws of its being.' 'There is nothing so revolutionary, because there is nothing so unnatural and so convulsive to society, as the strain to keep things fixed, when all the world is by the very law of its creation in eternal progress; and the cause of all the evils of the world may be traced to that natural but most deadly error of human indolence and corruption—that our business is to preserve and not to improve.'

Such was the view taken, and maintained at first with some consistency, by the ministry which came into power in November 1830. They saw that a new period had arrived, from which great changes must take their date. They saw what opposition would be raised by those who feared change; and what difficulties by a host of sufferers from existing evils, or unreasonable expectants of impossible good. They could laugh when Sydney Smith said, in a speech on the Reform Bill: 'All young ladies will imagine, as soon as this bill is carried, that they will be instantly married. School-boys believe that gerunds and

supines will be abolished, and that currant-tarts must
ultimately come down in price; the corporal and sergeant
are sure of double pay; bad poets will expect a demand for
their epics; fools will be disappointed, as they always are.'
Ministers might laugh at the expectations of the fools and
school-children; but they were aware that a multitude of
evils which must be redressed now and obviated for the
future, must be dealt with in another manner than the
sufferers themselves had any idea of, or were at all likely to
approve.   Not only had they to carry through some arduous
work in which they were supported by the demand and
the sympathy of a majority of the nation; they had also
much to do which was not less imperatively demanded,
but in doing which they must adopt methods which their
supporters had to be taught to understand.   To appreciate
their position, irrespective of the Reform Bill, let us briefly
survey the state and prospects of the country when Lord
Grey and his friends came into power.

The much-dreaded cholera proved the smallest of the
prominent evils of the time.   Its first assault was the
most violent; and then it attacked few but the vicious, the
diseased, and the feeble; and it carried off, in the whole,
fewer victims than many an epidemic, before and since,
which has run its course very quietly.   Before its disappearance from the United Kingdom, in fifteen months, the
average of deaths was one in $3\frac{1}{4}$ of those attacked; and the
total number of deaths in and near London was declared to
be 5275.   No return was obtained of the number in the kingdom.   When it is remembered how many deaths happened
in the noisome places of our towns, and in damp nooks of
wretched country villages and in the pauper haunts of
Edinburgh and Glasgow, and among the hungering Irish,
it is clear that the disease could hardly work any appreciable effect in the open places, and among the comfortable
classes of the kingdom.   If a person of rank or substance,
or in healthy middle age, was attacked here and there, it
was spoken of as a remarkable circumstance; and the
cholera soon came to be regarded as a visitation on the
vicious and the poor.   Happily the preparations which
depended on the apprehensions or the benevolence of the
rich were made before that change in the aspect of the

new plague—the cleansing and white-washing—the gifts
of clothing and food; and the impression was made on all
thoughtful minds that improved knowledge and care on
the subject of health were the cause of our comparative
impunity under the visitation of this plague, and that a
still improved knowledge and care were the requisites to
a complete impunity hereafter. Though our progress from
that day to this has been slower than it ought to have
been, the awakening of society in England to the duty
of care of the public health must date from the visitation
of the cholera in 1831–2.

The state of the rural districts was fearful at the time
of the accession of the Grey administration. Everybody
knew about the rick-burning and machine-breaking; and
the thoughtless and narrow-minded called for soldiery and
police, stringent laws and severe punishments. More
thoughtful persons, however, looked also at the condition
of the agricultural interest generally—the complaints of
distress, renewed from year to year, the increase of pauperism and poor-rates, and the growth of crime, as well as
of misery; and they saw that the evil was one which
stringent laws and severe punishments could not cure, nor
even reach. They saw that the real mischief lay in the
antiquated and corrupted poor-law, which they knew to
be what it was declared to be by a French commission
sent over to inquire into its operation—'the great political
gangrene of England, which it was equally dangerous to
meddle with and to let alone.' Under this system, in its
union with the corn-laws, the condition and prospects of
the country were truly such as to make sagacious statesmen
tremble. No previous administration had understood the
mischief in all its extent and its bearings; but the facts
were, that while rents were nominally very high, no
landowner was sure of his income; that the farmers were
subject to fluctuations in their receipts, which discouraged
all prudence and self-education for their business; that
land was badly tilled, or actually going out of cultivation;
that the quality of labour was deteriorating incessantly,
from the practice of paying wages more and more out of
the rates; that the labourers were becoming more and more
reckless and demoralised, as they came to form a huge

pauper class; that the honest and independent of their order were drawn down faster and faster into pauperism; that the class of small shopkeepers were becoming, in increasing numbers, unable to pay rates, and compelled, instead, to apply for relief; that country parishes were exhibiting themselves, with less and less shame, as scenes of unprincipled jobbing and scandalous vice, where every one who could, thrust his hand into the public purse, where the honest and independent became the victims of the knavish and reckless, where the unchaste might prosper while the chaste must starve, where the capitalists of the parish must sink under the coalition between the magistracy and the paupers, and where ruin impended over all. The amount of money expended for the relief of the poor in England and Wales had risen in half a century from under two millions to above seven millions per annum; and this vast expenditure went to increase instead of to relieve the pauperism of the country. Here was this enormous tax, becoming ruinous by annual increase, less production from the land, less industry among the labourers, more vice, more misery, a great race of illegitimate children growing up, riots by day, fires by night, the stout heart of England sinking, and likely to be soon broken; and all from the existence of a poor-law system for whose repeal or alteration there was no popular demand, while it was certain that every item of it would be clutched fast to the last moment by parties and persons the most difficult to deal with, from their lack of either enlightenment or public principle. Next to the reform question, the gravest which presented itself to the handling of the new ministry was undoubtedly that of the poor-law.

If it was proposed to lighten the pressure upon the poor-rate by the resource of emigration, the question was, how was it to be done?—where were the people to go? The true principles of colonisation were on the eve of being announced, but they were not yet understood; and there was the story of the Swan River settlement, new and disheartening, within every man's knowledge. The Swan River settlement dates from 1829 as a British colony. The accounts given of the district, on the western coast of New Holland, by Captain Stirling, who became its first governor, caused the grandest expectations. And the fault of the failure did not lie in any deception about the natural advantages of the place. The fault was in ignorance of the first principles of colonisation. Vast tracts of land were sold or granted to individuals. The colony was to be exempted, as a favour, from any importation of convicts. The settlers were to be allowed 200 acres of land for every labouring man, woman, or child above ten years of age, that they should import into the colony; and forty acres of land were given, up to the end of 1830, for every amount of £3 imported into the settlement in any shape. Thus land superabounded in proportion to capital; and the capital brought in, though so scanty in proportion to the land, abounded in proportion to the labour. The richest of the colonists could obtain no labourers; and they sat down upon their lands, surrounded by their rotting goods, their useless tools, and the frames of houses which there were no hands to erect; without shelter, and certain soon to be without food, if more labour could not be obtained. Instead of more, there was daily less, as the few labourers who were on the spot made use of their first exorbitant earnings to possess themselves of enough of the cheap land to make them their own masters. Now it appeared that the secret of the success of other settlements, pitied for their liability to convict immigration, was in their convict labour; and the Swan River colonists petitioned the government at home to send them convicts to save them from destruction. Some of the settlers wandered away, as they could find opportunity, to other colonies, stript of everything, or carrying the mere wrecks of their expensive outfit, and declaring of the famous Swan River district, 'It is a country to break one's heart;' and, people at home heard such tales of perplexity and disaster as shook the popular confidence in emigration as a resource, and might well make the government hesitate in regarding it as a remedy, in any degree, for the intolerable pressure upon the poor-rate.

And what was the state of older colonies? The moral sense of the nation must be met in regard to the abolition of slavery. From the time of the issue of the famous circular in Canning's day—from the time that the cause of

the negro had been taken up by the powers at home—it
was certain that a radical change must take place in the
relation between the proprietors of men and their legal
human property; and none who saw what a vast universe
of morals lies above and beyond the range of the law,
could for a moment doubt what that change would be.
But there were enough of men, as there are in every community, who see nothing above and beyond the existing
law, to make the process of change appear in anticipation
very difficult and hazardous. Those interested in human
proprietorship would perhaps no longer try to push Clark-
son into the dock at Liverpool, or even dare to murder
missionaries at such a distance as Demerara; but they had
to be reminded that laws could be altered or abolished,
and taught that eternal principles exist which compel the
destruction of bad laws: and unwilling pupils like these
are very slow at learning their lesson. This mighty work,
of the abolition of slavery, lay clear before the eyes of the
ministers, needing to be done, and soon. Another colony
in the west—Canada—was in an unsatisfactory state; but
the call for reform there appeared to be less pressing than
it really was, and no adequate attention was given to it for
yet a few years. As for our great Indian dependencies,
there was no option about attending to them and their
needs, for the Company's charter was about to expire; but
it was a question of mighty importance to future ages, as
well as of vital consequence to many millions of living
men, what the terms of the great East India proprietorship or administration should be from this time forward:
whether the new doctrine of commercial freedom should
spread to the nations of the east, by our practice of it
there; or whether any of the time-hallowed monopolies
of the most majestic of merchant companies should be
contended for against the rising popular will.

Nearer home, there was that difficulty, without limit as
to depth and extent—the state of Ireland. The form in
which the spirit of outrage now showed itself was opposition to the Church. It had become impossible to collect
tithe in Ireland; and men saw that to collect tithe in
Ireland would never be possible again. Here was the
insulted Church to be vindicated—for there was as yet no

debate whether to maintain it—and, at all events, the
starving Irish clergy to be succoured; many of whom
had pawned or sold their furniture and clothes, and were
working like labourers to raise potatoes to feed their
children, or were thankful for the gift of a meal of porridge
for their families from a neighbour.　In England, too, in
places where the clergymen were strict about their dues,
an imitation of Irish methods of dealing with tithe col-
lectors began to be heard of; and the affair was becoming
urgent.　Chancery reform, and many improvements in our
judicial system besides, were needed and demanded.　The
severity of our criminal law had been for many years
condemned; and one relaxation after another had been
procured; but much more remained to be done than had
yet been effected.　The infliction of punishment was still
perniciously uncertain, from the law ordaining severer
penalties than the tribunals chose to inflict; and a complete revision of the criminal law, in order to bring it into
harmony with the spirit of a new age, was a great work
pressing to be done.　There was another noble task—new,
beneficent, but not on that account the less urgently
necessary—for which the nation looked confidently to the
new administration, and especially to the Henry Brougham
who was so deeply pledged to the cause: the work of preparing a national system of education lay before the new
rulers.　The struggle and success of the people in the
reform question was a plea for it; the growing evils of
the poor-law system were a plea for it; the hope of the
operative classes, and the despair of the rick-burners
and the machine-breakers were pleas for it.　But these
pleas, and all others, were in vain.　It was not that
Henry Brougham, during his four years of power, made
efforts which were defeated, as efforts on behalf of education have been since, by sectarian or other differences: it
was not here that the disappointment lay; but in Henry
Brougham never approaching the subject at all, during his
four years of power.　This affair lay before the new administration, when they came into office, with the others
just enumerated; and it was the greatest of them all.　It
alone was left untouched, and must be omitted in the
narrative of what was done between 1830 and 1834.

There was, besides, the currency question, sure to turn
up, under all administrations, with every vicissitude of
the national fortunes; and now more sure than usual,
from the approaching expiration of the bank charter.
There was the usual eagerness everywhere for the reduction of taxation; and more than the usual expectation,
from the confidence felt that a reforming ministry would
deal freely with sinecure offices and pensions which a Tory
government could not be expected to touch.

The opportunity must be taken, while the spirit of
reform pervaded the nation, and the enlightened will of
the middle classes was in its completest union and vigour,
to reform the municipal institutions of the country. A
liberal cabinet, anxious to raise the national mind and
character by an extension of self-government, could not
but know that it was as desirable to purify and enlarge
municipal administration and powers as to amend the
parliamentary representation. And this work, which would
have been necessary if they had had nothing else to do
than to carry parliamentary and corporation reform, was
made yet more indispensable in their eyes by the necessity which they foresaw of introducing a principle and
practice of centralisation, new to administration in England, and requiring, not only a careful watch over itself,
but a set-off of enlarged local powers in some other direction. They foresaw that the perplexing and overwhelming task of poor-law reform could be accomplished no
otherwise than by taking out of the hands of local administrators the powers which had been so long and so
grossly abused, that the wisest and best individuals could
not be the reformers of the system in their own neighbour-
hoods, but only its victims. These powers must now be
confided to some central body, and by them locally administered. Whether this necessity was a good or an evil
one, might be and was debated by the two orders of politicians by whom the great question of centralisation and
local administration is for ever debated; but, while some
insisted that business was much better done when done
for the people by well-trained officials, sending out their
functionaries from a central office, and others contended
that no such advantages could compensate for the loss to

the people of the habit and the privilege of managing their local affairs for themselves, the new government felt that a municipal reform, which should enlarge the local powers and public interests of the people, would be the best safeguard they could give against the possible evils of such centralisation as they must establish in the prosecution of some other indispensable reforms.

Such was the series of works which lay before the new ministry, when they should have accomplished their distinguishing achievement of parliamentary reform. The mere list is an indication that we have arrived at a new period of history, and that our method of narration must change accordingly. Hitherto, while governments went on from year to year, legislating for the time—adding, amending, abrogating, from session to session, as natural occasion arose—our history could not but take something of the form of the chronicle, as it will again before its close. But at the incoming of a new period, so marked by a great act of regeneration or revolution—whichever it may be called—the chronicle method can do no justice to the matter to be conveyed. The story of the Reform Bill could not be fitly told but in regular sequence; neither can the story of the other reforms which it held in intimate relation. We have catalogued the ordinary stars as they set; but now that a magnificent new constellation appears in our political firmament, we must do something more than name the stars, and let them go down in the list. They must be signalised, so that all may know what has arisen. The story of these enterprises will therefore be given in sequence, after a glance at the condition of the new administration in regard to its powers and its impediments.

Lord Grey's administration was strong in political character. All its members had been not only liberal while in opposition, but consistent for a long course of years in contending for the precise objects which they now came into power for the purpose of achieving. They were strong in the popular support from the beginning; this strength went on increasing during the two years occupied by the reform struggle, and the meeting of the first reformed parliament; but it must, as every member of the government could not but know, end in weakness. The enthusiasm with which ministers were regarded in 1832 could not last. From the nature of the human mind, it must subside; and, when idolatry has once begun to decline, it is certain that the idol will soon be found to be clay. Lord Brougham was ridiculed for saying, after the meeting of the first reformed parliament, that the government was too strong. Whatever was the sense in which he meant this, the event proved that it would have been better for the government not to have had so overwhelming a majority as they could number. A patriotic minister wishes to have as strong an opposition as is consistent with the stability of his government, that his measures may be well sifted, and all objections considered before it is too late; and that he may thus share the responsibility of his acts with his sharp-sighted opponents. This kind of aid and support from the foe, was especially needed by the Whigs, from their inexperience in office, and their absolute lack of training for power. Thus was Lord Brougham justified in saying that they were too strong in the new parliament; and five years afterwards, there was nobody who would not have agreed with him. At the moment, however, this popular support was a vast power for good. It fixed the kind-hearted but feeble king; it saved time when the pressure of work was extreme; and it saved the country from reflex agitation from the political storms on the continent.

Here, perhaps, ends the list of the powers of the new ministry. They were representatives of liberal principles of policy; they stood high in political character, and were sustained by unequalled popular support. Some would have said beforehand that they must be strong in the ability of the respective members; but it did not prove so. While there was not a man among them who might not have been called able in his way, there was no one of them of commanding ability in office—no one great statesman. Lord Brougham was the man whose splendid talents were looked to for magnificent results; but he proved himself no statesman; and it was only because his supposed statesmanship was wanted that he was raised to the woolsack while known to be no equity lawyer. Some of his colleagues have since, after considerable training, shown high ability in office—of which Sir James Graham is an eminent example; but this training was exactly that in which they were unavoidably deficient, while it was essential to enable them to work together, and to render their respectable amount of individual ability compensate for the absence of commanding power. This want of training and of business habits is particularly incapacitating in the case of men of aristocratic station, who, if they have not the discipline of official life, can hardly have any business habits or talents at all; and again, the evil was here aggravated by the new ministers having, for the most part, spent their lives in opposition. Men in opposition inevitably form and utter rash judgments, from having only partial information on subjects of which they are called to judge. They inevitably commit themselves, so as to stand virtually pledged to courses of which they may think very differently amidst the lights of office. Thus hampered as to even the principles of much of the work to be done, they are in still greater difficulties as to the procedure.

Untrained as they were, it was absolutely necessary for the Whigs to retain the services of the underlings of former administrations. It was a bitter, a well-nigh fatal necessity; but a necessity it was. That men as new as their masters, clerks as inexperienced in official routine as the ministers, could not have carried on the business of the departments, needs no showing. The men who were at the desks must be continued, in order to get through the work of every day. These men were of like politics with the late administration; or rather, they were as much stronger in political opinion than their late *chefs* as underlings are wont to be in proportion to their superiors: they were very confident that their late masters would soon come back again; and they regarded the new Whig rule as an irksome and vexatious interval between two organic periods of strong government. According to the testimony of the perplexed new ministers and their friends, the disasters from this cause were innumerable and very serious. They were misled, quizzed, kept in the dark, left unaided at critical moments; in short, served faithlessly or not at all. It may be said, and it was said, that a gieat part of the capacity for government consists in securing good service. The Whig ministers pleaded that a man must himself understand the business he wants to have done before he can secure good service from fresh hands. However this may be, the fact was that they were incessantly complaining of hardship and misadventure from this cause. It is certain also that their power, popularity, and usefulness, were seriously impaired by the imperfection of the work they produced, and the flaws in the schemes they proposed. Perfection of detail might have sufficed in the absence of commanding ability of statesmanship, and commanding statesmanship might have overborne the impediment of imperfect routine execution; but here, where both the compensating powers were absent, it is a strong proof how enthusiastic was the national trust that the Whig ministers were enabled to carry the noble series of reforms for which they have a claim to the acknowledgments of far future generations.

CHAPTER VII.

Civil List — Pensions — Regal Income — Pauperism — Confusion of Poverty with Pauperism — New Poor-law—Its Principles — Its Machinery—Reception of the Measure—Its Passage and Operation —Factory Children.

BEFORE the Wellington administration went out, the House of Commons had resolved that a select committee should examine the civil list, in order to separate the proper expenditure of the crown from a large and various expenditure of another kind which ought to be under the control of parliament, but was not so, from its coming arbitrarily under the head of civil-list expenditure. The king and his new ministers went heartily to work to carry out the pleasure of the Commons and correct the abuses of the old system. The conduct of the sovereign on this occasion was very honourable to him. As an honest, plain-minded man, it was probably more satis-

factory to him to have a certain defined income, paid
and accounted for quarterly, than to be troubled with a
dozen kinds of revenue, necessitating a vast complication
of accounts, and causing him to be continually vexed with
applications and complaints about pensions and fanciful
claims, and harassed by periodical inquiries and censures
in parliament about the pension list. He might see how
much ease and relief he would gain by turning over the
whole business to parliament for re-arrangement; but that
he did see this from the station of the throne was such
a proof of good sense, and the grace with which he
surrendered everything to the judgment of his ministers
and parliament was so entire, that his popularity was as
much strengthened as it could be by any one act. He and
the queen relinquished all their annuities; and he placed
at the disposal of his faithful Commons his whole interest
for life in all hereditary revenues, droits of the crown, and
casual income from any source whatever, trusting to their
judgment and affection to make sufficient provision for the
dignity of the royal function, and for the comfort of
himself and his consort.

Now was the time for the reformers and economists of
the House to speak their minds about the pension list,
and to learn all that could be told about it. From this
time forward there was to be no more mystery about the
granting of pensions. The yearly amount was to be fixed;
and all secrecy was to be put an end to. There are many
at this day who think it a matter of regret that the
occasion was not used for establishing an honourable
system of rewards for public service, not official, such as
might befit a people now awakening to a sense of the
value and dignity of science, literature, and art. For the
best benefactors of society—its sages, philosophers, authors,
and artists, men whose pursuits are the least likely to
obtain pecuniary recompense—there is in England no
appropriation worthy of government to offer, or of them
to receive. The amount left at the disposal of the
sovereign is destined for any kind or degree of real or
imagined service, and is far too trifling to be of use in the
encouragement of lofty pursuit, or the reward of exalted
service. It has to be offered with an apology, and received

with shame; and there are few of those whose claims are
strongest, that would choose to receive as an act of favour
or favouritism from the minister that which they would
regard as an honour and unmixed blessing if conferred by
parliament, out of a liberal appropriate fund. Here and
there, at present, a great natural philosopher receives a
pension which does not pay for his apparatus; and a poor
author has a pittance which hardly provides him bread, fire,
and candle, while he is penning his thoughts—rendering
services to the world which no money can ever pay; and
such pensioners know that their names stand among some
so unconnected with all proper purposes of a pension list,
that the wonder is how they ever got there. It is not to
the credit of England, and was not in 1831 an honourable
result of sixteen years of peace, that hundreds of thousands
of pounds should be annually appropriated for military and
naval purposes, while only a pittance of a few hundreds was
really disposable for honour and encouragement to the
wisdom, knowledge, and ennobling arts by which the
human race is, if at all, to be exalted above the liability
to war. This was the proper opportunity for establishing
a National Reward Fund; but it was missed, and the
occasion has never been even looked for since.

The pensions charged on the civil list for England
amounted at this time to £74,200; those for Scotland, to
£31,222; those for Ireland, to £53,795—total, £159,217.
All these were legally void by the death of the sovereign
who had granted them; but there was no one who wished
that they should not be renewed to the individual
recipients, if the system of granting could be amended.
It was now proposed to reduce the amount charged on the
civil list to £75,000 for the three countries together—the
amount to be made up by the oldest pensions on the list,
in order that the king might have some power of bestow-
ing grants before the end of his reign by the dying off of
the oldest pensioners. Parliament was to deal with the
rest as it thought fit, after they had been transferred to
the consolidated fund. This chief point, and some less
disputed matters, being agreed upon, their majesties'
financial affairs stood thus: In return for all that they
had surrendered, they were to receive, in quarterly pay-

ments, during the life of both, the sum of £510,000, under the five following heads :

First Class,	For their majesties' privy purse . . .	£110,000
Second „	Salaries of his majesty's household . .	130,300
Third „	Expenses of his majesty's household . .	171,500
Fourth „	Special and secret service	23,200
Fifth „	Pensions	75,000
		£510,000

If the queen survived her consort, she was to have an income of £100,000, and Marlborough House and Bushy Park for residences. This opening of a system of rational management of royal income and expenditure is worthy of record. The country had suffered much in purse and patience from the extravagance and debts of royal personages; and it is suffering even now; for there are tracts lying waste in our British American colonies, not only useless in themselves, but a positive impediment to cultivation—tracts made over by the Duke of York to certain jewellers and others, his creditors. Since the arrangement here chronicled, there have been no complaints of royal extravagance, no instances of royal debt; and, though we English do not admit that we are a nation of shopkeepers, it is certain that we have so much respect for high probity in money-matters as to feel that the honour of the crown is eminently enhanced by the faultlessness of the last and the present sovereign in living within their incomes.

The alarming increase of pauperism throughout the kingdom has been noticed. This increase was complained of, and adverted to in terms of apprehension, year after year, in parliament and elsewhere; and when the annual poor-rate exceeded seven millions, with a clear prospect of augmentation, men began to ask, in their clubs and by their firesides, where this was to end, and who could be sure of not sinking down from being a rate-payer to becoming a rate-receiver. Parliamentary committees were found to be useless. A more stringent search was needed than such a body could institute. In 1832, the crown appointed a commission of inquiry, consisting of nine persons, among whom were the Bishops of London and

Chester, under whose direction the condition of every parish in England and Wales was investigated and reported. These reports, in their mass, and in the nature of their details, were enough to overwhelm any faculties, and to extinguish hope. Those whose business it was to receive the documents and consider them, as they came in, week after week, for two years, could scarcely help regarding the nation as a group of people, some busy and some gay, on an island destined to be overflowed by the deep, and round whose whole circuit the waves were advancing, inch by inch, while only those who were immediately disturbed were fully conscious of the danger. There was one solid ground of hope, however—one fixed point presented—from which improvement might proceed. There were two or three parishes in England blessed with the presence of a sensible man, sagacious enough to see into the causes of parochial evils, and powerful enough to obviate them. To half-a-dozen quiet country residents like these, men aiming only to do the duty which lay before their doors, our country mainly owes its rescue from the most appalling danger which has ever threatened its social condition, and its comparative purification from the worst complication of vice, perhaps, ever caused by any institution, except that of slavery, for which she has in any age been answerable. The amount of rate was a broad fact which every man could understand, and which any one might know from the newspaper; but, fearful as it was, it was that which pressed least upon the minds of the commissioners and of those whom they admitted to a sight of the reports. Among a multitude of painful facts, the most mournful was the pervading and unceasing oppression of virtue and encouragement of vice. The poor-rate had become public spoil. The ignorant believed it an inexhaustible fund which belonged to them. To obtain their share, the brutal bullied the administrators, the profligate exhibited their bastards which must be fed, the idle folded their arms and waited till they got it; ignorant boys and girls married upon it; poachers, thieves, and prostitutes extorted it by intimidation; country justices lavished it for popularity, and guardians for convenience. This was the way the fund went. As for whence it arose—it came, more and more every year, out of the capital of the shopkeeper and the farmer, and the diminishing resources of the country gentleman. The shopkeeper's stock and returns dwindled, as the farmer's land deteriorated, and the gentleman's expenditure contracted. The farmer's sons, waiting, at the age of five-and-thirty, for ability to marry in comfort, saw, in every ditch and field on the estate, lads under twenty whose children were maintained by the rates which were ruining their employer. Instead of the proper number of labourers to till his lands—labourers paid by himself—the farmer was compelled to take double the number, whose wages were paid partly out of the rates; and these men, being employed by compulsion on him, were beyond his control —worked or not as they chose—let down the quality of his land, and disabled him from employing the better men who would have toiled hard for independence. These better men sank down among the worse; the rate-paying cottager, after a vain struggle, went to the pay-table to seek relief; the modest girl might starve, while her bolder neighbour received 1s. 6d. per week for every illegitimate child. Industry, probity, purity, prudence—all heart and spirit—the whole soul of goodness—were melting down into depravity and social ruin, like snow under the foul internal fires which precede the earthquake. There were clergymen in the commission, as well as politicians and economists; and they took these things to heart, and laboured diligently to frame suggestions for a measure which should heal and recreate the moral spirit as well as the economical condition of society in England.

To thoughtful observers it is clear that the same grave aristocratic error which has before been adverted to—that of confounding in one all ranks below a certain level of wealth—was at the bottom of much poor-law abuse, as it has been of the opposition to its amendment. Gentlemen in parliament who talk over poor-law matters, and gentlemen in the country who discuss and administer the law, and gentlemen of the newspaper press who desire, with real benevolence, to advocate the cause of the poor, have been too apt to confound under this name classes more widely distinguishable, in fact and in principle, than any other ranks in our society—except only that of sovereign and subject. Except the distinction between sovereign and subject, there is no social difference in England so wide as that between the independent labourer and the pauper; and it is equally ignorant, immoral, and impolitic to confound the two. This truth was so apparent to the commissioners, and they conveyed it so fully to the framers of the new poor-law, that it forms the very foundation of the measure; and all effectual opposition to the working of the system since it became law, has proceeded from blindness to this great fact and fundamental principle. Here are two classes to be dealt with —the indigent, and the independent labourer, who, however oppressed by poverty, is a noble member of the state, and can lift up his head in the consciousness that he fulfils the part of a citizen, and is beholden to no man for a degrading charity. In the pauper class are many whom the state is willing to maintain, because they cannot maintain themselves—the sufferers under helplessness, from whatever cause; and it included also, at the time of the reform of the poor-law, a much larger number who were not suffering under any natural or accidental helplessness at all. These were the people whom a hasty and ignorant humanity call 'the poor,' and for whose support and comfort they pleaded; pleaded as if that support and comfort were to come out of the pockets of the rich alone. Now, the very first aim of the commissioners was to consider the poor—the independent and virtuous and most suffering poor. While magistrates were giving to pauper applicants at their own houses an additional loaf for every child, that loaf was provided by the more high-minded labourer, who toiled to raise the rate demanded of him, while he and his children were hungering together. Both the poor man and the pauper were to be cared for; but neither of them at the expense of the other. The law ordered, and it still orders, that every man shall be fed; but every law should provide, as all moral principle does, that the pauper, while supported by public charity, should be placed in a lower condition—if only that were possible —than the man who abstains from putting out his hand to the public purse. Clear as this principle is, and much as it has been preached since 1832, there is still existing a surprising blindness to it.   Appeals on behalf of the pauper are incessantly made, in forgetfulness of that class of the poor which should be considered and cherished with all possible honour and care; and those who are engaged in thus considering and cherishing an all-important class in our state, are reproached with hardness of heart towards the poor, on account of restrictions which are absolutely necessary as safeguards of the integrity of the people and the capital of the country.   In the very few parishes where such restrictions had already been enforced, it was clear that justice and mercy were, as they must ever be, coincident.   In those parishes, while all necessitous persons were relieved, idleness, and not industry, was discouraged; prudent marriage was not rendered impossible by a premium on profligacy; the land was not deteriorating, nor the capital of the district wasting away; farmers employed such labour as they wanted, and could choose it of a good quality; and the independent labourer was respected, while the pauper was pitied and fed.

Under the guidance of these few examples, and enlightened by a prodigious accumulation of evidence, the commissioners offered their suggestions to government; and a bill to amend the poor-law was prepared and proposed to the consideration of parliament early in 1834.

The first principle of the new law was that of the old —that every necessitous person had a claim to relief. The matter was to be much simplified now by the repeal of the worst restrictions of settlement.   If one main object of the reform was to encourage industry, it was clearly desirable to remove the impediments to the circulation of labour.   Settlement by hiring and service was to exist no longer; labour could freely enter any parish where it was wanted, and leave it for another parish which might, in its turn, want hands.

In observance of the great principle that the independent labourer was not to be sacrificed to the pauper, all administration of relief to the able-bodied at their own homes was to be discontinued as soon as possible; and the allowance system was put an end to entirely.   The

shameless petitioner was no longer to carry home so many
shillings or loaves for so many children, while his more
honourable neighbour not only went without, but bore
part of the cost. Henceforth, the indigent must come
into the workhouse for relief, if he must have it. There
stood the great house—with shelter, clothing, and food for
the destitute who chose to claim it; but, in justice to the
independent poor, and to society at large, there were
conditions belonging to this relief which ought never to
have been objected to by reasonable persons, however
irksome they might and must be to the idle, dissolute, and
extremely ignorant, who form a large proportion of the
pauper class. One condition was, that the able-bodied
should work—should do a certain amount of work for
every meal. They might go out after the expiration of
twenty-four hours; but while in the house they must
work. The men, women, and children must be separated;
and the able-bodied and infirm. The separation of the
men and women—husbands and wives among others—
was absolutely necessary to common decency, in an
establishment like a workhouse; and that of husbands
and wives was required by every consideration of justice
to the state, which could not rear a race of paupers within
the workhouse, to the prevention of virtuous marriage
without. That the aged and infirm should be separated
from the able-bodied was necessary to their own quiet and
comfort. Their diet included indulgences which others
could not have; and the turbulence of sturdy paupers
was no fit spectacle for them. That the children should
be segregated was necessary to their moral safety and
educational training. No part of the new law has
occasioned more complaint and opposition than this workhouse classification; and no part is more clearly defensible
from every point of view, or more evidently necessary.
Because the workhouses could not be permitted to be
rookeries for pauper families to roost in, they were called
prisons; though every man could go out with his family
any day, and was kept in only by the inducement of a
maintenance. As for the effects of the separation and
training of the children, a curious light is thrown upon
the subject by a discussion which took place a few years

after the reform was instituted—a discussion among certain barristers on circuit, a large number of whom were dining together, when some circumstance led them to compare their observations on workhouse schools. From the encouragement given to dissoluteness by the old poor-law, the first series of children in the workhouses of some of the rural districts were almost all illegitimate. The question discussed by these barristers was, what the effect on the disrepute of illegitimacy was likely to be, in the course of another generation, of the manifest superiority of the children educated in the workhouses over those of the neighbouring peasantry born in wedlock. The practical conclusion was, that the children of the independent labourers must be educated up to the work house schooling point, and as much beyond it as possible.

In order to a complete and economical classification in the workhouses, and for other obvious reasons, the new act provided for unions of parishes—the rating and expenditure of the rates remaining a separate concern. Thus, instead of half-a-dozen small, expensive, and ill-arranged establishments in as many different parishes, one central house, properly prepared for its purposes, would answer all objects, and be under a completely conspicuous management. To afford the necessary control over such a system —a system so new and unwelcome to a host of local authorities and managers—a central board was indispensable, by whose orders, and through whose assistant-commissioners, everything was to be arranged, and to whom all appeals were to be directed. The central board was to consist of three commissioners ; and the assistant-commissioners were at first twenty-one, diminishing to nine as the new organisation was completed. No change was proposed in regard to the rateability of property, or the mode of collecting the rate. The business of the new act was with the application of the rate when collected. The distribution was left to guardians and select vestries; and, in the absence of these authorities, to overseers. The discretionary power of magistrates was much contracted, none being left which could interfere with the main aim of the reform—the subordinating the condition of the pauper to that of the independent labourer.

Of the changes proposed by the new law, none was more important to morals than that which threw the charge of the maintenance of illegitimate children upon the mother. Hitherto the father had been made chargeable upon the oath of the mother as to his paternity. It was now proposed that the law should take no cognizance of the father at all. The Lords, however, modified this arrangement by giving an appeal to the quarter-sessions against the father. This appeal was rendered sufficiently difficult to leave the practical operation of the law pretty much what it was intended to be, till a change was made in 1839, by which it was rendered more easy to reach the father. This change was occasioned by feelings of humanity, which many wise persons still think misguided. When the law was framed, there was much wonder abroad that the Bishop of London, and many moral and humane persons about him, and not a few thoughtful women, were in favour of an arrangement which left the father of an illegitimate child 'unpunished,' and threw the whole burden upon the mother. The Bishop of London and his coadjutors were presently proved to be right by the demonstration of facts. The decrease of illegitimate births was what many called wonderful, but only what the framers of the law had anticipated from the removal of direct pecuniary inducement to profligacy, and from the awakening of proper care in parents of daughters, and of reflection in the women themselves. The first case or two occasioned a shock of surprise and dismay among those who had not understood the change in the law; and after that, the offence seemed almost to disappear in some districts where before it had abounded. As for the thoughtful women who did not object to the new arrangement, their feeling has been nobly expressed by one of them—Mrs. Jameson—in a passage which will not be forgotten; a few sentences in which she indicates the benefit to the whole sex, when woman is made, even through apparent hardship, mistress of herself—the guardian of her own mind and morals, instead of the ward of man.

Extracts from the reports had been given to the public from time to time, and all reasonable means used to prepare the mind of the nation for the new measure. Up to the last moment, it was impossible to conjecture how it would be received, and, therefore, how it would work; for there never was a measure which more absolutely required, for its successful working, the countenance and co-operation of the intelligent portion of society. One certain thing was, that the measure itself supposed and necessitated a repeal of the corn-laws—by its alterations in the provisions of settlements, its general release of labour from thraldom, and its reliance on general laws; while there was too much reason to apprehend that, carefully as this was explained and proved to the ministers, they would not admit it in parliament, if they did in their own minds. The apprehension was but too well founded. Lord John Russell and Lord Althorp, who brought forward the measure in the Commons, presently after refused even to receive evidence regarding the operation of the corn-laws; and Lord Melbourne, premier of the administration which set the bill to work, made a declaration in the Lords—only less memorable than that of the Duke of Wellington against reform of parliament, because Lord Melbourne was the lesser man —that he had heard many mad things said in his life; but that the corn-laws could be repealed was, before God, the very maddest thing he had ever heard. Yet the framers of the Poor-law Amendment Act knew, and always avowed to the Whig ministers, that the measure could never have a fair chance of working till the corn-laws were repealed; and in the interval they must pray for a succession of good harvests. On the occurrence of the first deficient harvest, it would probably be necessary—as they said in the freedom of conversation—to march soldiers to superintend the enforcement of the law. Nor did any condemnation of the measure lie in this assertion; for the state of things under the old law was so desperate that any determination short of desperation in the enforcement of the Amendment Act might be a mere matter of prudence. Except for the complication of the corn-laws with this measure, there was nothing to make it a party affair. Everybody was suffering under the existing system; and while the proposed reform was brought forward by a liberal ministry, men were more eager for it than the landed interest, in and out of the House. If it was probable that the country justices would resent the restriction of their powers in

their own province, it was certain that their neighbours
the farmers—of the same politics—were sinking under
the burden of the rates, and would welcome any prospect
of relief. As it was not a party matter, it was impossible
to divine how the newspapers would go. The only thing
considered certain under this head was, that the *Times*—
the great paper of all—was wholly in favour of the reform.
One of the editors had, a few days previously, sent a
message declaratory of intended support, to some of the
managers of the measure. Up to the last moment, though
the prospect was wholly uncertain, everything looked well.

And at midnight of the 17th of April, everything looked
better still. The chancellor of the exchequer, Lord Althorp,
had obtained leave from the Commons to bring in the bill.
His speech, plain, earnest, and impressive, had produced a
strong effect upon the House, and his proposal had been
respectfully greeted and warmly supported. The members
went home, feeling convinced that the evils of the poor-
law system were virtually abolished, and that this 'great
political gangrene of England' was successfully dealt with
at last. When each of them took up the *Times* from the
breakfast-table, the next morning, to gratify himself with
the study of its advocacy of the measure—an advocacy
sure to be more finely expressed than any that could be
heard elsewhere—what was the amazement to find a
thundering article against the measure! It became known
afterwards that the change in the mind of the *Times* had
taken place at the very last moment. It was naturally
declared and believed to be owing to evidence received
of the hostility of the country justices to the measure;
and the country justices were not only the great provincial
support of the *Times* newspaper, but composed an influence
too important to be lightly regarded. Whatever might be
the reason, the *Times* newspaper certainly did, at the last
moment, change its mind about supporting the new poor-
law. The fact—of the suddenness of the change—in
connection with the temper of the new opposition, is
worth noting, as illustrative of the character of newspaper
support or opposition in our day. The side which the
Times would take was a chance pregnant with good and
evil consequences which will influence the fate of whole

generations. The hostility has been so venomous, so unscrupulous, so mischievous in one direction, and so beneficial
in others, so pertinacious, so vigilant, and so remarkably
based upon the aristocratic error before alluded to—of
confusing all ranks below a certain level—that it could
not be passed over in the history of a time when the press
is admitted to be our fourth estate.

Before London had breakfasted, a wealthy member of
the Commons was in the city, with a friend, and had
bought the *Morning Chronicle;* and comrades were beating
about for writers of the leading articles—writers well
familiarised with the new measure. The consternation
of the ministers was not small. There was to be a cabinet
council that day; and the lord chancellor wrote a note to
Lord Althorp, to insure his attendance, as it was to be
considered whether the *Times* should be propitiated or
defied. Some expressions were added, not very compli-
mentary to the editor who had lately offered support.
Some tidings having arrived from Lord Althorp which
rendered the note unnecessary, it was torn up, and the
scraps thrown among waste papers under the table. Some
mischievous person picked them up, pasted them in order,
and sent them to the person remarked on, who was not
propitiated by what he read. From that hour, the virulence with which the leading paper pursued the lord
chancellor, the new poor-law, and the parties concerned
in its preparation, exceeded any hostility encountered by
the Whig government from any other quarter, and certainly had no small effect in impairing their much-weak-
ened influence and popularity, and in impeding the working
of poor-law reform. The mischief done was by the dis-
honesty of the paper in constantly misrepresenting the
enactments and operation of the new law; in imputing
to it the faults of the old system which it was actually in
course of remedying; in fostering the prejudices, and per-
petuating the mischievous powers, of the least enlightened
of the country justices; in upholding the cause of the unworthy among the indigent, by confounding them with
the worthy among the poor; in short, by a partial and
unscrupulous and unintermitting hostility to a measure
which had its faults, but which was not only necessary in

its time, but an eminent glory of its time, and which it would have been a moral benefit to Englishmen to appreciate better than they have done. The good effected by this hostility has, on the other hand, been very great. Bad as has been its temper and principle, it has acted in the name of humanity, and it has done some of the best work of humanity. Nothing in the shape of an abuse, a hardship, or a levity in the treatment of the poor, has it ever let pass. It has incessantly been unjust, and more cruel than the persons and usages it denounced; but it has induced a spirit of watchfulness and a sense of responsibility in official men; it has evoked a spirit of humanity in society, for which the whole class of sufferers may be grateful, and for the sake of which the most feeling moralists may subdue their natural and well-grounded resentment, and cheerfully acquiesce in the results which will remain when the warfare and all its disgraces, on every hand, are forgotten.

On the 14th of August 1834, the royal assent was given to the Poor-law Amendment Act, amidst prognostications of utter failure from the timid, and some misgivings among those who were most confident of the absolute necessity of the measure. These last knew that it was either now or never. When a member in the Commons complained of the short time allowed for the consideration of the Lords' amendments, Lord Althorp declared that he would be a bold man who should bring forward the bill in another session, after it had once been dropped. It is true—and the fact was repeatedly brought forward in the course of the debate—the abuses of the poor-law were almost all under forty years old; and the present object was rather to restore the principle and revert to the operation of the law of Elizabeth than to establish a new system; but still, there was the great and fearful fact before all men's eyes of the demoralisation of the peasantry; of their moral and social state being so bad, in many parts of the country, that it was a grave question whether they could be retrieved. It must be now or never. It appeared from the reports that a remnant still existed of the peasant order as it was before the corruption of the poor-law; a few hearty old men between sixty and eighty, sprinkled

through the country parishes, who had, for the forty years
of misrule, talked of the good old times, and turned away
from the pay-table with a disgust which would operate
well now, while the new purification was going forward.
Of these, there would be fewer every year; and the advantage of their presence was certainly an additional reason
why the reform should not be delayed. The bill became
law; the law came into speedy operation; for a time, long
enough to secure the reform, the seasons were kind, and
events were favourable. Everybody was not convinced—
and everybody is not convinced yet—of the blessedness of
the retrieval we have enjoyed. There are many who
charge upon the new law the abuses of the old, and the
difficulties which attend upon the very institution of a
poor-law; there are many who charge upon the law itself
some gross faults in parts of its administration; there are
many who will never be satisfied till every poor person is
thoroughly comfortable in his own home—a virtuous aspiration, but one not to be fulfilled by a poor-law of any
nature; but there are also many who think with a kind of
shudder what our condition would have been by this time
under the old law, or a less stringent reform. The facts
which all men might know, if they would, are, that before
two years were out, wages were rising and rates were
falling in the whole series of country parishes; farmers
were employing more labourers; surplus labour was absorbed; bullying paupers were transformed into steady
working-men; the decrease of illegitimate births, chargeable to the parish, throughout England, was nearly 10,000,
or nearly 13 per cent.; clergymen testified that they were
relieved from much of the pain and shame of having to
celebrate marriages where the bride was on the point of
becoming a mother, or where the parties were mere
children, with no other prospect than the parish pay-table;
and, finally, the rates, which had risen nearly a million in
their annual amount during the five years before the poor-
law commission was issued, sank down, in the course of the
five years after it, from being upwards of seven millions
to very little above four. After that time, when a long
period of severe distress ensued, the new law was found
insufficient—pending the maintenance of the corn-laws, it

must be remembered—to deal with the needs of our large manufacturing towns, as any other poor-law would have been. Of this we shall have to speak under its own date, as also of the changes found to be necessary in the application of the Amendment Act; but, from first to last, its operation in the rural districts has been not only salutary, but nothing short of salvation. This reform must ever be regarded as in the first rank of the honours of the Whig administration, and of the pregnant victories of the peace.

The poor-law inquiry was not the only one which disclosed facts of guilt and misery in our social state which might have lain concealed under the excitements of war, but which became gradually revealed amidst the quietude of peace. The poor-law commissioners had discovered how brutal and wretched was the condition of the children of rural labourers in too many districts of the country; of children who struggled with the pigs for food during the day—doing nothing useful, learning nothing which raised them above the beasts of the field ; and at night huddled down on damp straw, under a roof of rotten thatch ; or went out to carry poached game, or fire the farmers' stacks. Another picture, equally mournful, was presented from the factory districts. Throughout the manufacturing districts, in ordinary years, there ought to be a sufficient provision for all who are not behind their times; like the poor handloom weavers, who would have power-looms put down, to give them work. Such cannot be effectually aided ; but among other classes, if there were sense, knowledge, and goodness, there need have been no poverty at the time we speak of. This knowledge and goodness, however, are what the nation has taken no pains to cultivate in the mass, and to diffuse among the classes which are least able to desire them for themselves ; and hence has arisen the misery, the unspeakable disgrace, of the corruption of the parental relation among large numbers of our people. At the time now under review, it became known that parents sold their children to excessive labour ; and it has since become known that a considerable number have sold them to death through the burial-clubs —actually poisoned them for the sake of the burial-money, after entering the clubs for the very purpose. When Mr.

Sadler and Lord Ashley brought forward the subject of the oppression of the factory children in 1833, the question of legal protection to these children was as difficult a one as could be brought under the notice of any ministry and parliament. It is admitted by the most sagacious to be an insoluble difficulty. By guilty neglect we had brought ourselves into an inextricable embarrassment, which has become only more apparent, and not less perplexing to deal with, during all the discussion which has taken place from that day to this. Amidst much legislation which has been ventured upon, the question is apparently as far as ever from being settled—the great question, whether effectual legislation is possible **between** parents and children, and in defiance of the great natural laws which regulate the operation of labour and capital. By our guilty neglect we had placed in abeyance the still greater natural laws of the human heart, which alone can overrule economical laws ; and now we were reduced to try the fearful experiment whether, by interposing thus late with feeble arbitrary decrees and arrangements, we were likely to mitigate or aggravate the existing evil.

Here were children—little creatures whose life should have been spent in growing, in body and mind—employed all day and far into the night, in the monotonous and stupefying work of spinning in the mills. Most of the mills were found to be fairly wholesome ; the owners were not oppressors ; the pay was good ; the work was not in itself severe, or otherwise objectionable ; and all representations of the case as, generally speaking, worse than this, were found to be untrue. But it was too true that the parents let out their children to that class of middlemen, the spinners, from whom neither the care of parents nor the consideration of educated masters was to be looked for ; and the children were kept too long standing—too long awake—too long on the stretch over work which was not in itself of a hurtful nature. People who thought only of the children's instant welfare, and not of the considerations of justice and of actual practicability with which the case was complicated, clamoured for a law which should restrict the hours of labour, and determine the ages of the persons who should be employed in the

cotton and silk mills. Economists showed how vain had
always been, and must ever be, laws to regulate labour
and wages. Statesmen knew how vain it was to interfere
by law with private relations; and the mill-owners complained of the injustice of arbitrarily raising wages; while
this was exactly the prospect which delighted the operatives. They began to see before them a long perspective
of legal protection and privilege, by which they as well
as their children should obtain the same wages for less
and less work, while too few of them perceived that any
law which should deprive them of the free disposal of their
own labour would steal from them their only possession,
and be in fact a more flagrant oppression than any law
had inflicted on their order for centuries. Such was the
diversity of opinion in society in 1833, when a demand
was made in parliament for an act which should regulate
the labour of children in factories. The ministers were
fully aware of the difficulty in which they stood, and they
endeavoured to satisfy all parties, at the expense of the
smallest amount of mischief. They sent out a commission
to obtain evidence and report.

When the time came for the commissioners to report
and suggest, it was clear that their convictions were just
what might have been expected. The evil of overworking
children was clear. Though there were fewer swollen
joints, shrunken limbs, and distorted spines, than had
been represented, there was far too much of stunted growth,
and far too little of the character of natural childhood,
among those who were called 'the victims of the factory
system,' but who were, in fact, the victims of their parents'
poverty or heartlessness. But could a cure be found in a
mere law? The commissioners thought not. They foresaw that there would be false swearing about the children's
ages, and deception in many ways that no law could
obviate or detect; the parents from whom children needed
protection being exactly those who would have least scruple
about deception and perjury. But the commissioners had
not to decide whether there should be a law or not. It
was evidently settled that there should be one; and what
the commissioners had to do therefore was, first, to suggest
the best kind of law under the circumstances, and next, to

introduce and promote by it the measures in which they believed the remedy really to lie. About one of the remedies they could do nothing—that free importation of food which ought naturally at once to accompany a free circulation of labour, and to obviate all restrictions on it. The next most important, the education of the children, they thought they could introduce under the head of factory arrangements. The measure of education would be but small, and its quality but poor, if instituted in a way so indirect as this, and as an ostensibly subordinate object; but the commissioners thought that any educational training was better than none, and that they could but try for this collateral success, convinced as they were that the measure must fail in its professed object. They therefore proposed that the children should be secured from working for more than half the day by being placed at school, and certified to be there during some hours of the other half.

The Factory Bill of 1833 has received so many alterations since, that it would be useless to give a minute account of its provisions. It is enough to say that, except in silk-mills, no child under nine years of age was to be employed at all; children under eleven were not to be employed more than nine hours in any one day, nor more than forty-eight hours in one week; and after a time, this provision extended to children under thirteen years of age. School attendance was provided for, the cost—not to exceed 1d. in the 1s.—to be paid out of the child's wages, if the mill-owner desired it. Medical supervision was ordered; and four factory inspectors were appointed, to watch over the operation of the act. This was the beginning of that legislation protective of factory labour which has gone on to this day; the opening of a great controversy which is far from being concluded, and whose consequences lie deep in a future which no man now living shall see.

END OF VOL. II.

LONDON :

PRINTED BY WILLIAM CLOWES AND SONS,

STAMFORD STREET AND CHARING CROSS.